Low-Sugar Low-Ca Bowls

Easy & Tasty Breakfast & Snack Recipes for a Healthy Lifestyle & Natural Weight Loss

Alkaline Keto Diet Book 7

By Elena Garcia

Sign up for new books, fresh tips, super healthy recipes, and our latest wellness releases:

www.YourWellnessBooks.com

Disclaimer

A physician has not written the information in this book. It is advisable that you visit a qualified dietician so that you can obtain a highly personalized treatment for your case, especially if you want to lose weight effectively. This book is for informational and educational purposes only and is not intended for medical purposes. Please consult your physician before making any drastic changes to your diet.

All information in this book has been carefully researched and checked for factual accuracy. However, the author and publishers make no warranty, expressed or implied, that the information contained herein is appropriate for every individual, situation or purpose, and assume no responsibility for errors or omission. The reader assumes the risk, and full responsibility for all actions and the author will not be held liable for any loss or damage, whether consequential, incidental, and special or otherwise, that may result from the information presented in this publication.

The book is not intended to provide medical advice or to take the place of medical advice and treatment from your personal physician. Readers are advised to consult their own doctors or other qualified health professionals regarding the treatment of medical conditions. The author shall not be held liable or responsible for any misunderstanding or misuse of the information contained in this book. <u>The information is not intended to diagnose, treat, or cure any disease.</u> It's merely an inspiration to live a healthy lifestyle. If you suffer from any medical condition, are pregnant, lactating, or on medication, <u>be sure to talk to your doctor</u> before making any drastic changes in your diet and lifestyle.

Contents

Introduction

Are you ready to discover the new, super healthy, and nutritious way to help you look and feel amazing?

If your goal is to enjoy more energy, live a healthy lifestyle, and (if desired) lose weight – you have come to the right place!

Low-carb, low-sugar smoothie bowls are one of the best natural health tools you could try! The best part? No complicated cooking is required. You can now make super delicious and nutritious meals that actually taste good, even on a busy schedule.

The smoothie bowl recipes you are just about to discover (and hopefully try!) are very high in nutrients and rich in good fats. They will help you stay full for hours without feeling hungry or deprived.

And, if you feel like snacking – be sure to turn to our smoothie bowls as well! This booklet will show you a wide variety of delicious smoothie bowls, from naturally sweet, to spicy and savory!

You no longer need to worry about complicated meal plans. Instead, allow yourself to enjoy some healthy and balanced flexibility!

All the smoothie bowl recipes you are just about to discover are:

-very low in sugar (because they focus on fruits and veggies that are naturally low in sugar) – they are much healthier than traditional smoothies, and smoothie bowls that more often than not, are loaded with sugar, honey, and high-sugar fruit

-dairy and soy-free (we use healthy coconut milk and some nut milk as well) – once again, there are many smoothie books on the market, labeled as "healthy"; however they overdo dairy and soy *(one of the quickest ways to create an imbalance and mess up your hormones, not to mention – digestive problems that dairy products can cause).*

-naturally gluten-free and grain-free – perfect for a lighter and healthier lifestyle you love!

-Low in carbs, but still very filling and extremely nutritious (perfect for weight loss diets)

-Rich in good fats for sustainable energy! (if you want to lose weight, the best thing you can do is to reduce carbs while adding in some good fats- this is what this book is designed to help you with. Quickly and inexpensively)

-Rich in mind-body energizing chlorophyll and other superfoods- many recipes sneak in some healthy greens and other powerful superfoods to help you shine!

Our smoothie bowls are jam-packed with vital nutrients, vitamins, and minerals – to help you stay healthy and have beautiful, glowing skin and strong hair. They can also help you strengthen your immune system as they are very rich in Vitamin C, Magnesium, Zinc, and chlorophyll.

They are just perfect for helping you:

-enjoy more energy and feel amazing

-stay full for hours and avoid those annoying food cravings

-get you closer to your weight loss, health, and fitness goals without feeling deprived!

The best part?

-you don't need any fancy ingredients

-the recipes are beginner-friendly, so even if you hate cooking, you will do very well with this book

-most recipes can be used as a meal replacement

-our smoothie bowls are also very creative, and kids love them (perfect way to introduce your kids to healthy eating)

Included are:

-simple food lists/shopping lists (downloadable and printable to help you save your time) so that you know what to put in your smoothie bowls – we have done all the thinking for you.

-extra wellness tips and guidance (even if you are new to making smoothies and smoothie bowls – we got you covered)

-SOS motivation – to help you stay on track, take inspired action and experience all the incredible results of low sugar smoothies.

This mini recipe book is a practical "no-cook cookbook" designed for busy people who value their health and wellbeing.

I am very excited to have you on board, so let's get started!

Yes, as I mentioned earlier - not all smoothie bowls are made equal! Some of our recipes are naturally sweet (perfect as a quick, guilt-free dessert), and some are spicy or savory.

We love giving you different options to pick and choose from!

What I really like about our way of making smoothie bowls is that unlike traditional smoothies and smoothie bowls, they don't use any high sugar fruit (or use it in moderation).

That makes them perfect for people who need/want to follow low-sugar, low-carb diets.

Another benefit is that they can be customized very easily. Whether you like sweet, spicy, or savory- we got you covered!

I believe that just by making one big nutritious smoothie bowl a day, you have the power to truly revolutionize your health and feel amazing. It's also the best empowerment for you and your loved ones. It feels so good to know that you are doing the best you can to give your body what it needs to thrive while preventing disease.

The moment you decide to focus on abundance and enriching your diet with nutrient-packed, fresh foods, you will automatically crave less fast-food and processed foods. It's as simple as that.

This book is the 7th book in the Alkaline Keto Diet Series (where our recipes focus on empowerment, lifestyle change, and flexible, Alkaline-Keto inspired dieting).

Other books in this series include *Alkaline Ketogenic Juicing, Alkaline Ketogenic Mix,* and *Alkaline Ketogenic Lifestyle for Massive Weight Loss.*

The main focus of all our *Alkaline Keto books* is to inspire you to add more nutrient-rich foods to your diet to help you transition to a healthy lifestyle without feeling overwhelmed.

You can check out other books in the series on Amazon:

www.yourwellnessbooks.com/books

If it's the first time you are hearing the term "Alkaline"- don't worry. It's not about changing your pH, and it's definitely not about over-complicating your life. Alkaline foods are foods that are rich in Alkaline minerals (such as, for example, Magnesium). As such, they are a great tool to help your body stay in balance and give it the nourishment it needs to stay healthy and heal faster.

They are also naturally low in carbs and sugars, and so, we will be using them in our smoothie bowls.

The best alkaline foods to use in your smoothie bowls are healthy greens, low-sugar fruit, and some veggies.

With that being said, let's have a look at our food lists!

Low Sugar & Low Carb Food Lists

You can visit our private website and get your printable food lists (in PDF) at:

www.yourwellnessbooks.com/smoothie-bowls

(any technical issues with your download, please email:

info@yourwellnessbooks.com)

Recommended Fruit – Focus on Low Sugar & Low Carb As Much As Possible

The Best Fruits for Your Smoothies & Smoothie Bowls:

- Limes
- Lemons
- Grapefruits
- Avocado (yes, it's a fruit)
- Tomato (yea, it's a fruit)
- Pomegranate

The following fruit is also allowed in moderation, to add to taste, if needed

- Blueberries
- Sour cherries
- Raspberries
- Oranges
- Strawberries
- Other berries
- Green apple
- Pineapple

Recommended Greens – Super Healthy & Nourishing

All leafy greens are alkalizing and detoxifying to your body. This is why we will be working very hard to sneak them into our smoothies and smoothie bowls.

- Spinach
- Kale
- Microgreens
- Swiss Chard
- Arugula
- Endive
- Romaine Lettuce

+ Other:

- Parsley
- Mint
- Chive
- Dill

Veggies

Veggies to use in your smoothie bowls:

- Red bell pepper
- Green bell pepper
- Yellow bell pepper
- Zucchini
- Broccoli
- Asparagus
- Colliflower
- Garlic
- Onion
- Cucumbers
- Radishes
- Artichokes

More Superfoods and Herbs to Spice It Up

The following herbs and spices will make your smoothies taste delicious while adding in more healing benefits:

- Himalaya Salt
- Curry
- Red Chili Powder
- Cumin
- Nutmeg
- Italian spices
- Oregano
- Rosemary
- Lavender
- Mint
- Chamomile
- Fennel
- Cilantro
- Moringa

Natural Sweeteners and Supplements (Optional)

Stevia is very helpful if you want to make a sweet smoothie without using sugar or sugar-containing foods or supplements.

If you are looking for natural supplements to optimize your healthy smoothies and smoothie bowls, you can also try:

- Green Powders
- Moringa Powder
- Maca Powder
- Ashwagandha Powder

Again, these are all optional. However, if you are interested in learning more, please visit our private website, where I share more complimentary info with my readers. I have listed my favorite brands, green powders, and other health supplements to help you save your time:

www.YourWellnessBooks.com/resources

Healthy Fats

- Olive oil (organic, cold-pressed)
- Avocado oil
- Hemp oil
- Flaxseed oil
- Coconut oil
- Sesame oil

Please note, there is no need to purchase all of them, one or two is enough; my two favorites are coconut oil and olive oil.

***Wellness tip – whenever your body craves sugar or carbs have 1 tablespoon of coconut oil instead.
It always does the trick for me!

Then, you feel back on track, and you can proceed to making a nutrient-packed alkaline keto green smoothie with good oils to keep sugar cravings away for good!

Nuts and Seeds

These taste amazing in smoothies and will help you stay full for hours.

- Almonds
- Cashews
- Brazilian Nuts
- Macadamia Nuts
- Walnut
- Pine
- Pistachio
- Hazelnut
- Chia seeds

Of course, if you have any nut allergies, skip them in your smoothies. I have noticed that chia seeds work for most people (even those allergic to almonds or cashews), but, be sure to follow your own agenda, and talk to your health practitioner if needed.

Plant-Based Milk & Other

- Almond milk

- Coconut milk

- Hazelnut milk

- Coconut water

- Herbal infusions and tea

- Organic Apple Cider Vinegar

If you have any questions about the food lists/ingredients for your smoothie bowls, please email me at:

info@yourwellnessbooks.com

You can also sign up for our free wellness newsletter at:

www.yourwellnessbooks.com/email-newsletter

and then reply to my first email and say hi.

Why Low Carb, Low Sugar Smoothies? How Can They Help You?

Low carb, low sugar diets are proven to:

-manage your sugar levels, prevent diabetes

-normalize your hormones and auto-immune system

-improve your neurological health

Here are other benefits of low-carb, low-sugar smoothies:

-you will experience reduced hunger and reduced cravings

-you will be burning fat and reducing carbs and so normalizing your insulin levels

-you will protect your heart while raising the good cholesterol

-you will enjoy the anti-age benefits, as low-carb foods promote longevity and vitality (while nobody ever promised us we will live forever, by making a decision to stay healthy, we make sure that the time we are here on earth, we feel good and are vibrant).

The goal of this book is simple- I don't want to "push" any specific kind of a diet bandwagon or make you feel bad for eating a certain way.

Instead, I want to inspire you and give you simple, healthy, and delicious tools (low-sugar and low-carb smoothie bowls) to help you get closer to your health, wellness, and fitness goals every day.

Your Wellness Books Email Newsletter

Before we dive into the recipes, we would like to offer you free access to our VIP Wellness Newsletter

www.yourwellnessbooks.com/email-newsletter

Here's what you will be receiving:

-healthy, clean food recipes and tips delivered to your email

-motivation and inspiration to help you stay on track

-discounts and giveaways

-notifications about our new books (at massively reduced prices)

-healthy eating resources to help you on your journey

Sign up link (copy this link to your phone, tablet, or PC):

www.yourwellnessbooks.com/email-newsletter

Problems with signing up? Email us :
info@yourwellnessbooks.com

About the Recipes-Measurements Used in the Recipes

The cup measurement I use is the American Cup measurement. I also use it for dry ingredients. If you are new to it, let me help you: If you don't have American Cup measures, just use a metric or imperial liquid measuring jug and fill your jug with your ingredient to the corresponding level. Here's how to go about it:

1 American Cup= 250ml= 8 Fl.oz.

For example:

If a recipe calls for 1 cup of almonds, simply place your almonds into your measuring jug until it reaches the 250 ml/8oz marks.

I hope you found it helpful. I know that different countries use different measurements, and I wanted to make things simple for you. I have also noticed that very often those who are used to American Cup measurements complain about metric measurements and vice versa. However, if you apply what I have just explained, you will find it easy to use both.

Recipe #1 Easy Tropical Bowl

This smoothie bowl is quick and easy to make. Cinnamon and stevia make it naturally sweet, while coconut milk and oil contribute to its soft creaminess. Perfect breakfast or snack idea!

Serves: 2

Ingredients for the Smoothie:

- 1 small avocado, peeled and pitted
- 1.5 cup coconut milk (unsweetened, all-natural)
- 1 grapefruit, peeled
- 1 teaspoon Organifi green powder blend (optional)
- 1 tablespoon coconut oil
- 1-inch ginger
- Half teaspoon cinnamon to taste
- Stevia to sweeten, if needed

Ingredients for the Toppings:

- A handful of crushed cashews
- 2 pineapple slices, cut into smaller pieces
- 2-4 tablespoons coconut flakes (natural, unsweetened)

Instructions

1. Blend all the smoothie ingredients until smooth. Pour the smoothie into a bowl.
2. Mix in the rest of the ingredients (from the Ingredients for the Toppings section) by placing them on top.
3. Enjoy and serve! So yummy, filling, and healthy!

You can check out our favorite supplements and recommended green powder brands at:

www.YourWellnessBooks.com/supplements

Recipe #2 Delicious Vitamin C Power House

This recipe is full of Vitamin C to help you strengthen your immune system and feel amazing! It also sneaks in some greens to make it even healthier!

Serves: 1-2

Ingredients for the Smoothie:

- Half cup of blueberries or raspberries (fresh or frozen)
- 1 grapefruit
- Half cup baby spinach leaves
- A few fresh mint leaves
- Optional: a half teaspoon of green powder blend, such as Organifi
- Optional: stevia to sweeten

Ingredients for the Toppings:

- A handful of crushed almonds
- 1 tablespoon chia seeds
- 2 slices of apple

Instructions

1. Blend all the smoothie ingredients until smooth. If you are making this smoothie on a hot summer day, feel free to add some ice cubes. Pour the smoothie into a bowl.

2. Mix in the rest of the ingredients by adding them on top.

3. You can enjoy your smoothie bowl now or store it in the fridge for later.

Recipe #3 Magnesium Bomb Smoothie Bowl

This amazingly refreshing smoothie bowl is jam-packed with Magnesium to help you optimize your performance.

Serves: 2

Ingredients for the Smoothie:

- 1 small avocado, peeled and pitted
- 1 small lime, peeled
- half cup coconut water
- half cup coconut milk
- 2 tablespoons chia seeds
- 1 tablespoon flaxseed or coconut oil
- Stevia to sweeten, if needed

Ingredients for the Toppings:

- A handful of Brazil nuts, chopped
- 2 dates, peeled and pitted
- Cinnamon powder to sprinkle on top
- Optional – Organifi green powder to sprinkle on top

Instructions:

1. Blend all the smoothie ingredients until smooth. If you are making this smoothie on a hot summer day, feel free to add some ice cubes. Pour the smoothie into a bowl.
2. Mix in the rest of the ingredients by placing them on top.
3. You can enjoy your smoothie bowl now or store it in the fridge for later.

Recipe #4 Pudding-Style Dessert Smoothie Bowl

This smoothie bowl is just perfect if you are craving something sweet. You can enjoy it without compromising your health or weight loss goals.

Serves: 1-2

Ingredients for the Smoothie:

- Half avocado, peeled and pitted
- Half orange, peeled and pitted
- 1 cup cashew milk
- Half cup raspberries or blueberries (fresh or frozen)
- 2 tablespoons cocoa powder
- Optional: stevia to taste, if needed

Ingredients for the Toppings:

- A handful of crushed cashews
- 1 tablespoon cocoa powder or dark chocolate crumbs to sprinkle around
- 1 tablespoon plant-based protein powder of your choice
- 1 teaspoon cinnamon powder to sprinkle around

Instructions:

1. Blend all the ingredients until smooth.

2. Add the rest of the ingredients on top.

3. You can enjoy your smoothie bowl now or store it in the fridge for later.

Recipe #5 Green Health Freak Smoothie Bowl

Hemp seeds are an excellent all-natural source of protein. In this recipe, they team up with green superfoods to help you enjoy more energy and have healthy-looking, glowing skin.

Serves: 2

Ingredients for the Smoothie:

- 1 small avocado
- 1 cup coconut milk (or any nut milk of your choice)
- Half a lemon (or lime)
- A handful of fresh arugula leaves
- 1 green apple
- 1 tablespoon hemp seed powder

Ingredients for the Toppings:

- A handful of crushed cashews
- A handful of coconut flakes
- 1 teaspoon cinnamon powder

Instructions:

1. Blend all the ingredients until smooth.

2. If needed, blend in some ice cubes too.

3. Pour into a bowl.

4. Add the rest of the ingredients by placing them on top of the smoothie (they also serve as decoration).

5. Enjoy!

Recipe #6 Creamy Cherry Treat Bowl

Cherries are a fantastic ingredient for natural sweet smoothie bowls! They are also very rich in Vitamin C and Potassium to help you enhance your muscle strength and metabolism.

Serves: 1-2

Ingredients for the Smoothie:

- Half cup of cherries, pitted (fresh or frozen)
- 1 grapefruit, peeled
- 1 cup coconut milk or cashew milk
- A few slices of peeled cucumber
- 2 tablespoons chia seeds
- 1 tablespoon coconut oil

Ingredients for the Toppings:

- Handful of almonds
- Handful of cashews
- 1 teaspoon cinnamon powder

Instructions:

1. Blend all the ingredients until smooth.
2. Pour into a bowl.
3. Mix in the rest of the ingredients by placing them on top.

4. You can enjoy your smoothie bowl now or store it in the fridge for later.

Recipe #7 Easy Green Bowl

Chlorophyll is the secret power of vibrant health. So, start adding it to your smoothie bowls and watch your energy skyrocket! You can also use powdered chlorophyll or green powder mix that contains different herbs. For example, Organifi is a blend created by well-known health expert Drew Canole. It can be a great solution if you want something you can throw into your smoothie bowls that offer an all-in-one blend.

I recommend you visit:

www.YourWellnessBooks.com/supplements
 to learn more about it.

Serves: 2

Ingredients for the Smoothie:

- 1 handful of fresh cilantro leaves
- 1 tablespoon mint
- 1 cup of coconut milk
- 1 tablespoon Organifi green powder (optional)
- 2 drops of liquid chlorophyll (optional)
- Half cup blueberries (fresh or frozen)

More Ingredients for the Toppings:

- A handful of sunflower seeds

- A handful of hemp seeds

- 1 slice of lemon or lime

- A few raisins

Instructions:

1. Blend all the ingredients until smooth.

2. Pour into a bowl.

3. Mix in the rest of the ingredients by placing them on top.

4. You can enjoy your smoothie bowl now or store it in the fridge for later.

Recipe #8 Sweet Potato Fill Me Up Smoothie

When it comes to healthy carbs, like sweet potatoes, there is nothing to fear. They will help you start the day feeling energized and will fill you up for hours. With some added Omega-3 and protein from the flax seeds, you will enjoy an incredible snack or a healthy breakfast, even on a busy schedule.

Serves: 2

Ingredients for the Smoothie:

- 1 big sweet potato, cooked and peeled
- 1 cup of almond milk, unsweetened
- ¼ tsp. nutmeg
- ¼ tsp. ground cinnamon
- 1 tsp. flax seed
- A handful of arugula leaves
- Optional: ½ tsp. moringa powder
- Himalayan salt to taste

More Ingredients for the Toppings:

- A handful of green olives, pitted

- A handful of black olives, pitted

- A handful of crushed cashews

Instructions:

1. Blend all the ingredients until smooth.

2. Pour into a bowl.

3. Mix in the rest of the ingredients by placing them on top.

4. Serve and enjoy!

Recipe #9 Creamy Guilt-Free Bowl

This delicious smoothie bowl is just perfect for a quick, pick-me-up afternoon snack.

Serves: 1-2

Ingredients for the Smoothie:

- Half cup blueberries, fresh or frozen
- 1 cup coconut yogurt (natural, no added sugar). You can also use coconut cream or thick coconut milk. If you are allergic to coconut, any plant-based yogurt will do here.
- 1 tablespoon chia seeds
- A handful of baby spinach
- 1 grapefruit, peeled

More Ingredients for the Toppings:

- A handful of crushed almonds
- A few dried apricots
- Cinnamon powder and stevia to taste, if needed
- 2 tablespoons almond or coconut powder

Instructions:

1. Blend all the ingredients until smooth.

2. Mix in the rest of the ingredients by placing them on top.

3. You can enjoy your smoothie bowl now or store it in the fridge for later.

Recipe #10 Easy Spicy Bowl

Flax seeds are very nourishing, and nori adds even more amazing alkaline nutrients such as Vitamin C, Vitamin A, Potassium, and Magnesium to this mix. It tastes great, too! Perfect as a quick brunch or lunch recipe, or a side dish.

Serves: 2

Ingredients for the Smoothie:

- Half cup arugula leaves
- 1 small avocado, peeled, and pitted
- Half lime, peeled
- 1 cup coconut milk or almond milk
- 1 tablespoon flax seeds
- 2 nori sheets roasted and crushed
- Chili powder to taste
- Himalayan salt to taste

More Ingredients for the Toppings:

- Handful of pistachios
- 3 tablespoons of finely chopped red or green pepper
- Optional: a few black olives, pitted

Instructions:

1. Blend all the ingredients until smooth.

2. Mix in the rest of the ingredients by placing them on top.

3. Serve and enjoy!

Recipe #11 Healthy Immune System Bowl

This recipe will help you take care of your immune system while taking care of your eyes and skin. It's jam-packed with Vitamins A and C, Vitamin B6, copper, folate, and potassium.

Serves: 2

Ingredients for the Smoothie:

- 2 big carrots, peeled
- 1 green apple, cut into smaller pieces
- 1 cup hemp milk or other nut/ plant-based milk
- A handful of arugula leaves
- 2 tablespoons of chia seeds

More Ingredients for the Toppings:

- A few raisins
- A handful of cashews, crushed

Instructions:

1. Blend all the smoothie ingredients until smooth. Pour into a bowl.
2. Mix in the rest of the ingredients by placing them on top.
3. Serve and enjoy!

Recipe #12 Matcha Tea Energy Weight Loss Bowl

If you need a quick boost of energy, matcha and vitamin C is a great combination! This smoothie bowl is light and energizing. Perfect as a quick snack, dessert bowl, or healthy breakfast.

Serves: 2

Ingredients for the Smoothie:

- 1 teaspoon matcha green tea powder
- 1 big grapefruit, peeled
- 1 avocado, peeled and pitted
- 1 cup thick coconut milk (unsweetened)
- 1 inch of ginger (peeled)
- 1 tablespoon chia seeds
- Stevia to sweeten

More Ingredients for the Toppings:

- A handful of blueberries
- A few raisins or apricots
- 1 teaspoon cinnamon powder
- 2 tablespoons crushed cashews

Instructions:

1. Blend all the ingredients until smooth.

2. Pour into a bowl. Mix in the rest of the ingredients by placing them on top.

3. You can enjoy your smoothie bowl now or store it in the fridge for later.

Recipe #13 Coconut Almond Keto Fat Bomb Bowl

This smoothie is perfect if you are craving something sweet.

It's low-sugar, low-carb, packed in nutrients, and totally guilt-free.

Serves: 2

Ingredients for the Smoothie:

- Half lime, peeled
- ½ cup shredded coconut
- 1 cup coconut milk, thick, unsweetened
- 6 tablespoons of almond butter (or any nut or seed butter, unsweetened)
- 2 tablespoons coconut oil
- 1 teaspoon vanilla powder
- Cinnamon powder and stevia to sweeten

More Ingredients for the Toppings:

- A handful of crushed cashews
- Coconut powder to sprinkle over

Instructions:

1. Blend all the ingredients until smooth. Pour into a bowl.
2. Mix in the rest of the ingredients by placing them on top.
3. Serve and enjoy!

Recipe #14 Sesame Street Bowl

Sesame seeds are a great source of Vitamin E and natural protein as well as iron and Omega-3. They help remove toxins, balance hormones, and promote healthy skin and hair.

Serves: 2

Ingredients for the Smoothie:

- 2 tablespoons sesame seeds
- 2 tablespoons tahini
- 1 avocado, peeled and pitted
- 1 cup coconut milk
- 1 tablespoon coconut oil
- 1 teaspoon vanilla powder

More Ingredients for the Toppings:

- A handful of crushed cashews
- A handful of crushed Brazil nuts
- 1 tablespoon cinnamon powder

Instructions:

1. Blend all the ingredients until smooth.
2. Mix in the rest of the ingredients by placing them on top.
3. Enjoy and serve!

Recipe #15 Easy Green Bowl

This simple recipe is incredibly nutritious. The best part? It sneaks in some greens to help you shine!

Serves: 1-2

Ingredients for the Smoothie:

- A handful of fresh spinach leaves
- 1 green apple, cut into smaller pieces
- 1 cup almond milk
- 1 teaspoon cinnamon powder
- 1 teaspoon vanilla powder

Ingredients for the Toppings:

- A few grapes
- A handful of walnuts, crushed
- Optional – more cinnamon powder to sprinkle on top

Instructions:

1. Blend all the ingredients until smooth.
2. Mix in the rest of the ingredients by placing them on top. You can enjoy your smoothie bowl now or store it in the fridge for later. Enjoy!

Recipe #16 Tasty Mediterranean Olive Bowl

If you like Mediterranean flavors and spices, you will love this. Who said smoothie bowls must be sweet? Also, this one is super nutritious and perfect as a quick lunch recipe (or a delicious side dish).

Serves: 1-2

Ingredients for the Smoothie:

- 1 avocado, peeled and pitted
- 1 cup almond milk, unsweetened
- Half cup organic tomato juice
- 1/4 cup mixed Italian herbs
- 2 cucumbers, peeled and cut into smaller pieces
- A handful of arugula leaves
- Himalayan salt and black pepper to taste

Ingredients for the Toppings:

- A handful of pistachios
- A handful of black olives, pits removed
- A handful of green olives, pits removed
- A few fresh basil leaves

Instructions:

1. Blend all the smoothie ingredients in a blender, until nice and creamy.
2. Pour into a bowl.
3. Mix in the rest of the ingredients by placing them on top.
4. Serve and enjoy!

Recipe #17 Nutritious Raw Soup Bowl

Another option for a quick lunch smoothie. It offers a myriad of nutrients such as B vitamins and iodine from nori and Omega-3s from chia seeds. Perfect to help you stay energized and nourished.

Serves: 2

Ingredients for the Smoothie:

- 2 nori sheets, soaked in water
- 1 cup coconut milk
- 1 avocado, peeled and pitted
- 1 small cucumber, peeled and cut into smaller pieces
- A handful of kale leaves
- Himalayan salt and black pepper to taste

More Ingredients for the Toppings:

- A handful of pistachios
- A handful of crushed cashews
- Optional: a few chili flakes, if you like it spicy

Instructions:

1. Blend all the ingredients until smooth. Pour into a bowl.
2. Mix in the rest of the ingredients by placing them on top. Enjoy!

Recipe #18 Hemp Energy Smoothie Bowl

Hemp seeds are full of Omega 3 and 6, antioxidants, Vitamins B1, B2, B6, Vitamin C, Vitamin D, calcium, fiber, iron, and zinc. Perfect for natural energy and a healthy immune system!

Serves: 1-2

Ingredients for the Smoothie:

- 1 cup of hemp milk
- 1 tablespoon hemp seeds or hemp seed powder
- 1 tablespoon sugar-free nut butter (can be almond, sesame, or almond)
- 1 large handful of fresh arugula leaves
- Half avocado, peeled and pitted
- Pinch of Himalayan salt and black pepper to taste

Ingredients for the Toppings:

- A handful of chopped chives
- A handful of chopped basil leaves
- 1 teaspoon oregano
- A few slices of avocado
- Optional: chili flakes, or chili powder if you like it spicy
- Optional: a few black or green olives

Instructions:

1. Blend all the ingredients until smooth.

2. Pour into a bowl.

3. Mix in the rest of the ingredients by placing them on top.

4. You can enjoy your smoothie bowl now or store it in the fridge for later.

Recipe #19 Simply Sweet Chia Bowl

This delicious smoothie bowl is one of my favorite healthy desserts. It's also great for breakfast!

Serves: 1-2

Ingredients for the Smoothie:

- Half avocado, peeled and pitted
- 1 cup almond milk or coconut milk (unsweetened)
- 3 dates, pitted
- 1 teaspoon cinnamon powder
- 4 tablespoons chia seeds
- Stevia to sweeten
- 2 tablespoons coconut oil

More Ingredients for the Toppings:

- A handful of fresh blueberries
- Any nuts or seeds of your choice

Instructions:

1. Blend all the ingredients until smooth. Pour into a smoothie bowl.
2. Add the rest of the ingredients on top.
3. Place in a fridge for 4-8 hours.
4. Serve and enjoy!

Recipe#20 Easy Green Weight Loss Smoothie

This green vegetable smoothie is the number one recommendation if your goal is weight loss. It may take some time to get used to green vegetable smoothies, especially if you are more accustomed to drinking "sweety-carby-fruity" smoothies (not that good for you, unfortunately).

But trust me, after a few green smoothies, and fantastic energy they provide, you will be wondering how you could ever live without them.

Himalaya salt really makes it taste delicious. Now, I like to keep my recipes as simple as possible, without too many ingredients.

But to let you know the variations of this recipe- you could also add in some cilantro, curry, and chili pepper if you like spicy smoothies.

If you go for this variation, you may also heat up the smoothie and serve it as a beautiful, warm soup (and add some coconut or other full-fat cream on top). Enjoy!

Servings: 2

Ingredients for the Smoothie:

- 1 cup coconut or almond milk (unsweetened)
- 1 big cucumber, peeled and pitted
- A handful of arugula leaves
- A few lime slices
- 1 tablespoon coconut oil or flaxseed oil
- Pinch of Himalaya salt to taste
- Pinch of black pepper to taste

Ingredients for the Toppings:

- A few slices of red and green pepper
- A few green olives

Instructions:

1. Place all the ingredients in a blender.
2. Blend well.
3. Serve and enjoy!

Recipe#21 Spirulina Infused Spanish Gazpacho

This recipe is one of the most nutritious recipes I have ever created. Why? Well, it's because of the superfood called spirulina.

Spirulina is a green superfood naturally rich in calcium, iron, magnesium, and phosphorous. It acts as a powerful antioxidant and is rich in anti-inflammatory properties. In this recipe, it teams up with other healthy ingredients to create this original smoothie bowl recipe.

Serves: 2

Ingredients for the Smoothie:

- 2 medium-sized cucumbers, peeled and chopped
- 1 green bell pepper
- 1 big garlic clove, peeled
- 2 tablespoons extra-virgin, cold-pressed olive oil
- 1 cup organic tomato juice
- 1 teaspoon spirulina powder
- Half cup almond milk
- Pinch of Himalayan salt
- Pinch of black pepper

Ingredients for the Toppings:

- A handful of green and black olives
- A few onion rings
- A few cashews

Instructions:

1. Place all the ingredients in a blender and process until smooth.
2. Pour into a bowl and add in the toppings.
3. Serve and enjoy!

Recipe#22 Healing Celery Bowl to Help You Shine

Here comes another delicious veggie smoothie bowl recipe. Celery is very rich in vitamin C, fiber, alkaline minerals such as potassium and is also very hydrating and replenishing.

Serves 1-2

Ingredients for the Smoothie:

- Half cup of celery leaves
- 1 tablespoon avocado oil
- A handful of raw cashews
- 1 cup coconut milk or cream (unsweetened)
- Pinch of black pepper to taste
- Pinch of Himalaya salt to taste
- A handful of fresh cilantro leaves

Ingredients for the Toppings:

- A few avocado slices
- A few cucumber slices
- A few green olives, pitted

Instructions:

1. Place all the ingredients in a blender and process until smooth.

2. If needed, season with Himalayan salt and black pepper.

3. Pour the smoothie into a bowl.

4. Add in the toppings, serve and enjoy!

Recipe#23 Super Low Carb Bowl

This is a simple superfood smoothie that will help you boost your immune system by enriching your diet with vitamin C and a myriad of alkaline minerals.

Serves 1-2

Ingredients for the Smoothie:

- 2 big limes, peeled
- 1 cup of coconut or almond milk
- A handful of kale leaves, washed
- 1 tablespoon coconut oil
- 1 teaspoon cinnamon powder
- Stevia to sweeten, if needed

Ingredients for the Toppings:

- 2 tablespoons chia seeds
- 2 tablespoons crushed cashews

Instructions:

1. Place in a blender.
2. Process until smooth.
3. Pour into a bowl, add in the toppings and serve.
4. Enjoy!

Recipe#24 Bullet Proof Creamy Coffee Bowl

This smoothie is perfect early in the morning to help you concentrate better at work. It combines the antioxidant properties of blueberries with good fats and a bit of coffee. It's creamy, nutritious, and delicious.

Servings: 2

Ingredients for the Smoothie:

- 1 strong expresso (use organic, quality coffee)
- 1 cup thick coconut milk or almond milk
- Half avocado, peeled and pitted
- 1 tablespoon chia seeds or chia seed powder
- 2 tablespoons coconut oil
- Stevia to sweeten if needed

Ingredients for the Toppings:

- A handful of blueberries
- A few mint leaves
- A handful of coconut flakes
- 1 teaspoon cinnamon powder

Instructions:

1. Blend all the ingredients in a blender until smooth.

2. Pour your smoothie into a bowl.

3. Add in the toppings, serve and enjoy!

Recipe#25 Nutritious Aroma Smoothie

This recipe is very nutritious, and it can also be served as a quick, raw, or almost raw soup (you can add some eggs or protein to make it more filling).

Servings: 2

Ingredients for the Smoothie:

- 1 cup thick coconut milk (full-fat)
- 1 tablespoon coconut oil
- Half avocado, peeled and sliced
- Half lemon, peeled and sliced
- 1 cup fresh cilantro leaves, washed
- Half teaspoon Himalaya salt to taste

Ingredients for the Toppings:

- 2 tablespoons crushed cashews
- 2 tablespoons crushed macadamia nuts

Instructions:

1. Place all the ingredients in a blender.
2. Process until smooth.
3. Pour into a smoothie bowl.
4. Add the toppings, serve, and enjoy!

Recipe#26 Creamy Relaxation Bowl

This smoothie uses healing herbal infusions such as chamomile and rooibos. Chamomile is famous for its sleep and calm-inducing properties, while rooibos is full of healthy, alkaline minerals, such as Magnesium. It's also naturally sweet, and so is this smoothie.

Servings: 2

Ingredients for the Smoothie:

- 1 cup rooibos tea (cooled down, use 1 teabag per cup)
- 1 cup chamomile tea (cooled down, use 1 teabag per cup)
- 1 small avocado, peeled and pitted
- A few dates, pitted
- Half cup thick coconut milk
- 1 tablespoon coconut oil
- Stevia to sweeten if needed

Ingredients for the Toppings:

- A few raisins
- A few cashews

Instructions:

1. Place all the ingredients in a blender.
2. Process until smooth.
3. Pour into a bowl and add the rest of the ingredients.
4. Serve and enjoy!

Recipe#27 Double Your Energy Bowl

This smoothie can be served as a quick lunch or brunch to help you double your energy and feel amazing. No more afternoon energy crashes!

Serves: 2

Ingredients for the Smoothie:

- 1 cup of fresh dairy-free yogurt or full-fat coconut milk (no added sugar)
- Half cup water, filtered
- 2 cucumbers, peeled and chopped
- Half an avocado, peeled and pitted
- 1 cup iceberg lettuce
- A pinch of Himalayan salt to taste
- A pinch of black pepper to taste
- 1 tablespoon coconut oil
- A few lime or lemon slices

Ingredients for the Toppings:

- A handful of cashews
- A handful of green olives
- 1 tablespoon fresh chive or dill

Instructions:

1. Place all the ingredients in a blender.
2. Process well until smooth and creamy.
3. Taste to see if you need to add some salt.
4. Pour into a bowl.
5. Add in the toppings.
6. Serve and enjoy!

Recipe#28 Spicy Keto Bowl

This recipe uses hemp oil, which is great to re-balance hormones, soothe anxiety, and improve the mood. Perfect for a delicious, low-carb and low-sugar smoothie like this one!

Serves 1-2

Ingredients for the Smoothie:

- 1 tablespoon of hemp oil
- 1 cup thick coconut milk
- Half avocado, pitted and peeled
- A handful of cilantro leaves, washed
- 1 teaspoon spirulina powder
- Pinch of Himalayan salt
- Pinch of curry powder
- Optional (if you like it spicy) a pinch of chili powder

Ingredients for the Toppings:

- A few red bell pepper slices, minced
- A few onion rings
- A few spicy olives, pitted

Instructions:

1. Place all the ingredients in a blender.

2. Process well until smooth.

3. Taste to check if you like the taste or if you need to add a bit more of Himalayan salt or curry powder.

4. Now, pour into a bowl and add in the toppings

5. Serve and enjoy!

Recipe#29 Easy Relaxation Bowl

This smoothie is great for digestion and relaxation.

Thanks to coconut oil, it also helps prevent sugar cravings.

Serves 1-2

Ingredients for the Smoothie:

- 1 tablespoon of mint leaves
- 2 tablespoons of coconut oil
- 1 teaspoon of fresh vanilla powder
- 1 cup chamomile infusion, cooled
- Half cup blueberries, fresh or frozen
- Stevia to sweeten, if needed

Ingredients for the Toppings:

- A handful of almonds, crushed
- Cinnamon powder
- A few raisins

Instructions:

1. Blend all the smoothie ingredients until smooth.
2. Pour into a bowl and add in the toppings.
3. Serve and enjoy!

Recipe#30 The Healthy Skin Glow Bowl

This bowl is designed to help you have a glowing, healthy-looking skin. All this while helping your body get back to balance through optimal nutrition.

Serves 1-2

Ingredients for the Smoothie:

- 1 tablespoon coconut oil
- 1 cup of cashew or other nut milk of your choice
- Half cup broccoli, steamed (you can also use steamed zucchini or cauliflower)
- 1 big tomato
- 1 small garlic clove
- A handful of fresh cilantro leaves, washed
- Himalayan salt to taste

Ingredients for the Toppings:

- A handful of cashews
- A few avocado slices
- A few cucumber slices

BONUS – Green Smoothies for Detox and Weight Loss

Vitamin C Alkaline Keto Green Power

This delicious smoothie is jam-packed with vitamin C coming from alkaline and keto-friendly fruits like limes and lemons. Now, I understand that looking at the ingredients of this recipe; you may be feeling a bit "turned off." Yes, alkaline keto smoothies are very different to usual "sweet fruity smoothies."

But, give it a try. It tastes great! Very similar to natural, Greek yogurt. You can also use this smoothie recipe to season your salads. Most salad seasonings are full of crappy carbs, sugars, and a ton of chemicals, while this smoothie is 100% natural! Another suggestion is - you could use this smoothie recipe to make a smoothie bowl by adding in some nuts and seeds. Once you have tried this smoothie, you will get my point for sure!

Servings: 2

Ingredients:

- 1 big avocado, peeled, pitted and sliced
- A small handful of spinach leaves
- Half lemon, peeled and sliced
- 1 cup of coconut milk
- 1 teaspoon coconut oil
- Pinch of Himalaya salt

- Pinch of black pepper

- A few slices of lime to garnish

Instructions:

1. Place all the ingredients in a blender.

2. Process until smooth.

3. Serve in a smoothie glass and garnish with a few lime slices.

4. Drink to your health and enjoy!

Green Mineral Comfort Smoothie Soup

This recipe can be used both as a smoothie as well as a soup.

Whenever I am pressed for time, I make it for dinner, to enjoy something warm, and I keep the raw leftovers to have a healthy green smoothie in the morning.

Servings: 1-2

Ingredients:

- 1 big cucumber, peeled
- 1 small avocado, peeled and pitted
- A handful of parsley
- A handful of cilantro
- 1 cup of thick coconut milk
- A handful of raw cashews or pistachios (peel removed)
- 1 tablespoon of olive oil
- Himalayan salt to taste
- 1 chili flake (optional)

Instructions:

1. Blend all the ingredients in a blender.

2. Serve raw as a smoothie, or heat it up (using low heat) and serve as a gentle, detox, comforting soup.

3. Enjoy!

Green Fat Burner Smoothie

This recipe combines the best fat-burning ingredients ever, helps you concentrate for long hours while feeling lighter.

It's also great if you suffer from water retention. Personally, I love drinking this smoothie in the summer.

Servings: 2

Ingredients:

- 1 green tea teabag (or 1 teaspoon green tea powder)
- 1 horsetail infusion tea bag (or 1 teaspoon horsetail infusion powder)
- 1 cup of water, filtered
- 1 big avocado
- 1 big grapefruit
- Half cup of coconut milk
- 1 teaspoon cinnamon powder
- Stevia to sweeten

Instructions:

1. Boil 1 cup of water.

2. Add in the green tea and horsetail infusion.

3. Cover.

4. In the meantime, process the remaining ingredients in a blender.

5. Add in the cooled herbal infusion and process again.

6. If needed sweeten with stevia.

7. Serve chilled and enjoy!

Massive Green Power Plants Smoothie

If you don't like spinach or kale, I highly recommend you try arugula leaves. They taste delicious, both in salads and smoothies.

Servings: 3-4

Ingredients:

- 1 cup arugula leaves, washed
- 1 small avocado, peeled, pitted and sliced
- 2 cucumbers, peeled and sliced
- 4 tablespoons fresh lemon juice
- 2 tablespoons olive oil
- 2 cups hazelnut milk (unsweetened)
- Himalaya salt and black pepper to taste

Instructions:

1. Place all the ingredients in a blender.
2. Process well until smooth.
3. Serve and enjoy!

Easy Guacamole Smoothie

This smoothie can be used as a dip to be served with some veggies.

It makes a great meal replacement if you are pressed for time and are looking for an easy and nutritious meal.

Servings: 1-2

Ingredients:

- 2 tomatoes, sliced
- Half avocado, peeled and sliced
- A handful of arugula leaves
- 1 small garlic clove, peeled and minced
- 4 tablespoons lime juice
- Half cup water, filtered
- 2 tablespoons olive oil
- Himalayan salt and black pepper to taste

Instructions:

1. Place all the ingredients in a blender.
2. Process well until smooth. Serve and enjoy!

Questions?

You can email me at:

info@yourwellnessbooks.com

Low-Carb Low-Sugar Smoothie Bowls is the 7th book in the *Alkaline Keto Diet Book* series.

The first book in the series is called: *Alkaline Ketogenic Mix*: *Quick, Easy, and Delicious Recipes & Tips for Natural Weight Loss and a Healthy Lifestyle.*

It's a step-by-step beginner guide to help you transition to a healthy alkaline-keto way of eating without feeling deprived.

Other books in the *Alkaline Keto* series focus on specific recipes or cooking methods, for example: *Alkaline Ketogenic Salads, Alkaline Ketogenic Smoothies & Juices,* or *Alkaline Ketogenic Green Smoothies.*

There is no recommended reading order – feel free to pick up your next alkaline keto book by focusing on your favorite recipes, or a specific alkaline keto cooking method you wish to dive deeper into (for example salads or smoothies).

You will find all the Alkaline Keto Diet books on Amazon & listed on our website. You will also find them by searching for "Alkaline Keto Elena Garcia" on the Amazon website (US or other countries).

www.amazon.com/author/elenagarcia

www.yourwellnessbooks.com/books

(FYI, there is also a romance/erotica writer who uses the name Elena Garcia on Amazon, however, it's not me. I only write wellness and weight loss as well as healthy eating books!).

By searching for *Alkaline Keto Elena Garcia*, you will be able to find other books in the series.

If you are looking for specific alkaline keto supplements, programs, or other tools and brand recommendations (readers ask me all the time), I have listed everything on our website to help you save your research time:

www.YourWellnessBooks.com

Extra Resources to Help You on Your Wellness and Weight Loss Journey

-Alkaline Cleanse – discover how to lose weight and get rid of sugar cravings without feeling hungry or deprived:

www.YourWellnessBooks.com/cleanse

-Keto Meal Plans & Keto After 40:

www.YourWellnessBooks.com/resources

We Need Your Help

One more thing, before you go, could you please do us a quick favor?

It would be great if you could leave us a short review on Amazon.

Don't worry, it doesn't have to be long. One sentence is enough.

Let others know your favorite recipes and who you think this book can help.

Your review can inspire more and more people to turn to the low carb & low sugar lifestyle so that they can finally achieve their wellness and weight loss goals the way they deserve.

Your honest review is critical.

Thank You for your support!

Join Our VIP Readers' Newsletter to Boost Your Wellbeing

Would you like to be notified about our new health and wellness books? How about receiving them at deeply discounted prices? What about awesome giveaways, latest health tips, and motivation?

If that is something you are interested in, please visit the link below to join our newsletter:

www.yourwellnessbooks.com/email-newsletter

As a bonus, you will receive a free complimentary eBook *Alkaline Paleo Superfoods*

Sign up link:

www.yourwellnessbooks.com/email-newsletter

(any technical issues, please email us at:

info@yourwellnessbooks.com)

More Books & Resources in the Healthy Lifestyle Series

Available at:

www.yourwellnessbooks.com

Conclusion

Until next time, wishing you all the best on your journey!

Elena & Your Wellness Books Team

Conclusion

HUMPHREY JENNINGS

Also by Kevin Jackson

Invisible Forms

Kevin Jackson

HUMPHREY JENNINGS

PICADOR

First published 2004 by Picador
an imprint of Pan Macmillan Ltd
Pan Macmillan, 20 New Wharf Road, London NI 9RR
Basingstoke and Oxford
Associated companies throughout the world
www.panmacmillan.com

ISBN 0 330 35438 8

Picture Credits
All photographs property of, and reproduced with permission of, Mary-Lou Legg except:
Horse's Head – reproduced by permission of Jean-Pierre Haik;
Lee Miller contact sheet – courtesy Lee Miller Estate

1 3 5 7 9 8 6 4 2

A CIP catalogue record for this book is available from
the British Library.

Typeset by SetSystems Ltd, Saffron Walden, Essex
Printed and bound in Great Britain by
Mackays of Chatham plc, Chatham, Kent

For my parents

AJ   ADLJ

Whoever wants to do dreamwork
must mix all things together

Albrecht Dürer

Contents

Contents

Acknowledgements

My greatest debt is to Dr Mary-Lou Legg, whose contributions to this biography – interviews, phone calls, letters, arranged introductions, diplomacy, book loans, impromptu history lessons, lunches and many other acts of kindness – have greatly exceeded the claims either of daughterly loyalty or of friendship. If there is merit in these pages, much of it is due to her.

I have also drawn freely on the following recorded interviews, some of them filmed for Kevin Macdonald's documentary *Humphrey Jennings, The Man Who Listened to Britain* (Figment Films, 2000) (a few of the older witnesses, sadly, have since died):

*

With other members of Humphrey Jennings's family: his daughter Charlotte Jennings, his brother Rodney Jennings, and his granddaughter Anna Clarke; with his surviving friends and colleagues outside the world of film-making: Mrs Mary Boggeis, M. Henri Cartier-Bresson, Mrs Elsie Duncan-Jones (*née* Phare), Mr David Gascoyne and Mrs Judy Gascoyne, Mr Conroy Maddox, Dr Kathleen Raine, Mr Humphrey Spender, Mr Harry Waugh; with his fellow film-makers from the GPO and Crown Film Units, and from Wessex Films, and with members of their families: Lord Attenborough, Mr Ken Cameron, Mrs Frances Cockburn, Mrs Megan Dalrymple, Sir Denis Forman, Mrs Nora Lee (formerly Dawson), Mr John Legard, Mr Joe Mendoza, Sir John Mortimer, Mr C. Pennington-Richards, Mrs Diana Pine, Mr Julian Spiro, Mrs Jenny Stein (*née* Hutt); with the people of Cwmgiedd and Ystradgynlais, particularly Mr Ewart Alexander, Mr V. L. Evans, Mr David Roberts and Mr Eddy Thomas – and with Mr Cyril Demarne, the veteran firefighter, who was assigned to assist Jennings for the making of *Fires Were Started*; with various Jennings experts and enthusiasts: Mr James Birch, Professor Angus Calder, Mr Terence Davies, Sir Christopher Frayling, Mr John Gray, Mr Patrick

Keillor, Mr Mike Leigh, Professor David Mellor, Dr Rod Mengham, Mr Andrew Murray, Lord Puttnam, Professor Michel Remy, Professor Jeffrey Richards, Mr Hisashi Okajima, Dr Dorothy Sheridan, Mr David Thomson, Mr Dai Vaughan.

Work on this book was greatly enriched by an enjoyable collaboration with Kevin Macdonald on *The Man Who Listened to Britain*; my warmest thanks to him, to our researcher Kier Roper-Caldbeck, to our line producer Fran Robertson and to our crew, Neve Cunningham (camera) and Cath Patton (sound). I am very grateful to Tim Gardam of Channel 4 for having the vision to commission this film, and the will to broadcast such serious, uncommercial matter at prime time during the Christmas season, 2000.

As for many of my other projects David Thompson provided a wealth of otherwise unobtainable videos, particularly on Jennings, John Grierson, the GPO Film Unit and Mass-Observation. Geoff Andrew of the NFT invited me to curate a season of Jennings's films in January 2000, and so enabled me to make a close study of the complete *oeuvre* as it was meant to be seen – on the big screen. Zahid Warley and Lawrence Pollard of the BBC went out of their way to track down relevant tapes of radio broadcasts. Professor John Haffenden, the biographer of William Empson, kindly provided me with a copy of the Jennings/Empson correspondence. The tenants of two Walberswick houses in which Jennings spent his early years preferred to remain anonymous, but were more than generous with their time and hospitality.

Dr John Constable and Mrs A. Fitzsimmons arranged for me to have access to the I. A. Richards collection at the Pepys Library, Magdalene College, Cambridge, and the Librarian, Dr Richard Luckett, graciously permitted selective quotation from the archive. Mr David Jones allowed me unlimited access to relevant Perse School files, and to its collection of the school magazine, *The Pelican*. I would also like to thank Miss J. S. Ringrose (Pembroke College Honorary Archivist) and the librarians of Pembroke College, Cambridge; the Mass-Observation archive at the University of Sussex (including a second thankyou to Dorothy Sheridan – my guide as well as my interviewee); the British Film Institute Library, London, and the Beinecke Library, Yale University. Dr Mike Saler of the University of California, Davis, provided a copy of his unpublished seminar paper on *Pandæmonium*; I don't agree with his largely negative view of the work, but am glad to have read his arguments. Apologies to anyone I may have forgotten or let slip through my notes; no slight intended.

Sue Phillpott, copy-editor supreme, saved me from (literally) hundreds of minor errors and not a few major ones; invaluable help.

Other declarations of gratitude for encouragement, assistance and advice with aspects of this book are due to Professor Martin Wallen and Professor Robert Mayer of OSU, Stillwater; Dr Jonathan Miller; Mr Tony Penrose; Mr Alex Linklater, Mr Erich Sargent, Mrs Kate Gavron; Dr Toby Haggith; Professor Ian Christie; Professor Lisa Jardine; Mr Philip French; and, among the friends not already mentioned: to Gilbert Adair, John and Caroline Alexander, Alastair Brotchie, Peter Carpenter, Mark Godowski, Richard Humphreys, Ian Irvine, Glyn and Evie Johnson, Tom Lubbock, James Malpas, Richard Milner, Roger Parsons, Michael Schmidt, Paul Schrader, Iain Sinclair, Peter Straus, Peter Swaab and Clive Wilmer. My deepest personal debt, as always, is to Claire Preston.

All of the above must be exempted from any part in my failures of taste, intelligence and industry throughout.

K.J.

Prologue: Poros, 1950

At about eight o'clock on the morning of Sunday 24 September 1950, the English film director Humphrey Jennings set out by ferry from Athens for the nearby island of Poros. Jennings was forty-three years old, and had made almost thirty films, some of which had been seen by huge audiences both at home and abroad. And yet, though widely admired and respected within the British film industry, he was very far from being a household name. The main reason for this obscurity can be stated very simply. He had spent most of his professional life not in the glamorous and highly publicized world of features, but as a jobbing documentary film-maker, working mainly for the General Post Office and other government-sponsored bodies. In the previous few years, he had mostly been involved in projects backed by the Central Office of Information, on such unenticingly worthy subjects as the modernization of British coal-mining.

His latest film, provisionally entitled 'The Good Life', was to be about the contemporary state of European health and medical care, and was one of a series of six documentaries commissioned by the United States Economic Cooperation Administration called *The Changing Face of Europe* – a series designed partly to explain to American taxpayers how well and wisely their dollars were being spent under the terms of the Marshall Plan, and partly to advocate the ideals of European unity and technical cooperation. In the previous three weeks, Jennings had been both scouting for locations and shooting footage in France, Switzerland, Italy and northern Greece; but his unit had returned to Athens the day before, forced into idleness by a camera breakdown. The American sponsors of the European series had demanded that it be shot in Technicolor, a process which at the time relied on a camera as large, heavy and unwieldy as a domestic refrigerator. Jennings had never worked with Technicolor before – in fact, he had made only four shorts in colour at all – and the unfamiliarity of this technology would surely have compounded all the usual difficulties of filming on location. Still, morale appears to have been good. The director and his crew had posed for jovial snapshots drinking and chatting outside tavernas, riding donkeys up into remote villages in the hills and fraternizing cheerily with the locals on the ferries between the islands. And, apart from a little toothache (his teeth were always appalling – 'green', people remember them with a shudder), Jennings was obviously in high spirits. He was greatly taken by the Greek people – 'friendly & cultured & enthusiastic beyond anything I have ever seen,' he wrote to his wife and young daughters back in London[1] – and, as a lifelong connoisseur of landscape and architecture, he was no less favourably impressed by the Attic scenery:

> the hills beyond the Parthenon are fresh and green & smell of pine – a particular resin which they mix with the white wine *rhezina* – the colours exactly Cézanne's palette – orange rocks – blue sky & sea – light blue – dark blue – fresh yellow greens in the young trees – olive greens & darker greens too but less of them. Behind all the fundamental fresh colours – blue & white – the marble & the sea – the white wash of the houses the sky – the national flag blue & white . . .[2]

Not wanting to waste time – he had long been notorious among his colleagues for driving himself and his crews hard – Jennings had decided to spend the day of compelled leisure on a recce for possible locations both for his own film and for others in the same series, accompanied only by his production secretary, Dillon Barry. The day began with a minor accident: Jennings had actually intended to set off for a different island, but was misdirected to Poros by the sailors at Piraeus. The subsequent catastrophic events are drily recorded in an official memo by Miss Barry.

> We spent about three quarters of an hour in Poros which is really only a village with a naval post attached, and then walked along the road to the cliffs which looked out to sea and to the other islands.
>
> We climbed over some rocks at the foot of the cliffs where the road ended, and went round the corner of the bay in which Poros lies. We had lunch at 1.15, having brought bread and grapes etc. in Poros.

At about 2.15 we started to climb the cliff which was not very high, as Mr Jennings wished to see the view of the islands from the top for a possible shot requested for the Transport film.[3] The cliff was I suppose about 30 to 35 ft., but this estimate of height may not be very accurate.

It was not a difficult climb, but Mr Jennings must have taken hold of a loose stone as he reached the top, because he suddenly fell from the cliff past me as I was half way up, and onto the rocks below.

He was lying on his side with his head against a rock, and half way in the water. I climbed down and lifted him out of the water. He was unconscious and breathing with difficulty and covered with blood which seemed to come mainly from a cut on his hand. I raised his head and put a tourniquet on his wrist and went back over the rocks round the corner of the bay and called a boat.

The boat took us to Poros Military Hospital across the other side of the bay. The doctor from the Naval station arrived about ten minutes later, and I think by then it must have been about 3.45.

The doctor who spoke English asked if my blood group was the same as Mr Jennings, and as I did not know he gave a transfusion of what they said was plasma. I thought that if we could get a sea plane from Athens we might get Mr Jennings to a main hospital, so I had wireless messages sent to the E.C.A. [Economic Cooperation Administration] headquarters, the British Embassy, Max Varnel the Unit Manager, two friends of Mr Jennings and the naval authorities in Athens. I was told that the naval authorities were holding a plane and awaiting a notification from the Embassy.

Meanwhile the doctor said that his pulse rate was improving but that the danger was that his head was swelling and it was impossible to determine the extent of the fracture. Later a surgeon came in and tied the vein in his hand, and although he did not speak English it was apparent from his attitude that there was very little hope.

After about an hour from the time we arrived at the hospital his breathing suddenly grew very slow, and stopped. I notified Athens and a Greek naval vessel took Mr Jennings back at three o'clock in the morning.

The police authorities there took a statement from us, but as the questions were asked by the naval commander who spoke very little English and were taken down by a police officer who spoke no English, and also with the help of a Greek Admiral who came in later and spoke French, I cannot really remember what were the questions asked.

*

Jennings's older daughter, Marie-Louise, came home to the family's two-bedroom flat in Camden, North London, the next afternoon, heard the telephone ringing in her parents' bedroom and picked up the receiver. The caller was Ian Dalrymple, Jennings's long-term producer and close friend; he asked quietly if he could speak to Mary-Lou's mother, Cicely. Mary-Lou handed over the phone and went into the living-room. Seconds later, she heard a scream – a terrible scream, she recalled half a century later, 'like something out of a Greek tragedy'.

The Jennings family were not the only ones to receive the grim news with horror and disbelief. Denis Forman, now Sir Denis, was at his desk at the British Film Institute in London when the phone rang for him, and found it hard to credit what he heard. It was not merely that Jennings had always been a dazzlingly, exhaustingly vital presence – restless, energetic and, above all, torrentially talkative. He had seemed almost indestructible: a man who had taken in his stride the bombs, the fires, the flying glass and falling masonry of the Blitz, apparently without suffering so much as a scratch; who had insouciantly filmed giant conflagrations of his own making for his film, *Fires Were Started*, from rickety planks several storeys above street level; who had gone ashore under heavy fire with the Marines during the invasion of Sicily and returned cheerful and unscathed. To have survived all those wartime hazards with such effortless aplomb, and then to be killed on a tranquil Greek island while working on a film about the promises of peace ... small wonder his friends were as incredulous as they were stunned.

The British press reported Jennings's death in short, respectful paragraphs, recalling his valuable wartime propaganda work and dutifully mentioning the Order of the British Empire which he had been awarded in recognition of those efforts. Yet few of those who read the brief obituaries would have gleaned much of an idea of who Jennings had been, or what his country and the world had suddenly lost. In fact, he had been many things in his day; far too many, some thought, for his own good. Among other vocations, he was a painter and draughtsman; a poet; an exceptionally learned, searching and innovative critic of literature and art; an experimental photographer; a leading light of the British Surrealist movement – indeed, one of the handful of people who brought Surrealism to Britain; a co-founder of the influential and occasionally notorious domestic anthropological project known as Mass-Observation; an occasional actor; a scrupulous and original editor of Shakespeare; a translator; and an intellectual historian – the author of an extraordinary literary collage of eyewitness accounts of the Industrial Revolution, *Pandæmonium*, unpublished at the time of his death but now acknowledged by those who have browsed its haunting pages as a masterpiece of imaginative history. Accomplishments enough for several lifetimes; but accomplishments known, for the most part, to a coterie of family, friends and colleagues. Often unaware of his other gifts, his encyclopaedic mind and blazing enthusiasms, most of those who knew him for an artist of any kind valued Humphrey Jennings primarily for the paid work he did month by month, year by year, to keep his family fed and housed: they thought of him as a uniquely gifted film-maker.

Under such circumstances, Jennings's small measure of fame might very easily have perished within months of his accidental death. Strangely, quite the opposite happened. In the fifty years that have passed since then, many others have come to share the view of Jennings as a unique and outstanding talent, and though it would be foolish to suggest that he is a household name in any but the most cinephile of households, his critical reputation is now far higher and more widespread than it was on the day he set off for Poros. To take just a few soundings: the novelist and film critic Gilbert Adair has called him 'our greatest documentarist'. The director and critic Lindsay Anderson went a good deal further, and offered the much-repeated verdict that 'Humphrey Jennings is the only real poet the British cinema has yet produced.' And in 1969, a writer for the British Film Institute's journal *Sight and Sound*, Daniel Millar, said of his film *Fires Were Started* that it was quite simply 'the highest achievement of British cinema; and Jennings is not only the greatest documentarist but also, counting Hitchcock and Chaplin as American, the greatest film maker this country has produced. *Fires Were Started* is the only British film which looks and sounds as if it came from the land of Shakespeare.'

There are plenty of other critics, film-makers, cultural historians and fans who would hold the truth of this bold claim to be self-evident. Since I share this view of Jennings's cinematic achievements, I hope to contribute something towards fleshing out and publicizing its truth. I hope, too, that I may be forgiven a lapse into superlatives by proposing that the following chapters will attempt to describe and assess the life and work of the man who remains Britain's greatest film-maker.

One

1907 to 1926: Childhood in Walberswick, School Years at the Perse

Frank Humphrey Sinkler Jennings, who would devote many years of his mature life to pondering the imaginative history of the Industrial Revolution, spent his childhood in a setting that bore almost no visible trace of the machine age. As an adult, he lived and worked almost entirely in cities – Cambridge, Paris, London and the great industrial centres of northern England – but the rural landscape of his first nine years stayed in his mind, not so much as the melancholy lost paradise of Romantic artists but as a fertile creative resource quite free of nostalgia, a stock of resonant visual images and themes to which he would return again and again in his films, his paintings and his writings. In recent years, some of his admirers have suggested that Jennings might well be seen as a member of an unofficial East Anglian school of artists, a characteristic celebrant of the region's distinctive geology, history, social composition and even (it's sometimes fancifully said) unique qualities of light and cloud. 'East Anglia,' writes the critic David Thomson in his entry on Jennings in *A Biographical Dictionary of Film* – probably the best and most suggestive brief résumé of the director's career published to date – 'offers one of the most self-contained and enduring of educations in English social history and art: it is the world of agricultural peasantry, of Constable, Benjamin Britten and [the subject of Ronald Blythe's book] Akenfield.'[1] Whether or not Jennings would himself have acknowledged precisely these affinities is arguable; but his keen awareness of the region's history and geography, and his recognition of their importance for his emotional and intellectual development, are beyond dispute.

He was born on 19 August 1907 in the small village of Walberswick, on the coast of Suffolk. Even today, Walberswick is a remarkably unspoiled resort – a comfortable home for the somewhat better-off class of retired person, a popular summer retreat for those in search of the more tranquil kind of English holiday. Though the village contains some sadly undistinguished bungalows, houses and shops built in the last half-century or so, much of its domestic architecture is still reassuringly picturesque, verging (as so often in England's coastal resorts) on the mildly eccentric as one approaches the array of beach houses and somewhat ramshackle wooden vacation houses near the shoreline and landings. Walberswick's old church is partly ruined and of relatively scant aesthetic interest, but just a short walk takes you to the neighbouring village of Blythburgh, where the skyline is dominated by one of the most magnificent churches of a region famously rich in great ecclesiastical architecture. In the last four or five years of his life, Jennings paid return visits to these scenes from time to time, and re-established one kind of creative link with his childhood by making a number of landscape drawings and paintings in which Blythburgh Church dominates the view. And in the early days of the Second World War, when the threat of German invasion seemed imminent, he wrote about the district, too, in a sequence of much-revised prose-poems – never published in his lifetime – which would ultimately have been part of a large ambitious work mingling autobiography and social history, entitled 'Beyond the Life of Man'. The first of these fragments is called 'The Sea':

> The range of the sea goes so many miles inland: a cottage at Ilketshall (12 miles back) has a model trawler on top of the clothes-line pole in the garden. The sea-washed stones from the beaches and out of the fields are split in half like an apple broken by hand and the split inside faces look out from the church-tower and the church walls in patterns and letters of texts. The great Suffolk churches were built in the midst of civil war, in the 'golden age of farming', when 'the sailors sat in their shops at Dunwich and saw the ships in Yarmouth bay'. And today – the day of invasion – out of a huddle of thatched and tiled cottages – out of a few corrugated-iron roofs – out of a group of wind-directed fir-trees – these great church-towers stand up with a protestant clarity of voice like the music of Handel: Blythbrough [sic], Southwold, Walberswick – landmarks of the simplest, most unconscious lives.[2]

As Jennings's text suggests, just across the river from his native Walberswick is the village of Southwold. Unlike Walberswick, Southwold had succumbed at least a little to the march of the machine, and it was here that the boy Jennings first encountered a form of technology that was to fascinate him for the rest of his life: the railway engine.

SOUTHWOLD (before the war) was a small coast town to which the railway came late – perhaps the latest of any township in East Anglia. It lived round the Church and the lighthouse – both in the midst of the town – standing behind the Swan Hotel in the High Street: the church on Church Green, surrounded by properly trimmed grass, well-kept graves, and tidy stone paths. The lighthouse standing just like a house in a side street, flanked by houses, and painted a luminous white. White indeed was Southwold – easily the white light fled off the curved lighthouse stack, off simple bay-windows and rounded street corners: off the breasts and the cheeks of the figurehead at the corner of Church Green – off the neck of the white Swan looking down the High Street as it leaves the shops and goes away with wide lawns down towards the salt marshes. And there too the ancient guns of the battle of Sole Bay still lay on the grass outside the Guardroom – and a moment's eyeclosing evoked the square sails of the fleets and the echoing puffs of white smoke in the bay.

South among the marshes the mouth of the river Blythe – a possible harbour for fishing smacks and with some dredging even for Scots trawlers and Dutch Hollyboats, and here there was a steam-ferry to join the Southwold and Walberswick sides of the river.

Later in 'Beyond the Life of Man', Jennings recalls an old rumour about the exotic origins of the Southwold railway:

The Railway was said locally to have been built for Japan and to have been rejected. It was nick-named the *Crab and Winkle*. True or not, it was a good popular guess to connect it with Japan, for the misty river and the heron-haunted marshes and the scented fir-woods through which it ran are indeed leaves from a Japanese screen or back numbers of the Art magazines of the period. And the Japanese themselves made wood cuts of the first railways in their own landscapes, and at the Swan lately I found a Japanese tourist magazine advertising their railroad system – but most of all the desolate beaches of Dunwich and Walberswick reminded me of the exile of Genji at Suma . . .

And to the text of this prose poem Jennings appended a report of the opening of the first Japanese railway at Yokohama, on 15 October 1872.

The proximity of Southwold to Walberswick opens up the tantalizing possibility – though no more than that – of a passing youthful encounter between Jennings and one of his near-contemporaries. In December 1921, a family by the name of Blair moved to Southwold and stayed there until the outbreak of the Second World War. Throughout those years, the Blairs' house was often used as a temporary refuge cum operational base by their sickly, impoverished and apparently feckless son Eric, a former imperial policeman later to become universally known as a writer under his pseudonym 'George Orwell'. Blair/Orwell picked up a little money during some of his humiliating visits home by tutoring small boys in Southwold and Walberswick;[3] by that time, though, Humphrey was in his early teens and well beyond the need for a tutor, and there is no unequivocal record of an early meeting between the two non-conformists. In adult life, Jennings would come to be a great admirer of Orwell's political writings, and there are a number of interesting affinities between these two fiercely independent-minded left-wing patriots. Some sort of passing acquaintance in later years does seem reasonably likely, since Orwell and the Jennings family shared friendship with the poet Ruth Pitter; the most probable place of meeting would have been in or near the Jenningses' next family home, in Kensington, West London. Orwell's second wife Sonia certainly knew Jennings well for a short period, paying frequent visits to the set when he was filming *Fires Were Started* in 1942.[4]

'Beyond the Life of Man' also includes an evocation of Walberswick itself:

At Walberswick there was a white wooden windmill: the ground it stood on is still called *Millfield*: and as the church is up at the top end of the village it made another centre to Walberswick as the lighthouse did to Southwold. It had nearly unbroken wooden sails – and a flight of steps and a balcony: all painted white. In windy weather the sails began to turn a little and the mill itself to swing round into the wind, and for a moment looked as if it would begin work again and the whole world come right in an afternoon. But of course it never did, and then in the 1920s it was burnt right down to the ground.

Walberswick church stands on the edge of the common: not so exact as Southwold, less full of wonder than Blythburgh. Once upon a time it too caught fire, and the chancel was still a ruin. Inside simple and clean. The harvest festival the only time of magic. Then the fishermen's nets were hung on the wall. Apples near at hand in careless rows on the grey window ledges: stooks of corn piled against the pulpit: prize marrows and shining pumpkins on the steps of the choir: beyond these momentary glimpses of the golden loaves on the altar itself. Nets to catch, apples to eat, corn to grind, marrows to prize. To bring together is to transform.

Despite the odd sharp, unillusioned touch in these reminiscences, it is plain that Walberswick, quaint enough in the early twenty-first century, must have been almost idyllic for an adventurous, energetic child in the early twentieth, when Humphrey's parents first set up home there. Jennings once referred to his childhood as 'wild' and 'lonely', and yet far from looking back in self-pity he seems to have relished both of those conditions. In a letter he wrote to his wife-to-be Cicely in the early days of their courtship, he recalled:

At home I lived almost alone on the seacoast seeing Mother at meals having nobody much to play with: in my memory & close to all that is deepest & dearest are sand-dunes with prickly bits of sea holly & dry tufts of grass – overhanging blackberry branches to which as one reached the ground squelched [sic] & my sandalled feet felt the cold black greenish slime rising – and the smell of gorse – O, gorse with the prickly sticky-out bits that caught one's ankles as one leapt along the path & rabbits disappeared. And beyond all the rather terrifying marshes ... & the joy of finding a mushroom.[5]

At the time of the Jenningses' arrival, Walberswick was little more than a scattering of cottages, inhabited by fishermen and their families

– fishing being the mainstay of the local economy – and by the handful of artists and bohemians who had been holidaying or settling there from the 1890s onwards. The painter Wilson Steer and the architect and designer Charles Rennie Mackintosh were among the pioneers of Walberswick's artistic colony, and it's probable that it was largely the village's artistic reputation that had initially attracted Mr and Mrs Jennings.

Indeed, the evocation of Blythburgh in 'Beyond the Life of Man' begins precisely with those local painters. A fragment headed 'Blythburgh 1910' (in some drafts, '1914') recalls:

> It was a time of artists and bicycles and blue and white spotty dresses.
> They had a little boy who was carried in the basket of his mother's bicycle and they used to picnic on the common between Walberswick and Blythburgh.
> In the summer the gorse on the Common [*deleted*: was] bright yellow and a spark from the train as it passed would set the dry bushes on fire.
> How hot the flames of gorse, how hot even the day itself!
> How cool the inside of Blythburgh Church – the shade of a great barn, from whose rafters and king-posts the staring angels outspread wooden wings.
> The solemnity of a child.
> The intensity of the sea-bird.

Walberswick was also the sort of place in which local 'characters', slightly sinister to a child's wary eye, could occupy a prominent place:

> At Walberswick there was a man called Gentleman Jim – a tall spectre of a seaman in a black top-hat, with curly hair and gold ear-rings and bloodshot eyes. He wore a roll-top jersey, and had a walking-stick and walked with a limp. He lived in a house at the top of the green. He was said to see ghosts. To see the black dog – in the lane, on the dingle, on the beach at night. On the beach where the white breakers show their teeth even on the darkest night, where the swell invisibly shifts the grinding shingle, throws up driftwood and margarine, mine-floats and dead Germans.[6]

That final jarring note of horror, which carries the passage from the past of childhood timidity to the wartime present of composition, is

something of a hint as to Jennings's larger intentions for the unfinished 'Beyond the Life of Man'. For the adult Jennings looked back
on the landscape of his earliest years not only with an artist's eye for
visual detail, but with the eye of an historian: a British socialist historian – comparable in his own way to, say, the Raymond Williams of
The Country and the City, or the E. P. Thompson of *The Making of the
English Working Class* – fully alive to the arduous labour and the acts
of coercion and resistance that had shaped that superficially peaceful
rural world. A short preface to the text makes its ambition explicit:

> This is the story of a struggle taking place almost unnoticed in
> the background (in the clamour) of greater struggles (wars) – or
> so they seemed at the time. Because – distant as it appeared – it
> will be found in the end to be profounder, more enduring than
> they. Greater than the war against Napoleon, or the war against
> Hitler. Moreover it began long before they were even dreamt of
> – profounder because its conquests will exist when theirs have
> been forgotten.

A brief, hasty table of contents, littered with typing errors and
scratchings-out, suggests something of what Jennings had in mind
for this uncompleted work, especially when it breaks away from a
relatively ordered numerical scheme ('1. A desperate area of the world
2. The battle with the landlords   3. Fire, war and destruction –
lawsuits and murder . . .') and all but shrieks in anguish:

> No one has any conception of what the so-called
> commonpeople have put [up] with for as far back as memory and
> books and
> and what they still put up with
> Noone haxzny concetption of the re al life of the people
> today – nothing like the papers or the films or the novels
> or the paintings or the peoms . . .

A long prose passage, reworked many times, elaborates on this
breathless outburst:

> All the memorials of this part of the world, as far back as the
> written word stretches, are reports of disaster – fire, flood,
> encroachments of the sea, poverty, oppression, decline, war and
> the military, destruction of common rights.

To the east is the sea. The sea-coast consists of sand-dunes, shingle, clayey cliffs, which are continually eaten away by the waves at their base and so slide into the main. Then the winds and the tides will silt up the river's mouth or break down the dykes and inundate the marshes and meadows and farmsteads far inland with winters of great flood. Then storms at sea will cast vessels on the banks of the Ness and batter them to pieces. Then fire will catch the dry gorse on the common and spread from roof to roof. Then the townsfolk will come out on the marsh with bill-hooks and flails and defend the commons against the Lord's men.

Unwritten the story of the people's resistance, uncelebrated in words their struggle and labour. But the church towers from the past, the jetties and piers, the mills and lighthouses, the farms and cottages, the roads and the ridiculous railway – in whatever state they may be now – we must never forget that they were made and built and created and tended by the people – not by those powers for whom they were put up or whose names they may bear or whose money allowed them to call them theirs – into the actual making they had little or no part – it was the people and the people alone who had the knowledge and strength and skill and love to fit the sails in the windmill, the thatch to the barn, the wings to the wooden angels, the flashing reflector to the lighthouse lamp.

It is a striking shift of emphasis: where a more jaundiced left-wing commentator might see only the traces of aristocratic and bourgeois exploitation, Jennings also notes common skill, knowledge, strength and 'love'. His interest in and respect for such practices never received the sustained exploration he seems to have been planning, but glimpses of such admiration are scattered across his work in different forms.

Take, for instance, his concern with agricultural labour and tech-nology. Two of his rare and tentative ventures into colour film-making deal directly with the subject – the lyrical *English Harvest* (1939) and the more jocular short of about the same time, *The Farm* – while his most substantial film of the early days of war, *Spring Offensive* (1940: also known as *An Unrecorded Victory* – both titles are misleadingly bellicose, was a semi-dramatized documentary about the largely unre-garded part Britain's farmers were playing in keeping the besieged country fed, and specifically about the Government-backed movement to reclaim the unproductive farmland which had fallen into disuse since the First World War. It was filmed entirely in East Anglian locations, an experience to which Jennings alludes in a fragmentary prose-poem entitled 'Description of a Postcard'.

> Working at Southwold in the spring of 1940, an officer who arrested us said he himself came from this part and when we talked about the Railway he said that Reg. Carter's comic postcards were still on sale although the Railway had been out of action for fifteen years or so. So before leaving went and bought a packet including one in particular which I remembered from childhood. What is the fascination of this image? What are the lines of life into which it leads?[7]

(The poem is followed by a three-line note: 'Description/Analysis/ Reconstruction'.) Jennings went on to revisit the sort of farms and farmers he had seen in childhood for a number of his most important wartime films, including *Listen to Britain* and *A Diary for Timothy* (in which 'Alan' the farmer is one of the four leading characters), as well as for his last completed film, *Family Portrait*, which includes a contemplative account of the ways in which farmers and agricultural scientists must start to learn from each other.

All of which might, to be sure, have been largely a matter of chance – more an indication of the kind of assignments Jennings received from his masters than of a personal commitment to the subject. It's in the artistic work he did for himself that we find the most unambiguous evidence for his enduring engagement with the agricultural world, as well as the proof that his regard for that world was not simply that of the town-dweller innocently or ignorantly nostalgic for the harsh daily round of the countryside. He was always fascinated, for example, by the historical development of ploughs, which he would frequently paint and which are the subject of a poem he wrote two years before his death, in 1948. It opens with a connoisseur's catalogue of various forms the machine had taken:

> The gallows. the vine, the gang, the beet, the subsoil, the hoe,
> The Norfolk wheel,
> Whether in Tull's tune-book, Jefferson's design, on the Illinois
>   prairie or pagoda ground

All, all I see reflected in the giant shadow plough;
The gallows coloured green, the vine coloured red, the gang-
    plough lemon yellow, sombre purples and browns,
And the Norfolk wheel itself deep blue, standing alone on the
    snow.[8]

Still, preoccupied as he may have been by all aspects of agriculture, Jennings was not a farmer's son, and the most obvious physical evidence of the circumstances that shaped him is the actual fabric of the house in which he grew up. Humphrey's father Frank Jennings, born in 1877, was an idealistic architect with only a limited amount of formal training – he had served a kind of apprenticeship to a practice in Bury St Edmunds and never became a member of any professional architectural association – who specialized in something that was, in its day, unusual to the point of eccentricity: the loving reconstruction of period buildings. Frank was particularly fond of working on those neglected Tudor houses which, long before the days of Listed Buildings, the National Trust and all the (sometimes mixed) blessings of 'the heritage industry', were often simply pulled down and used for firewood. Frank Jennings would take these structures apart beam by beam, number the parts, and carefully reassemble them at a new site for his clients. His own house, the Gazebo, was just such a reconstruction; and Mr Jennings must have been a sound builder, since it is still standing. In the early months of 2000, the house's present owner was kind enough to let me wander round its garden, looking at the exterior. Though extensions have been built on to the house since Frank Jennings's day, altering its original outline, the purity of his antiquarian ambitions is still quite visible, and the unbriefed visitor would find it hard to credit that the Gazebo has only been standing in its present site for a century.

So strong was Mr Jennings's desire for authenticity of detail in his architectural practice that he was always reluctant to compromise a house with modern furniture or any twentieth-century home comforts. It was not until after 1945 that he would countenance indoor plumbing, electricity or the telephone in his own homes. His granddaughter, Mary-Lou Legg, remembers visiting him in the depths of a freezing winter in a house – Garrett's Farm, in Essex – which had no front door, because he had not been able to find one of precisely the right kind. In other regards, though, she looks back on the experience of staying with him fondly. 'He was a fascinating, sweet-natured man, a brilliant talker who lived in the past,' she recalls. 'He lived in the medieval or Tudor world.' So complete was Mr Jennings's abstraction from the contemporary scene that it could sometimes involve him in scrapes with the authorities. During the First World War, he was twice arrested on suspicion of being a German spy after being found wandering around gazing intently at architraves. His air of abstraction must have been intensified by the fact that an ear infection had left him with poor hearing; friends and family learned to raise their voices when talking to him.

Independent-minded and principled as Frank undoubtedly was, the dominant partner in the marriage was Humphrey's mother, Mildred Jessie, *née* Hall. 'My mother believes she carries the keys of the universe in her pocket,' Humphrey said of her in later years. The daughter of a solicitor, she was born in Lewisham, South London, in 1881; her father died young, from tuberculosis. Before her marriage to Frank, Mildred had trained as a painter, first at the Slade School of Fine Art and then in Munich, showing considerable talent. Her younger son Rodney remembers her as especially gifted at pen-and-ink drawings, pencil work and watercolours – never oils – and as having a particular flair for landscapes and houses; she also possessed a sharp eye for the design of textiles and other kinds of craft and art.

Mildred's parents were hostile to the idea of her marriage to Frank Jennings, feeling that his family background was disreputable – a pattern which repeated itself almost exactly in the next generation, when the family of Humphrey's chosen bride also put up a fight against the nuptials, and out of much the same sort of anxiety. One of the reasons for Mildred's sojourn in Munich, chaperoned by her mother, was to keep the young lovers apart, and Mr and Mrs Hall somehow managed to extract a promise from the couple that they would not communicate by any means for a period of two years. The time duly served, and the lovers stubborn in their constancy, the reluctant Halls had little choice but to give in. Frank and Mildred were married in 1906.

One key difference between husband and wife was Frank's hopelessly negligent attitude to business finances; he was lax and forgetful about collecting fees, all but incapable of establishing favourable rates

for his work. Thanks to the erratic nature of his income, Mildred –
naturally possessed, anyway, of a much sounder business sense –
frequently had to be the family breadwinner, and she began her
commercial career in 1909 by opening a pottery shop in the village:
the Walberswick Peasant Pottery Company. As Rodney Jennings
recalls, the business began as a kind of collaboration with her sister-in-
law Rose Jennings, and its first project was the importing of peasant-
made pots from remote regions of Transylvania and Romania – both,
at the time, part of Hungary. 'About 40 per cent of the pots were
broken by the time they reached Walberswick, but they were so cheap
that it was still possible for my mother to make quite a lot of money
in the four or five years before the war.' Mildred soon diversified her
trade by incorporating a line of hand-thrown dishes and other goods
that she would bring back from her regular trips to Brittany. She
would often take her oldest son along on these trips, thus helping to
lay the foundations for Humphrey's excellent spoken French and for
his lifelong involvement with many aspects of French culture, from
modernist painting and *surréalisme* to *haute cuisine*.

In 1920, with the help of an old friend from Slade days called Mrs
Bradbury – 'the Bradburys at that time owned *Punch* magazine, and
Mr Bradbury was a director of the Bank of England, so they were very
wealthy' – Mildred refinanced the business and reopened her shop in
West London, at 12 Holland Street, just off Kensington Church Street.
The Jennings family moved in above the business (though they kept
the Gazebo on as a summer home until the late 1920s, when they sold
up and bought a dilapidated farmhouse in Essex – the same freezing,
doorless place recalled by Mary-Lou).

> 12 Holland Street is a very extraordinary house, because it was
> built for one of the ladies-in-waiting at Kensington Palace, when
> Kensington Palace was built, so it's very early eighteenth-century.
> It's completely panelled in wood inside, and the rooms were
> divided only by pannelling, so when the doors slammed – as they
> always did, because the house was a bit rickety after all these
> years – pictures tended to fall off the walls . . .

Since the supply of Hungarian pottery had dried up, Mildred Jennings
began to commission British potters to work in the same style, and to
diversify the business towards small furnishings. When Humphrey was

home from school and university, he would sometimes help with the paintwork on these pieces: 'But he never followed the traditional patterns of design,' Mary-Lou recalled, ' – he would make them rather surrealistic. I don't think they sold very well.'

With the move to London came the first glimmers of the only, and not very long-lived, period of moderate prosperity for the family. Frank Jennings teamed up with a White Russian – 'not a very good architect, but a good businessman' – and opened offices in Westminster. Several large commissions eventually came their way, including one for a block of flats on a former estate near Putney Heath – a project made remarkable by Frank's insistence, at the time thought rather cranky, that none of the existing trees should be cut down and that development should take place around them – and another for some offices in and around the City. The most eminent of these is the CBI's headquarters on Tothill Street. Frank was, his son Rodney insists, a very good architect, whose great strength (or failing) was his steady adherence to traditional principles.

But the comfortable years were an anomaly. Though decidedly middle-class by occupation and values, the family enjoyed little in the way of traditional bourgeois comforts and security, and by the standards of the day they counted as genteel paupers. 'My mother-in-law [i.e. Mrs Stuart Legg] once said that grandmother Jennings was the first woman she'd met of her class who didn't have servants,' Mary-Lou Legg recalls. 'You had to have a pretty low income to be middle-class and not have servants.' Some of their economic problems began with the philoprogenitiveness of the preceding generation: Frank Jennings was the youngest of fourteen children, and so inherited very little money. The happy London days apart, he was seldom able to make good through industry and talent his native lack of wealth. Humphrey would follow his father's example by being serenely negligent about finances – and, as a result, chronically strapped for cash – almost all his life.

Frank had never been on good terms with most of his huge family, who came from Newmarket, and were mainly trainers and breeders of racehorses. 'He came from a completely unaesthetic background,' Mary-Lou Legg recalls. 'He would say that they were all absolutely appalling, the Jenningses, and that they only owned one painting, and that was of someone who had gone mad.' The two or three siblings

for whom Frank had any fondness were the ones who shared something of his taste for the arts – though it should be said that the artistic
Jenningses made up amply and vigorously for the lazy philistinism of
their forebears, and in some highly colourful ways.

Frank's brother Jack, for example, was initially apprenticed to a
top-class saddler in London, but had soon frittered away his allowance
and, in debt and disgrace, was packed off to Australia, literally with a
shilling to his name. In Australia, he applied himself to work in the
goldfields with a certain amount of profit, but instead of building on
his early finds he took off for the South Sea Islands where, as his
nephew Rodney recalls, he began 'collecting what we would now call
Native Art . . . and he ended up being the first curator of the Sydney
Museum, at the age of about 30'.[9] He returned to England and spent
the rest of his life as a reasonably solvent collector and dealer, selling
mainly to Americans. 'He had a wonderful nose for anything made of
wood,' Rodney Jennings recalls, 'he knew *immediately* the provenance
of anything made of wood.' Rodney, who recalls him with affection
as 'a marvellous man', would sometimes see Uncle Jack taking his
idiosyncratic breakfast at Henekey's pub in London: a large glass of
port, soaked up by the free biscuits at the bar.

Then there was Uncle George, who as a young man declared his
ambition 'to be a painter' and was duly packed off for an apprenticeship
with a house-painter. Somehow worming his way out of this career
trap, George took off for India, where he did much the same thing as
Uncle Jack, buying up some marvels of Indian craft and art which he
brought back for sale in Europe, only to have most of it stolen while
he languished, ill, in Brussels. This illness left him with impaired
hearing, which worsened to near-deafness in later life. Thwarted in his
attempt to become a dealer, he applied himself to landscape painting –
'he followed the Corot School, the Turner school'[10] – and lived for a
number of years in Paris, refining his skills, apparently to good effect.
Here, perhaps, is one familial seed of Humphrey's ambition, realized
for only a short period in the early 1930s, to live in Paris and paint.

Most beloved of all the Jennings siblings was Aunt Rose, or Marie-
Rose, just a year older than Frank and far and away the most
glamorous of Humphrey's forebears. (Rodney adored her.) In the
1890s, Rose had enjoyed a passionate affair with her brother-in-law.
Alarmed and scandalized, the family had pulled a few strings among

their better-connected racing friends and sent her off to stay with the
Esterházys in Austria. Rose Jennings's response to this banishment was
characteristically high-spirited: she promptly had an affair with Prince
Esterházy. She subsequently travelled around Eastern Europe in grand
style, buying china, peasant prints and the like. Aunt Rose was to be a
benign presence in Humphrey's life, and there is a family rumour,
unsubstantiated but wholly plausible, that she generously introduced
Humphrey to a prostitute when he was eighteen: 'She knew,' says
Mary-Lou Legg, 'that a young man had to be educated properly.'

Before these more independent-minded souls of Frank's generation
kicked over the traces, the Jenningses were otherwise flawlessly free of
any taint of nonconformity, taste for learning or abstract interests.
While there is some inconclusive evidence that the Newmarket branch
of the family may have descended from Sarah Jennings, the wife of
the first Duke of Marlborough, the most illustrious of Humphrey
Jennings's undisputed forebears was his grandfather Thomas – 'Tom'
– Jennings, a celebrated trainer of racehorses. The most famous of
Tom's mounts was Gladiateur, who in 1865 became the first French
horse to win the Derby, and thus became known – at least by the
French – as the 'Avenger of Waterloo'. (Gladiateur's tail is preserved
to this day as an exhibit in Newmarket's museum of racing.[11]) The
racing world was an international community at that time, and Tom
Jennings travelled a great deal on the continent. Another Jennings
family legend has it that he was largely responsible for establishing
Italian horse racing, during a period when he worked as a trainer for
Vittorio Emmanuel II; still another, that he was employed in the same
capacity by the King of Sardinia. At any rate, he was highly successful
at his trade, and established a fortune of some £30,000, part of which
went to the establishment of his Newmarket business, the La Grange
Stables (today owned by a keen racing family from Saudi Arabia).

Tom Jennings met his wife, Sarah Carter – who, despite the
impeccably English-sounding name, was in fact French – on a trip to
Chantilly, which at the time had close connections with Newmarket.
She was barely out of the convent at the time, and presumably had
the attractiveness of youth, though Rodney Jennings recalls that the
one surviving family portrait of her makes her look rather bleak and
frightening, like a less relaxed version of Queen Victoria. (The matching portrait of Tom shows an equally severe presence, who with his

square frame, chubby face and broad shoulders could hardly be more unlike his tall and gangling grandson Humphrey.) It is this grand-mother that Humphrey's friends usually had in mind when they made the vague observation that he came 'from a French family'. The couple bred enthusiastically, and as the years passed the Newmarket home became cluttered with sons, daughters, nieces, nephews, sons-in-law, daughters-in-law ... Meals were taken at a large communal table, where Tom would lay down the patriarchal law.

Fortunately, by the time Frank came along, Tom Jennings was growing old and tired, no longer quite the overpowering tyrant he had been to the earlier offspring – hence Frank's relative freedom to make his way in the world of architecture. Nonetheless, Tom was remem-bered by Frank as a brutal man. He forced him to learn to ride before he was five, and had him blooded at a fox hunt by the time he was six.

> My grandfather [says Mary-Lou Legg] told me that he would have
> to ride with a string of racehorses on the heath at Newmarket,
> and he would have to be the boy that got down to open the gate,
> and you had to be back up on your horse very quickly to gallop
> over and open the next gate. It was extremely exhausting. So he
> could ride very well indeed, but he hated that whole world.

When Frank was barely eleven, he was sent off by his father to handle the export of a brace of horses to the continent – a task which involved legal complications no boy of that age could reasonably be expected to have mastered. The experience was so wretched that he vowed to have nothing to do with horses again.

Plainly, Humphrey Jennings took after his father Frank – and his uncles Jack and George – in following a career in the arts rather than horsemanship. Yet his rejection of the horsey world was by no means absolute. The horse mania of the grandfather's generation resurfaced in various unpredictable ways in the work of the grandson, who may never have ridden to hounds or in a steeplechase or point-to-point, but who nonetheless carried on the Jenningses' tradition of equestri-anism by translating it into the abstract realm of words and images. Humphrey frequently drew, painted, photographed and filmed horses – most of his admirers will immediately think, for instance, of an unforgettable image of a panicked horse racing away from a blazing warehouse in *Fires Were Started*,[12] or of the more stolid dray horse plodding through the early dawn in *Listen to Britain*. Many of his most accomplished canvases and drawings depict the heads of horses, horses in their stables, or horses at full gallop; and indeed – though one should not attribute too much in the way of authorial premeditation to such slight works – his very first films for the GPO Film Unit, *Post Haste* and *The Story of the Wheel*, are both well stocked with pictures of horses, riders and coachmen. Moreover, in an autobiographical note for the Surrealist magazine *Contemporary Poetry and Prose* written in the mid-1930s, he describes himself as someone who had 'survived the Theatre and English Literature at Cambridge [and] is connected with colour film direction and racehorses'. That connection was wholly ancestral, not first-hand, so it's curious that he should have felt compelled to declare his horsiness in such an unlikely quarter. Surrealists were not noted as keen equestrians.

It is also striking that the very first poem Jennings published in *Contemporary Poetry and Prose* (June 1936) concludes with a detailed study of a horse, albeit of a visionary kind that would have perplexed if not enraged his grandfather:

> When the horse is impassioned with love, desire, or appetite, he
> shows his teeth, twinkles his coloured eyes, and seems to
> laugh.
> He shows them also when he is angry and would bite; and
> volumes of smoke come from his ears.
> He sometimes puts out his tongue to lick. His mouth consists of
> the two rays of the eternal twins, cool as a sea breeze.

This fondness for making equine images in his own work was matched by an interest in the presence of horses elsewhere in art. Jennings was deeply impressed, in an unconventional way, by the work of Britain's greatest horse painter, George Stubbs, on whom he wrote an unpublished review-essay in 1939 or thereabouts, reclaiming that artist for intellectuals as more than a supplier of robust sporting pictures for the philistine county set: 'After all "George Stubbs, Painter" is emphatically not the property of riders to hounds only. The passionate attack upon reality which in fact this book [a reprint of Stubbs's *The Anatomy of the Horse*] represents is far closer to the so-called atheist science of Leonardo than to the conservatism of the

English country gentleman.'[13] It is a startling claim, and the pity is that Jennings never pursued and justified it at greater length; had he written any such essay, it would almost certainly have made reference to a quirk of sensibility in the early days of the Industrial Revolution, when Western humanity had, he often suggested, made a partial return to animist modes of thought by imagining machines as a new form of labouring beasts. Significantly, the earliest sketch for *Pandæmonium* was published under the title 'The Iron Horse'.

But the single most thought-provoking of Humphrey Jennings's reconsiderations of his equestrian heritage is a prose fragment entitled 'The Prism', which displays his characteristic flair for teasing out otherwise unsuspected connections, literal and metaphorical, between apparently distinct historical developments:

> 'A figure in white marble of Tregonwell Frampton, keeper of the running-horses to King William, standing with a prism in his hand.'

> The choice of Newmarket as a racing-centre appears to have been due to Charles II. That is to say, about the time that Newton at Cambridge was experimenting with the break-up of white light into prismatic colours, and with the application of abstract analyses to natural phenomena in general. So in racing the owners' colours replace feudal heraldry. Their colours are abstract colours: colour and no more: colour in bands, diamonds, oppositions (abstract, even prismatic shapes) but just colours. Then from the experiments of Newton came the three-colour analyses of Young, Clark Maxwell, Helmholst: impressionism, pointillism, cubism. In the 18th century the jockeys were already dressed as Harlequins. Curious how checks should be considered horsey! Undoubtedly the success of racing is connected – lies in its not pretending to be more than it is: frankly mercenary: and yet how romantic.[14]

*

Perhaps by way of reaction against the harshness of Frank's own upbringing, Humphrey's parents allowed their young son a great deal more freedom than most children of the period enjoyed. Humphrey – and, when he came along, Rodney – was permitted to run around freely as he pleased, and to scramble around on the beach and on the groynes even when the sea was high and dangerous. He was also allowed to drink coffee and wine, and even to smoke, from an early age. Such domestic liberties suggest that the Jenningses were happy to look on their son as a small adult rather than a child in need of constant cosseting, and must surely have played their part in fostering the child's native courage and sense of his own worth. The bold boy-explorer of the beaches grew up into the fiercely independent-minded investigator of ideas. Humphrey's self-esteem would also have been enriched by the fact that, for the first eight years of his life, he was the undisputed king of his parents' tolerant affections, since Rodney was not born until 1915; though, it's fair to add, those parental affections may have been less than completely doting. Mary-Lou Legg recalls her grandmother as rather a distant, self-engrossed personality, more taken up with her artistic or spiritual interests than her family; in some respects, a cold woman. Still, Mildred Jennings always encouraged her son to take it for granted that – like others, did they but know it – he could succeed at anything to which he turned his mind or hand.

> My father [says Mary-Lou Legg] was brought up with the idea, certainly my grandmother had the idea, that children ... that *anybody* could read anything, that anybody could do anything. I remember that when I was about eleven I had the flu when Grandmother Jennings came to stay with us. I told her that I was bored and wanted something to read, so she came back and gave me Plato's *Republic*. Well, my father was brought up like that. He felt he could do anything; she felt she could do anything. So he really had a flying start on a lot of people.

Most of those who lived and worked with Humphrey Jennings will comment on the exceptional self-confidence and volubility with which he would assert his views, whether he was insisting angrily on the right order of shots to compose a sequence, praising or damning a painting, book or person, or arguing a political case. Those who disliked this side of his character could find him arrogant, bossy or dogmatic. These are not, however, necessarily unsuitable or even unappealing traits in a film director, who, more than any other type of artist, has to think and behave like a military leader – maintaining unit discipline, making important decisions at a second's notice, constantly struggling against interference from above while tackling the countless unexpected setbacks with which all but the happiest productions are plagued. Ditherers and habitual seekers of second opinions seldom thrive in the trade.

What is remarkable, however, is not that some people were antagonized at times by Jennings's highly developed sense of the absolute correctness of his own views, but that so few seem to have been more than briefly irritated. Even in social gatherings, there was plainly an agreeable aspect to Jennings's firm sense of his own value. If he was an inveterate holder-forth, there were plenty of people more happy to listen and be enlightened, at times enthralled. The traditional figure of the know-all or the bar-room philosopher is that of a man (far less often a woman) whose boorishness is in direct proportion to his ignorance. But Jennings did know a very great deal about a great many subjects, and his displays of arcane knowledge do not usually seem to have been offered in the spirit of aggression or one-upmanship but more as gifts, ceaseless and prodigally bestowed on the nearest bystanders. He simply took it for granted that a sound-recordist, a miner's family or a nervous Crown Film Unit apprentice would be as fascinated as he was by some recondite detail of architecture, geography or mechanics.

Listening to reminiscences of Jennings in his most characteristic pose – holding enthusiastically forth – one is struck both by the fondness of such recollections and by the innate sense of democracy that they imply. The emphasis returns again and again: when it came to intellectual matters, Jennings instinctively treated everybody the same. It is exactly what one would expect (or at least hope) of the man who directed *Fires Were Started* and *Listen to Britain*: films in which everybody from a factory girl to the Queen is presented with comparable fondness and respect. Jennings, who made a careful study of Freud's writings in the 1930s, might well have enjoyed the speculation that his egalitarian vision of his fellow-citizens was firmly grounded in an experience of good (or, in more recent, duly chastened terminology derived from the great British analyst Winnicott, 'good enough') mothering – the kind that leaves a child refreshingly free of that neurotic self-hatred which cripples every project and nourishes contempt for others.

Unemotional as she may have been, Mildred was certainly conventionally maternal enough to have kept records of baby Humphrey's development: family snapshots, preserved in black albums painted with her own decorative designs, rather Celtic and Arts and Crafts-influenced; notes on his first words, and his first drawings. It would be pleasant to record that these drawings show precocious accomplishment of a Picassoesque order, and clear promise of his future vocation as a painter, but to the untutored eye at least they seem no more or less remarkable than the enthusiastic scrawls of any reasonably well-adjusted child. It is, however, worth noting one aspect of his infantile artwork: Jennings was left-handed, and remained so, since his parents, unlike a lot of their contemporaries, were far too enlightened to try to train or bully him out of it.

At some stage of his education, as his friend Jacob Bronowski recalled in a memorial essay published in 1959, the young Humphrey had made life easier for himself by devising a way of writing which involved turning the paper 'so that he wrote almost vertically, as if he were writing Chinese'. Jennings was rather proud of his invention, which, Bronowski observes, anticipated a way of writing that was commonly recommended to left-handed children by the late 1950s. Bronowski also notes that Jennings's left-handedness, like that of Leonardo da Vinci, left its traces in some of his paintings, such as the study of a bonfire which Bronowski bought from him around 1931–2: 'the direction of the painting was from the bottom right-hand corner to the top left-hand corner'.

★

After a few years at the Gazebo, Frank Jennings built – or reconstructed – a second house on the other side of the village of Walberswick. Again, it is a handsome structure, and its present inhabitant is delighted with the place. She is well aware of the Jennings family, and owns an old book on local history which comments on Frank Jennings's architectural practice; she showed me around the interior, speculating plausibly that Humphrey must have occupied the smaller of the two bedrooms on the first floor, looking out over the lane, while his parents' room looked over the garden.

Despite Walberswick's pastoral remoteness from the modern world, there was one contemporary event too vast and dreadful for any villager, however young, to ignore. Humphrey was seven at the outbreak of the First World War. In 'Beyond the Life of Man' he recalled some of the impressions those days made on him:

> I remember as a child by the ferry watching the soldiers testing horses for France. Farm-horses – chasing them naked down to the river while the men on the banks hallooed and shot off guns in the air. I remember the Scots fisher girls on Blackshore gutting the herring and singing in Gaelic. Scaly hands running in fish-blood, the last vessel dropping her sail at the pier's end, the last fish kicking the net. But today there is nothing – nothing of the girls or the boats or the nets or the songs or even the fishmarket itself. Utterly gone – only the wind and broken glass and rough tiles made smooth by the sea. Only still visions of bloodshot eyes brimming over with fear.

(The 'Scots fisher girls' were migrant workers brought down to work as herring-gutters.)

The most direct impact of the Great War on the Jennings family came in 1916, when Frank was called up into the Royal Flying Corps. He had already been rejected by the Army on grounds of deafness, but the embryonic RAF found use for him as a ground technician, and exploited his architectural training by setting him to work at technical drawing. His departure made the domestic finances even more precarious, and it was only the income from Mildred's shop that kept the wartime wolf from the door. Shopkeepers are, of course, traditionally assumed to be among the most conservative elements of any society; not so with the owners of the Walberswick Peasant Pottery Company.

Frank Jennings's rebellion against the brutality and philistinism of his father had a political as well as a personal dimension. Both of Humphrey's parents held progressive views, and for much of their adult lives were supporters of Guild Socialism, a now largely forgotten ideology of the early twentieth century which had its deepest intellectual roots in the writings of the great Victorian artists and social critics John Ruskin and William Morris. Their son was well acquainted with the works of both writers from an early age, and their words stayed with him, echoing throughout the course of his life. The published text of *Pandæmonium* ends, fittingly and movingly, with an extract from Morris's *A Dream of John Ball* (1888), in which the visionary sleeper awakes to the glum reality of his own London:

But as I turned away shivering and downhearted, on a sudden came the frightful noise of the 'hooters', one after the other, that call the workmen to the factories, this one the after-breakfast one, more by token. So I grinned surlily, and dressed and got ready for my day's 'work', as I call it, but which many a man besides John Ruskin (though not many in his position) would call 'play'.[15]

Though he may have briefly relapsed into a more Tory outlook during his schooldays, Jennings appears at all other times to have been a loyal, if idiosyncratic, partisan of that noble strain within British left-wing politics that has been inspired by these writers and by other literary critics of capitalism. His most famous statement on the subject was published in 1947 in a brief autobiographical note for an article in the popular left-leaning magazine *Our Time*, which ended: 'Home ground. East Anglia. Politics: Those of William Cobbett'.

Guild Socialism was the short-lived brainchild of three unconventional left-wing thinkers: Holbrook Jackson, Arthur J. Penty and – most significantly – A. R. Orage (1873–1934), writer, teacher, critic and editor from 1907 to 1922 of an extraordinary journal of literature and politics, *The New Age*. Orage's influence on Mr and Mrs Jennings was to be profound and long-lasting, first in politics and later in spiritual matters; his evocation of the socialist milieu in which his own political views were developed stresses its eclecticism, exoticism, even occultism. The socialism of his day was, he said,

a cult, with affiliations in directions now quite disowned – with theosophy, arts and crafts, vegetarianism, the 'simple life', and almost, one might say, with the musical glasses. Morris had shed a medieval glamour over it with his stained-glass *News from Nowhere*. Edward Carpenter had put it into sandals, Cunninghame Graham had mounted it upon an Arab steed to which he was always saying a romantic farewell. Keir Hardie had clothed it in a cloth cap and a red tie. And Bernard Shaw, on behalf of the Fabian Society, had hung it with innumerable jingling epigrammatic bells – and cap. My own brand of socialism was, therefore, a blend or, let us say, an anthology of all these, to which from my personal predilections and experience I added a good practical knowledge of the working classes, a professional interest in economics which led me to master Marx's *Das Kapital* and an idealism fed at the source – namely Plato.[16]

All of which sounds painfully like the kind of herbivorous 'crank' socialism at which Orwell snarled in *The Road to Wigan Pier*; so it is worth recalling a more generous assessment of the movement by one of its recent historians, Wallace Martin:

> The Guild Socialists attempted to deal with man's religious instincts, his artistic proclivities, his desire for ownership and professional pride, as well as his inherent tendency to place his own advantage ahead of that of the community. They attempted to take account of all the phenomena of civilization, rather than economic phenomena only, in formulating their political system. They failed to achieve their ends, but their efforts are worthy of mention.[17]

The pages of Orage's journal were also hospitable to still more exotic theories than those of Guild Socialism. In the early 1920s, he became a disciple of the Armenian guru Gurdjieff, and left Britain to pursue that form of esoteric discipine known to Gurdjieffians simply as 'the Work'. These influences soon filtered down to Mildred Jennings, who in the 1920s took herself off for frequent visits to Gurdjieff's Institute for the Harmonious Development of Man at Fontainebleau near Paris, and ultimately led her, after the schism between the two teachers, to become a fervent disciple of Gurdjieff's sometime acolyte and apologist, the Russian mystical teacher P. D. Ouspensky.

The burden of Gurdjieff's teaching is hard to paraphrase, not least because he tended to expound it in the form of gigantic and all-but-unreadable parables such as *Beelzebub's Tales to His Grandson*. Perhaps it would be best, here, to hand over that task to Rodney Jennings, who sets out the core of the doctrine in the way that he believes his mother understood it, and as he learned it in his youth from studying Gurdjieffian and Ouspenskyan texts – 'Oh, they're fabulous books to read, I read them again and again and again'; he particularly commends Ouspensky's *New Model of the Universe* and *In Search of the Miraculous* – and from knowing Ouspensky quite well ('an extraordinary man, who hardly ever spoke except to answer a question'):

> Gurdjieff thought that all people are machines, complete machines, and all our actions in the world are purely mechanical – even those of people of genius. And if you wish to avoid being mechanical

you've got to change your way of thinking, behaving, walking, feeling, moving ... Gurdjieff got his information from a wide number of sources: from the Sufis, from many extraordinary journeys in Russia, Asia, Asia Minor, and built this system of *action*. He said that there were three ways of going towards, how shall I say, a higher level of existence – [via] the Yogi, the Monk (prayer and faith), the Fakir (who just sits and does nothing for years), and that each of these works on a different, what he called, centre – the intellectual centre, the spiritual, and the moving centre, and they conquer each one of those centres. And then Gurdiieff said, there is a fourth way – to work on all those centres at once, which is by far the quickest, and means that you don't have to cut yourself off from ordinary life in a monastery or retreat ...

So he insisted, for example, that people should work extremely hard physically, all day long, and sometimes at twice the speed they should do [*sic*]; that they should attend lectures, extremely difficult lectures, and show that they understand them through question and answer; that they should do extremely complicated dances and exercises, like the Dervishes, involving extremely complicated counting systems. Now, it's an incredibly tough system, and Gurdjieff said that people will only succeed with that system if they have found that they have failed in life and are desperate and must find something new ...

Whether or not Mildred felt she had succeeded in the quest, she was certainly in quest of something new, and, having amicably drifted apart from Frank, went to live in an Ouspenskyan community in Chorley Wood, in Hertfordshire, staying there until the end of the Second World War. (Frank, in turn, took up with another woman, built himself another house near Saffron Walden in Essex, and seems to have been fairly content with his new domestic arrangement. He lived there until his death in 1961.) Humphrey seems to have little to say about this aspect of his mother's life, and though he was well read both in the classical literature of mysticism and in its contemporary interpretations by the likes of Jung, it would be misleading to claim that there is any very clear strain of occult doctrine in his mature work. But the influence of Orage told deeply on his adolescence in a very different and wholly practical way. It was almost entirely thanks to Orage's suggestion that Mr and Mrs Jennings decided to send their eight-and-a-half-year-old son away to a boarding school; a very particular boarding school.

*

On 4 May 1916, Master F. H. S. Jennings was admitted to the Perse School, Cambridge. He seems to have been living at this time at a small farmhouse just to the south of Cambridge, probably owned by friends of his parents. Orage had proposed the Perse as a suitable place for Humphrey because he was an admirer of the school's already renowned headmaster, the extraordinary classicist, polymath and visionary Dr W. H. D. Rouse – a generous and energetic man still quite widely remembered in the twenty-first century as, among other things, the co-founder of the Loeb Classical Library of parallel-text editions, and translator in 1937 of the *Odyssey*, about which he corresponded in detail with Ezra Pound, who gives him an approving mention in Canto 74. (Pound, the 'demon pantechnicon' of literary modernism, was a most unlikely kindred spirit, since Rouse's literary tastes, like many of his social views, were decidedly conservative. The correspondence petered out as Pound's letters grew more splenetic, obscene and deranged.)

William Henry Denham Rouse was born in a Baptist mission house in Calcutta in 1863, the son of the Indian Secretary of the Baptist Missionary Society. It is sometimes said that he remained a missionary all his life, though his cause was the secular one of classics teaching. In 1880, when the family returned to London on leave, he studied briefly at the Regent's Park College, and in 1881 won a scholarship to Christ's College, Cambridge, going up in 1882. He took a good First in Part One of the Classical Tripos – recently reformed to include history and philosophy – and a better one in Part Two. In 1888 he was elected to a six-year fellowship at Christ's, and began work on the daunting task of co-translating with R. S. Conway four volumes of Karl Brugmann's monumental Indo-European *Grammar*. This was the beginning of a prodigious publication list, which included a major book on *Greek Votive Offerings*, manuals of Greek and Latin composition, editorship of *The Year's Work in Classical Studies*, the *Classical Review* and many school Latin texts.

But there were few vacancies for classicists in a world where senior fellows tended to hang on to their appointments till death, and in 1894 Rouse was obliged to become a schoolteacher, first for brief spells in

Bedford and Cheltenham and then, in 1895, at Rugby, where one of his pupils was Arthur Ransome, later to write the children's classic *Swallows and Amazons*. Throughout his early years as a teacher, Rouse continued to publish scholarly works that combined erudition with innovation, including two on Greek iambics and Latin elegiac verse which indicate that he was already beginning to elaborate that more intellectually stimulating method of teaching ancient languages that became the standard at the Perse. For reasons that are not altogether clear (they may have included objections to his less than wholly orthodox religious beliefs), this remarkable body of work went largely unrewarded in material terms, and Rouse's many applications for headmasterships, supported by impressive references, were all failures until, in 1902, he was invited to take charge of the Perse School.

Some of his friends warned him against accepting the post. When he arrived, the school was in an almost irreversible state of crisis. The number of pupils had plunged from 213 in 1900 to 106 in 1902. Finances were in a parlous state, so that by 1906 the Governors, confronted with an overdraft of £1,130 and debts in the region of £400 as well as a predicted deficit in income for the following year of more than £1,000, were on the point of closing it down. But they rallied, believing that Rouse's intellectual merits made him worth the risk.

Their faith was amply rewarded. By 1910, Rouse had not only built up the school's numbers and restored much of its financial health, but had made it known internationally as a unique centre of education offering an unprecedented combination of traditional and progressive teaching. Rouse's single greatest innovation was the so-called Direct Method of teaching Greek and Latin, a technique partly inspired by developments in Germany. Where their less fortunate contemporaries were still undergoing the age-old miseries of drilling in declensions and conjugations, boys at the Perse were thrown into lively dialogues accompanied by action: '*Surgo*,' a boy would say, matching action to word by standing up. '*Surgit*,' his classmates would yell, pointing at him as he did so. Before long, they would be capable of reasonably fluent debate – first in Latin, then in Greek – and certainly of reading with ease extracts from Thucydides, Plato, Homer and Herodotus. According to one admiring account, Rouse had somehow managed to resurrect the spirit of the ancient world in the dusty confines of a sixth-form room.[18] It was an exercise which, for Rouse, went well beyond

mere pedagogy. At a time when the study of classics was coming
increasingly under attack from the educational authorities, he not only
kept up a stout defence of the ethical centrality of ancient learning but
felt that, in the Direct Method, he was baptizing his pupils in the living
waters of great speech.[19] Not everyone was convinced, and school
inspectors would murmur darkly about the relative neglect of science
subjects, but for many, Rouse's time at the school, which lasted until
1928, was little short of an Arcadia.

At the time when Master Jennings arrived to take part in Rouse's
Great Experiment, halfway through the Great War, the school was
housed about five minutes' walk from the railway station at Gonville
Place, near the Catholic church, in a set of redbrick buildings put up
in 1890 and comprising a hall and twelve classrooms, though no
science labs, gym or dining-room. Accommodation for the boys, from
1911 onwards, was mainly in the boarding-houses at 90 and 92 Glebe
Road – respectively 'School House' and 'Hill House', the latter
exclusively for Jewish boys until 1948. (The food, Rodney Jennings
recalls, was conventionally horrible, though redeemed from time to
time with wonderful curries and other Indian food – a material
memory of Rouse's own boyhood.) In 1910, Rouse had also built
himself a house on five acres of land at Cherry Hinton, just south-east
of Cambridge, and tried to run the place along ruralist Utopian lines
suggested to him by his readings of Morris and Ruskin: 'The pigs,'
he liked to say, 'bring in more money than the boys.' Younger boys
were taught at the preparatory school in nearby Bateman Street,
under the eye of Miss C. Burrows, head from 1910 to 1934. (Rouse's
long-cherished ambition to move the school to a more spacious site
in the Hills Road went unfulfilled in his lifetime; he died in 1950, and
the official opening of the Hills Road buildings, the school's present
home further out from the town centre, did not take place until 1961.)

Every morning, the boys would see Rouse – a small, portly, bearded
figure – arrive on his bicycle, with its unique leather book-pouch made
to fit inside the frame. A keen horseman and a derider of the motor car
– he called it a 'hell-waggon' – he sometimes came on horseback. He
would then preside over assembly from his desk below the fellowships
board in the hall. Already, events across the Channel were beginning
to cast their bleak shadow across the tranquillity of school life: more
and more frequently, the shields commemorating recent academic and

sporting achievements would be updated with the words 'Killed in Action' or 'Died of Wounds'. After leading prayers, Rouse would make the day's announcements, and once a year would commemorate, in graphic terms, the courageous death of a distinguished Old Persean, E. H. Palmer, an Arabic scholar in the T. E. Lawrence mode, who had perished courageously in the desert mountains of Sinai. Lessons would then begin, and continue until a quarter past four, when Rouse would lead another set of prayers and conclude with the blesssing.

However much the school inspectors might doubt Rouse's enthusiasm for these subjects, mathematics and science were indeed part of the curriculum, as at other schools. There were the inevitable games, an Officer Training Corps, a Scout troop, a certain amount of music and – the Ruskinian hand of Rouse, again – some instruction in handcrafts. Apart from its triumphs in classics, though, the Perse was mainly noted for excelling in modern languages. All the boys started French by eleven, Latin by twelve, Greek (for the real classicists) at fourteen and German at sixteen. As with the dead tongues, all modern language instruction was in the Direct Method – not a word of English permitted throughout – and wherever possible by native teachers, so that former Perse boys were often complimented on their accents later in life.

The staff in Jennings's day included the classicist R. B. Appleton, who joined the school in 1909, and despite being paralysed from the waist down and confined to a wheelchair, maintained the strictest discipline of any master – though bolder spirits referred to him teasingly as 'Tabby' Appleton, since his hair had gone conspicuously grey in patches. Dr Rouse taught only boys in the fifth and sixth forms, by which time they were already more than capable of tackling Homer. French was taught from 1903 onwards by M. Léon Chouville, aka 'Shovel', who conveyed the correct values of French vowels musically, by having his classes sing the eight open sounds in chorus as the ascending and descending scales of an octave, and then added anatomical depth to the exercise by chalking up diagrams of the mouth, throat and tongue on the blackboard. (Scholars of the early history of British anthropology may care to know that M. Chouville's salary was paid by Sir James Frazer's French wife Lilly.) German instruction was in the formidable hands of M. de Glehn, a native of Alsace who until the war had been known as Herr von Glehn, and continued to be known to the boys as 'Vonny' for years afterwards. A stern, slightly alarming figure who favoured ginger Harris tweed plus-fours, he was given to seizing the ears of boys at whom he had just fired a question and hanging on grimly until they had answered.

From 1920, history was taught by F. C. Happold, by all accounts a humane and intelligent man of wide-ranging interests (he later wrote a scholarly study of mysticism, published by Penguin Books) who had the rare gift of exciting his students with a sense of what it had been like to live at a particular historical period. One of Happold's techniques, which fired enthusiasm even in the more sluggish, was to have his pupils form pairs and construct 'development charts' showing how costume, transport or architecture had changed across the centuries, thereby incidentally acquainting them with the tools of independent research.

But, by common consent, the most exceptional of all the Perse's fine teachers at this time was the English master H. Caldwell Cook, who joined the school in 1911. Cook was the author of an influential work of educational theory, *The Play Way*, which advocated his principle of 'learning through pleasurable doing', and stressed the value of encouraging children to participate in dramatic and choral activities. He not only taught his pupils the art of writing clear and easy English prose, but set them to composing – and enjoying – blank verse, ballads and sonnets. In 1912 he set up an institution remembered by all Old Perseans of the day, the Mummery, a sort of improvised Elizabethan theatre based in two rooms of a nearby Victorian villa, Pendeen House. Here, the boys threw themselves into reading and acting plays by Shakespeare and other dramatists. For the youngest, he devised a series of 'speeches' sessions, in which pupils would deliver five-minute orations on subjects of their own choice, and would then be marked by a jury of their peers, first for basic interest and then for eloquence. Possessed of independent means, Cook drew no salary for over a decade, furnishing the Mummery from his own pocket. In these initiatives, he was working very much in the ethos of his headmaster, who always placed a premium on good speaking and on reading works of literature out loud. On the front of Rouse's desk in the sixth-form room was pinned a notice in his own calligraphy:

> Learn to read slow; all other graces
> Will follow in their proper places.

★

And yet, for all the academic excellence and, in some cases, compassionate interest of the Perse's staff, the experience of attending an English public school was for Jennings, as for countless thousands of other boys sent away from their homes at a tender age, largely miserable:

> I came to school at 8½ & hated it. I couldn't make friends & was bullied & hated boxing which was compulsory: the agonies I went through trying to avoid certain boys & pretending not to be seen when they passed! . . . as a schoolboy I was a wretched fellow compared . . . to the mass of white curls that picked blackberries & chased rabbits.[20]

As he worked his way up the school, however, his earlier boyish energy and independence of mind began to return, and before long he seems to have been making quite a dazzling impression on his fellows. One of them, Marius Goring – who went on to become a successful film actor and worked with Jennings on *The True Story of Lilli Marlene* – wrote:

> He was brilliant in mind and exuberant in body; I had watched him win the Senior Quarter Mile . . . and thought 'No hope: he belongs to a superior race.' There was nothing, it seemed, he could not do: he was original, and he conformed; his Classics were first-rate, he understood . . . Mathematics; his English was astonishing; his wit in the School journals and concerts was unsurpassed.[21]

Among this golden boy's many blossoming talents was a knack for poetry, though it is fair to say that his very first appearance in print shows little sign of his future literary flair. 'The Scrum-Half', a parody of Oliver Herford's 'When I was but a kitten small' (itself a parody of Robert Louis Stevenson's 'When I was down beside the sea'), appeared in *The Pelican*, the school magazine, for May 1920, co-credited to 'HUMPHREY JENNINGS IIIc, 12.4.' and 'PATRICK HUGHES, IIa, 11.2.'.

> When I was but a scrum-half small,
>   They gave to me a Rugger ball
> To put inside the scrum.
> One day they heeled it out with glee;

> I passed it out to our wing-three,
>   And he did make things hum.
> And then a mighty cheer arose –
> Just as the ref.'s shrill whistle blows –
>   We've beaten them, by gum!
> And now I am a Cambridge blue,
> The best scrum-half that ever threw
>   A ball inside the scrum.[22]

A cod-scholarly editor's note informs the reader: 'The phrase "by gum" is an editorial emendation for rime's sake.'

Jennings was soon to move on to more serious verse, though *The Pelican* – not a markedly highbrow publication – provides a more detailed account of his prowess on the rugby pitch. Its 'Critique' column for March 1925 reports that F. H. Jennings 'Has played some good games when the school pack has been winning, but is quite unable to stop a forward rush. Has a useful, if not powerful kick. Tackling quite good on occasions.' The March 1926 'Critique' is also less than fulsome in its assessment, reporting that Jennings 'Has played soundly through the season. Rather slow in getting the ball away, owing, partly, to slow heeling by the forwards. Has developed a good kick. Keeps cool, though his tackling is not always reliable.' A contemporary eyewitness rated him more highly, calling him a 'vociferous Ist XV scrum half – he would shout which side he was putting the ball in – "Coming in LEFT, Perse" – and deliver the ball to his stand-off by dramatically throwing himself full-length on the ground!'[23]

The same issue of *The Pelican* records his two greatest triumphs as an athlete:

> F. H. Jennings provided a great thrill in the cross-country by jumping the barbed-wire fence at the finish and winning, after running second most of the way. He ran an excellent and well-judged race, and well deserved his win. He was also responsible for the second thrill, winning his half-mile in the relay races in the record time of 2 mins 8⅖ secs.

A contemporary amplifies on the nature of his cross-country feat:

> This was a race of over three miles which started from a lane near Little Shelford and involved crossing fields, hedges, plough,

wading Hobson's Brook and running parallel to the Railway Line, crossing the Long Road and then a field and fence or two before the finish in the school field. Jennings told us before the race that he intended to win it and would beat any near challenger by leaping the last fence. This he did and a great cheer went up . . .[24]

By this time, he was already acknowledged as one of the school's outstanding all-rounders: 'one of the Junior Prefects; Hon. Secretary of the Perse Players; and Committee of the Union Society; and a Lance-Corporal in the OTC'.[25] Nor, it is slightly surprising to learn, was Lance-Corporal Jennings a reluctant or bolshy idler in the ranks:

> He was a most enthusiastic NCO in the OTC. We used to have an inter-House competition for drill, turn-out etc. We had 1st War Lee Enfield .303 rifles and bayonets. For easier handling the latter had pieces of wood, one each side, held in place by steel screws. Jennings said South House would have white wood and burnished screws on the bayonet handles. We spent ages scrubbing these small pieces of wood and using copious amounts of bleach pinched from the Lab. before we got a respectable looking white wood![26]

But such assiduousness must have been relatively short-lived, since Jennings – or so the story runs – was eventually dismissed for misconduct both from the OTC and from the Scouts.[27]

Meanwhile, his poetry was growing more adult in its preoccupations, and melancholic love – wholly literary in its inspiration, one suspects – was taking the place of rugger as his muse. Probably written under the guidance of Cook, his verses were competent, derivative, and judged entirely suitable for publication in Heinemann's *Public School Verse*, volume IV, 1923–4 – Jennings's first, unheralded appearance on the national scene.

Song

O I had gotten me a love
That was as fair as fair
Her eyes were as the sky above
And flaxen was her hair.

But, out alas! this love of mine,
　　That now is gone away,
She loved not scented larch nor pine
Nor hollyhock nor columbine;
'The which,' she said, 'are loves of thine.'
　　And so she said me nay.

And I will not seek after her,
　　Nor any other maid,
But I will love the forest fir
　　And sit beneath its shade.

And the green larch shall be for me
　　A love that is divine;
And every other forest tree,
And columbine that blooms so free,
And hollyhocks along the lea –
　　These shall be loves of mine.

Probably the most accomplished of his adolescent efforts in this vein of frigidly competent academic pastiche was published in *The Pelican* for July 1924:

Walberswick

The lavender in pewter jugs,
　　Upon the window-sill,
The heather, in the stoneware mugs,
　　We gathered on the hill;
The tall and laughing hollyhocks
　　I see them, smell them, still.

For it is always in that place,
　　For me, September days
When every flower has a face
　　Parcht
Torn and yet smiling, pollenless
　　Along the garden ways.

And the summer, yes, the summer
　　Is coming once again . . .
Let summer pass, then I'll go back

To garden, lane and fen:
I'll live among the hollyhocks,
    And throw away the pen,
It's then I'll go to Walberswick
    When Autumn's here again.[28]

Still all but thoroughly hand-me-down, though the broken metre in
the second stanza is an odd, idiosyncratic touch; and if the note of
bookish yearning ('And throw away the pen') for a lost pastoral haven
is a shade incongruous in a teenager – it smacks of Housman's blue
remembered hills – the verses seem to have at least some faint basis in
his own boyhood experience of East Anglia, and maybe in the feeling
that the family's move to London four years earlier had severed some
obscurely important connection to his native ground.

Perhaps he was already growing aware, as he proceeded up the
school, of the extent to which his verses so far had been little more
than classroom exercises in poetic diction. At any rate, far and away
the strangest of Jennings's surviving bits of literary juvenilia is a spoof
book review published in *The Pelican* for May 1926. He takes for his
text a slim volume entitled *Various Verses* (revised edition) by one
'William Brantom'. He begins:

There is some good in all things, and of Mr. Brantom's verse it
may be said that it is calculated to inspire hope into the breasts of
rising poets; nothing after all could be so bad as the lines:

Though exercise is good yet some schools ought
To think far more of work and less of sport,[29]

And, after a handful of citations from Brantom's poetastry – a miniature *sottisier* of amateur versifying – 'F.H.J.' concludes with the
observation:

Like Thomas Hardy and Wordsworth, he dates his poems, so the
growth of his muse will be an easy matter for his future
biographers. The last word on this amazing collection is the
author's own:

The trifles that annoy,
And happiness destroy;

> Could not life's joys allow,
> If we would sense employ,
> And would ignore . . .

By nothing is England so glorious as by her poetry![30]

This more playful, satirical, contrary side of Jennings's temperament must also have been given free rein in his many contributions to the Union, the Perse School's senior debating society. Thanks to reports in *The Pelican*, we know that on 6 June 1924 he seconded the motion 'That, in the opinion of this House, modern civilization is incompatible with the existence of the Fine Arts'. In subsequent debates, he spoke for the motion 'That this House would approve of a bill, prohibiting the display of advertisements and hoardings'; opposed the motion 'That this House would approve of the introduction of prohibition into this country'; and proposed 'That this House welcomes the return to power of a Conservative Government'. In 1925, he went on to propose 'That, in the opinion of this House, the abolition of slavery is the abolition of Civilization' (20 February), and to support the motions 'That . . . the evil outweighs the good efforts of wireless' (27 February) and 'That . . . Trades Unionism is a public menace' (23 March).

It is not hard to make out a pattern here: almost consistently, Jennings took the conservative, even the violently reactionary side on issues from trades unions to slavery. Does this indicate a temporary rebellion against the socialist principles of his parents? A retreat into the conservatism common to public school boys? Or – as his daughter Mary-Lou Legg is inclined to suspect – simple youthful mischief, a desire to show off wit and rhetorical verve by arguing the case that he personally found less tenable, rather as Samuel Johnson was fond of arguing? Whatever the explanation, it is the only time in Jennings's life that he seems to have spoken up for the side of the Lords instead of that of the People. And even if he was sincere in espousing conservative political views for a while, his fellows regarded him as anything but conservative in other respects. He had, in fact, a reputation for eccentricity and wild beliefs:

He was a great believer in 'mind over matter'. Pontificating in the dorm one night he said the human brain could control all matter. Someone asked him if he could move one of the iron bedsteads without touching it. He had a go. We gathered round and he stared and shouted 'Move, bed, move' umpteen times. There was no doubt about his concentration, beads of sweat appeared on his forehead. We were all silent. He tried hard for some time but the bed never moved. We all thought he was potty, of course![31]

But of all the different activities he engaged in during his years at the Perse, from military training to amateur telekinesis, none was so influential on the future course of his life as his participation in school drama, and no teacher more important than the man who schooled the Perse boys in dramatic method: Caldwell Cook. It was with Cook that Jennings had his first lessons in acting, dancing, building and painting scenery and recitation; Jennings also became the co-editor of *The Player Magazine – The Unofficial Organ of the School House Players*.[32] On a personal level, Cook was also very kind to him, and he looked back on the English master as a mentor.

I never think of anyone being ill without remembering once when I had tonsilitis at school & when the worst was over Caldwell Cook ... brought me Galsworthy's 'Awakening' & 'Pickwick Papers'. 'Awakening' was in the lovely illustrated edition & had pictures of little Jon sitting in bed with measles reading 'Bevis' and playing red Indians and pirates. Also my grandmother sent me oranges: & Jon it appeared loved oranges in *his* convalescence.

I think I was particularly fond of 'Awakening' (as I still am) because all the lovely things that happened to Jon had never happened to me – at least I didn't feel they had. At the time I was thirteen: Jon was only seven or so & in him I seemed to see myself – or what I might have been. Anyhow little Jon in bed & oranges & Mr Mantelini & the look of the white sickroom at school make my heart ache even now – for some strange reason. I *loved* having tonsilitis.[33]

According to school records, Jennings took some part in half a dozen or so main productions during his time as a pupil. As an actor, he began by playing roles in farces, including the part of Lady Kidderminster in a schoolboy adaptation of the comedy *In the Cellar* (27 March 1923), and he went on to play 'Pepper-Popp, wife of Ali Baba' in *The Sultan's Mustachios*, which he co-devised with one F. A. Aldworth. More serious fare soon followed. By the Christmas of 1923 he was designing the costumes for the Chester Miracle Play, in which he took the part of Noah, and in the next three years he designed sets for *Trial by Jury* and a play about St Simeon Stylites, as well as playing Bottom in *A Midsummer Night's Dream*.

The Perse Players also gave him his first experience of dramatic writing. According to a manuscript written some time later by his history teacher Mr Happold, 'The Perse Players 1920–1928', one of the pupils' earliest ventures into play-writing was a work entitled '*The Duke and the Charcoal Burner*, which, with Humphrey Jennings as the moving spirit, had been written and acted by Form IIIc in 1920–21'. Happold implies that this was no great shakes; but goes on to say of its sequel: '*Jane in Search of a Husband*, on the other hand, I regard as a significant play in the annals of the Perse Players. The authors, Humphrey Jennings, Frank Aldworth and Ivan Turner, were all boys who had shared in the writing of *The Duke and the Charcoal Burner*, but were now more mature and more certain of their powers.'

The dramatic sphere in which Jennings excelled almost effortlessly, though, was neither writing nor acting but set design. One of his contemporaries, Brian Lacey (now Professor Lacey B.Sc., MD, F.R.C.Path., C.Biol., F.I.Biol.), writes: 'He was then very obviously highly talented and an artistic person. He could in a few minutes sketch out designs for plays including Polish scenes or Negro spirituals which when amplified for a production served splendidly without significant alteration.'[34] Jennings was well aware of his own abilities as a designer. Much later, he would go on to work on many large-scale productions, both professional and amateur, and was still designing sets in his first days at the GPO Film Unit. He sometimes thought of stage design as the career in which he was most likely to win renown, and there can be little doubt that he could, at the very least, have made a fair living at the trade had he been slightly more diplomatic in his dealings with directors and management.

Like other fortunate contemporaries at the Perse, Jennings would be able to put off choosing a career for another three years at least. He crowned all his varied achievements by winning an exhibition to read English at Pembroke College, Cambridge, and left school triumphantly in the summer of 1926 – though, unlike some Old Boys of an artistic and non-conforming nature, he continued to be in close contact with the Perse for several years to come. The year 1926 was also the one in which, for the first time since the Armistice, events from the larger world forced their way through the school gates. When the General Strike was declared in May, at least one of the Perse's masters joined the ranks of the middle-class volunteers who were helping to keep services running: he left his second-form boys behind to go and drive the train to Bletchley and back.[35] Was Jennings, like so many of his near-contemporaries at the university, also excused classes for the purposes of strike-breaking? Or did school duties, or some reawakening of his parents' socialist principles, keep him at his desk? The record is silent.

After a decade of study at the Perse, Jennings was, then, equipped with an exceptionally fine training in modern languages and classics, unconventionally advanced skills in English composition and a vivid and well-formed historical sense. He had shone as an athlete, an orator, an actor and designer, and had published his first poems. In other words, he had enjoyed the kind of early success which often leads to a terrible sense of anticlimax,[36] or even humiliation, on arrival at a major university, where all the golden lads and girls from provincial sixth forms suddenly discover that each and every one of their new friends is every bit as brilliant as they are, and probably more so. But this was not to be Jennings's fate. As an undergraduate of Cambridge University, the Perse's marvellous boy would simply have a larger and more public stage on which to triumph.[37]

Two

1926 to 1929: Cambridge and Courtship

A vignette from Cambridge University, eight years before Jennings matriculated: Armistice Day, Monday 11 November 1918:

Shortly after 11 a.m., the hour at which the Great War finally ended, a mob of undergraduates – mainly medical students – stormed the offices of the *Cambridge Magazine*; they smashed windows, destroyed furniture and hurled paintings by leading members of the Bloomsbury Group – Duncan Grant, Vanessa Bell and Roger Fry – from the windows. No doubt they despised the bolshy nature of the art, but the true object of their unbridled rage was the mild figure of C. K. Ogden, sometime classicist and freelance free-thinker, who had used his editorship of the previously unremarkable *Cambridge Magazine* to assert a form of liberty of the press unique in Britain. From October 1916 he ran an extensive digest of foreign – including enemy – newspaper coverage of the war. Many patriots were outraged by this, and by the generous amounts of room Ogden always gave to the opinions of those who were less than wholly enthusiastic about the prosecution of hostilities, though he had some odd defenders, too. The Foreign Office maintained a surreptitious subscription to the magazine and found it immensely useful, while Grand Old Men from Thomas Hardy to Gilbert Murray conspicuously raised their hats to Ogden's lonely crusade.

Later, in the evening of 11 November, Ogden came along to the offices with his friend and protégé, I. A. Richards, to inspect the damage and see if Richards could identify any of the culprits. But as they were chatting on the stairs, Odgen mentioned an article he had recently read in the philosophical journal *Mind*. They fell to talking long and intently, under the gaslight, while the noise of drunken revelry raged outside and a giant victory bonfire blazed in Market Square, cheered by town and gown alike; and by the time they bid each other farewell in the small hours of 12 November, they had sketched out the basis of one of the most influential English-language books of the twentieth century, *The Meaning of Meaning*.

This much-repeated anecdote[1] owes some of its pregnancy to the romance of intellectual otherworldliness, like the tale of the ancient Greek mathematician telling the invading swordsman about to strike a lethal blow to go away and leave him to his circles. But it also says a great deal about the nature of the Cambridge that Jennings was about to join – and not only because I. A. Richards would soon be his most important teacher.

It is easy for the browser in reference books and chronologies to form an idealized picture of interwar Cambridge as a magnificent, almost unparalleled treasure-house of the intellect. However slack and slothful the university may have been at other periods of its history, the sheer concentration of brainpower gathered in that damp and cheerless market town between 1918 and 1938 must surely provoke awe: it can look like a new Athens of innovative thought spanning the whole range of human endeavour, graced by names that changed not only their immediate disciplines but the whole world.

In philosophy, there were the likes of G. E. Moore, Bertrand Russell and – briefly in 1925, then more or less permanently after 1929 – the troubled and seductive genius of Ludwig Wittgenstein. In economics there were world-class talents of the order of A. C. Pigou, Dennis Robertson, Joan Robinson and others, all of them to be eclipsed in fame by John Maynard Keynes. In the natural sciences, the field is so crowded with accomplishment that it is almost impossible to draw up even a lengthy short-list without omitting several major names. Ernest Rutherford, Director of the Cavendish Laboratory from 1919, was, in the words of one historian of science, the man who in 1911 had 'introduced the greatest change in our idea of matter since the time of Democritus'.[2] He had gone on to assemble around him what has been called 'the largest number of gifted experimental physicists gathered together which had ever been known',[3] including the Russian expert in low-temperature research Peter Kapitza and a certain Niels Bohr, while in 1928 the young Dr P. A. M. Dirac of St John's College had published, aged twenty-six, a paper on the quantum theory of the electron which fully deserves the usually inflated epithet 'epoch-making'.

Outside Rutherford's immediate circle were A. S. Eddington, the Trinity College astronomer, spoken of in awed terms as 'the modern Archimedes'; Frederick Gowland Hopkins, who had laid the foundations of human biochemistry, won the Nobel Prize, and assembled a team of biologists in its way every bit as impressive as Rutherford's physicists, including the famously rude J. B. S. Haldane, leading geneticist and author of a number of admirable works of scientific popularization, including *Possible Worlds*; Joseph Needham, embryologist and, in later life, principal author of one of greatest monuments of twentieth-century encyclopaedic scholarship, *Science and Civilization in China*; J. D. Bernal, pioneer of X-ray crystallography; and many others.[4] And this is not to mention the university's outstanding contributions to the fields of mathematics, law, history, anthropology and English literature.

Indisputably, then, Cambridge was a remarkable place, and a fine arena for keen young minds to stretch and hone their talents. And yet, to the average undergraduate much of this astonishing activity was hardly more conspicuous or significant than were Ogden and Richards's staircase semantics to the fledgling doctors rioting outside. For many students, especially those with rich backgrounds and assured futures, Cambridge was little more than an agreeably untaxing interlude between the privations of public school and a preordained career in business, law, medicine or – for an untypical minority – the Church; and college life mainly a thing of team sports, dinner in Hall, compulsory chapel and prodigious quantities of strong drink. Only a relatively small number of undergraduates shared in, or indeed were alive to, the remarkable place and time in which they lived; only a very few added something distinctive of their own to the intellectual wonder of the place at its best.

Humphrey Jennings was one of those few.

*

F. H. S. Jennings, exhibitioner elect, matriculated at Pembroke College, Cambridge, in Michaelmas Term 1926, and moved into a modest college hostel at 29 Ettisley Avenue. Before many weeks had passed, he had established himself as one of the most conspicuously gifted undergraduates of his day – though his distinction was perhaps more apparent to those outside Pembroke than to his fellow-collegians, since the college was traditionally one of the heartier of the university foundations, not much given to the sort of airy-fairy stuff like painting and plays at which Humphrey excelled. Still in his teens, he had already become that vivid character recalled by all who knew him even slightly in his later years: a garrulous, argumentative, short-tempered, exhaustingly energetic young polymath, thrillingly charismatic to some, intensely irritating to others, given to laying down the law on all sorts of matters – from recondite points of scholarship and aesthetics to the obligation for all persons of taste to support the contemporary arts by buying new paintings and books of poetry whenever possible. He worked enthusiastically at his formal studies and excelled at them, while continuing to paint, to write articles, to act, and to design costumes and scenery for theatrical productions both in the university and for the Perse, some of which were sufficiently accomplished to receive favourable notice in the national as well as the local press. One such review, in the *Sheffield Daily Telegraph*, spoke of 'a very young undergraduate of absolute genius, Mr Humphrey Jennings'. In a small way, he was already becoming known to the larger world.

Critics have sometimes bemoaned Jennings's penchant for spreading his talents too thinly, across too wide a range of media, suggesting that his refusal to be limited to any one art form or sphere of interest is the mark of a dilettante. It's debatable how far this multifaceted quality of his mind should be seen as a weakness rather than a virtue, but it is true that at this very early stage of his career Jennings himself could express considerable uncertainty as to the best arena for his many gifts. 'As to my progess in art,' he wrote to his friend Leonard Amey about 1927, 'I am as usual torn among painting, literature, and the theatre. I love each infinitely in turn and feel that I get on well in each – but where it will all end – in which, I don't know.'[5]

Many of the friends and acquaintances he made during these energetic undergraduate years would go on to exceptionally distinguished careers as writers, scholars, critics and actors. Perhaps the most brilliant member of the immediate Jennings circle was William Empson, later Sir William, the author of *Seven Types of Ambiguity*, *Some Versions of Pastoral*, *The Structure of Complex Words* and other works that established him (or so many of his successors have judged) as one of the finest English literary critics of the twentieth century – perhaps the finest of all – as well as a greatly gifted poet whose relatively slim body of work proved hugely influential on later generations as well as his own.[6] Before turning the full attention of his powerful and highly idiosyncratic mind to literature and language, Empson had been a mathematician, and it was characteristic of the Jennings circle to take a lively interest in both of the Two Cultures (as they became known after an acrimonious debate among a later generation of Cambridge men),[7] the arts and the natural sciences. Most of his friends were aware of recent developments in the 'softer' sciences of psychology, anthropology and linguistics, and some were also au fait with work in biology, chemistry and physics as well as mathematics. There are signs that Jennings was already musing on the history of technology in his student years, and such an interest would not have seemed at all eccentric to his open-minded friends. Other promising members of his crowd included the scientist and writer Jacob Bronowski, best known to the general public for his BBC television series of the early 1970s, *The Ascent of Man*, but also a student and editor of William Blake; the novelist Malcolm Lowry, famous for his harrowing, semi-autobiographical fantasia *Under the Volcano*; the poet, journalist and sociologist Charles Madge, who later joined forces with Jennings to found the Mass Observation movement; the painter Julian Trevelyan; and – one of the very few women to cut a dash in this predominantly male world (not least for her spectacular and legendary beauty, which was applauded by young men as she cycled into town from Girton) – Kathleen Raine, who read Biology as an undergraduate but became famous as a poet and scholar of Blake and the Western esoteric tradition.

It's almost certain that Jennings also knew Anthony (later Sir Anthony) Blunt, the art historian and Soviet spy, since he contributed to a short-lived undergraduate magazine co-edited by Blunt, *The Venture*.[8] Blunt, who was reading Modern Languages at Trinity, was one of a very small number of undergraduates to take much interest, let alone a keenly informed interest, in contemporary art. (The dons were hardly any better. Many years later, Sir Roland Penrose, founder of the Institute of Contemporary Arts, recalled that in the 'provincial' Cambridge of that day only Mansfield Forbes and John Maynard Keynes had any awareness of modern art, or, come to that, of any of the visual arts whatsoever.[9]) Though Blunt was often disliked by his contemporaries – intellectually patronizing and chilly – it's likely that he and Jennings would have found occasion to converse from time to time. On the other hand, there is no evidence that the relationship was particularly close, and it's highly improbable that Jennings – never a member of the Communist Party, or indeed of any other political organization save a trades union – ever found himself being enticed by Blunt towards playing a part in that bloody Revolution of which all good Marxists were dreaming. Nor was Jennings homosexual, unlike most of the Blunt coterie.

Blunt's co-editor on *The Venture* was Michael (later Sir Michael) Redgrave, who was already showing signs of the theatrical talent that would soon establish him as one of Britain's most distinguished actors. Besides their dabblings in student journalism, Redgrave also collaborated with Jennings on plays – an anticipation of their wartime work together on the film *A Diary for Timothy*, for which Redgrave spoke E. M. Forster's commentary. Meanwhile, another future colleague of Jennings in the documentary movement, Basil Wright, was organizing pirate screenings of films from the far side of the Channel – the sort of films that were the favourites of young intellectuals of the day: among others, René Clair's *The Italian Straw Hat* (1927), F. W. Murnau's *Faust* (1926), Pudovkin's *Mother* (1926) and Eisenstein's *Battleship Potemkin* (1925).[10] Like Redgrave, Wright took part in some of the dramatic productions on which Jennings worked, including the famous production of Arthur Honegger's *King David* in 1929, for which Wright played the humble part of a messenger.

It was, in short, a quite outstanding generation, a Golden Age of undergraduate promise and accomplishment; and yet Jennings managed to shine even in this dazzling circle. In later years, several of his university friends would write memoirs recalling the effect this extraordinary and unconventional young man had had on them. Initially, his contemporaries were most struck by his unusual physical appearance and almost alarming displays of barely contained nervous energy and excitement:

> He was rather tall, very angular and bony, with a wild crop of straggly fair hair, usually quite uncontrollable. He had a large, sharp nose and an extremely prominent Adam's apple which jumped around all over the place when he talked – which was a great deal of the time.
>
> He was an acutely restless person, and found it almost

impossible to sit still except when painting. He habitually paced
the floor as he talked – 'Terrific, terrific,' – jerking and gesturing
in a thoroughly Mediterranean fashion. Humphrey had many
distinctly personal physical habits. For instance, he was at the
time greatly addicted to China tea, which he drank in quantity
and at all hours. He would hover over the sugar basin like a blue
jay, suddenly dive with his long bony fingers, pick up a cube of
sugar, dunk it in his tea, and then, holding it delicately between
his thumb and his index finger, he would suck at it, thus
interspersing his conversation with loud sibilant noises as he paced
the room. Finally with a flick of his finger the lump went down
and a few moments later he would reach for another.[11]

As this passage suggests, the next thing to strike contemporaries
after his ectomorphic build, unruly hair and fizzing energy was the
fervent, torrential quality of Jennings's talk. 'He had a manner,' Jacob
Bronowski noted, 'which was full of what I can only call impersonal
excitement; he always came alive in conversation, but what gave him
life was the conversation, not the people.' Gerald Noxon, a slightly
younger Cambridge contemporary who first met Jennings in 1928,
offers more detail:

> To say that Humphrey was a brilliant talker is a truth that does
> not in the least convey his impressive gifts in this area, which were
> beyond those of any other person I have known. When Humphrey
> addressed himself to a subject, he did so with a lucidity, a force-
> fulness, and a kind of internal illumination generated by his
> immense enthusiasm. To be sure, he often spoke in outrageous
> hyperbole, made fantastically sweeping generalizations, made
> deductions totally unjustified on the basis of the known fact, but,
> BUT, nobody was more aware of these flights of fancy than Hum-
> phrey himself, and he was always the first to acknowledge them.
> In fact he knew exactly what he was about. It was all part of his
> technique of verbal exploration of the subject, of creating channels
> of communication with all those around him, even if he had to
> shock, outrage and even seriously anger them in the process.[12]

As to Jennings's favoured topics of conversation or, more precisely,
monologue – in an unpublished memoir composed many years later,
William Empson wrote of the characteristic Jennings peroration:

it was heady, bouncing talk, though almost entirely about the art and literature of the sixteenth and seventeenth centuries. He talked about other things to other people, but in this area we had interests in common, and I think he would have agreed that they were fundamental to his world-view as a whole. Western man was still working out the Renaissance, and what you made of that had to appear in your popular films and your abstract paintings. The theory that the Renaissance never occurred had perhaps already been invented, but he would have brushed it aside as a minor but typical 'treason of the clerks'. 'Triumphs, Triumphs, it's all Triumphs' – I actually do remember him saying that, with a breezy gesture, in the middle of a non-stop harangue of documentation.[13]

For Kathleen Raine, Jennings was, with the possible exception of Malcolm Lowry, 'the only one . . . of my then contemporaries to whom the word genius can be truly applied'. Her autobiography, *The Land Unknown* (1973), records:

I think I learned more, in those years, from the inspired talk of Humphrey Jennings than from any other person. I see him, in memory, as an incarnation of Blake's Los, spirit of prophecy; whom in appearance, with his full flashing eyes and mane of yellow hair, he much resembled. Humphrey used to declaim, with 'the mouth of the true orator', long passages of Blake's prophetic books . . . He talked of Triumphs, of Gray's Progress of Poetry, of Inigo Jones . . . While the rest of us were reading Freud, Humphrey was already reading Jung's *Secret of the Golden Flower*; he quoted from Lao Tze, and not only in Arthur Waley's translations . . .

Such disinterested fervour could be inconvenient, and might even appear mildly comic. Julian Trevelyan remembered:

His enthusiasm was immense; I remember his waking me up at eight in the morning to show me a picture he had painted in the night. At his best his work had a purity that one associates with Ben Nicholson but without the dehydrating good taste. But his work was erratic: he had, so to speak, to talk himself into a picture.[14]

★

Though the undergraduate Jennings does not seem to have been arrogant in the conventional sense, he had, equally, no false modesty about his accomplishments. At around this time, he wrote to Leonard Amey: 'I can imagine this letter being found in an old drawer – a hundred years hence – being certified by you or your descendants to be in my handwriting and to be presented to a museum as the earliest known literary opinions of Jennings, the famous critic and designer! I know I am born to be famous.'[15] This unabashed, mildly embarrassing vision of future fame as 'critic and designer' reads oddly now, since Jennings is remembered as neither of these things. It suggests that, at this stage, he was foreseeing a career that might somehow combine his theatrical activities with some pioneering academic work in literary criticism, a field of the humanities which was already undergoing rapid and far-reaching changes and was about to undergo yet more.

Though his training at the Perse would have qualified him to read Classics or any number of other subjects, Jennings's chosen Tripos[16] was English Literature – still a novel subject at the time of his matriculation. The earliest fully working prototype of the new English Tripos had come into being less than a decade before, in 1919; and it was only in October 1926, the same month he matriculated, that the university first granted tenure to the dozen young or youngish lecturers in Early and Modern English.

'Cambridge English', as it later came to be known, has a unique place in the development of English literature as a discipline, and for good and ill its powerful influence on the teaching of the subject lasted for generations, not only in Britain – where graduates of the English Tripos went on to preach the Gospel according to Magdalene (or Downing) College in both schools and universities – but in Common-wealth countries and, particularly, in the United States, where the modified (and, one might argue, impoverished) form of Cambridge-style 'close reading' formulated by the likes of John Crowe Ransom, Allen Tate and Cleanth Brooks, and known as the 'New Criticism', dominated the teaching of English Literature well into the 1960s and beyond. Over the decades, countless thousands, perhaps even millions of English-speaking schoolchildren and undergraduates have been exposed to some version (however diluted, coarsened or caricatured) of the reading methods developed in Cambridge in the 1920s – a rare, in some respects unique, instance of an apparently minor parochial reform in an academic discipline giving rise to a cultural movement of international scope.

The full story of the creation and growth of Cambridge English has yet to be written, though there is a rich enough literature of personal reminiscence and partisan claims and counter-claims, a good deal of it flavoured by the writers' attitude to the Puritan orthodoxy enforced by F. R. Leavis from his stronghold at Downing. At the most general level, however, the story can be told fairly simply, and runs something like this. Before 1914, English Literature was not only a minor subject studied on the margins of other disciplines, but was barely recognized as a proper subject of undergraduate study in Cambridge at all. (Other British universities, notably St Andrews, were well ahead of Cambridge in this regard.) On the one hand, there were the philologists, attached to the faculty of Modern and Medieval Languages, who were concerned only with vowel changes in Middle English and the like. On the other, there were the textual scholars and literary historians, busy producing editions of Bishop Percy's Folio Manuscript of Ballads, or writing contributions to the intellectually undemanding 'English Men of Letters' series. Neither faction's members concerned themselves much, if at all, with the aesthetic value of the texts they edited or used as evidence in their arguments (to the pure philologists, such questions were quite irrelevant); and outside the lecture halls, the sort of writing that passed for literary criticism generally ran to gossip, florid paraphrase or pure gush.

Here, to pick one offender from the crowd, is the long-forgotten Mr Stopford Brooke, from his *Studies in Poetry*:

> The best examples of Keats's Odes need neither praise nor blame. They are above criticism, pure gold of poetry – virgin gold. Of them it may be said – with all reverence yet with justice, for these high things of poetry come forth from the spiritual depths of man – The wind bloweth where it listeth, and thou canst not tell whence it cometh or whither it goeth – so is every poem that is born of the spirit.[17]

And so he goeth on. As one historian has written, the 'idea of *criticism*, the subtle and detailed analysis of verbal effects in relation to their meaning within a passage as an exercise for examination, scarcely existed anywhere, even in the traditional disciplines of Latin and Greek'.[18] It was more than time for a change, especially now that the colleges were suddenly being filled by ranks of demobbed men back from the trenches, often wounded in body or mind, sometimes bitterly impatient with everything that smacked of the smug, easy world before the apocalypse of 1914. (One of the wounded young men who came back, F. R. Leavis, had carried a copy of Milton with him throughout his time in the trenches. It is hard to guess at the almost perversely painful sense of integrity that later led him to repudiate Milton.)

So, put in very broad strokes, the revolution that took place in Cambridge English immediately before and during Jennings's time as an undergraduate was intended to sweep away the twin ills of stultified pedantry and impressionistic, highly subjective rhapsodies in the mode of the nineteenth-century critic Walter Pater. In place of the older disciplines of philology and literary history, it encouraged literary criticism – wide-ranging and thoughtful reading in the English litera-ture of the previous six centuries, together with some complementary study of other European literatures and the history of ideas. Above all, it placed at the centre of undergraduate literary studies the habit of paying minute attention to 'the words on the page'; that is to say, it encouraged English undergraduates to develop a heightened awareness of literary (and indeed, non-literary) uses of language by inviting them to consider nuances of meaning and tone in individual words and phrases, as well as the significance of poetic metre and poetic form. Once firmly grounded in precise knowledge of what was actually there on the page – and alerted to the fascinating possibility that literary texts may be saying more than one thing at a time, and usually are – the student could then proceed to broader reflections on the signifi-cance of major conventions or genres such as tragedy, the pastoral, the satire and so on. This practice of close reading and writing was called, and continues to be known in Cambridge and elsewhere as, Practical Criticism – often familiarly abbreviated, by generations of teachers and students alike, to 'Prac. Crit.'.

Like another well-known revolution, the Cambridge English revo-lution began in 1917 – though, again like that other uprising, it had been preceded by years of discontent and sporadic premature acts of rebellion. It was in 1917 that, in response to proposals and other forms of persuasion on the part of those already teaching some form of the subject, the university finally granted English its own Tripos. Its two principal architects were H. M. Chadwick, a former classicist who had been appointed Professor of Anglo-Saxon, and his younger High Table colleague at Clare College, the historian Mansfield Forbes. Forbes was a truly remarkable man, considered by some to be the closest to a saint they had ever encountered, and whose contribution to the world was far greater than his skimpy publications list might suggest to later generations.

Chadwick, a man who – unusually, many thought – combined great humane learning with considerable independence of mind and sound common sense, was appalled by the worst excesses of the philological school and thought philology quite inappropriate as a subject for undergraduate study. These were views which, unsurprisingly, won him a great many enemies in Cambridge. Without his alliance with Forbes, Chadwick would have had little chance of making English, as he hoped, replace Classics as the centre of a humane education for the brightest young men and women of Britain. Fortunately for Chadwick, Forbes, who enjoyed a substantial private income and took an active interest in many arts, was also a man (as one account puts it) of 'social genius': brilliant at winning support for Chadwick's new Tripos, still more inspired as a one-man recruitment agency or appointments board for the clever young people who would teach it.

Chadwick and Forbes were joined in their crusade by two other, very different, men. One was Sir Arthur Quiller-Couch, or Q, at the time by far the most famous man in Cambridge and one of the few academics well known to the nation as a whole. Q was not merely a best-selling novelist and prolific writer of essays and journalism, but editor of the *Oxford Book of English Verse*, owned by every British household with even the most modest claims to literacy, as well as a sportsman, a prominent Liberal politician and a noted wit. In 1912, he was appointed to the recently created King Edward VII Chair in English Literature (whose first occupant, A. W. Verrall, had unexpectedly died only a year after its foundation in 1911). His appointment was made by the Prime Minister, Asquith, at the urging of Lloyd George, who credited Quiller-Couch with having kept Liberalism alive in his home territory of Cornwall for many years. Before long, Q's chatty and entertaining lectures had become so much a part of the Cambridge scene that some considered him to be a landmark comparable to the Senate House.

The second ally of Chadwick and Forbes was the Reverend
H. F. Stewart, a distinguished scholar of Pascal and Boethius, a noted
theologian and a man of consummate political skill. It was in the
garden of Chadwick's house in Gresham Road in the Easter term of
1916 that Stewart and Quiller-Couch met with Chadwick and talked
the new Tripos into existence.

There was one small obstacle in their way: apart from its creators,
hardly anyone in Cambridge appeared adequately qualified to teach
the new Tripos. Well aware of the insecurity of their position – the
town was already echoing with elderly sneers about the 'novel-reading
Tripos' – the innovators rapidly set about putting together the rudiments of an English faculty. The informal, haphazard means by which
teachers were recruited by Forbes and co. would horrify modern-day
academic bureaucrats. One day during the long vacation of 1919, for
example, Chadwick dropped by the house of E. M. W. Tillyard –
another former classicist and one of the earliest English recruits – and
said: 'There's a man called Richards. All I know about him is that
he's got a first in Moral Science and a red nose. But Forbes says he's
all right, and I've put him on the lecture-list.' Which was how I. A.
Richards, less than a year after his staircase seminar with Ogden, came
to be lecturing on the theory of criticism at the start of Michaelmas
term 1919; and, less directly, how one man's particular vision of what
literary criticism might and should be came to predominate in the
early days of the Tripos. Tillyard had been startled by Chadwick's
suggestion: 'Richards, it was rumoured, was primarily a philosopher;
he lived an ascetic life in an attic and he was the friend of C. K. Ogden,
reputed at that time in stiffer Cambridge circles a blasphemer and a
pacifist.'[19] But despite these initial misgivings, Tillyard soon came to
admire Richards profoundly, and gave him a good deal of the credit
for the initial success of the Tripos.

After 1923, a series of momentous appointments followed: among
them men and women whose names are still familiar to many students of English, including Basil Willey, F. R. Leavis, T. R. Henn and
G. F. W. ('Dadie') Rylands. (Some present-day academics will be
startled to hear that of all those who created Cambridge English –
Forbes, Richards, Q, Tillyard, Aubrey Attwater, Willey, F. L. Lucas
et al. – not one possessed a doctoral degree. Happy days.)

Meanwhile, the founders were hard at work drafting and redrafting a new form for the Tripos, which eventually resulted in the statute of 1926. Jennings's year was the first to be able to take English for both Part One and Part Two of the Tripos, instead of combining English with some other subject, such as History or Classics. The mood among Forbes and his fellow-conspirators was one of 'elation'. In the words of Tillyard: 'There was, to begin with, the not very moral elation of having to do with a popular and growing subject: it was exhilarating to be on a winning side. Some of our enemies had said that the vogue of English was a piece of post-war folly which would soon die down.'[20] Basil Willey, one of Tillyard's first generation of pupils, recalls that the students were as thrilled as their teachers: 'We felt ourselves to be a happy band of pioneers, united by a common faith, despised perhaps by the older academics, but sure of triumph in a glorious future.'[21] The signs of that triumph were plain to the least perceptive eye. William Empson recalled of I. A. Richards's teaching that 'more people would at times come to his lectures than the hall would hold, and he would then lecture in the street outside; somebody said that this had not happened since the Middle Ages'.[22]

Distinguished, learned, innovative and inspiring as the other pioneers of the subject might be, it would be hard to deny that the early days of Cambridge English were dominated by I. A. Richards – and, more remotely, by both the poetry and the critical dicta of Richards's friend T. S. Eliot. Tillyard, for one, acknowledged that Eliot was 'the man really responsible for introducing into Cambridge a set of ideas which both shocked and satisfied', while Richards said that Eliot was 'the one hope for the then brand-new English Tripos . . . I was soon full of dreams of somehow winkling Eliot out of his bank and annexing him to Cambridge.'[23]

Richards's effect on undergraduates was more like that of a religious leader than a mere lecturer. His awe-inspiring presence towers over accounts of the period, both biographical and fictionalized: Richards appears as the 'amazing genius' B. K. Wilshaw in Edward Upward's novel *No Home But the Struggle*; elsewhere, Upward recalled, 'We were terrifically thrilled at I. A. Richards's lectures.' One of the best evocations of the Richards cult at this time is found in Christopher Isherwood's heavily autobiographical novel *Lions and Shadows*, which describes Richards – a 'pale, mild, muscular, curly-haired young man' with a 'plaintive, baa-lamb voice' – as 'the prophet we had been waiting for ... to us, he was infinitely more than a brilliant new literary critic; he was our guide, our evangelist, who revealed to us, in a succession of astounding lightning flashes, the entire expanse of the Modern World'.[24]

Richards's written words proved as potent as his spoken words. Between 1919 and 1929 he wrote five books and about twenty articles, and, as his biographer says, 'His fame and influence rest largely on the achievement of this decade.'[25] The five books were *The Foundations of Aesthetics* (1922), *The Meaning of Meaning* (with C. K. Ogden, 1923), *Principles of Literary Criticism* (1924), *Science and Poetry* (1926) and – best known of all – *Practical Criticism* (1929). They were widely read, excitedly discussed, and helped colour an entire generation of educated speech: 'In our conversation,' Isherwood recalls, 'we substituted the word "emotive" for the word beautiful; we learnt to condemn inferior works as a "failure in communication" or, more crushing still, as "a private poem".'[26] Richards was the first critic to bring to the study of literature the insights of modern philosophy (notably that of another eminent Cambridge sage, G. E. Moore) and modern science (particularly psychology and neurophysiology), and the first to attempt to make the evaluation of literature a procedure as strenuous and rigorous – in aspiration, if not in sober reality – as the ground-breaking work in physics being carried on in the Cavendish Laboratory. Distance has robbed the enterprise of a good deal of its enchantment, but for undergraduates of the 1920s it was a brave new world. Nor were these youngsters peculiarly susceptible, faddish or naïve. There is a general consensus that the students attracted to the study of English in the later 1920s were better and brighter than those who came immediately before and after. As Tillyard says, 'It was in those years too that there was a unique crop of able people taking the Tripos: people better equipped than those of the earliest years and yet retaining their freshness.'[27]

*

In short, it was a uniquely exciting time, a glorious time for Jennings to be reading English at Cambridge – though one should temper these superlatives a little by noting that much of the intellectual excitement in English was happening in other colleges than the one he had just joined. (And though I. A. Richards would later be Jennings's personal supervisor, he was away from Cambridge between March 1926 and September 1927, during Jennings's first undergraduate year.[28]) At hearty, sporting Pembroke, his studies would no doubt have been of a rather more old-fashioned nature than those of his peers at, say, Magdalene, King's or Clare. Basil Willey, who played a notable part in the development of the 'English Moralists' section of the Tripos, was part of the Pembroke fellowship, but Jennings's director of studies there was Aubrey Attwater (1892–1935): a solitary high Tory in a discipline taught mainly by those of Liberal or 'progressive' views, who nonetheless, thanks to his generous and convivial nature, managed to be friends with everyone regardless of their political or intellectual allegiances. Attwater had taken a First in Classics in 1914, been President of the Cambridge Union Society and had also won the Charles Oldham Shakespeare prize. The outbreak of war put paid to his ambition to read for the bar, and he immediately enlisted as a subaltern with the Royal Welch Fusiliers – the same regiment joined by the soldier-poets Siegfried Sassoon and Robert Graves. Seriously wounded in the hip by a bullet early in 1915, Attwater was sent for treatment at Craiglockhart, the Scottish military hospital recently brought back to popular memory by Pat Barker's fine *Regeneration* trilogy of novels, which were inspired by the encounter between two patients, Sassoon and Wilfred Owen, and their humane and brilliant doctor W. H. R. Rivers, one of Cambridge's most attractive polymaths of the natural sciences.

Attwater's bullet wound left him permanently disabled, with a terrible limp, and eventually brought about his premature death at the age of forty-three (by coincidence, the age at which Jennings was also to die). Instead of salvaging his earlier plans for a legal career, Attwater returned to Pembroke, where, there being no obvious vacancy for him as a classicist, he became an enthusiastic teacher for the new English Tripos. It was Attwater who suggested that Pembroke should take the lead in offering scholarships in the subject, and Jennings was one of the early beneficiaries of this proposal.

E. M. W. Tillyard wrote that Attwater always put him in mind of the figure of lame Vulcan in the first book of the *Iliad*, hobbling around with a cup of nectar after an Olympian row and telling his mother to cheer up. Attwater was, Tillyard recalls, a lovable man, a great peacemaker, and one in whose company it was difficult to remain angry long. Moreover, as 'a classicist and a Tory he was looked on by the more conventional dons as that supremely desirable thing, a safe man, and was thus a powerful means of adding respectability to a new and disreputable subject'.[29] Attwater's strategic value to the new Tripos was immense. Tillyard wrote with obvious affection and compassion of his physical appearance – his rosy face, which paradoxically left the impression of unhealthy pallor; his atrociously bad teeth, disfigured with thick deposits of tar; his wispy hair and moustache; his sensitive eyes and high-pitched laugh, both of which seemed to Tillyward sadly expressive of the constant physical pain he struggled to ignore.

Attwater occupied the same rooms in the Hitcham Building of Pembroke's Ivy Court which had once been occupied by, among others, Thomas Gray and William Pitt. He crammed the walls of these rooms with a large and constantly growing collection of books, partly for the pleasure of collection, partly because he found it difficult to walk to the town's other libraries. In the words of his *Times* obituarist, this collection soon grew into 'one of the best private libraries in Cambridge. Attwater bought his books judiciously and yet gaily; seventeenth-century quartos, early nineteenth-century colour-books, the latest novel – all found a place, somehow or other, on his bulging shelves. Perhaps [the obituarist adds on a slightly more sombre note] it was his voracity for reading and collecting which prevented him from producing books himself.'

Attwater also filled the cupboards of his comfortable rooms with copious quantities of sherry and spirits, which he liberally dispensed to his constant stream of visitors – for his rooms were open to students and colleagues alike at all hours of the day and night. Some of these visitors were members of a play-reading group he had founded, the Spenser Society,[30] initially for the benefit of his own students but subsequently opened to students of other disciplines, too. The choice of plays tended towards the jovial rather than the mandarin: J. R. Planche's *The Vampire*, John Gay's *The What D'Ye Call It* and Fielding's *Tragedy of . . . Tom Thumb the Great* were some of the more popular texts.

In many respects, then, Attwater was more a clubbish gentleman scholar of the pre-war school than a pioneering intellectual of the harsher and more psychologically, linguistically and philosophically inclined approach to literature being formulated by Richards and his associates. Denied the chance to participate in team sports himself – and growing increasingly corpulent on college food and his own wines – he was a regular spectator at Henley, Twickenham and Lord's; and every September, before the start of the new academic year, he would take himself off to Stratford-upon-Avon to see the latest productions of Shakespeare. As his obituarist concedes, he was disinclined to publish much, and his major concrete legacy to literary scholarship was a single chapter in the *Companion to Shakespeare Studies*, since he refused the proposal of Q and others that he should undertake a revision of the Temple edition of Shakespeare. His real ambition was to write a major history of his own college, and he was still at work on a short preliminary version of the Pembroke book at the time of his death in 1935. It was eventually seen into print by Attwater's friend at the Cambridge University Press, the Johnson scholar S. C. Roberts.

But in a university like Cambridge, where until quite recent years it was possible to regard excessive publication as a form of self-advertising vulgarity, meagre scholarly output is not always or necessarily the mark of the intellectual dud – Forbes, a teacher of undisputed brilliance, left almost no literary remains. Nor is there any reason to view with scepticism the verdict of Attwater's obituary, which described him as an excellent scholar and an inspiring teacher: 'For formal lecturing he had no love; it was the individual teaching in his own rooms that mattered . . .' The erudite Tillyard, too, considered him as 'very learned', and he was widely respected for his learning. Jennings, never one to suffer fools gladly or disguise his contempt for incompetent figures of authority, left no written complaints about him, and, though Attwater may have been an unlikely mentor for the independent-minded, absolutely modern young man, it's quite possible that he helped steer Jennings towards two of his principal interests as a postgraduate scholar: Thomas Gray, the declared topic of Jennings's Ph.D. thesis, and the earliest poem by Shakespeare, *Venus and Adonis*, which Jennings edited for a small press edition in 1930. Like Attwater, he was to win the Oldham Shakespeare prize.

*

Whether under Attwater's direct tutelage or (more usually) in the pursuit of his own private intellectual concerns, Jennings read hungrily.

As William Empson attests, his particular fascination at this time was for the literature of the sixteenth and seventeenth centuries, though Jennings by no means confined himself to research in those areas. One account of his studies from 1926 to 1928, both official and personal, indicates that he was reading Plato and Aristotle, the Greek tragedians, Ben Jonson, Milton ('the greatest English poet'), various eighteenth-century novels and plays, John Stuart Mill, Dickens, Trollope, Hardy, Shaw ('the greatest dramatist – on St. Joan alone, if need be'), Ruskin and Oscar Wilde. 'I remember ten days ago reading De Profundis from cover to cover on top of a bus and in the National Gallery much to the amazement of the officials.'[31] He was also interested in Tudor fireplaces, the influence of Captain John Smith's voyages on seventeenth-century design, English porcelain, eighteenth-century Spanish art and twentieth-century line drawings.[32]

At least some of these concerns look forward to his work on the Industrial Revolution, Pandæmonium. Leonard Amey recalled:

> He deplored the whole mechanization of modern life and sketched the idea of a masque whose climax should be the entry of the Devil on a reaping machine. Masques seem to have fascinated him at this time. He had a scheme for taking over a school end-of-term concert and ending it with a masque of Coe Fen, involving a policewoman as the tutelary genius and featuring the new Fen Causeway bridge, whose design he liked. He was continually drawing costume designs for masques and theatrical productions, a good many of which came to nothing. There was, for instance, a series for Hamlet in full Elizabethan style.[33]

A look at the university's lecture lists for 1926–7 indicates some of the riches the freshman Jennings would have sampled. This was the year in which E. M. Forster delivered his Clark Lectures on 'Aspects of the Novel', which later became a best-selling book. But the bill of fare for English students also included Quiller-Couch on Aristotle's Poetics, Mansfield Forbes on 'The Reading, Analysis and Value of Poetry, with Special Reference to the Poets of the Romantic Revival Period', E. M. W. Tillyard on 'The History of Criticism' and Milton, Dr Leavis on 'Modern Poetry', Mr Rylands on 'Development of the Ode, the Sonnet and the Elegy in English Poetry', Miss Enid Welford on 'The Renaissance in England', Mr Lucas on 'The Victorian Poets', Mr S. C.

Roberts on 'XVII Century Prose' and Mr Attwater on 'Dramatists Contemporary with Shakespeare'. An enviable list, and one which offered plenty to keep Jennings at his books. If he succumbed at all to that common tendency of first-years to luxuriate in unaccustomed leisure, the public record remains unblemished: on 23 June 1927, the *Cambridge Reporter* announced that, in the intercollegiate examination in English Literature, just four men had taken Firsts. The last on the list was 'Jennings, F. H. S., Pemb.'[34]

★

But he was no less busy on other fronts. On arrival at Pembroke, Jennings wasted little time in infiltrating the undergraduate theatrical world, and by the end of his first term was already busy designing, acting and dancing in an Amateur Dramatic Club production by a fellow of King's, Frank Birch, *The Christmas Revue (With Nothing at All about Christmas in It)*. As if this were not enough to sate his appetite for theatrical jollities, he also returned to the Perse for a production entitled *Le Théâtre des Souris Blanches* (The White Mice Theatre), which was, as *The Pelican* explained, 'a Christmas divertisment [*sic*] invented by R. R. Broome, F. C. Happold and F. H. Jennings'. The report added: 'A new stage was provided, designed to give an intimate contact between players and audience' – all very well for the front rows, but frustrating to those at the far end of the hall, who could only make out the performers' heads.[35]

Much of Jennings's subsequent theatrical work, both as an undergraduate and in his early postgraduate career, was for productions by Dennis Arundell, at the time a fellow of St John's and later famous as a writer, opera director and actor. Some of Jennings's activities were fairly minor: in February 1927, for example, he played the presumably undemanding part of 'A Man in a Bowler Hat' in a 'Nursery' production of *Dragons – A Symbolic Play in Three Scenes*, written and directed by Basil Wright. (One of the other two plays on the evening's triple bill was *Three Stories*,[36] a one-act melodrama written by William Empson.) Later in the year Jennings played 'Jack Ketch, the Hangman' in another ADC Nursery production, *The Tragedy of Punch*, a 'fantastic play' by Russell Thorndyke and Reginald Arkell. But some of his contributions were much more substantial. He both designed the costumes and (since, it is curious to recall, women undergraduates at

Cambridge were at this time forbidden to take part in such diversions)
played the female lead – opposite Michael Redgrave – in a production
of Thomas Heywood's *The Fair Maid of the West*, directed by Arundell
for the Marlowe Society. In later years, Empson wrote a memoir of
this bit of cross-dressing, which, he said, had prompted him to some
characteristically unconventional speculations about the young Jennings's character and sexuality:

This heroic girl [the Fair Maid] sailed to America and made the
rough types do much better there: my impression is that she
founded the British Empire, but in any case she behaved like the
Queen: 'Elizabeth – there's virtue in that name!' Humphrey was
the Fair Maid; I had a walking-on part, and forget whether I said
anything, but there was never a dull moment. He was on the tall
side and lanky, or what I think is meant by gangling; there were
no rumours of his giving homosexuality a trial, whereas our
friends would have seen no need to be discreet if he had; but
anyway, the absence of sex in his treatment of the part was what
you would expect of the Fair Maid, who was more in the line of
Joan of Arc than of the Queen. But he was immensely queenly.
Of course, female actors were then simply forbidden, so that his
taking the part was not at all out of the way; even so, the force
and naturalness of the result struck me as needing an explanation.
'Don't poke, Humphrey,' the producer would say (whoever can
the producer have been? [Empson is presumably half-remember-
ing Dennis Arundell] An older man, and one felt they hardly
existed); this was a very classy phrase, usually needing to be said
to a future duchess before she attended her first Hunt Ball. Often
he would stand very upright and glare straight at the audience, or
smile at it graciously; but then he would withdraw into himself,
and the long neck would protrude horizontally, while he gazed
at the floor. How often did he do this in his own clothes,
I wondered, without being noticed? The play went off very well,
and I wish my memory was less capricious about it. But I felt I
solved the sex-problem of Humphrey; the reason why the part
suited him was that, though quite unaffectedly a leader, he was
not at all a bully. He was not interested in 'mastering' people, or
'possessing' them, let alone frightening or bribing them – in fact,
he was rather unconscious of other people, except as an audience;

he did have a good deal of consciousness of whether he was swinging round an audience to vote on his side. It is in a way a saintly quality, and I daresay I had been taught to admire it by the Julius Caesar of Bernard Shaw, though I am pretty sure I did not think of the parallel at the time. Of course women, like men, are often bullies and possessive, but the position of a woman leading the councils of a group of armed men selected for a fight makes the contrast sharp . . .[37]

Further small-scale projects and acting roles followed. Again for the ADC, he played the part of Timothy Spratt, in *At the Same Time* by A. P. Herbert. In December 1927, he went back to the Perse once again to design costumes and decor for a school nativity play, *The Finding of the King*, and played 'The Innkeeper of Bethlehem'. Marius Goring stage-managed the production. The reviewer for *The Pelican*, one 'K.G.T.', observed:

The most important part in the play was taken by F. H. Jennings, as the inn-keeper. At the beginning of the play he is very prominent, with his absorbing covetousness and his sophisticated incredulity, but in the middle of the play, when the stage is filled with the shepherds and with all the trains and panoply of the eastern kings, when even the very heavens are filled with the angelic host, he is left on one side, and forgotten. Consequently, the audience tend to lose the full effect of his sudden adoration at the foot of the crib. Jennings, however, if he may be forgiven a slight tendency to overact, played his part admirably; the gradual change in his mind, the final and complete surrender to a power that he could not understand.

K.G.T. concluded that the general effect 'was magnificent. The scenery, designed by Jennings, the acting, so well rehearsed by Mr Happold, the orchestra and choruses, so well trained by Mr Broome, all combined to give the whole a wonderful sense of unity . . .'[38]

*

Meanwhile, he continued to apply himself fiercely to his studies. In October 1927, starting his second year at Cambridge, he moved into lodgings closer to college, at 2 Botolph Lane. This year, the *Cambridge Reporter* was advertising a series of lectures by I. A. Richards called, simply, 'Practical Criticism'. There is no direct evidence that Jennings was among those who flocked to hear them, but – especially in the light of his later relationship with Richards – it would have been uncharacteristically lazy and incurious of him not to have attended, and taken part. It was in this series, soon to become an established part of Cambridge legend, that Richards performed the experiments – he had, in fact, been developing them with Forbes at least as early as 1925 and possibly a good deal earlier – that helped establish his fame and were published in 1929 under the same title, *Practical Criticism*.

In essence, what Richards did was very simple: he handed out unattributed copies of a variety of poems and asked his friends and students to reply with 'protocols' – anonymous written responses which he would analyse and comment on in turn, coaxing out the underlying attitudes and habits that caused readers to damn, praise or claim indifference. It was, in short, an attempt to discover – in reasonably objective, if not exactly scientific, terms – how and why it was that people read as they did. Thanks to a combination of personal testimonies, we know that a number of the published protocols are by Forbes and Leavis, though there are none by Empson. And F. H. S. Jennings, of Pembroke?[39] Since Richards destroyed all the original scripts, it is impossible to use handwriting to judge; and we know too little of Jennings's academic written style at this time to make more than a guess as to which, if any, of the published protocols issued from his pen.

*

It was in the middle of his second year that Jennings engaged in his first really large-scale theatrical production. In February 1928, he designed and Arundell directed Purcell's *King Arthur* for the New Theatre in Cambridge. The play was considered a great success, and Jennings was singled out for praise. The press declared: 'Humphrey Jennings is a discovery. He has a quality all of his own, belonging neither to the Bakst nor the Lovatt Fraser school, while his sense of colour is as delicate as his sense of line'; 'Particular mention must be made of the scenery and dresses of Mr Humphrey Jennings, because they seem to . . . show a touch of something very like genius'; 'The scenery and dresses . . . would have done honour to any opera house in Europe or the United States. It would be a pity if the talents of

[Arundell and Jennings] were not some day given the fullest scope in a large theatre.'[40]

With these plaudits still fresh in his memory, Jennings took advantage of the Easter vacation of 1928 to go off on a brief trip to Italy with a Pembroke friend, staying in Rome and Florence – where, no doubt worn out by his hectic term, he took to sleeping for twelve hours a night. Almost exactly a year later, while staying at his parents' country house in Essex, the sound of villagers singing in the moonlight brought back memories of nights in Rome: 'Our hotel was in a little cobbley alley – very cabbagey and smelly in the day, but a heavenly misty blue at nights – and one night as we stood on a balcony high up, there came up the cobbles just such another party of men singing O exquisitely the most lovely folk tunes: we stood like statues . . .'[41]

On his return to Cambridge, he was faced with the imminent prospect of his first major examinations – Part One of the English Tripos, sat then as now at the end of the candidate's second year as an undergraduate. Predictably, his name was among those of the five men who would take a First (though not with special distinction: it was Miss E. E. Phare of Newnham College who achieved that pinnacle). Pembroke duly acknowledged the coup and awarded him the Parkin Scholarship – named, somewhat arbitrarily, after one Charles Parkin, a benefactor who had left the college land and some £5,000 in 1771. (There was no direct connection between this bequest and the scholarship, which appears to have been worth £100 per annum.[42]) Another of the perks of scholarship was a set of rooms for his third and final year – D15 in Old Court, above the Hall. Perhaps feeling a burst of affection towards his alma mater for this recognition, he now produced the only physical evidence of college spirit: he designed the cover for the June 1928 issue of Pembroke's little magazine The Pem (a sorry publication which consisted mainly of grotesquely humourless attempts at humour, and provides strong evidence for the existence in that college of a conspicuous hard core of braying hoorays) – an unremarkable outline sketch of two tail-coated male figures flanking an elegant female, with what look like stage curtains above and a college crest: a hint of May Ball festivities.[43]

To round off what must have been an immensely satisfactory year for a young man mindful of future fame, he went back to the Perse School one last time to design a revue, devised in honour of Dr Rouse,

who was finally retiring as headmaster.[44] Humphrey's whereabouts for
the summer vacation are unknown, though he probably spent at least
part of it at his parents' Essex house. One can only hope that he
relaxed, since his third and final year was going to be strenuous even
by his own exacting standards.

*

October 1928, the beginning of his last Michaelmas term, brought
him yet more laurels. The *Cambridge Reporter* announced[45] that on
25 October the prestigious Charles Oldham Shakespeare Scholarship
had been jointly won by a postgraduate, Lionel Charles Knights BA of
Selwyn College (better known in later life as the eminent scholar and
critic L. C. Knights), and by Jennings of Pembroke. The same month
also saw the real beginning of his career (always a fitful one, to be sure)
as a published writer. At a meeting in Jacob Bronowski's rooms in Jesus
College, Jennings and a group of his friends resolved, like so many lively
young students before and since, to found a magazine, this one to be
called *Experiment* – a name charged, in young Cambridge, with all the
glamour of the natural sciences. Most of the subsequent meetings of
the *Experiment* group took place in the rooms of Viscount Ennismore –
who, as a supporter of the Labour Party, was democratic-minded
enough to wish to be known by his family name, William Hare. It was
in Ennismore's room that the first editorial board was chosen by ballot.
The original intention had been to appoint three editors, but since there
was a tie for fourth place, it was decided to appoint no fewer than five:
Jacob Bronowski, William Empson, Ennismore, Humphrey Jennings
and Hugh Sykes Davies, later a fellow of St John's and, like Jennings, a
prominent member of the British Surrealist movement. According to
Bronowski's memoir of this time, neither Ennismore nor Jennings was
to take much practical part in the magazine, Ennismore because he
was too busy with political activities and Jennings for various reasons,
not least his continuing preoccupation with the theatre.

Very few undergraduate magazines have ever boasted quite such
an illustrious cast of contributors as *Experiment*. Apart from the editorial
team, local writers and artists who worked on the publication included
John Davenport, Malcolm Lowry, George Reavey, James Reeves,
Kathleen Raine, Timothy White, Basil Wright, Richard Eberhart, Henri
Cartier-Bresson and Julian Trevelyan – all later to enjoy distinguished

careers in their various fields. Contributions from outside Cambridge were even more impressive: somehow or other, the editors managed to solicit work from the likes of Conrad Aiken, Richard Aldington, Paul Éluard, James Joyce, Vladimir Mayakovsky and Boris Pasternak.

According to Bronowski, Jennings had no relish for the drudgeries involved in bringing out even a small magazine, and soon withdrew somewhat from the editorial circle. He did, however, contribute an article to the first issue in November 1928, on 'Design and the Theatre', and wrote two more substantial articles for the second issue, in February 1929: 'Odd Thoughts at the Fitzwilliam' and 'Notes on Marvell's "To His Coy Mistress"'.

The first of these begins in a jocular, mildly eccentric manner:

All the family agreed in disliking the baby. The theatrical manager thought that Art was all very well in museums but likely to cause trouble in the theatre. The producer said he might want a spectacular set now and again but he could always hire the costumes. The author said that the play was the thing and that anyway with his stage directions you wouldn't want a designer. The actor said he had got along pretty well so far and wasn't going to wear talc dresses now. The public didn't say anything, and the baby sat in the corner drawing . . .[46]

The last article provides the earliest evidence of the approach to literary criticism that Jennings had been developing in his first two years as an undergraduate: it shows that he had been reading the works of I. A. Richards's friend T. S. Eliot ('These notes are intended to be to the "Coy Mistress" very much what Mr Eliot's own notes are to The Waste Land: suggestions for further interpretation of thought and for a fuller development of visual imagery . . .'[47]) It also suggests that his way of thinking about poetry was very close to that which his friend and co-editor William Empson was shortly to reveal to the world in Seven Types of Ambiguity (1930), full of bold imaginative leaps, out-of-the-way historical knowledge and the ambition to truffle out the full range of connotations from the humblest words:

Shakespeare's use of 'bed' in the second quotation is of course connected with oyster beds, and again suggests richness: but also Troilus is describing Cressida, and to the audience purity and constancy are the question: hence the pearl, symbol of spotlessness (see the fourteenth-century poem 'Pearl'). Marvell's 'Indian' combines both these uses, only he brings in neither spice nor pearls; neither the Coy Mistress's purity nor her richness are in question; she is seated by the Ganges appropriately finding rubies . . .[48]

When not engaged in teasing out resonances in seventeenth-century poetry, Jennings was hard at work on designing. His theatrical career was going from strength to strength; indeed, he was about to make theatrical history. In November 1928, he was invited by Arundell to design the first British production of Stravinsky's *The Soldier's Tale*, starring the internationally famous ballerina Lydia Lopokova – the wife of John Maynard Keynes – and Michael Redgrave. A reviewer in the *Cambridge Evening News* wrote: 'Humphrey Jennings's decorations are uneven, his set for the first scene being extremely good, but the palace set, while not being obtrusive, seemed hardly in the spirit of the music at this point. His design for the Devil's costume in his various metamorphoses was incredibly ingenious.' *The Pelican*, understandably loyal, was warmer, noting: 'Another Old Boy who has brought the fame of the Perse into the public eye is F. H. Jennings . . . He has . . . been busy designing for the A.D.C., and his work for Mme Lopokova in Stravinsky's 'Soldier's Tale' was greatly appreciated.'[49] (The same issue noted, in the Union Society annual report: 'Mr F. H. Jennings (Ex-Pres.) spoke against the motion "That in the opinion of this House the Modern Age lacks all sense of proportion".') It was thanks to his continuing connection with the Perse that his life was to undergo its most dramatic change to date.

*

Sometime late in 1928, Jennings met a tall, dark and strikingly beautiful young woman called Cicely Cooper. Born on 25 April 1908, she was a year younger than Jennings, and came from an Anglo-Irish family of considerable distinction. In more grandiose moments, they claimed descent from both William the Conqueror and one of the High Kings of Ireland. More modestly, they could justifiably point out that the Cooper, or Synge Cooper, family is directly descended from the enlightened eighteenth-century Church of Ireland Bishop Edward Synge, and rather more distantly related to the playwright J. M. Synge.

Curiously, the Jenningses and the Synges appear to have come into oblique contact a couple of centuries earlier. Bishop Synge had known Handel, and had been present at the first performance of the *Messiah*, the libretto for which was written by one Charles Jennens of Warwickshire – a direct forebear, it seems. Synge wrote to Handel to express his admiration for the piece, and Handel in turn wrote to Jennens, explaining that there was an Irish bishop who was tremendously excited by their collaboration.[50] Another branch of the family was the Burkes of Galway, who according to legend were descended from Spanish sailors shipwrecked in the Armada and washed up to settle in Ireland. If there is a grain of truth in this, a seasoning of Mediterranean genes may account for Cicely's olive skin, grey eyes and very dark hair – characteristics shared by her younger brother Arthur.

Cicely's father was Richard Synge Cooper, a civil engineer who, at the time, was in charge of new works for the London Midland and Scottish Railway and enjoyed the curious privilege of being entitled to sit in George Stephenson's chair at Euston Station. He was also, his granddaughter Mary-Lou remembers, 'an extremely strange and difficult person, a very bad father to all his children, and often angry – he was the sort of man who threw food out of my window . . . and so was my father'. At the time of Cicely's birth, the Coopers were living at 19 Birdhurst Road, Croydon. She was christened Cicely Mary Wilhelmina Raimond Cooper – after, respectively, her grandmother Cicely, her mother Molly, her grandfather William Burke and her uncle Raymond. As the only daughter, the middle child between four brothers, and the first female Cooper born in that line for a generation, she was doted on and in some respects indulged. (Largely an obedient child, she was capable of small acts of rebellion: 'When she was younger, my mother had hair right the way down her back. And then she had it cut, Eton cropped, the way girls did in the 1920s, and my grandfather took one look at her at the breakfast table, buried his head in his hands and wouldn't look at her.') And she could charm others, too. When her parents sent her on holiday with her grown-up cousins Edward and Effie Cooper at their house in Dunboden in Ireland, the couple asked, perfectly seriously, whether they might adopt her.

As far as it went, Cicely was given a good education: she was sent to St Paul's Girls' School in London, noted then as now for its academic excellence. Gustav Holst, famously, was the school's Director of Music, and his lessons supplemented her already considerable home education in music. Mr Cooper had been a keen amateur musician since his youth – he had played the French horn – and numbered Dennis Brain, the horn player, and the celebrated early-music specialist Arnold Dolmetsch among his friends. Cicely played both piano and violin and had a good, if rather idiosyncratic, soprano voice. She particularly enjoyed singing Elizabethan songs, including the pastoral 'Have You Seen But a White Lily Grow?'. Another favourite was 'The Ash Grove' (a song movingly used in a sequence of Jennings's 1942 film to *Listen to Britain*[51]). Since, however, she was poor at mathematics, her father – himself an outstanding mathematician – angrily refused to allow her to sit for the School Certificate at sixteen.

Instead, in 1924 Mr Cooper sent her to Brussels for a year to perfect both her French and her music. In later years, she would sometimes admit that her time in Brussels was perhaps the only truly happy period of her life – mainly because she had finally escaped the horrors of negotiating that miniature civil war which was family life. Mr Cooper's rages, which found their ostensible justification in the loss of some properties in Ireland and in the fact that his sons were a disappointment to him, were mainly directed against his poor wife. He tried to recruit Cicely as an ally against her, but Mrs Cooper made her own bids for Cicely's comfort and support. Though she grew stoical and emotionally secretive in her mature years, Cicely once confided in Mary-Lou the sheer misery of being a child forced and wheedled into ever-shifting alliances with and against her father and mother.

Cicely could find some compensation, though, in the doting love of her brothers: Jos and Dick, eight and four years older than her; Edward and Arthur, four and eight years younger. With her two younger siblings she formed 'Cicely and her troop', teaching them to read and generally imposing some order on their lives; soon they took to calling her 'Pip', after a cartoon in the *Daily Mail* about the adventures of 'Pip, Squeak and Wilfred'. The nickname stuck, and 'Pip' was Humphrey's pet name for Cicely in their affectionate periods. The youngest children played elaborate, imaginative games together: Arthur invented the characters of 'Bogdan and Boris', who lived in a country of warring tribes where the people spoke cod-Russian and spies communicated furtively in code. They spoke in a slang largely of their own devising, heavily peppered with Irish words learned from their mother and from holidays on Ireland's west coast.

At eighteen, like other women of her class and like her mother before her,[52] she 'came out' – in other words, was presented as a debutante at court and participated in all the dances, tea parties and other festivities of 'the Season', as this annual marriage market was and is known. Terribly shy, Cicely found it at best tedious, at worst an ordeal; and her usually flawless sense of fashion let her down at crucial moments. For her appearance at Buckingham Palace she wore a short silk dress with short sleeves, matched with a train, long kid gloves and an ostrich feather at the back of her head, held in place by a band. The overall effect was bizarre in the extreme. Nor did she find much to interest her in the nice young men with whom she was obliged to make small-talk – the phrase 'chinless wonders', though unkind, is probably appropriate – especially since the sparkling, adventurous talk of her brothers made these prospective suitors seem dull and ignorant.

For, difficult as it must have been, the Cooper household was also a stimulating environment for an intelligent girl – 'very exciting, slightly eccentric', is how Mary-Lou Legg characterizes it. All Cicely's brothers were immensely well read, and (as those games with codes and lingos might have foretold to the shrewd observer) grew up to be exceptionally good linguists. Joshua became a Russian scholar, later working for the Foreign Office and for the now legendary Bletchley Park code-breaking unit during the Second World War; his translations of four classic Russian plays were published by Penguin, and are still in print. Arthur Cooper became a Chinese and Japanese specialist, though he was also fluent in Icelandic and in Irish; he accumulated a substantial library of Irish books. Arthur also went to work at Bletchley Park; he was in Singapore when it fell to the Japanese, but managed to work his way back to England by way of Australia. The second-youngest brother, Edward, had the most difficult relationship with his father. Identified as a 'difficult' child, he had been sent to the Perse School – oddly, in view of Mr Cooper's generally reactionary outlook – because of its progressive reputation. Edward became an actor and enjoyed some early success, especially with his appearances at Stratford, but he volunteered to fight in the Spanish Civil War, for the Republicans, and died at the age of twenty-five.

It was through Edward's budding talents as a performer that

Humphrey and Cicely first met. She had come to see Edward act at
the Perse: Humphrey, who had designed the costumes, saw her in the
audience, and the following day went to Cambridge station to see her
off. Years later, she would say that he fell in love with her 'because
she was wearing beautiful boots'. This sounds like a slightly rueful
joke, but there is no doubt that her fashionable, expensively groomed
appearance was something of a revelation to the Jennings circle, who
seldom tended towards elegance in dress even if they could afford it.
'She went to Cambridge in Paris frocks with a white Pekinese under
her arm,' says her daughter Mary-Lou. Why did she fall for him? In
part, perhaps, because he was the first young man she had met who
could talk as well and about as many different things as her brothers;
the first who was not just a well-mannered dolt. At any rate, for both
young people it was the *coup de foudre*. Their courtship began almost
immediately, though in a circumspect manner: it was to be quite a
while before Jennings's friends met the woman in his life.

When the encounters came, they were not always easy. Jacob
Bronowski recalled that Cicely 'was as impersonal as [Jennings] was,
but had less conversation; she therefore seemed to us rather remote'.
A more likely explanation for her quietness was that the relentlessly
talkative Jennings and his friends simply overwhelmed her. (Bronowski
came to know and like her better towards the end of 1930, when she
offered to take down some dictation for him.) Kathleen Raine's first
impressions of Cicely were a good deal warmer: 'She was tall,
statuesque, and as silent as Humphrey was voluble. She had been a
debutante, and her wonderful simple clothes were in the style of *Vogue*;
which I first saw on her table. Her little white straw hats shaded her
beautiful eloquent grey Irish eyes. She was everywhere accompanied
by her fierce Pekinese dog.'[53]

A good deal of the courtship between Humphrey and Cicely
was conducted by post. She was living at her parents' house, then
49 Tregunter Road, London SW5, and working as a typist in an office
in the West End; they could see each other only for a few hours at a
time in London at weekends, when they would generally go to the
cinema as one of the few places where they could be respectably and
cheaply alone together. In later years, Cicely would recall that Humphrey, a rural child, had hardly ever been to the cinema at this time
except to see the likes of 'Felix the Cat'; she had more sophisticated

tastes, and claimed to have introduced him to the films of René Clair (though these were also part of the standard pantheon for the film buffs Jennings knew at Cambridge, so perhaps she was just one of his tutors in this area). So discreet were the lovers that even Cicely's brother Edward knew nothing about the romance in its early months. Starry-eyed as they may have been, both partners were sensible enough to realize that Mr Cooper was, to put it mildly, unlikely to regard Humphrey – poor, eccentric, and of doubtful background (his parents did not even keep servants!) – as a suitable husband for his only daughter.

Cicely hoarded the letters that marked the progress of their love, and more than sixty of Humphrey's letters, cards and notes to her have survived. He, on the other hand, kept none of her letters, much as he praised her for them; I leave it to the reader to decide later whether this was indicative of an unromantic callousness in the young Jennings in particular or of a thoughtlessness common to his sex in general. Whatever the reason for his neglect in this respect, it renders what remains of their epistolary courtship something of a dramatic monologue, in which Cicely's attitudes and opinions can only be guessed at from odd hints and references. For all its one-sidedness, though, this collection of letters is uniquely revealing. Up to this point in his life, Jennings's personal voice is all but inaudible, to be inferred only from the traces it left in the memories of his friends or odd bits and pieces of unripe poetry and prose. Now, suddenly, for the space of four or five months, it pours out in an unstoppable stream. In many ways, it is the most fully formed statement we have of what Jennings the man thought and felt, second only, if at all, to the letters he wrote Cicely at the height of the Second World War.

*

The turning-point in their relationship came early in the New Year of 1929. His first note, on 9 January, is decidedly flirtatious but still safely within the bounds of respectable communication between a young gentleman and a young lady:

Dear Cicely,
    It is deliciously rare for anyone to ask me what I draw: everyone always remarks that it is 'so nice to be artistic' and

leaves it at that. Anyway perhaps you would like the enclosed trifle – rather theatrical as I warned you. Once again thank you all so much for your lovely dance.

>　　Humphrey.

Whether she was principally charmed by the note, the modest enclosure (not preserved) or the sender, Cicely was obviously not averse to being wooed by this self-declared young artist. Just six days later, their relationship seems to be on quite a different footing:

> My beloved,
>　　I will come up on Saturday morning arriving at King's X 9.56 . . .
>　　O darling I do so long for you . . .
>　　Your loving Humphrey

And just two days after that, on 17 January, comes the first of his many full-length letters to her, one which suggests that he, at least, is convinced that they are now launched on a serious long-term affair. There is a touching display of old-fashioned manners and filial duty here: dangerously free-thinking as he may be in other respects, Humphrey has felt obliged to tell his mother all about his new love. He had presented himself to Cicely not only as a Cambridge under-graduate but as an artist, and the intelligence of her response had greatly pleased him.

> My darling Cicely,
>　　I wanted to get Mama's letter before replying & now I haven't time for a long letter. Mama has behaved like a darling: is very glad I told her & thinks it extremely sensible for us not to shout it about – she is going to write to you.
>　　So you were an elusive child who wouldn't make friends and who wrote poetry eh? How I love you for that and what a perfect description of myself at the same age (English master included)!
>　　Never mind about Monday night: it wasn't naughty – only natural . . .
>　　I have been working like mad (for me) at a book on the Chinese method of drawing which you would love: there that's what it is – I turn round to tell you something & you are at No

49 or No 8 miles away – O Cicely I want you here here now now.

I want call [*sic*] you names & say how much I adore you . . . there is a Chinese remark (one of the ones on painting) that 'of that which is unfinished the possibilities are infinite'. Simply I want to be with you & work with you: draw you – I have immense things to tell you – O when?

Cicely, about coming down: I will try definitely and come up to town on Saturday week & stay Sunday if possible. But this Saturday is rather near to last vac for my tutor! I can't tell him I want a rest yet! . . .

I have been having the most hair raising toothache the last few days – really the 'goods' – however the dentist will see me today: don't worry. You see I do so want you to come *here* and see my rooms & favourite haunts & my books & me 'in action'. Damn its always having to be Saturdays & Sundays. It is all snowy here now: I woke up yesterday to find a white glare everywhere from my roof – I mean the thousands of roofs from my windows: you don't know the view yet! The snow was not the best of things for tooth ache & the photographer said it made a soft light which will probably mean a terribly suave picture – so you must be ready for anything . . .

. . . from your devoted and adoring Humphrey.

Cicely appears to have been Humphrey's first real girlfriend – at any rate, a few weeks later he confessed to her about the existence of a certain young woman – 'Well, she & I have known each other for years & have been rather fond of each other, what we thought was in love – but never really understanding one another – she was too respectable for one thing . . .' Cicely does not seem to have much minded about her respectable predecessor in Humphrey's affections.

From this point onwards, Humphrey's amorous letters touch on three main areas. First, the ecstasies, frustrations, comforts and miseries of his love for Cicely – sentiments which, apart from the occasional eloquence of their expression, are generally indistinguishable from those of a thousand thousand other smitten young swains. They prove only that this extraordinary undergraduate was in one basic respect perfectly ordinary. Then there are the descriptions, sometimes quite lengthy, of Cambridge streets and courts, trees and clouds, wind and rain. A cynic might assume that these passages amount to no more than a literate mating dance – a display of visual sensitivity and verbal dexterity for the admiring benefit of his new girlfriend. The desire to woo Cicely may indeed have played its part here, but Jennings would continue to include such passages in his letters and diaries for the rest of his life, so it would probably be more accurate to see these vivid accounts of nature and architecture as spontaneous expressions of his relationship with the visible world – the written counterpart to his many drawings and paintings. The earliest example will do duty nicely for dozens of such passages:

> My most beloved Cicely,
> It rained this afternoon & then about four o'clock the rain stopped and for a short time – half an hour or so before dusk Cambridge was exquisite – 'l'heure exquise'. There was enough sun to warm the air for a little, beads of rain lay on the grass & among the trunks of trees and on stretches of college lawns there was a blue grey mist which melted into the bright yellow of a few willows near the river & the dull red of old brick walls behind the colleges.
> Patches of stone in the bridges stood out almost white, the rest lay back warmly grey matching the curling smoke from the thousand chimneys of men's rooms . . .

Most revealingly, there are the passages reporting on his daily life, his hopes and anxieties, his beliefs and ideas; especially the last. There are notable silences in these accounts. He barely so much as mentions his academic work or anything to do with his private studies until the very brink of finals, though he's always ready to tell Cicely what he's reading for pleasure. With one or two notable exceptions, such as allusions to his parents or the Goring family, he doesn't write much about friends or acquaintances – he's not much of a gossip. Nor, for a man coming perilously close to graduation day, does he often talk with much precision about his plans for the future. In other respects, though, his letters to Cicely are a gratifyingly detailed account of his daily life as a third-year undergraduate. On the whole, extracts from these documents may be left to tell their own story.

20 January 1929:

You must not think me sad but I am easily tired when I come childlike to lay my head on your lap you must bear with me. For that is the essence of being a man; the divine energy in us leads into far and rough places where as Milton again says 'that immortal garland is to be run for, not without dust and heat'. That to my dusty spirit & 'heat oppressed brain' is waiting Cicely with cool hands and marble poise is the blessedest thing I know . . .

. . . contrary to all that I have been planning, I have decided – I will not stay at Cambridge beyond June: you don't want me to, do you? It is all very well but terribly cramping: at once too conservative and too brilliant . . .

. . . As you see I have been reading quantities of Milton this week: all connected (in my mind at least) with Blake & Sassoon and my book on drawing . . . I want to read it all *with* you & not give you the snippets from exam work . . .

. . . I am not a letter writer I am afraid. You write so easily Cicely & slide so perfectly from one thing into another. There's the damn university again: they have made me so critical that I can't do anything . . .

1 February:

My darling Cicely,

You know those lines in Chesterton's 'Flying Inn' about

> The smell of Sunday morning
> God gave to us for ours

It's true; but here above the morning roofs (as Shakespeare wd. say) and the smoky chimneys I don't notice it. Grapefruit, gent's relish, a clean shirt and China tea make my Sunday morning smell and glorious they are: I hope you have a weakness for Patum Peperium or The Gentleman's Relish – it is one of the few genuine remains of Merry England.

The rest of the world however are at chapel or playing golf or reading the Observer: we *have* to go to chapel on a Sunday: isn't that babyish? Think of me with my South-Sea beliefs calling myself a miserable sinner once a week: I go to evensong which only lasts half an hour and study Wren's plaster ceiling as they sing those two glorious pieces Magnificat and Nunc Dimittis.

When you have finished 'Disenchantment'[54] (what a description that is of the last advance through the fog) you should go on
to Sassoon's 'Memories of a Foxhunting Man' and Edmund
Blunden's 'Undertone of War': 'Journey's End' is a detailed study
of the same business . . .

. . . About typing I take you at your word: next vac I shall be
writing two theses for College Prizes & things: if you could take
down what I shout and make me work when I feel lazy it would
be splendid. It's precisely the actual physical writing that I can
never get done: I do so much prefer talking – but you know
that . . .

. . . This week I have been drawing, drawing, I *will* learn some
anatomy: which reminds me, do you know a decent book on it?
I really mean an *indecent* one in French or German: the photos
are the main things. The whole of figure drawing is based on a
passion for the human body as thrilling machine, but the models
in English anatomy books always look as though they were
ashamed of God for not giving them [illegible] dresses from birth.
The pathetic & paradoxical result is that they always look
undressed – such are the paths of respectability.

At the present I am drawing from photos of the Russian
ballet: glorious poses & intelligent photography – but rather small
to draw from: when your photo comes I shall draw that . . .

5 February:

. . . Mrs Goring behaves angelically to me like a mother & is
rather worried about what I'm going to do in June: she still thinks
I am coming up for a fourth year & wants to know what I am
arranging – it's so awkward not being able to say anything to one
so near my heart: never mind. I was reading the life of Blake
again yesterday. He fell in love with his wife almost at first sight
& on its all coming out he said he would not see her again till he
had made enough money for them to marry: I feel I ought to do
that really . . .

. . . I feel very quiet and walk slowly in the gardens & along
the backs [the banks of the River Cam, which flows through
Cambridge] reading Plato's Republic & the Memoirs of a Foxhunting Man. The world seems restful and attentive: it is waiting
for spring . . . So among the freshness of the early world of the

Greeks & in the exultant New Jerusalem of Milton & Blake I sit and read, with 'England's green & pleasant land' around & *our* kingdom before me in my mind. What a description of England that is – 'Green & pleasant land'! . . .

. . . Picture me with one shaft of electric light falling straight down on my ruffled hair in the centre of a smallish grey coloured room, with a sofa along one wall & bookcases along two others. The sofa & the table in the centre are covered in papers & books & the bookcases have overflowed on to the floor. The window is long & low with no curtains: the black night stares in through dirty panes. How almost hermitlike. I sit by a gas fire & think of you long and long.

Since writing the last sentence I have made some tea & read some more Plato: O those astonishing Greeks . . .

8 February:

You mustn't take 'The Venture' as the high water mark of Cambridge culture: I will send you its rival magazine 'The Experiment' when it comes out. Between the two you will be able to see what a crowd of 'clever young men' we are! Ugh! I am afraid I contribute to both:[55] only Cicely my darling you do not I hope think of me as a clever young man. 'The Granta' is Cambridge's 'Punch': a remarkably good weekly. I am doing some more odd jobs for them when I have time! Thank you so much for the Duncan Grant cutting: I had seen it but had wanted to keep it & hadn't: there is an excellent phrase in it about 'composing with the brush' which I wanted to remember. As the Chinese say 'the law of bones by means of the brush'.

Mrs Goring has come round about my going down in June: she was rather afraid I think that I should be selling my soul to keep alive. Having assured her my soul was reasonably safe & that anyway I am tired of Cambridge, she agreed. Only of course it all depends on what turns up. Don't worry though. I'm not. . . .

*

For all the excitements and demands of courtship and scholarship, Jennings still managed to find enough time to keep up with his stage work. From February until May 1929, such spare time as he had was usually given over to the challenging task of designing scenery and

costumes for Arundell's forthcoming production of Honegger's dramatic oratorio *King David*. Jennings first mentions it in a letter sent to
Cicely on 11 February, and it is a running topic of comment for the
next three months. There are, to be sure, plenty of other things on his
mind; letter of 13 February:

> . . . They say there are starving wolves at the gates of Rome!
> Think of it: there's one for Civilization. I secretly hope there is a
> wolf in England somewhere. It would upset our placid bourgeoisie
> so . . .
>   . . . As far as I can see I shall be terribly busy from now on
> right up to June . . . in the meantime I have been seeing all sorts
> of people about jobs & there seem to be some possibilities . . .
>   My room gets I think untidier & untidier if that is possible:
> what a man to look forward to! But out of the muddle there
> comes from time to time slowly a drawing or something which is
> perhaps worth while. Anyhow the drawing business is getting
> slowly a little better: at least so people tell me – due my angel
> entirely to you . . .

Then on the 15th, after a rueful account of 'my wrapped up, down-
at-heel, hurrying figure with a thousand things to do, people to see, &
no no time':

> . . . 'King David' is beginning, as they say, to take shape – that
> means that we have made long lists of scenes, scenery, colours
> for lights & costumes, entries & exits etcetera. Now I am sorting
> old dresses & rolls of unused stuffs from past shows. This goes on
> in cold draughty 'rooms' in [St] John's [College]: everything deep
> in dust – no fire. Nothing looks so tawdry as dresses off the stage.
> Mrs Rootham shouts how many of each there are & what colours:
> I with trembling fingers write on the back of an envelope odd
> remarks like '2 Doz Chinese pyjamas' or 'six fishermen's jumpers
> in odd blues'. Then with some of these under my arms, wrapped
> up to the neck I trail across cobbled courts slippery with ice – the
> drift snow blowing playfully around corners – & back to the
> warmth of home.
>   Here one sits up till 2 a.m. doing tentative sketches of odd
> characters in pencil with dabs of poster colour & inks. Some of
> these look possible and are taken next morning to Dennis Arundell

who is usually in bed in a purple dressing gown, with a typewriter on his bedspread clouds of cigarette smoke. He is giving lists of lights to somebody: and gives vague criticisms – with an occasional 'Yes I like that one' – to the drawings which are finally taken back to Mrs Rootham and the dress-makers begin. But that stage is not due till March.

... As for my drawing. I am beginning I think to see things – people especially – as exciting machines or balanced groups – if only I could put it down. The finished thing – or even a [illegible] sketch is so dead compared to the momentary vision: it is steadier vision I want – and infinitely greater control in my fingers. One can only pray & practise ...

As term draws to a close, there is a quite unexpected early brush with the world of films; letter of 25 February:

Dennis ... broke to me a scheme he has with Fox Films for producing a film of a novel by 'Q' wants me to be 'Art Director' & is going into details now. In fact if we (mainly I) can get the estimate for sets & dresses low enough to suit Messrs Fox I start right away next vac. Isn't that thrilling? But you've no idea of the work – I have been at it about three or four hours & my head is going around with specifications of doors, windows, plastered walls etc. I know nothing about this type of business whatever: Dennis doesn't know much: it *is* fun. This of course if it comes off is a proper paying job. Don't breathe a word though till it's settled ...

27 February:

... at the present moment I have something like fifty costumes to design – among other things – in the next ten days or so: it [*sic*] this film coming on top of 'King David' – a film of the Civil War 1642 with fights on the backstairs of farmhouses, inns burnt down and escapes from haylofts: incidentally, how *does* one give an estimate for an inn kitchen to be burnt in the film-studio? That is the sort of thing I find myself suddenly asked. It *is* exciting: and even now I am managing to get some English done – & then there is the Chekov [*sic*] show ...

Humphrey shelters from the traditional end-of-term sportsmen's debauchery much as Ogden and Richards once sheltered from the Armistice Night riots; letter of 6 March:

> ... Tonight the University – or most of it – is drunk: that is to say, today was the last night of the 'Lents' and everyone has been having Bump suppers:[56] along the dark & stony streets there come bursts of shouting, little hurried knots of men & the occasional glare of a bonfire. At the present moment outside my door (carefully locked) unsteady men in boiled shirts & boating blazers are shouting out the names of men on the staircase. Your true heart is sober if lazy ...

Finally, an undated letter, sometime in the spring:

> My darling love,
>
> I feel terribly to blame for writing so little, particularly as I haven't really been doing anything much: I think the strenuous-ness of the earlier weeks has left me a little generally tired. Don't be worried or anything, I am not ill, only rather given to mooning around as I used to in the old days up and down Charing Cross Road. Like old Jolyon[57] I went out today and bought a pair of shoes I don't really want and am feeling a trifle better. I am also reading 'The Man of Property' again: a sure sign that I am taking life easily ...
>
> I think never have I wanted you to be by me so much as when this afternoon I stood on King's Bridge and watched the glow of sunlight on the weathered stone and yellow lazy river.

On 16 March he wrote: 'There is an awful idea nowadays that one should do so much work – get it over – & then enjoy oneself. That is all wrong. One should enjoy one's work ...'

*

The Easter vacation separated the young lovers more drastically than ever. Cicely went with her parents to France, staying at the Modern Hotel, St-Jean-de-Luz, and then, after a few weeks, in Paris. It was, so Mary-Lou Legg believes, more than simply the usual family vacation: Mr Cooper was alarmed by what he knew of the courtship, and was trying to keep Cicely out of harm's way. Meanwhile, Humphrey went to the country home his father had recently bought: as the letterhead gives it, Garrett's Farm, Shalford Green, Nr Braintree, Essex. A derelict Tudor farmhouse, Garrett's Farm stood isolated in the middle of a field, and was 'filled with beautiful objects: oak furniture, mediaeval pottery and glass, and oriental rugs'.[58] Like other Jennings residences it was wholly devoid of modern amenities, and even colder than usual – this was the house for which Mr Jennings had not been able to find a front door entirely to his exacting tastes, and had therefore decided to have no door at all. There were no electric lights, and no indoor lavatory; the earth closet was at the end of the garden, and torn-up newspapers served as toilet paper. In spring and summer, though, it could be idyllic.

In the course of the next few weeks, with none of Cambridge's duties and pleasures to distract him, Jennings's already copious out-pourings to Cicely become a minor flood – more than a dozen long letters, often festooned with sketches in pencil and ink or watercolours. He tells her at great length how much he loves the countryside – '. . . this Paradise. O Cicely all I want is you to share the ecstasy of this place . . .' He describes thirty-mile rambles in unseasonably hot weather ('like July') to Thaxted and other Essex villages; goes into the minutiae of country life both alone and, when they come up for odd weekends and other visits (housemaid in tow: the Jennings family fortunes were going through a healthy patch), with his parents and brother Rodney. He continues to work on his designs for *King David*, and he tells Cicely the story of a lecture he gave to the village guild of March (just north of Cambridge) immediately before coming on to Garrett's Farm; describes the embarrassment of having to stay at the local vicarage, with its terrifyingly pious children who demanded prayers before and after every mealtime, and the clergyman, who in response to his observation that all pictures are to some extent relative thundered 'There is nothing absolute but GOD!' He mentions his reading – Hardy's *Dynasts*, Galsworthy's *In Chancery* – and, as ever, ruminates on his drawing and painting, several times comparing his work to that of Duncan Grant.

On 25 March he wrote to Cicely: 'I always distrust the sentimental hours of dusk & moonrise: in fact sentimentality altogether – not to be confused with sentiment – sentimentality is always sad & cuts *feeling* off from *life*. Sentiment – but damn these definitions – you must sit on me when I preach, beloved.'

1 April:

Have been painting most of today: one of my too rare attempts
at oils – I mean it wd. do me good to do more – nothing
complimentary. Result rather Henri Matisse – that's because of
the elm trees here. Matisse paints tree trunks & outgrowing
branches inimitably – & yet I find myself imitating the general
style & getting no more . . . hardly then. In the meantime my
hands are covered in paint: I always was one for getting messy
. . . 'King David' continues very slowly though heaven knows I
work at it hard enough: and all the time as Rodney remarked
naively yesterday 'The Tripos loses'! . . .

    I haven't read the D. H. Lawrence I'm afraid. In fact – O my
darling – I have never read anything of his – isn't that awful?
Especially as I am sure from what people have said he is *our* kind
of writer – but I will; I will – my knowledge of the moderns you
know is unspeakable . . .

3 April:

Have just come in from sketching: the wind having dropped
somewhat. Sun & clouds too irregular to do much: also I am
working without Vernon Blake (my book on the way to hold a
pencil etc.) which always hinders me. Making toast again: I live
on it I think. On my grave shall be written: HE LOVED
WOODFIRES AND TOAST: only I won't have a tombstone:[59] so
it wouldn't be possible . . .

6 April:

In the old days I was pretty lonely anywhere & it didn't seem
much different: I got away from spending money and noisy
people. Now I am wretched unless I am with you, but doubly so
here. Father & mother have gone back to town. Thoughts,
thoughts tangle themselves in my poor head (I am smiling
darling!) The idea of being ill makes me so I think. Foul thoughts
– born of a public school education – vague abortions of imagination, and in a way the worst – monotonous mental images come
up like scum to the surface when my mind stands still . . .

16 April:

I read 'The Indian Summer' (feeling with one of Papa's cigars in my mouth very like old Jolyon himself) and some Plato and more of Vernon Blake on drawing: then I draw for a little or listen to Bach or go & fetch the milk – slowly with a pause at gates and walls to look at the view – or 'note the values'. The weather is warm enough to be comfortable. Our maid – with a strange Rembrandtesque face – is down here so there are no beds or cooking or washing up to be done. I have to 'clear the table if you please' for meals – always covered with my papers & precious little jars of poster colour . . .

But far and away the most revealing letter of this Easter period (written in more than usually illegible pencil in the course of a country walk) is one that gives a sketch – so to speak – of his philosophical position of the time. It's a rambling disquisition, full of dogmatic assertions and throwaway remarks on political and social themes, of ideas on individual and group psychology, of his views on cultural history and religion. Plainly, a holiday letter to a still-new girlfriend should not be read as a fully worked-out manifesto or credo. For all its scrappiness and occasional gaucheness, though, it touches on many of the themes to which Jennings would return in his working maturity, and is the most substantial surviving account of the young man's preoccupations. It begins with a response to some unspecified distress suffered by Cicely, apparently to do with the strictness of her upbringing:

. . . Your Easter Sunday letter came this morning: O my dear, how I understand everything – not that the same sort of thing happened to me: rather the opposite, I have been allowed to do almost anything – but the result of great freedom, especially intellectual freedom has made me lonely and self-centred in rather the same way, I think.

About being a heathen & the Fontarabbia procession: the underlying trouble is that the same religion won't do for everyone. The idea of believing without thinking is an admirable one, in its place, but of course doesn't suit us because we are used to putting everything to intellectual tests. But it was a good one during the Middle Ages for people who couldn't think anyway: it stopped them trying to think, which was really a good thing since a plowman or a farmer who goes on day after day without

thinking is likely to be a better plowman or farmer than one who
is on the verge – as it were – of ideas.

After all, the morbidness & introspection we hate so . . . is the
result of having a brain 'in thinking order'. The trouble is that
democracy has muddled up the farmer & the gentleman & the
result of teaching farmers to think is that they cease to be farmers!
There is you see, at the bottom of democracy, a snobbish idea
that it is better to be a gentleman than a farmer; without realising
that in a well-ordered world there is plenty of room for both and
both are equally essential . . .

Compare this early statement with one of Jennings's very last written
fragments, a draft for the introduction to *Pandæmonium*, contrasting
the labourer on an assembly line with a Tibetan Holy Man: 'in fact the
factory man is living on the vision of others and the Buddhist Yogi
on the production of others. In some societies (civilisations) the two
have been mixed, in others clearly distinguishable. The relationship
of production to vision and vision to production has been mankind's
greatest problem.'[60] The letter to Cicely continues:

Men are not born equal, they are born *complementary*. This brings
us to that inside personality you describe: which no sensible man
has ever doubted for a moment. Once again it is the vice of
democratic & intellectualised 'education' that it tries to make
people do what they – their real inside selves – don't want to do.
Hence the misery of 'work' at school. The world has got shuffled
& people are all doing the jobs they have been taught to do
rather than those that their 'selves' wish to. It can't be helped but
it *is* damnable for the few who still want to do what they *know* to
be the right work – artists for instance: their place is usurped by
people taught (O irony!) to 'do art'.

You will think this a condemnation of the intellect my love:
but it isn't really. I want the intellect to be in the right place. The
inside self is after all not very intellectual: it *knows* what it wants,
likes, dislikes but there is not very much that is rational about it –
that is the trouble and the delight of it.

The truth of the matter is that there are two underlying
principles everywhere, which, when found in humans are called
intellect & emotion (gentlemen & farmers if you like), both
essential but working in diametrically opposed ways . . .

(Anyone who has seen *Family Portrait* will immediately see how the germs of that late film's philosophy are already present in the undergraduate Jennings's mind.)

When a tree grows, the force of life pushes it up, the force of gravity pulls it down: both are necessary or the tree would not exist. Without life there would be no tree; without gravity it wd be infinitely large. Now emotion tends to be overwhelming & it is the business of the intellect to restrict it to a reasonable size. In fact space, time, and all that is, *is*, simply through the *tension* between these two forces (this is Einstein simplified). The best things are not *overdone* one way or another: they are in the middle . . .

His argument then ventures more deeply into questions of depth psychology – describing, though not naming as such (he sticks with the phrase Cicely has proferred him, 'inner self'), his idea of the unconscious mind – and seems to be open to the idea that the unconscious may be as much collective as individual. Perhaps, as Kathleen Raine's memoir suggests, he had already been reading Jung?

But there is another thing. For us now, it is essential that both intellect & emotion should be *genuine*. Most people substitute 'useful information' for intellect and sentimentality for emotion. Exam knowledge rather than real perception, Mendelsohn [*sic*] rather than Bach.

   And the more intellectual people *try* to become, the more sentimental they *do* become, because sentimentality and emotion are utterly, utterly opposed. Haven't you often felt that your real inside self is not only you but part of something wider? Notice that in questions of *emotion* people *agree* much more than in questions of *intellect*. The inside *selves* of two people are much *closer* than their intellects: so that in a way our innermost selves are *outside* 'us' (because bigger than 'us'): to them belong the real urges, such as to paint, to love (as *we* love – for life *together* & not memories *apart* – this is exactly what you feel about it being wrong to love anyone in a *pitying* way). The intellect when it has more than its full share of a person (if you see what I mean) goes *in* and *in* and finds nothing but the *traces* of past emotion: these it mistakes for real emotion & brings them to the surface saying 'Look, don't you remember when that happened?' Result: senti-

mentality.[61] While all the time, the real emotional inside self –
being as I say, greater than 'us', has got covered up, or disappeared
– at any rate *cut off from life*. That is what has happened today. At
Fontarabbia there is a last attempt still being made to keep up
what were hundreds of years ago genuine emotions: in the
'springtime' of Christianity: but it is now autumn & everywhere
else the intellect is greater than emotion – so both ways it is
unbalanced, & the leaves are falling.

I don't think of the children at Fontarabbia as muddled – only
out of place: but not more out of place than the overcivilized
clerks at their desks in the city: that is the other extreme. To
discover what really *is* our place, is our business. There is no *place*
for us in human society, at present, because everyone else is
wrong: the *whole* pack wants reshuffling. So the best we can do is
to be genuine to each other and to the inside selves = to my
Essex landscape.

Now from my point of view as a painter (this sounds very
selfish darling but pardon it & wait) I must be true to the vision
in me & do as it says, only with my intellect – technique, work,
etc – shaping and forming the more abstract vision down to the
size (here it is again) of a picture. Now to love, you with me
means an enlargement – as it were of the 'great inner self' –
agreement as I said being easier here than in the intellect – so that
having found you my darling has doubled my poor little worth as
a painter already . . .

Sadly, the leisure that permitted him to compose such a probing
rumination was rapidly drawing to a close: the final term at Cambridge
was almost upon him, with *King David* to see through to completion,
the hurdle of Part Two examinations to be cleared, and beyond that
the biggest problem of all – the choice of life. Idealistic enough to
define himself as essentially a painter, Jennings was also realistic
enough to understand that a far less appealing career – that, say, of
'the overcivilized clerks at their desks in the city' – might well be in
store for him unless he was very lucky or very shrewd. The thought
of Arundell's film project for Fox may have been sustaining him; if so,
he was in for a disappointment.

★

Jennings went back up to Pembroke on 18 April 1929. His first letters of the term are gloomier than usual, and full of worries about what he is to do after graduation. On the 21st he wrote to Cicely: 'I am hating Cambridge: so damn sophisticated & hearty – I should say soph. *or* hearty – after your spontaneous grace & gentleness, Cicely . . . My love for the film business seems rather "off": Fox people terribly vague damn them – something will turn up I suppose.'

23 April:

I shall I suppose end up by going to the appointments board & asking them to get me a film job – they said they wd. introduce me to somebody – but my darling I should hate doing films really; for a long time anyway. This sounds terribly selfish. I ought to take any job that wd. bring us enough to be married on, and live respectably ever after – only wd. it be happily ever after if I was doing something I hated?

I want to draw & I think you want me to draw – & that is the business of a lifetime not of leisure hours. It needs quiet, concentration, & regular work at it. Only how is this to be achieved if there is no money? The ideal thing would be to live partly at Essex & partly abroad wouldn't it? It is not a question of wanting art more than you or anything melodramatic like that: simply the will to draw must be obeyed: to obey it I must not be spending *all* my time doing something else. I have a scheme up my sleeve which I will tell you if it seems possible – isn't that horrid? . . .

Unless the 'scheme' was for a year or so of postgraduate research, nothing seems to have come of it. As an undated letter from around the same time showed, he was seriously considering his chances of an academic career:

I am still terribly bothered about what to do in June: I would rather like to come another year but that would only have any point if I was trying to get a fellowship – that is if I were to stay up for another four years or so. Couldn't you get a job here? Or wouldn't you like that? In my heart of hearts I would of course prefer to be in town drawing but there is no money in that I'm afraid. A fellowship would mean about 300 a year for a time: always assuming they gave me one! I presume a terrible amount from the authorities! If you could think of something lovely to do in town in June that would also mean some money & *not* 8 hours in an office please tell it me. Though why *you* my darling should think of it for *me* I don't know . . .

Fortunately, Jennings had something in hand to keep his mind off the yawning void of life after 'varsity.

King David finally reached the stage on 10–11 May 1929 at the Guildhall, in a presentation of the Cambridge University Musical Society; Honegger himself was booked to conduct, but was delayed from travelling to Cambridge by illness, and was understudied on the first night by Dr C. B. Rootham. This was *King David*'s first production as a dramatic pageant in Britain, and it drew a great deal of attention from the national press, not all of it favourable. The *Morning Post* observed glumly that the 'work is long, and the Cambridge production too heavy-footed', while the *Daily Mail* was harsh on 'the scrappiness of Honegger's music'. But the *Daily Telegraph* was kinder, and in the long review published by *The Times*, otherwise fairly lukewarm (describing some of the work as 'tedious'), Jennings received warm praise as having been 'extraordinarily successful in designing a framework . . . which was at once appropriate to the play and did not clash with the undisguised walls of the Guildhall and the gilded organ pipes which rose above it at the back. His costumes, though less consistently good than those for *King Arthur*, produced an excellent general effect.'[62]

With *King David* at long last out of the way, it was time for Jennings to give his full attention to his Part Two examinations, and particularly to brush up on the Italian studies he had been neglecting.

15 May:

This is Wednesday evening; I am re-arranging my books – for no particular reason, only I hate dirty or squalid bindings & whenever I rearrange these are eliminated. I have – strange to say – also been working at the accursed Italian set books . . .

. . . I have just finished in Dante the exquisite account of Paolo & Francesca & how they fell in love. Terrible simplicity: they were reading the adventures of Lancelot du Lac together –

several times the story made them look for a moment at each
other & blush: then when there was a kiss given in the story
Paolo leant over & kissed Francesca: 'that day we read no more.'
And they my beloved went to the second circle of hell!

. . . I have just heard in what order I get my papers next week
– the Essay comes first so after that I shall get sleepier & sleepier
until on Thursday morning I have the French & Italian – of which
I know utterly nothing. What a fellow – I have had two years to
try & read some of these books & I don't *yet* possess them
even! . . .

17 May:

My darling,

Once again only a line. Masses of French & Italian: what will
happen on Monday (not to speak of Tuesday & Wednesday &
Thursday) I daren't think: I am feeling particularly silly à ce
moment so you might pardon this scribble. O my dear I do feel
so lost without you, utterly – things go on round me, but I don't
seem to do anything: only with you am I alive, Cicely.

I have papers right up to Thursday evening, so I am afraid it
must be Saturday before I will try & send you what I owe you –
O finances finances. At the present moment my ignorance on
whatever the examiners may feel like questioning me is more
abysmal I think than ever before – never mind. The weather has
of course been exquisite & I have been putting in some painting
in spite of the Italian & the rest . . .

The following Tuesday evening, now in the thick of Part Twos, he
writes:

It is terribly hot here of course just as I am in the middle of
things: my papers have been so-so so far: two reasonably nice
ones and one terror, which I did atrociously: you mustn't expect
anything my darling.

I spend the rest of the day doing absolutely nothing (in
which case I might have written more often?) and at night sit
completely naked in my rooms drawing myself in the mirror: it is
scorching . . .

In the same letter he refers to himself, for the first time, as her 'husband': 'Since seeing you, I have spent exactly half a crown! So you see your husband *can* save if he wants . . .'

And from this point on the private record gives way to the public. Despite his procrastination over his Italian studies, his misgivings about that 'terror' of a paper and all the time being 'lost' from the Tripos in theatrical work, Jennings covered himself in academic glory once again; and having given so much of his scholarly attention to the Renaissance convention of the Triumph,[63] he must have been more than commonly gratified by the triumphant conclusion of his undergraduate career.

In June, he gained the highest academic honours open to Cambridge students: a First with Distinction in Part Two of the English Tripos, which was set for the first time that summer. His success was far from solitary. The year 1929 was a triumphant one, the 'great year'[64] – as Tillyard called it all of three decades later – for the English faculty in general, which was widely considered to have vindicated itself beyond reasonable question by its spectacular results. Of those who sat Part Ones in 1929, ten took firsts, including William Empson, Alistair Cooke (the celebrated journalist and broadcaster) and Muriel Bradbrook, who went on to a prominent academic career in Cambridge English. The results for Part Two were even more astonishing. Of the fifty candidates no fewer than eleven took Firsts; and of these, five took distinctions: 'F. J. R. Bottrall, F. H. S. Jennings, G. W. Rossetti, T. H. White and Elsie Phare'.[65] (Once again, Pembroke rewarded the academic success of its sons: Jennings was awarded a Foundation Scholarship, and he and Bottrall both received college prizes.) Tillyard remarked, with only mild ruefulness, that it was curious that none of these should have achieved high scholarly distinction in later life – this being no sad reflection on the English Tripos, which 'exists not primarily to turn out dons but to construct people'. Bottrall, after a period as Professor of English at Singapore, opted for a career with the British Council; Rossetti went into university administration and died young; Miss Phare, later Mrs Duncan-Jones, produced a book on the poet Gerard Manley Hopkins but then devoted herself to motherhood; T. H. White became a schoolteacher for a while, then launched himself as a popular professional writer, best known today for *The Goshawk* and *The Sword in the Stone*. As for F. H. S. Jennings . . . Tillyard notes that this candidate 'had a brilliant career in the film industry, cut short by an early death'.[66] It's pleasant to learn that at least one of Jennings's lecturers took a kindly interest in his later achievements.

A man who graduates from Cambridge with a starred First can be forgiven for believing that the world is all before him, and that he can do whatever he wants. F. H. S. Jennings BA (Cantab.) was well aware of his abundant talents; his only problem was in choosing what he wanted to do with them. But if this is too sombre a note on which to close Jennings's undergraduate career – or careers – let Jacob Bronowski redress the balance. After noting in his article 'Recollections of Humphrey Jennings', published in the January 1959 issue of the journal *The Twentieth Century*, 'the directness and the angular intimacy which endeared [him] to me', he concludes:

> I suppose that I spent more time with Jennings than with anyone else at Cambridge except James Reeves, who was at my college; we must have had tea together (it was the only common meal we could all afford) at least once a week. We talked most often about poetry, but neither Humphrey nor I were sticklers for a subject; and to me, an innocent among the social niceties of Cambridge, even his manner was an education. He was quite unconscious of his own oddities (and of mine), so that I learnt from him that a man is most at home when he finds everything except himself absorbing.

And from Gerald Noxon:

> In his formative years at the Perse School Humphrey had been influenced particularly by certain English writers and artists of the past – by Shakespeare and Marlowe, of course, but more unusually perhaps by John Milton, John Bunyan, John Constable and William Blake. The works of these men remained in Humphrey's background as a permanent frame of reference. Their kind of Englishness was Humphrey's kind of Englishness. To say that Humphrey Jennings was a typical Englishman is, of course, a contradiction in terms, for the most characteristic quality of the English is their nontypicalness, their eccentricity. In fact, he was most English in his eccentricity, which happened to include a complete lack of what are often considered English characteristics – snobbishness, intellectual and social, hypocrisy, insularity,

arrogance and indifference. For in spite of his brilliance and his sophistication, Humphrey remained utterly nonsnob, utterly candid, utterly noninsular, essentially humble, and completely and enthusiastically involved and in love with art and life everywhere.[67]

Three

1929 to 1934: Postgraduate Years and Married Life

Jennings's career as an undergraduate is neatly book-ended by two great social catastrophes, one local to Britain, the other on a global scale: the General Strike of May 1926 and the Wall Street Crash of October 1929 – the beginning of a worldwide economic depression that blighted countless millions of lives for much of the coming decade, and ultimately helped precipitate the war that gloomier souls were already prognosticating. It was one of the least auspicious moments in modern history for young men and women to set off on their careers, even if they were doubly blessed by exploitable talents and fortunate birth; and though Jennings was too well padded by his middle-class status ever to face the grinding horrors of hunger, homelessness and unrelieved indigence known to many of his fellow-Britons, he was all too soon to face the realities of genteel poverty – short bursts of insecure and uncongenial employment, humiliating shortages, cold and discomfort, loneliness, reliance on family gifts and other small forms of charity, and nagging uncertainty about the economic future. It did not help that he was never much good at handling money, being too idealistic to chase it and too self-indulgent in small luxuries like old books and new art objects to hang on to it.

Still, however discouraging the world picture, in closer focus the situation was happy enough to encourage the animal optimism natural to youth. On paper, at least, the early days of Jennings's graduate career showed every sign of living up to the abundant promise he had displayed as an undergraduate. In addition to his Foundation Scholarship from Pembroke, the *Cambridge Reporter* declared that on 17 August 1929 he had been one of three successful candidates for the Goldsmiths' Company's senior scholarships for that year. His proposed topic of research was the poetry of Thomas Gray. The two prizes added up to no more than a modest income, but for a while, at least, he would not have to worry about being forced away from the world of ideas and scholarship and into some more mundane form of employment.

He also had every reason to be happy with his research supervisor, no less a magus than I. A. Richards; and Richards, to judge by his later testimony, was both impressed by and sympathetic to Jennings and his work. Sadly, Richards was to prove something less than the ideal supervisor from the point of view of accessibility: from autumn 1929 to December 1930, Jennings's first year and more, he was away at Tsing Hua National University in China; then from January to August 1931 he went off to lecture at Harvard, where he made an enormous impact on many of his listeners including the young poet James Agee, a fascinating man whose work in documentary prose, film criticism and screenwriting has a number of interesting affinities with that of Jennings.

Moreover, if slogging for his starred First while keeping all his other creative projects in the air had wearied Jennings in any way, he showed little sign of it, since his restless creative energies now found yet another outlet. Together with his friends Gerald Noxon from the *Experiment* crowd and the painter Julian Trevelyan, he now established the Experiment Gallery, a small exhibition space behind Christ's College devoted to the latest movements in painting and the other visual arts. A neat card sent out to interested parties declared:

EXPERIMENT GALLERY
Cordially invite you and friends
to their
FIRST EXHIBITION
*
Paintings by Frank Dobson, Troin, Bissil,
Emmanuel Levy, Gontcharova, etc
(in conjunction with Dr. Stanislaus Ossiakovsky,
Bloomsbury Galleries, London)
Julian Trevelyan, Humphrey Jennings
Louis Le Breton and Honi Bhabha

Polish and Czecho Slovakian Graphic

and an exhibition of

Modern European Glass
(in conjunction with Bernard Nelson, Ltd, London)

The exhibition will be open daily
from 11.30 to 1 and 3.00 to 5.00

The Experiment Gallery was meant to be a commercial enterprise, a way for Jennings to supplement his meagre income, though aesthetic idealism generally muddied the waters of commerce. Jacob Bronowski remembered that both Jennings and Trevelyan had remonstrated indignantly with him when he bought a large reproduction of a Matisse for his mother. Jennings furiously insisted that he should stay away from reproductions and support contemporary artists instead by buying original paintings.

In addition to the excitements of modern art and antiquarian literary research, Jennings had a far more fundamental reason to be cheerful. Unlike most of his contemporaries, he need never be plagued by those traditional banes of graduate student life, monasticism and dislocation, since, during the very same month in which he began his career as a junior academic, he also became a married man.

The wedding of Humphrey Jennings and Cicely Cooper was held at Kensington Register Office in October 1929: the groom was twenty-two, the bride twenty-one. Their marriage, which would seldom be an easy or uncomplicated one, met with difficulties from the very outset. Still disapproving violently of this 'penniless man', Cicely's father and mother refused to attend the ceremony; Mr and Mrs Jennings also stayed away since they considered the couple too young to marry, so that the only family guests were Cicely's brother Jos and her favourite uncle, Raymond Cooper, who acted as witness. More serious than this emblematic snub from the practical point of view, the Coopers denied Cicely the generous marriage settlement she could reasonably have expected had her choice of spouse been more acceptable to them. Over the next couple of years or so her father relented just enough to give her a few small sums of money, and made one or two other minor peace overtures: on at least one occasion, Cicely and Humphrey went to stay at the Coopers' Oxfordshire house – The Grange, Duns Tew, Deddington. But there was no full rapprochement between the families until some four years later, after the birth of the couple's first child, Marie-Louise, in 1933.

This estrangement was, however, something of a mixed curse for Cicely, since a large part of her decision to marry Jennings was that she was desperately eager to escape her impossible father and the social ordeals imposed on her by the customs of her class. Whatever Humphrey's shortcomings as a conventional breadwinner or 'good catch', at least life with him ought to be free of the kinds of emotional bullying and tortures by boredom she had been obliged to endure under her parents' roof.

Even so, the sudden plummet in her material circumstances came as a terrible shock. All at once, the glamorous young lady with the lapdog who regularly bought her hats and dresses from the leading designers in Paris found herself having to scratch by on Jennings's scholarship income of £2 a week. One of the more comic emblems of her newly poor status was the episode that took place when the couple moved into their flat above the Experiment Gallery. Marius Goring told the story of how 'their marriage bed was too big to go up the stairs of their flat; I helped him cut it in half and reassemble it inside'.[1] Inclined, anyway, to be depressive by temperament, Cicely soon found plenty of new things to be depressed about in married life. 'Living in Cambridge was tough for her,' her daughter Mary-Lou thinks. 'She couldn't succeed with her own peer group socially as part of her family, and nor could she succeed with my father's acquaintances. Though she was used to being around very bright people, I think she found people like Bronowski and co. really just too much – pretentious and tiresome, and they simply ignored her.'

Still, not all of Humphrey's friends were quite so rude as the worst of the *Experiment* gang, and those mature enough to make the effort to know Cicely better came to like and sympathize with her, and would later recall that the early years of their marriage were far from wholly devoid of domestic happiness. Limited as their funds may have been, the Jenningses usually managed to live in reasonably attractive surroundings. Kathleen Raine remembers that after their wedding

> they lived in poverty in a tiny house in Round Church Street [in fact, the couple did not move there until some time in late 1932 or early 1933], made elegant by Cicely's taste and Humphrey's skill. Humphrey (partly French) and Cicely, a perfectionist also, had nothing about them which was not beautiful. One basket chair only, but the stripes of the Basque linen of its cushions were right to a hair's breadth. On her small housekeeping allowance Cicely would not make 'rice pudding' but delicious *gâteaux de riz*; no more expensive, but infinitely better. Humphrey painted with the perfectionism of fine art the flimsy walls and doors and the

uneven floors of that little house where poverty itself was immaculate.[2]

Kathleen Raine was not the only one to be struck by the excellence of Cicely's cooking – an art which she had been obliged to acquire in haste. In the dark days before Elizabeth David reintroduced the gastronomically stoical British middle classes to the complex pleasures of cooking and eating they had cast aside some time in the later stages of the Industrial Revolution, it was quite unusual for young brides, unaided by paid help, to prepare dishes that required imagination, care, and a knowledge of French and Italian procedures and ingredients. She cooked mainly from a volume with the homely title *Les Recettes de Grandmère*, by 'Marcellys', published in 1931; it is easy to guess at her favourite recipes from the stains on the pages devoted to risotto, *blanquette de veau*, *crème caramel* and, of course, *gâteaux de riz*. Even during the most stringent years of postwar rationing, she would always be scrupulous about the niceties of the table.

Such culinary treats must have been one of the additional incentives that drew guests to their small flat; and all but the most intransigent intellectuals eventually followed Kathleen Raine's kindly example and grew more cordial towards this elegant and quietly gifted young wife. Jacob Bronowski, for one, changed his view for the better, and many years later continued to keep in touch with Cicely from time to time in her widowhood. A small fragment of correspondence between them has survived: this exchange of notes was prompted by the publication in *The Twentieth Century* of Bronowski's article 'Recollections of Humphrey Jennings' in 1959. In her letter to Bronowski, Cicely Jennings wrote:

I recall that you came to see me in our cottage in Bradwell's Yard behind Christ's ... to break the news that Humphrey had collapsed in Bowes and Bowes [the bookshop] and was being looked after by Kathleen (she and Hugh Sykes Davies had a flat in Trinity Street then). When I rushed round Prof. Piccoli was there, too. Humphrey refused to eat anything but pickles and bananas while he had jaundice, and in the end I had to ask his mother to come and stay with us, and she was more strongminded than I dared to be, and made him take beef-tea.[3]

But this short bout of illness was hardly typical of her energetic husband. His involvement with the theatre was as absorbing as ever, probably more so. Within three months of his marriage he was intensely busy in London, designing costumes and sets for two of Dennis Arundell's productions at the New Scala Theatre – Locke and Gibbons's *Cupid and Death* and Purcell's *Dido and Aeneas*. *The Times*'s review of the latter noted: 'The costumes effectively viewed both the Greek and the supernatural characters through 17th-century eyes. Aeneas and his followers wore full-bottomed wigs; the witches were country folk of a sinister aspect, and the lighting and grouping of these figures made a series of vivid pictures.'

*

Just a couple of months later, back in Cambridge, Jennings went on to design J. T. Sheppard's production of Euripides' *The Bacchae*, performed in Greek at the New Theatre (4–8 March 1930), with music by Handel arranged by Arundell. Not the least noteworthy aspect of the production was that it marked the stage debut of a sullenly handsome young Yorkshireman, an architecture student from Peterhouse College, one 'J. N. Mason', later to be known to a much wider audience as James Mason, the stage and movie star, who by 1946 was Britain's biggest box-office draw and who has been described by the film critic Philip French as 'possibly the finest movie actor this country has produced'.[4] It's doubtful whether anyone in the audience could have predicted this illustrious career at the time, since Mason had a non-speaking role as one of twenty dancers. Jennings's own credit in the very handsome programme is a short line towards the bottom after the cast list: '*Scenery and Dresses* designed by MR HUMPHREY JENNINGS'.

Jennings was obviously keen to move into production himself, and was full of ideas for possible projects. A letter to Julian Trevelyan in the summer of 1930 sketches out one of them:

You may remember Kathleen Raine and Hugh [Sykes Davies] were talking one night about Marlowe's 'Dido Queen of Carthage': I have been working on Marlowe the last month or so and especially on 'Dido' with the result that I want to produce it sometime. This I talked to Hugh about (seeing him at Cambridge the other day) and also questioned Robert Eddison about the

ADC [Amateur Dramatic Club] stage. The position is this: it is a rollicking play with a relatively small cast, which can and should be played in front of a decor *simultané*[5](very cheap this). As I am a member of the ADC I can produce a show there for a much reduced rent and borrow their scenery, lights etc. The casting is pretty easy. Now what better than this as an *Experiment* contribution to the Centenaire de Romantisme? There is no doubt that put on in the first half of next term for three performances and really well advertised by Gerald [Noxon] with *Experiment* names on the posters (John Davenport to play the heavy lover) – production and decor (if I may) by H. J. with [J. M.] Keynes and Manny [Mansfield Forbes] and [George] Rylands[6] really interested – we should more than pay expenses. Consider expenses:

Reduced rent (for a week: 3 days in the theatre, 3 days' performances) about	£15
Dresses for cast of 15 or as near as may be	£30
Paint three-ply props	£10–15
Publicity	£5–10
about	£70

against this, the ADC holds 200: average price . . . 3/6 if we got houses two thirds full it would be 400 × 3/6 equals £70. It seems worth risking if one could find the capital to do it on. If we had a matinée I could probably persuade my wretched school to come in vast numbers to it. It would obviously be best if run by Experiment. I have about £5 to put into it but no more. Consider with Gerald: he should be business manager obviously. ? run it in connection with the film guild. Circularise English lectures.

Go and see the Delacroix exhibition at the Louvre. Reply here inside the next fortnight (I mean I shall be here for so long).

Both penniless in Oxfordshire to you all: joy

Humphrey

An afterthought scrawled in pencil tells Trevelyan: 'Keep your eye on works by Cossion, Ghika, Bozes, Vines.'[7]

As the letter hints, some of Jennings's plans for the theatre were growing directly from his academic research – though his supervisor, had he not been in China, might reasonably have enquired as to why

his graduate student was spending so much time on Marlowe when he
was supposed to be investigating Thomas Gray. Perhaps Jennings was
attracted by the kind of hybrid career – part theatrical, part scholarly –
that he could see being pursued by the likes of Dennis Arundell. He
was certainly enjoying a measure of accomplishment on both fronts,
since it was at this time that Jennings published his first book: an
'original spelling' edition of Shakespeare's *Venus and Adonis*, from the
Quarto of 1593, for Gerald Noxon's Experiment Press. As Noxon
recalled, 'It was a paperback book because we wanted to sell it for
half-a-crown which we did in modest numbers.'[8]

There seem to have been some minor mishaps in the book's
production:

> Add to the many confessions of failure this (for Gerald) that I
> have done nothing so far about [the printer R. I.] Severs and
> 'Venus and Adonis' partly because our luggage got stranded with
> my copy in it and partly because I don't know if G. has given
> Severs any instructions: in any case he can set it up pretty quickly:
> let me know Gerald's infuriated reply.

The resulting publication, however, shows no signs of such travails. A
slim and austerely handsome grey-green volume – nothing but letter-
ing on the cover, a slightly archaic typeface for the text – Jennings's
Venus and Adonis was a production of which he could be justly proud.
In his brief introduction, he remarks: 'In case anyone feels a defence
of such a reprint is necessary, I will refer him to two books to which
I have been specially indebted: *Shakespearian Punctuation* by Percy
Simpson, and *A Survey of Modernist Poetry* by Robert Graves and Laura
Riding.'

The second of these books seems to have been a key text for the
Experiment group: its discussion of the differences between the texts
of Shakespeare's sonnet 129 ('Th'expence of spirit in a waste of
shame . . .') as they appeared in the *Oxford Book of English Poetry* and
the pirated 1609 edition was also familiar to William Empson, who
used them as the launch pad of his precociously brilliant critical treatise
Seven Types of Ambiguity, of which the thirty-thousand-word first draft
was written – so legend has it – in a single fortnight. It was published
the same year as *Venus and Adonis*. Empson, for reasons which are well
known to his admirers but can always stand repeating, had been

obliged to finish the book while living on his small private income in London. In an episode that now seems grotesquely comic – which is not to say that it should not be viewed as a disgrace to the institution responsible – Magdalene had stripped Empson of his Bye Fellowship and removed his name from the books after an inquisitive college servant had discovered him to be in possession of 'sexual engines': condoms.[9] According to one account – that of F. R. Leavis's wife Queenie – it had to be explained to the Master of Magdalene what these curious things were for.[10] Legend – unconfirmed, but delightful – has it that when Empson was invited to speak in his own defence to the governing body, he asked, 'Would you prefer me to go in for buggery?' The sentence was passed, and the most dazzling, humane, creative – and witty – Cambridge critic of the century was thus obliged to spend his career gracing universities from Tokyo to Sheffield rather than in the town where he and Richards had re-imagined the discipline of English. It was Cambridge's loss.

The two debut publications of 1930 had very different fates. *Venus and Adonis* sold modestly and faded still more modestly from print; *Seven Types of Ambiguity* helped change the nature of English literary criticism for the better part of half a century or more, and became one of those books that people are fairly sure they have read and understood even when they have not so much as held it in their hands. There is no major injustice here – such innovative thinking as Jennings brought to his edition must be teased out with imagination and learning, while Empson's slim but potent tract appeared to present its thrilled readers with a kind of magical key to all mythologies. Even so, it is a shame that a little of Empson's well-deserved critical glory has not, as yet, rubbed off on this aspect of Jennings's intellectual career. Empson himself was happy to acknowledge that he had discussed his work on ambiguity with Jennings, and that the finished text owed quite a bit to these lively exchanges. Empson also repented the apparent loss of a handwritten document in which Jennings set out some of his own innovative ideas.

> His theory about the Renaissance approval for Triumph was the sort of thing that especially needs presenting in a documented written text, so that you can find what holes need to be stopped in it, where it is liable to give bad advice, or instead might be

rough medicine for an emergency. He understood that very well, and here have to make a painful confession. He posted me (when I was living in Bloomsbury) a long statement of this theory, which I had asked for because it might help me in writing *Ambiguity*, and probably did use it though I can't now say where. At the end of this document, which he had clearly written straight down, he added casually: 'You might hold on to this, because I don't think I have written it all down anywhere else.' I am extremely sorry that I did not do what I was told, but the random stroke of his death was beyond foreseeing, and at the time I was sure that he would write down a better version of it soon after. All the same, to lose it was a betrayal, and I must never blame my own friends for betraying me, if I could do that to him.[11]

Sir William was too harsh on himself: the letter in question was not lost but merely mislaid, and has recently been unearthed by his biographer, Professor John Haffenden, who kindly provided me with a copy. The document is every bit as fascinating as Empson recalled. It was dated 3 January – presumably 1930, if he is right that he received it while he was at work on *Ambiguity* – and sent from Jennings's parents' home, Garrett's Farm, in Essex. Since the text is rather long, and deserves to be preserved and appreciated in full rather than in a series of extracts, I have chosen to reproduce it as an appendix (see p. 387). Though it will mean more to those who are interested in Jennings's total body of work rather than his films alone, it is perhaps the most fascinating literary work he has left us: not so much for its overarching thesis (which, alas, is nowadays the sort of cosmological topic that tends to attract mythologists, mystics and cranks rather than the literary scholars who are best placed to assess its soundness and pertinence) as for its evidence of Jennings's youthful appetite for grand explanatory narratives, occult tradition and anthropology, as well as its diagnosis of the condition of art and artists in the modern age. He would return to this diagnosis, or at least a version of it, ten years later on the eve of war, when he used a series of BBC radio broadcasts to outline a pet theory about the relationship between poets and their audiences from the neolithic (or its living representatives in the Trobriand Islands) to T. S. Eliot. Had he gathered his energies together and written the book, there is little doubt that it would have made a stir, and have earned its place on enlightened bookshelves between, say, *Seven Types of Ambiguity* and Maud Bodkin's *Archetypal Patterns in Poetry*. But that phantom book exists only in hints and phrases here and there; and for the first time in his life, the sheer range of Jennings's interests seems finally to have been damaging him in the way people had long warned. He was working or playing at so many different things that he lacked the focus to excel at any one.

★

Loudest among the siren calls away from the library was his love of painting. Throughout this whole time, notwithstanding the conflicting claims of academic research, stage work, friendships and matrimony, he continued to paint as often as he could afford the time and materials, and sometimes when he could afford neither. According to Gerald Noxon, the young Jennings had set himself to learn from, and if need be reject, the lessons of Picasso, Klee, Mondrian, Masson, Max Ernst and Magritte.[12] Noxon's account of this stage of Jennings's development as a painter bears out the common view that he was now growing more and more inclined to regard painting as the central creative activity of his life:

> I happen to think that Humphrey was a painter of great quality, although his work remained practically unknown except to a very small circle of friends. He was never much interested in showing his paintings, which he thought would not be understood, and in this he was quite right . . .
> . . . essentially his painting was for himself – it was an essential part of his explorer-adventurer technique in the arts. The use of brushes, paint and canvas came so naturally to him that self-expression and self-revelation through painting were an integral part of his daily existence. If people did like his paintings he was frankly delighted; if they disliked them or ignored them he was not in the least surprised or concerned.[13]

Perhaps it was the lure of the city that was the acknowledged capital of modern art; or perhaps it was simply the need for a respite from the chills and gloom of Cambridge in a place they both knew and loved; in either case, Humphrey and Cicely decided to spend part of the 1930 Christmas holidays in Paris, staying with Julian Trevelyan at his lodgings in the Villa Brune, Mont Rouge, Montparnasse. However unhappy Cicely may have been in her uncompromisingly intellectual new milieu, at least Humphrey could look back on his first year as a research student and young husband with a moderate sense of satisfaction. Nineteen thirty-one, and the next few years, would not be nearly so happy.

*

By the spring of 1931, *Experiment* magazine, as short-lived as hundreds of other less remarkable student publications, was plainly on its last legs, financially if not editorially. For the final issue, number seven – which also included a section from Joyce's *Work in Progress*, a text by Malcolm Lowry, Bronowski on D. H. Lawrence and a poem by Empson as well as his review of Auden's 'Paid on Both Sides' – Jennings contributed two articles, both of them in collaboration: 'Rock-Painting and *La Jeune Peinture*', co-credited to Gerald Noxon, and 'A Reconsideration of Herrick', for which he shares authorship with James Reeves. Noxon's account of the means by which the first article was completed casts a revealing light on Jennings's conspicuous failure ever to complete a substantial prose work:

> Verbal and visual communication came naturally to Humphrey, communication via the written word did not. When he first introduced me to the study of pre-historic cave paintings and I became greatly excited about them, particularly about their significance in relation to the development of the moving image, I begged him to write an article on the subject for *Experiment*. He agreed, but kept putting it off. In the end I had to become the co-author of the article in order to force him to get his ideas down on paper, so the piece finally appeared over both our names. It was mostly my writing and his thinking.[14]

The second article, on Herrick, appears to have grown out of an excited conversation between Jennings and Bronowski, who had become persuaded that Herrick's poetry was 'more profound than its manner suggested'. Bronowski corroborates Noxon's views in observing that this is one of the few critical pieces on poetry that Jennings managed to complete, 'no doubt because he had a co-author;

he himself was always too inventive in his reading of poetry, too subtle and too nimble-minded, to get down on the page all that he wanted to say – and did say in conversation'.

Both articles ripple with intellectual vigour; yet there are signs that, sometime in the course of 1931, Jennings may have been losing both direction and heart. His academic work faltered, and he established a dispiriting pattern of short-term employment, often unhappy and ill-paid, alternating with fitful attempts to resume his scholarly career, or paint, or establish himself as a professional in the theatre. For the first time in his life since his tearful, frightened days as a new boarder at the Perse, he seems to have lost some of that innate self-confidence and zest that had borne him along since his early childhood. From time to time, he can now appear gloomy, at times almost frantic, and one senses that he only recovered his former aplomb to the full once he had found greater regularity of life and livelihood in the film industry, about three years later. It's not surprising that Jacob Bronowski dates to 1931 his one glimpse of Jennings (otherwise 'always full of optimism') in a state of depression.[15]

One of the year's few bright spots was the chance to play the part of Bottom in Arundell's production of Purcell's operatic treatment of *A Midsummer Night's Dream*, *The Fairy Queen*. James Mason played Oberon, and also stage-managed. It was to be Jennings's last collaboration with Arundell.

Already dreaming of a spell of painting in Paris, Jennings soldiered on with his thesis on Gray until May, when he finally became so short of money that he had no choice but to look for some form of job. Cicely, who had helped run the Experiment Gallery, had also been in search of employment, and eventually found it in the short-term form of modelling for a wholesale dressmaker's salon in London – a job she left when it became clear that the path of further advancement in the business ran directly through the proprietor's bed. Eventually, the old school tie proved useful to Humphrey: his history master from the Perse School, F. C. Happold, had now taken up the post of head-master at Bishop Wordsworth's School in Salisbury. Jennings applied to Happold for a temporary position, and was taken on for a single term, until the end of July; Cicely retreated. It was the earliest of many periods of separation for the couple – periods which eventually produced a substantial and eloquent volume of correspondence.

This letter, undated (about early April 1931), was addressed to
Cicely Jennings, 28a Brunswick Square, WC1, from Bishop Wordworth
School, Salisbury:

My most darling Pip,

Why is it that whenever I get a job of work it turns out to be
special or peculiar or to have something wrong with it? ... You
remember I said that just before leaving here last weekend, the
man whose place I am taking had turned up looking pretty fit –
well there is a glorious mixup going on here now over that. He
wants to come back – and at the pay – but I have an engagement
for two months from May 4th. We can't share because the
Governors won't allow this. He on the other hand is not allowed
to do a full time-table by his doctor. Happold would like to send
him away till June 4th, but the poor man Macfarlane (his name
is) is extremely nervous and may break down at being told
anything difficult. H[appold] is being very good to me, and I don't
suppose I shall lose much ... at present (contrary to regulations)
we are sharing work and I am getting some extra painting done
... Don't worry about this, whatever happens. H is looking after
me and I am trying to avoid fusses with everybody: etc. Had a
letter from Gerald [Noxon] who says he wants to go to Rome,
and that he is going to Paris this week-end.

I have been wondering whether I couldn't get a job with
Curtis Moffats [a decorating company] or some such firm ...
house decorating is about the only thing anyone does in the
summer in London ... I shall certainly be back in July now, and
must try and make up a little money for this dratted man's
recovery ...

A pussy has come in at the window. All my love to my
darling Pip-py.

Humphrey

Another letter, apparently posted the next day, confirms one or
two details. He was to 'stay till June 4th (end of two months' contract)
at full pay. Also I now have Monday morning quite free: I am very
lucky I think. I am now doing three days' work a week & painting
the rest – or playing cricket ...' Then, in an undated letter probably of
21 June:

I don't feel like Paris now though it wouldn't necessarily be hotter than London. I want to sit down somewhere & be quiet to paint for a little. I will pay the domestic bills as soon as I am paid here & the other can more or less wait. So very glad you are liking jobs however vulgar. I feel extremely tired of 'taste' – being a person of taste – so if you find a thoroughly ugly flat or bungalow I shall be delighted . . .

Undated (probably 22 June):

'. . . if all goes well I shall be back with you on Friday week – the 3rd I think. I should then have about £45 in the world. I don't honestly know exactly what to do. I shd like to be in Paris now, but don't think it would be much in three weeks' time and later. In any case I want to be with you for some time. Suppose provisionally I come and sleep with you – I mean at almost anywhere which would be cheap – for the rest of July: that wd give time to look round . . . Paris [illegible: 'is'?] obviously the place to live: it is so much easier but I can't live without fucking . . . Never mind what the place is like so long as it is cheap: I don't care now for anything except cunts and paintings: if you are out part of the day I shall be able to paint . . .

. . . Feel dreadfully tired of all polite men, conversation and so on . . .

A fragment of a damaged card, dated 24 June, reads: 'Yesterday came a notice from the . . . [Cambridge University?] appointments B[oard] of a lectureship in Eng[lish] in the S. of Sweden £400 a year 6 hrs a week. An incredibly easy job. But I shd. prefer to starve in Paris. Only say what you think. In any case I am *so* looking forward to seeing you my dear Pip . . .'

*

Against all reasonable expectation, his 'ideal job' soon materialized. In August 1931 Jennings went to Paris, to work on designs for Cresta Silks. He found modest but agreeable lodgings at 12 rue de la Grande Chaumière – 'a nice little room with quite a good light, looking out on to the backyard, and quiet'.[16] He may also have been pleased by the hotel's literary associations – it was said that Strindberg used to stay there, and one of the rooms was equipped with multiple doors, which prompted speculations about the playwright's activities.[17] But Jennings soon found himself lonely in Paris: apart from the odd visitor from England, his only friends in town were a Mrs Brown and her daughter Jill, who lived in the Latin Quarter and gave Humphrey the odd meal. The prevailing tone of the nine surviving letters he sent to Cicely at 49 St George's Square, London SW1 is plaintive, and full of frank, sometimes bawdy, expressions of sexual yearning for his absent wife, as well as confessions of doubts and misgivings about his path in life and – more cheerfully, or at any rate less self-engrossedly – observations on the art he was seeing.

17 August:

Yesterday I saw Mrs Brown & Jill who gave me lunch, but there was nothing to do yesterday evening & I was very homesick. Now I am better, having begun some designs for Cresta . . .

. . . There is utterly nothing on in Paris and I could be very sad if I let myself but I sit in my room painting & reading and tell myself I must exist like that for a time . . .

I am now going to the Degas exhibition at the 'orangerie' – I am now there – or here: writing in the 'orangerie' having walked round the exhibition one or two times. Evidently D is very different to our conception derived from the usual pastels. His sculpture is here again: superb again I think it. And the pictures are almost entirely of one class: oils (no pastels) and oils by Degas with his eye on Ingres ('c'est grave – très grave – faites beaucoup de lignes'). You know the two great Ingres in London: M de Norvins at the N[ational] G[allery] and the head of an officer tucked away at the Tate: nearly all the Degas here have something looking back to that side (portraiture) of Ingres: esp. Degas' self-portraits. Treatment of staring or dreaming *eyes* especially – then the same eyes are given to his sitters & to washerwomen and tramps. And in these pictures the paint has a parallel quality of thick contemplativeness: Ingres-like finish & luminosity; Degas' staring & dreaming *at* the picture. No cleverness, no shimmer of ballet dress – but thought: great thought. And in the colour too: black grey-blues Indian reds: saturated colours . . .

. . . The sculpture I still feel to be different & greater: because more direct: almost Indian in the rhythm of dancers, with no pastel to weaken the outline or colour to fidget . . .

More often, Humphrey is just plain miserable. On 19 August he writes:

My darling Pip,

On my twenty-fourth birthday I am sitting on my bed feeling horribly ill, having managed to catch a chill yesterday I suppose & waking up this morning feeling faint & sick. Rather better now. I wouldn't mention it only last night I went to bed with so much to tell you of one thought & another & now I can't remember anything. I am not really settled here yet. . . .

. . . I am finding life very difficult & rather sad I must admit but if I can stick it I shall be the better for it, only it is all going to be increasingly difficult anyway. I feel intensely the necessity for not talking or arguing (and that applies as much to here as it does to England) really, for using one's energy properly, but I have a headache and can't explain . . .

. . . Not thinking very much or worrying, simply rather negative about everything . . .

21 August:

My darling Pippy,

Again writing in the Luxembourg: this time at the top end by the fountain in full view of the observatory: a great wind today which is blowing spray in gusts away from the fountain. This wind is the last of a tremendous storm that burst over us two days ago as I got your letter in the evening.

It didn't depress me as I have been or had been feeling more or less numb also. But now I am feeling much better in every way not at all ill & much happier. Paris seems emptier than ever [August was, as now, the traditional shut-down in Paris] every day but I am glad really; I can feel quiet & try to discover myself without arguments & other people's discoveries (of themselves) to distract me: I feel that in November (or whenever) I shall like to come back to England but that I shall continue to want to be very quiet & continue winter landscapes & father Christmas from last year. You know how I like English winter – but that will all be difficult I know . . .

I promised you a longer letter last time but I can't make one & must promise again. The wind in the Gardens continues & I drink chocolate at the Dôme or the Deux Magots with my tweed coat on – quite like Christmas again.

My balls feel as quiet & rich as the paintings of Poussin in exile.

Humphrey.

23 August:

I sit & paint & read all day so there is nothing to tell you: it is a very slow business. I am managing to exist on thirty francs a day for everything including paints which isn't so bad, & at that rate ... [my] money will last me including coming home until the second half of November. Anything from the St Andrew's Street rent had better be put by for existence in England between then & Christmas. A very long time my darling Pip, but I feel it's necessary (apart from the money) to get us both started ...

The Cresta things are intensely difficult.

On the 26th he told Cicely: 'I feel that England is such a desert one could perhaps treat it as a place to be quiet in – another Majorca ...' Then, also probably in late August: 'I find it very difficult to be the poor student and think that Jermyn St is in my blood really: I have always got my nose against a sweetshop window of one kind or another ...' And in a letter of about the same time:

At the Galerie Vignon I saw ... some magnificent early work (1925–7) by Miró: thrilling colour; and then at Paul Guillaume's some more new Derain landscapes which are rather a return to Matisse 1905 and far more like painting, details I thought for a moment almost like the Mirós.

'The Listener' which I read at lunch rather depressed me – a breath of English arguing as usual: at the same time I am always wanting to be back in another England on your breasts and in the country.[18] I can't think my money is going to go as far as I had boasted to you, mainly because when I feel lonely I can't sit in my room & going out inevitably means spending, but I am not worrying; only wondering what to do (& how to exist) when I come back. Please think for me, or rather if you have a good idea please say. Painting has spread itself into all corners of 'the morning day' and the other hours I miss you so ...

... I am thinking very hard about Toulouse-Lautrec (of all

people) . . . There are two very large paintings (almost scribbles)
by Lautrec in the Luxembourg (which with Seurat's 'Le Cirque'
are the only paintings to see there now) – black, white & one or
two colours direct on to brown canvas: again very Miró . . .

2 September:

I want you so physically: everyone is so demonstrative here
(rightly so) and their kissings and arms over under – [André]
Masson 'les adieux', 'les amoureux' – are like stabs. I can feel
from your letters that you are growing more independent, harder
and fuller (useless words) and that too makes me want you: we
are both growing up terribly fast (does that sound like 'adolescent
introspection'?) So you see I am really feeling both increasingly
awake and unhappy to be so far from your thighs.

To Toulouse-Lautrec and Roux you may add Mantegna &
Rembrandt which sounds the queerest jumble for me to be
looking at and to mean nothing.

Do not let your people's gloomy view of the future disturb
you: I see no future and that leaves it open. I feel that I have
always assumed that things will inevitably get better and people
more understanding, but don't now. People & things will continue
[to] be stupid & wrong for ever & ever and Mantegna will never
be understood except by a few people. Or Roux. Or us. Your
people are looking in vain for the horizon of compromise. We
shall only be really happy by having struck out . . .

*

However glum he had been in Paris, the period of exile was at least
short-lived. In early September, he wrote to Cicely suddenly announcing that he planned to return within a matter of days, asking her to
arrange for him to stay at her parents' Oxfordshire home, Duns Tew,
'for about a fortnight in order to finish the Cresta things & others'.[19]
He seems to have stuck to this new plan, came back to England
around the middle of the month, and by October he had moved for a
while to a large and well-lit studio flat at 9a British Grove, Hammer-
smith, London W6 – 'very close to [the New Zealand-born artist and
abstract film-maker] Len Lye'. Jennings and Lye were very different
personalities – Jennings the hyper-articulate Cambridge aesthete, Lye

an intuitive creator who liked to hide his intelligence behind a taciturn, tough-guy façade – but the two men seemed to hit it off well, and spent a good deal of leisure time in each other's company.

> It is nicely furnished including plate linen etc: rather Hugh & Kathleen's type of things. Pictures by Ben Nicholson and Frances Hodgkin[s]. Piles of lovely books: Seizin Press[20] stuff. Very comfy feeling about everything . . .
> We can go in when we like: I have the key: the owner (or lessee) John Aldridge is coming back for a day or two but can stay at Len Lye's if necessary . . .
> . . . I saw James [Reeves] yesterday & we went to the latest Marx Bros film which I had to admit was terribly funny: surrealism for the millions. Also to an excellent short at the Tatler with LL and Jane, of Voodoo dances in W. Africa, and to the 'Old Batchelor' at the Lyric which (you were quite right) was ghastly – I came out after two acts. I am painting most of the time: Mother never really liking the things – and getting on with my own as difficultly as ever. James has bought a picture of mine and LL will give me something in exchange. Quite happy. Want my Pippy . . .'

But this period of London residence was short-lived. Very soon he was back in Cambridge, once more picking up the threads of his neglected research, once more applying himself to painting. Little in the way of documentation has survived from this period, save for some letters to Cicely which oscillate between sincere gloom and willed cheerfulness and otherwise speak mainly of small domestic matters.

3 March 1932 – from Chesterton Lane, Cambridge (which seems to have been the home of Hugh Sykes Davis and Kathleen Raine during their brief marriage):

> My darling Pippy,
> . . . I work here pretty hard. And a little painting but feel very unsatisfied. I want you so already. Long talks and chess with Kathleen. Much Freud whom one must read cover to c before having a baby (which I think of so). Freud not at all frightening as I should have found him two or three years ago.
> A superb sunny day here: after which I am typing this at Bruno's [Bronowski's]. Waiting for him. Busy and comfy but

restless. Nothing else. Love to my dog – your dog. Tell me your thoughts . . .

Undated, from the same address, at about the same time; Humphrey is obviously engaged in house-hunting: '. . . so far . . . I can't find anything on the nice side of Cambridge. And in any case it seems very rare for a cottage to be let. Or to have a bath. I wish we could build. I am working hard at this stuff,[21] and am thinking of going to the Bodlean [*sic*]: perhaps that could be managed from Duns Tew . . .' Discouragement once again seeping in, he wrote to Julian Trevelyan in France asking for help with his latest escape bid:

My Dear Julian,
    I write to enquire whether you know anything about cheap villas, chambres meublées or such like in Provence (St Trpoez – damn – or near it) for the summer. Terribly cheap essential. Do you know anyone who owns one or anything like that. How long are you going to be in Paris? I sit about and paint and try not to lose my temper with this country and its ludicrous inhabitants. How are you? I hear Hugh got very drunk in Paris. You don't know of a nice job anywhere on the continent? This lack of money is very tiring.
    Very thrilled with Braque's new work and a new drawing by Roux reproduced in Cahiers [d'Art].[22] How is Paris? Do let me know – soon – about anything for the summer: it ought to be by the sea.
        Ever
            Humphrey.

With or without Trevelyan's help, the plans for a long stay in the South of France went ahead. In May that year Jennings returned to Paris, and then travelled on to Provence. Cicely joined him there, and the couple spent several months in the region, staying at La Tourelle, a converted windmill tower just outside St-Tropez, with Gerald Noxon and his new wife Betty. 'We lived there,' Noxon recalled, 'in joint ménage and monetary poverty for several months before returning to England to face the difficult realities of the depression, which had finally fallen with full impact on a disordered Europe.'[23] For the Jenningses, the stay was made possible by a small inheritance, probably from Humphrey's Aunt Rose. Though not substantial, it liberated them for the first and last time in their married life of the need to fret about money and gainful employment. Noxon remembered it not merely as an idyll, but as a highly productive time for Jennings:

> during that time Humphrey was one hundred per cent painter and artist. I think that he knew that he was enjoying a period of freedom from worldly responsibilities which would not last very long and he was determined to use every instant of it in a concentrated attack on the artistic and creative problems with which he was so seriously concerned.[24]

On their return to England, Noxon went to join their old friends and Cambridge contemporaries Stuart Legg and Basil Wright, who were both now working at John Grierson's Empire Marketing Board film unit – the prototype for the far more famous GPO and Crown Film Units, for which Jennings would make most of his films. Jennings, who wanted to stay out of regular work as long as there were a few shreds of the legacy left, went back to Cambridge with Cicely. They moved into 7 Round Church Street and Jennings continued to paint for as long as the inheritance cash held out.

*

At the beginning of 1933 the couple learned that their wobbly financial position was soon to be even more precarious: Cicely was pregnant with their first child. Fortunately, Humphrey soon found a way of supplementing the family income that was, at least in principle, more congenial than many others.

In 1926, an energetic and multi-talented amateur director called Terence Gray – independently wealthy, an Egyptologist by training, and a fan of German Expressionist drama and the stage designs of Edward Gordon Craig – had bought Cambridge's old Theatre Royal building (established 1816) out on the Newmarket Road and converted it into the Festival Theatre, tearing out the Georgian proscenium and installing a revolving stage with Britain's first ever cyclorama behind it. Gray's friend Harold Ridge, later to install the lighting at the Shakespeare Memorial Theatre in Stratford, provided the new space with one of the most elaborate and technically advanced lighting rigs in the world. (Since Gray was also something of a sybarite, he boarded over all the Victorian temperance mottoes and put in an excellent bar, lavishly stocked with burgundy, caviare and champagnes. He also established a Festival Grill, so that the theatre also became the best restaurant in town. Reviewers who were lukewarm about the productions seldom failed to wax eloquent over the catering.) Within a matter of months, the Festival Theatre had become an exceptionally distinguished institution with a far-reaching reputation as a home for experimental and avant-garde productions – it was, in fact, the most 'advanced' theatre in Britain.

Kathleen Raine has written in rapturous terms of the effect 'that magical place' had on her as an undergraduate already repelled by the tight-lipped scientism of the Cambridge poets and critics and yearning for something more numinous. Invoking the physical particularities of the place – its romantically dim foyer, green-lit auditorium, revolving stage and elaborate lighting plot – she suggests that Gray managed to import to the unpromising climate of Cambridge something of the same spirit that was animating Yeats at the Abbey Theatre in Dublin, Lorca in his travelling troupe of players in Spain, and the Čapek brothers in their experimental work for the theatres of Prague.

She evokes, particularly, the overwhelming power of Terence Gray's debut production of Aeschylus' *Oresteia*,[25] remarking how every detail of its presentation, from the striking of the gong before perform-ance down to the Edmond Dulac-style illustration on the programme cover, helped induce a sense of heightened awareness. Week after week, she and her contemporaries were caught up in the likes of *Desire under the Elms*, or *The Hairy Ape*, or *At the Hawk's Well*, or *The House of Bernarda Alba*, or *Rosmersholm*; and the performers who helped create these works included Ninette de Valois (Gray's cousin, and designer of the dance-drama for the *Oresteia*'s chorus, before going on to found the Sadler's Wells Ballet), Flora Robson, Robert Donat, Rupert Doone and Joseph Gordon Macleod.[26] Other famous names who launched their careers at Gray's establishment include Tyrone Guthrie and Jessica Tandy.

Gray had designed each short season to incorporate a historical drama, a modern play, a 'static' work (meaning, presumably, some-thing along the lines of Yeats's dramas) and a classical play; he claimed that he wanted to 'wage war on the old game of illusion and glamour and all the rest of the nineteenth-century hocus pocus and bamboozle'. To this end, he bridged the gap between audience and performers by installing a flight of steps at the front of stage, and all but did away with props. He took all sorts of liberties: costumes were designed on a character-by-character basis rather than in a single period or style; in *Twelfth Night*, Andrew Aguecheek and Toby Belch whizzed about the stage on roller skates; *Romeo and Juliet* was done in flamenco style; *Richard III* was set in a series of interlocking, revolving cubes, and spotlights threw huge, menacing shadows for the ghostly scenes.

Early in 1933, Gray began to employ Jennings more or less regularly as a scenery painter and all-purpose set-hand. Though this piecemeal employment by the theatre was not an ideal solution to their financial problems, it at least seems to have lifted Jennings's spirits a little, and some of his former panache is once again audible in a letter he wrote to Julian Trevelyan in Paris, dated 15 March:

> I want you if you will be so good to get me some photos. from the Galerie Simon (29bis rue d'Astorg) of any new work by Roux. Or rather not any, but about three mediumly large photos (they are 12f[rancs] or were) of figures (I presume he is still painting figures) not one of his vast compositions as a photto [sic] shows you nothing – and not still lives or 'compositions'. Work of 1932 or this year. The last one I have is the 'Femme accoudée' 1931. Please pack them flat. And I will pay you when I get them, which will be soon I hope. If you are coming back to E[ngland]. any time do let me know as I badly want some chassis [frames] and some paint – there is absolutely no English equivalent for Jaune Citron and I am lost without it. Perhaps also a photo of anything new by Miró: is he still doing criss-cross stuff? How is 'the world of the picture dealers'? And if I ever collected enough bearable pictures do you know anyone who would take them? . . .
>
> . . . I am sorry I can't sent [sic] you a photo of anything of mine: they are rather more like something now. In such time as I get to paint. I have been painting scenery – not designing simply painting – at the Festival, which is however closing at the end of next term. Not enough to live on but something. The University is ahem going Marxist . . . and England is busy persuading itself for the seven millionth time that it is beginning to face reality. We are rather snugly situated here, and managing to let existing slide off our duck's back. But off [sic] course there is always the rent to pay. Give Jolas[27] seventy kicks in the arse for his last

Transition. John Cullen[28] was here for a day or two: very 'young German'. The Auden's and Day Lewis' and so on are a positive menace. Bill [Empson] is well out of it in Japan.[29] And after Roux?[30] Anybody?

Another, undated, letter to Trevelyan from roughly the same period suggests that he had rejected the possibility of following Empson's example by working – presumably as a school or university teacher – overseas:

So Roux has been in Africa: what it is to use one's colonies. I have been two years turning down posts in Bombay and New Zealand.

You sound rather unhopeful. The position I gather is that in Paris people have some understanding of pictures but won't buy and in England other way around.

I can't see myself getting to Paris for a bit yet being hopelessly overdrawn . . .[31]

Such economic respite as the Festival Theatre had offered Jennings was, sadly, short-lived. Gray's pockets, though deep, were not bottom-less, and he had largely carried the company's financial losses from his own funds. Almost as soon as Jennings joined, there were rumours of imminent closure; and though these turned out to be exaggerated, his professional relationship with the theatre was becoming stormy. A cool if diplomatically phrased letter from Terence Gray, dated 24 April 1933, suggests that the director felt Jennings had been exceeding his modest brief as a scenic artist:

Dear Jennings,

Surely your experience of the theatre has shown you that, without unity of conception, a play can only succeed by accident. Giving artists an opportunity does not mean offering them the stage as a canvas independently of the play and its method of performance. A scenic artist needs a capacity for cooperation. In this instance the fault lies somewhat with me for not dealing with the matter at an earlier stage, but, unfortunately, you do not submit designs from which it is possible to visualise the finished article. You have a very individual style and one which is not readily adaptable to theatrical purposes. I have only recently begun to see how best it can be utilised in a production and have been seeking an opportunity of giving it free play.

Not long after issuing this rebuke, Gray resigned, handing over the management of the theatre to a new team who just about kept it afloat until 1939. Claiming to have no regrets – he had done everything he wanted to do – Gray took off for France to grow vines. Later in life he bred horses in Ireland, and then retired to Monte Carlo.

So once again, it was time for Jennings to go on the hunt for a new employer. In June that year he asked both I. A. Richards and Aubrey Attwater for testimonials, presumably in the hopes of finding a job teaching at a secondary school. Both of them complied in the warmest terms. Richards wrote, in a letter dated 16 June:

I have, in the last two or three years, seen a lot of Mr Jennings' work. It shows a *very* remarkable combination of elaborate erudition with speculative daring. He has recently been applying to the poems of Gray a method of conjectural interpretation which is largely his own invention. He has read very widely and carefully, submits what he reads to an intensive play of surmise and theory, and constructs as a result hypotheses whose range and novelty make any immediate decision of their value unwise. But his powers of assimilation, of perceiving possible and hitherto unnoticed connections, and of synthesising his perceptions into systems, are most impressive. His work is already highly interesting; it may become of real importance in illuminating the tradition of English literature.

As an expositor he is extraordinarily patient, clear and energetic. As a teacher, I believe that he would be most stimulating and impose a very high standard of industry, accuracy and critical reflection in his pupils.

Aubrey Attwater's shorter reference, dated 27 June, concluded:

I formed a very high opinion of his scholarship and his originality. He is widely read and has excellent powers of analysis and exposition. He brings to the study of literature a knowledge of art and artistic gifts which often enable him to handle topics from a fresh and stimulating point of view. He is one of the ablest pupils I have had during the last twelve years.

Despite such glowing references – or possibly because they made Jennings sound so terrifyingly overqualified for any but the most exalted academic positions – no offers were forthcoming.

★

On 3 September 1933, Marie-Louise Jennings was born in the Brunswick Nursing Home near Midsummer Common in Cambridge. On the birth certificate, Humphrey gave his occupation as 'artist painter'.[32] His daughter's given name was a muffled echo of his beloved aunt's, Marie-Rose – for some reason he took it into his head that this was hard to pronounce, and that Marie-Louise tripped much more fluently off the tongue. (Marie-Louise itself soon underwent a mutation into Mary-Lou, the version by which Humphrey and Cicely's older daughter – now the historian Dr M.-L. Legg, a specialist in the nineteenth-century Irish press and related matters – is still known by family and friends.) Mary-Lou recalls that, as the years went by, she became increasingly glad that her name was not nearly so outlandish as those of her contemporaries, who would be forced to go through life signing themselves 'Yancey', 'Bix' (after Bix Beiderbecke) or 'Mogador' (after a Parisian telephone exchange).

Marie-Louise Jennings's infancy and early childhood were highly unconventional by the standards of the day. Instead of the traditional whites and pinks, she was swathed in yellow; a couple of decades later, a young mother herself, she followed suit by also choosing unusual garments for her children. Since Cicely Jennings was a staunch believer in the teachings of the New Zealand paediatrician Truby King, Marie-Louise was also subjected to a regime of rest and feeding which later generations would tend to regard as harsh or even inhuman. Feeds were administered every four hours on the hour; infants were not to be touched or comforted between feeds, no matter how much they cried; in general, babies were treated like tiny mechanisms, with unhappy results for both parents and offspring. As Mary-Lou Legg has written, 'generations of men and women now over 65 suffer from anxiety about food and their digestive processes as a result of this treatment; they are impatient, and can be aggressive if they have to wait for meals and, indeed, for anything else'.[33] The strictness of the regime also made Cicely – expert cook though she was – anxious and vulnerable about everything concerned with the preparation and consumption of food.

The arrival of Marie-Louise displaced the quadruped member of the family, Cicely's lapdog. When Mrs Cooper came to Cambridge to see her new grandchild, she asked, 'Now, Humphrey, what can I do for you?' 'Take that wretched dog away!' he replied; so poor Ting-a-Ling was exiled to Oxfordshire, and Marie-Louise took his place. Even dogless, though, the young family's accommodation was still too cramped, and a few months after the birth they moved to a basement flat at 28 Bateman Street, off Hills Road near the railway station – now a fairly expensive middle-class district, but at the time shabby and generally impoverished.

Shortly after the move, Cicely Jennings once again left her husband for a while, largely because she could no longer stand the misery of her Cambridge life. Mary-Lou recalls: 'They were living in a basement flat, in a freezing cold Cambridge winter with no proper heating, no help, no money, a very small baby and my father probably being pretty intolerant, and probably going out spending the evening with friends and not thinking about the fact that she was stuck at home. So she went back to her mother.'

Several undated letters to Cicely, addressed from 28 Bateman Street, offer glimpses into this period of separation. One of them expresses Humphrey's violent opposition to having Marie-Louise christened:

> I am afraid I feel *totally* against the christening not because of 'family' feelings: but because of 'the church'. I don't want to argue, but it quite hurts me (really) to think of it. I understand perfectly your position & suggest that I should write carefully to your mother & explain. I feel happy enough about 'godparents' in themselves: but utterly anti-clerical: I am sorry – but it is I am afraid very bound up with painting & existence; even though I would like to disconnect it. Please understand: & do not – my pussy – think me merely a nuisance. I would like to write and relieve you of having to hedge.
>
> I do so long to see you: I hardly feel Marie-Louise exists for me yet . . .
>
> . . . I got some money for a picture yesterday – so don't be down-cast: and *don't* let's *discuss* it: it tires one so.
>
> Ever your loving husband & papa, Humphrey

Another such letter reports: 'I have been looking at [Herbert] Read's book 'Art Now' which is pretty awful & *so* inaccurate. He is now editor of the Burlington [*Magazine*] . . . I feel exactly as you do about the country & doubts all the time about England: but I feel all the time I am getting on.' And from an undated letter:

> The theatre is not particularly hectic at present but is rapidly becoming far more incompetent than under Gray: the other designer says he is going at the end of the term and certainly they won't get me to design anything for them: I have been watching the way they treat things. However the ordinary painting continues without too much trouble – touch wood.
>
> The wireless next door plays usually about supper time for an hour or more – quite bearable – and sometimes at lunch. It is sometimes a bit loud (but very expensive and well bred) but I have refrained from saying anything as I have no doubt that Marie-Louise and this typewriter will easily equal it from their point of view . . .
>
> All my love to you both. I am sitting by a nice coal fire with a vase of chrysanthemums – so you see it is not too uncivilised. Many many kisses.
>
> > Your loving
> > > Humphrey

And another:

> I go on as well as I can: very hard work everywhere: and I am afraid I am beginning to feel lonely at Bateman Street.
>
> I feed myself well & keep warm & get work done . . .
>
> I am shifting scenery every night for the Revue: which is hard work: get back at 11.30. Money is not so bad. Tell me a thing or two: or I shall feel you aren't ever coming back . . .
>
> I am afraid this long separation from you & privation from Marie-Louise is beginning to hurt me seriously – when can you come back? Do not answer 'Whenever the house is ready': please come next week: if you love me.
>
> I cannot go on alone.
>
> > Humphrey.

Among all the other details is a single reference which seems like a premonition: 'Stuart is working at his [illegible: 'Calson'?] film: fiercely Communist: I met his incredible Griersons & Paul Rothas etc.'

★

One of the options Jennings seriously considered at this time was finding a job in a major museum or art gallery.[34] Early in 1934 he sought advice and contacts from Richards, who turned to T. S. Eliot, who in his turn consulted Herbert Read. Instead of contacting Jennings, Read was inspired to write a mildly satirical article entitled 'How to Get a Museum Job', which he sent to Eliot with a note warning that – however far-fetched the joke might seem – the picture it painted of an art world dominated by snobbery, foppery and nepotism was all too scandalously accurate, and should not be allowed to fall into the wrong hands. Eliot forwarded the article to Richards on 19 February, warning him to give Jennings just the barest outlines of what Read had written and then to destroy the article at once. (Richards did not heed the advice, and the article can be found in the I. A. Richards archive at Magdalene College.) More kindly, he also offered to set Jennings up with an introduction to the art critic Bernard Berenson.

Eliot's circumspection here seems a little excessive. Though cheeky, Read's piece is hardly inflammatory: it simply urges the would-be curator to dress in appropriately attractive style – light flannel suits and bright ties are the ticket, Harris tweeds and beards are *verboten* – to cultivate an uncial style of handwriting, to indicate casually his familiarity with Ravenna, Santiago, Moscow, Cairo and Chicago, and to have at the ready a highly burnished new anecdote about Berenson. Whether it was the tenor of Read's spoof, or the sensible recognition that he lacked the finances to cultivate the right persona, Jennings did not chase this possibility any further. He did, however, maintain his contact with Eliot, who had escaped his purgatory as a bank clerk for Lloyd's and was now enjoying his twin professions as a commissioning editor for Fabers and editor of a highly regarded literary magazine, *The Criterion*. Probably at the suggestion of Richards, Jennings sent a large fragment of his Gray thesis to Eliot in the hopes that Faber might consider publishing it.

'A Passage in *The Progress of Poetry*', as he titled the piece, is a sort of Empsonian close reading of the second stanza of Gray's poem (lines 13–24) – to modern tastes, and indeed to the tastes of many intelligent eighteenth-century readers, rather a flat exercise in rendering some of the narrative sense of Pindar's first Pythian ode into the standard epithets of the late Augustans:

> Oh! Sovereign of the willing soul,
> Parent of sweet and solemn-breathing airs . . .

Jennings proceeds to dismantle these few lines minutely, and to demonstrate that every phrase, indeed almost every word of the poem has its origins in some earlier poem of the seventeenth or eighteenth century – particularly (so one strand of the argument runs) in poems on the subject of music: Milton's 'Vacation Exercise', 'Comus' and 'L'Allegro', Cowley's 'Davideis', Pope's 'Ode on St Cecilia's Day', Collins's 'The Passions', Jortin's[35] 'A Hymn to Harmony' and a direct translation of Pindar's original ode by West (1746); but also, and more generally, in Pope's *Iliad*, Akenside, Dryden, Lyttelton, Warton, Eusden, Green, Philips and (the then little-read) Aphra Behn. If nothing else, the thesis fragment proves how deeply and widely Jennings had been reading in the major and minor English poets of two centuries.

So far, a decent piece of detective work and an impressive display of scholarship, which establishes pretty clearly that Gray's poem is full of borrowings. But it is not Jennings's game to charge Gray with simple lack of originality, or of pilfering: his project is not demolition, but reconstruction. To be exact, Jennings explains that what he is doing is 'proposing a theory according to which Gray might have written, parallel to the theory according to which Wordsworth claimed to write. And I suggest that the language of Gray's poetry in general and of this passage in particular, is a selection of the invented language of poets . . .' Or, as his epigraph from Lautréamont puts it more pithily, '*Le plagiat est nécessaire*' (Plagiarism is necessary).[36]

To simplify slightly, Jennings's case is that Gray's poem should not be read as a sample of post-Popean diction about to go threadbare with over-use, but as a highly self-conscious echo-chamber of other poems, and that Gray is deploying this barrage of allusions, echos and direct liftings in the service of a thesis about Poetry and Conquest. For example, Jennings suggests, with one of those stabs of keen historical perception that so often glint in Empson's prose, that the apparently bland lines beginning 'On Thracia's Hills the Lord of War' – roasted by Dr Johnson as 'unworthy of further notice. Criticism disdains to chase a schoolboy to his commonplaces'[37] – are nothing of the kind. Here, he says, is a specific evocation, not of the mythical Mars, but of the real-life Alexander the Great, who, as both Pliny in his *Natural*

History and Milton in a sonnet[38] remembered, had burnt the city of Thebes but mercifully spared the house of a grateful Pindar. In other words, Jennings contends that what Gray was engaged in here was a species of what later generations of literary critics have called 'inter-textuality': and that the requirements of his theme obliged Gray to write in accordance with a particular theory of language. Jennings's conclusion is appropriately triumphant: one can sense the pride in his own completed act of intellectual Conquest:

> In Pindar's own odes poetry celebrates persons and events. But in this ode poetry celebrates Poetry or Poesie ... in Pindar, poetry is still the servant of Conquest, but in Gray it conquers Conquest and becomes a substitute for it. It will therefore not be enough for Gray's poetry to describe other poetry – the function of poetry as description has been conquered also – it must celebrate Poetry without making descriptions even of poetry. This can only be satisfied if the poem be made of quotations, for quotations do not describe, but are already descriptions, and therefore the poem does not describe. It presents. It presents Poetry.

*

Behind the scenes, as Jennings fiddled with his manuscript and spattered it with amendments, deletions and insertions, Richards was doing his very best to pull strings for his protégé. On 17 April 1934, he wrote a candid letter of encouragement to his friend at Faber & Faber:

Dear Eliot,

I seem to think very much as you do about Jennings. I agree he isn't in Empson's class or near it – but then I can't quite think of any young person who is. Candidly and confidentially, I should expect 90% of Jennings' stuff to turn out to be mare's nest preliminaries, but again – whose *isn't?* Looking around in the kind of way somewhat similar work is done by others, new and old, famous and unknown, I don't feel at all sure I can't honestly say that publishing him would not be a genuine and recognisable duty to the world. If I were asked, say by the Cambridge University Press, what I thought and I neither knew nor cared what they thought of me, I would urge publication strongly. On the ground that something of a distinct and unusual and coherent and energetic kind was being done in a field where most of the work is mere hum and ha-ing.

You will see from this how much I would like to press you to bring something of his out if you can; and that I only hesitate because it is wild stuff and silly stuff in parts and public opinion (academic) in these days shows a sort of senile nervousness in these matters, as though a few too audacious ascriptions were somehow a kind of danger to civilisation. My own feeling is that we *need* a lot more rashness if only it is learned and devoted and extreme enough. I have too a half hope, that if Jennings doesn't throw any direct light on Gray, discussion of what he says might help in bringing up the whole question of varying attitudes of poets both to words and the work of writing poetry.

So to conclude this, I do hope you may be able to do something with it. (Could you serialise some of it in the *Criterion*?)[39]

Evidently, Eliot thought he could. He wrote to Jennings from his editor's desk at *The Criterion* on 20 April, saying that he had been thinking a great deal about the piece, which he found 'extremely interesting',[40] and considered that the whole thesis deserved to be published – though he had his doubts about whether such a serious and specialist work could be expected to pay its way in the market-place. Eliot proposed, therefore, that the most sensible thing to do would be to publish an extract in *The Criterion* so as to see what sort of interest it might provoke. He went on to explain that, at about ten thousand words, 'Progress of Poetry' was far too long, but that if Jennings could bring it down to six thousand, he would be 'delighted' to print it.

Surprisingly, and for reasons which are not clear, Jennings did not reply. Six months later, on 2 October, Eliot's secretary wrote to him again chasing the matter up, explaining that she had tried to reach him at Cambridge but that the dead-letter office had returned it; it was only now, after his Cambridge friend Charles Madge had supplied his new address at '6, Brandram Road, Lee, SE', that she had been able to track him down. Eliot, with or without the urging of Richards, was obviously still keen to have the piece for *The Criterion*.

It never appeared. Perhaps Jennings had renounced all his ambitions as a literary critic, at least for the time being; perhaps he

was simply too busy. By the middle of 1934, a few months before his
twenty-seventh birthday, he had begun his first proper job. It was the
start of his life as family breadwinner. It was also, though no one could
have foreseen it at the time, the start of his career in the medium in
which he would achieve his most enduring works. Humphrey Jennings,
lapsed scholar, unrecognized painter, indigent man of the theatre, had
become a documentary film-maker.

Four

1934 to 1936: First Films and Surrealism

At the time Jennings joined the GPO Film Unit in 1934, just a few months after its official birth the previous September, documentary film-making in Britain was a relatively novel phenomenon; a craft or art which, if not quite in its infancy, was certainly little more than a youngster, albeit a noisy and attention-seeking one already showing precocious promise. Nor was there any doubt about the paternity. The universally acknowledged father of British documentary, then as now, was a harsh, fiercely charismatic figure some ten years Jennings's senior: the uncompromisingly serious Scottish film-maker, theorist, polemicist and teacher, John Grierson.

Jennings's relationship with Grierson was never to be close and seldom happy. Though both men, from time to time, have been accorded the epithet of 'genius', neither of them seems to have had very much regard for the other. Interviewed almost a quarter of a century after Jennings's death, and just a year or two before his own, Grierson set about damning his wayward protégé with faint praise before damning him outright:

> Jennings was a minor poet. I don't think he was a great poet . . .
> He was certainly, certainly a very considerable talent – stilted, I
> think, a little literary. He was fearfully sorry for the working class,
> which is a kind of limited position to be in, you know. Yes, he
> was safely, safely sorry for the working class, which did credit not
> just to his liberal spirit but to his lack of relationship with the
> living thing, sometimes. I think the word is that he didn't have a
> sense of smell. There's no doubt that he had good taste, visual
> good taste.[1]

'Good taste' was not a quality for which Grierson had an unalloyed regard – it was the dubious virtue of the aesthete – and his belief that Jennings's basic social attitude was one of comfortable sorrow for the lower orders was one he had not failed to make well known in documentary circles. 'Let's go down and see Humphrey being nice to the common people,' he sneered to the film-maker Denis Forman on one notorious occasion.[2]

For his part, Jennings could speak of Grierson as a coarse-minded dogmatist, a bully and a fraud; the differences of temperament and philosophy between boss and employee could hardly have been more pronounced, and though some reference books have tended to over-simplify matters by referring to Jennings as a leading film-maker of 'the Grierson school', the fact is that his mature films (all of them made a fair time after Grierson had left the Unit in 1937) have virtually nothing in common with Griersonian orthodoxy – indeed, can be seen as works of outright heresy. And yet some linking of the two men's names is not simply inevitable, but just. For all their mutual suspicion and antagonism, it is unlikely that Jennings would ever have become the film-maker he did but for the happy chance of being recruited to the unit Grierson had created – it might even be said, to the cinematic form he had created. However out of place he may have seemed there at times, Jennings learned its techniques, breathed its atmosphere, took on at least something of its sense of social mission.

In short, to appreciate Jennings's accomplishments fully and in true perspective, one must know a certain amount about the harsh mentor he rapidly outgrew.

*

John Grierson was born in Deanston, a small village on the River Teith near Stirling, on 26 April 1898. His father, Robert, came from a seafaring family, but had broken with tradition to become a 'dominie', or schoolteacher; his mother, Jane, also a teacher, was from a radical Ayrshire family. An outstandingly good student – one examiner spoke of the 'effortless superiority' of his papers – Grierson easily won a scholarship to the University of Glasgow, though he deferred his entrance to work as a telegraphist on Royal Navy minesweepers until his demobilization in February 1919. When he finally took up his bursary at Glasgow, he found himself, enraged and rebellious, like many other ex-servicemen suddenly thrown back to the condition of pupil after four years confronting the dangers and horror of war.[3] Unlike most of his contemporaries, he managed to channel his rage productively, becoming a fiery orator and founder of the university Labour Club. His student years coincided with that intense period of postwar activism by Clydeside socialist movements collectively known as 'Red Clyde'. As Grierson later told an interviewer, 'I grew up in the Clydeside movement. I've been in politics all my life. Nobody who ever grew up in the Clydeside movement forgets.'[4]

After a hectic and distinguished student career, which ended in a flurry of honours, Grierson took his Master of Arts degree in 1923, lectured in philosophy for a while, and then went off to the United States for a momentous two-and-a-half-year course of intensive research into the sociology and technology of mass communications media, funded by the Rockefeller Foundation and based mainly in Chicago and New York. It was in the States that he first latched on to the potential of the cinema, began to work as a journalist, and sought out the author of an influential recent work of sociology, *Public Opinion* (1922), the newspaper editor Walter Lippmann. Under Lippmann's influence he began to examine the workings of Hollywood, made a minute, frame-by-frame study of Eisenstein's *Battleship Potemkin* and became friends with Robert Flaherty, already famous for his *Nanook of the North* (1922). It was in a review of Flaherty's latest film, *Moana*, that Grierson introduced the noun 'documentary' to the English language.[5] By the time he returned to the UK in 1926, he was a man with a clearly defined mission: to create a British documentary movement.

The ground had already been unwittingly prepared for him by others. In response to the deepening depression, the British Government had set up the Empire Marketing Board to help stimulate trade between Britain and her colonies. Its success in this area remains, to say the least, debatable, but in cultural terms the EMB left an invaluable legacy, thanks in no small part to its quiet but deeply gifted secretary Stephen (after 1932, Sir Stephen) Tallents (1884–1958). Under Tallents's enlightened stewardship, the EMB became a major patron of the arts in Britain, employing a host of the best artists, architects, writers and film-makers. In some respects, Tallents was following the bold precedent established by Frank Pick at the London Passenger Transport Board.[6] In other respects, he was a pioneer. What Tallents created was, in effect, an entirely new philosophy of advertising and public relations. One of his most far-reaching innovations – which seems unremarkable enough now, but was derided or treated as idiocy at the time – was the policy of 'background publicity': briefly, that an industry or public body might sponsor all kinds of artistic work that would not strive to promote specific goods or services, but simply foster some general awareness of those things. (Flaherty was among those who had already acted on this principle: *Nanook* had been funded, not by a studio, but by the New York furriers Revillion Frères.)

Even before Grierson strode into Tallents's office, the EMB was already weighing up the possibility of film production, partly at the behest of Rudyard Kipling, no less, who had managed to bully or cajole the Board into giving him the job of producing a soundly imperial feature film, to be written by Kipling himself and directed by one Major Walter Creighton, a man who, whatever his military skills, was almost wholly innocent of the techniques of film-making. Recognizing that it might be prudent for the Major to have at least a few rudiments of the art under his belt, in 1927 the Board sent him off on a leisurely tour of European and American studios. It was Grierson who stepped in to fill the vacuum Creighton left behind him. He began by writing internal reports detailing in persuasive terms the possibilities for competing with American films, and suggesting the dramatic marvels that might be achieved through the artistic rendering of everyday actuality. He supplemented these reports with a series of instructional screenings, so that the Board could see what had been done elsewhere in the world, and particularly by the Soviet directors Grierson admired so passionately. Though, strictly speaking, the import of such communistic works was meant to be illegal, he showed and enthused loudly about the likes of Pudovkin's *Storm Over Asia*, Dovzhenko's *Earth* and Victor Turin's study of the construction of a railway in Soviet Asia, *Turksib*.

As he might have predicted, many members of the Board either slumbered noisily through these revolutionary splendours or sloped off home for supper. But Grierson was gaining influence and respect at a great rate, and in no time had entranced Tallents completely. Soon, the chance came for Grierson the theorist to make his practical demonstration of the power of non-fiction film-making. The shrewd Tallents began to drop broad hints to him about the possibility of a film on the Scottish herring fleets – a subject shamelessly contrived to catch the interest of the Financial Secretary of the Treasury, Arthur

Michael Samuel (later Lord Mancroft), a herring fanatic who had written a definitive study of the place of that nutritious fish in British history.

By July 1928, Grierson was out at sea, often fighting terrible storms and taking over the camera work himself, since his cinematographer Basil Emmott was a chronic sufferer from seasickness. (Grierson, the old minesweeper hand, was made of harder stuff.) The hazardous shoot took the better part of five months; fortunately, no one was seriously hurt. By the time Grierson called a wrap, he had exposed twenty thousand feet of film. (Major Creighton, meanwhile, had not yet so much as called for 'Action!' on the Kipling epic.) But his work had barely begun: having absorbed the lessons of Eisenstein and the other Russian masters, Grierson would now have to prove himself their equal in the art of montage. He started to cut the film in his basement flat in Belsize Park in London, then rented a basement at 12 Charing Cross Road as his editing room. He also hired a young assistant, Miss Margaret Taylor; their relationship was already more than professional, and Margaret would secretly (or so John liked to fool himself) become Mrs Grierson in 1930.

By the summer of 1929 the herring film, now called *Drifters*, was ready to show to the EMB Film Committee. It was a depressing experience. The Board members were shocked and perplexed by exactly the sequences Grierson regarded as his best – those which owed most to the lessons of Eisenstein. He argued his corner fiercely, but the Committee insisted that the offending material be cut. So Grierson took the print home, trimmed away his Eisensteinian sequences, hung them up carefully on pegs, then showed the castrated version to the Board members, who approved it for distribution. He went home again, no less carefully put back all the material he had taken out, and sent it off to the labs, where the first print was struck. The film that launched a thousand subsequent documentaries and changed the face of cinema for ever had been brought in at a total cost of £2,948.

Drifters had been made, but now it had to be seen to have been made, and as prominently as possible. Grierson soon got his chance, and handled it with characteristic slyness. Four years earlier, a small group of writers and intellectuals, including John Maynard Keynes, H. G. Wells and George Bernard Shaw, had founded Britain's first Film

Society, which had rapidly established itself as a favourite gathering-point for the progressive wing of the British intelligentsia. Grierson got wind of the fact that the Society was about to mount the UK premiere of the previously banned *Battleship Potemkin*; he therefore arranged for *Drifters* to be shown as the opening film for the evening's show – a suggestion that pleased the Society since they were clear in their minds that the 'big picture' was to be *Potemkin*.

On the evening of Sunday 10 November 1929, Grierson and Tallents made their way to the Tivoli Theatre, took their seats side by side, and waited, almost sick with anxiety, to see how their experiment would be received. They need not have worried. In the words of the *Birmingham Post*'s reporter, *Drifters* was 'rapturously received by the sophisticated audience', who were so thrilled by its montage techniques that by the time *Potemkin* was shown at the end of the evening, it seemed to them that Eisenstein's much-vaunted artistry was simply watered-down Grierson. Other reviews were similarly enthusiastic, and continued for weeks; cinemas across the country began to demand prints for their curious audiences. Grierson had triumphed, and in ways more far-reaching than he could reasonably have anticipated.

*

Scattered among the great and good at the Tivoli that night was a small group of bright young men in their late teens and early twenties. Within just a few months of *Drifters'* premiere, these youths would become the leading members of the newborn British documentary movement: Edgar Anstey (b.1907), Arthur Elton (b.1906), Stuart Legg (b.1910), Paul Rotha (b.1907) and Basil Wright (b.1907). Wright was the first to step forward and be counted:

> I saw *Drifters* at the Film Society on the Sunday. On Monday I started ringing up my friends, saying 'Do you know anybody who knows Grierson?' so I could get at him. On the Tuesday I received a letter from Grierson out of the blue saying that he'd seen an amateur film I'd made at some amateur film festival and would I go and see him?

He promptly went, only to be met by Grierson's scathing verdict on everything that was wrong with his tyro film, immediately followed by the offer of a job with the EMB at £2 a week. Just days later,

Wright was installed in a dank basement cutting a four-minute instructional film about cocoa from stock footage; the budget, Grierson warned him, was not to exceed £7. Humble beginnings for one of the single most admired and influential forces in world cinema; but documentary film grew up swiftly over the next few years. In Wright, Grierson had found not so much his first recruit as his first disciple, and other idealistic young men followed. Harry Watt, who joined up with Grierson in 1932, was one of many who found himself naturally using a religious metaphor when he summed up the relationship between the fledgling directors and their boss: 'Grierson was our guru, our 'Chief', our little god, the man who gave us an aim and an ideal, who battled for us and protected us, and at whose feet we sat. We were adult enough to laugh at his foibles and play-acting, to joke about his verbosity and Calvinism, but, basically, we adored him . . .'[7]

Such exalted views of Grierson were not always shared by the powers at the EMB. Despite the handsome profits brought in by *Drifters*, Grierson was forced to operate on pitifully low budgets and in humiliatingly poor conditions. His team's first home was a set of two tiny rooms off Wardour Street (that raffish Soho street which has traditionally been the London home of the British film industry). The lavatory doubled as a projection booth, and films were shown on a screen made of blotting paper. The Unit then moved into the top floor of 179 Wardour Street – slightly larger, but even more cramped thanks to the recent arrival of Elton (a former scientist) and Anstey (Jennings's exact contemporary at Cambridge, who had also read English) – just two of the fifteen hundred hopefuls who had eagerly applied for jobs with Grierson in the wake of *Drifters*. The strongly Cantabrian flavour of the Unit was often the subject of jokes, even by the dour Grierson, who later recalled: 'Stuart Legg and Basil Wright and Arthur Elton were first-class minds. And there was a time when we used to say that you couldn't get into documentary unless you had a double first, and from Cambridge, too, which was supposed to be great snobbery. . . .'[8]

Without knowing it, Jennings had made himself eminently well qualified; though whether he would have regarded life at the EMB as an attractive proposition is doubtful. Thanks to the Board's parsimonious attitude, salaries were kept low: £2 a week was standard, £4 the rarely achieved maximum. Thanks to Grierson's demand for single-minded devotion to the cause, there was also a climate of almost monastic celibacy: 'We were all normal, pretty well,' Harry Watt remembered, 'but we were absolutely forbidden to get married, and even the fact of us having girl friends was rather kept in the background . . .'⁹ Grierson also established a work ethic which, though informal, was merciless: 'We worked every God's hour there was and wandered out to the pub and had a sandwich and a drink and came back and worked again and very often if it was a rushed job, slept on the cutting room floor . . .'¹⁰

Slowly, however, the financial position began to look brighter, especially after Grierson's long-absent rivals, Major Creighton and Mr Kipling, finally turned in their feature, which proved to be catastrophically expensive (£17,740 – that is, three times the EMB's annual production budget) and artistically wretched. Mr Kipling's exceedingly bad film, *One Family*, concerned a pudding – a Christmas pudding cooked for the royal family with ingredients from every part of the Empire. Harry Watt's verdict – 'abysmally vomit-making' – nicely sums up the opinion of both press and public, and the film took just £334 at the box office. Understandably, the Board turned away from Kipling's grandiose plans for feature film production and towards the man who could turn in films that were cheap, profitable and – already – critically respected. By 1931, Grierson was in a position to send his young men and women – who had mainly been confined to learning their craft by re-editing existing footage – out into the world with cameras.

They came back with half a dozen short films, the so-called Imperial Six, on such topics as farming, logging and transport. Thanks to an odd piece of luck, Grierson was also able to offer employment to one of the world's handful of famous directors – his old friend Robert Flaherty, stuck in London while trying to make his way to the USSR. Less happily, and thanks to Flaherty's leisurely and painfully costly working habits, the author of *Nanook* squandered all but £100 of the large budget allocated to him on a set of pointlessly handsome shots that would never have cut together into a narrative. Legend states that Grierson used some of that remaining £100 to stand Flaherty a splendid dinner at which he gently sacked him, and used the rest to complete *Industrial Britain*, with Edgar Anstey – a film of which it is sometimes said that, notwithstanding the innovations of *Drifters*, it put the real faces of British working men and women on the screen for the first time.¹¹

A brief return visit to North America at this period had strengthened Grierson in his conviction that industrial sponsorship might be a
practical alternative to direct funding by the Government. He was
proved right: industry would become far and away the most important patron of the independent production companies that began to
proliferate in the 1930s. Encouraged by Grierson, the EMB directors
began to make films either directly for commercial concerns (Arthur
Elton, for example, made *The Voice of the World* for His Master's
Voice), or under the EMB's own banner. By 1933, Grierson's team
was expanding vigorously into overseas productions – Basil Wright
went to the West Indies to make a film about sugar, then to Ceylon
for tea; Anstey went off to Labrador. But all this activity was a decep-
tive index of the Unit's health. Beneath it was a financial crisis that
was worsening every day. First, the amount of revenue that could be
raised by the EMB was diminishing: since the advent of sound in
1929, fewer and fewer cinemas were willing to show silent films, and
the EMB still had no recording equipment. Second, and much more
seriously, the organization's secretary Sir Stephen Tallents was having
to fight hard to keep the EMB alive in the face of growing scepticism,
even hostility, from a Government that could not see that its activities
were doing much to ease the Depression. Already, it was being spoken of as a suitable candidate for abolition. Grierson rallied to Tallents's side by waging a propaganda campaign in the letters pages of
The Times and elsewhere, maintaining that the EMB represented the
only real possibility 'of freeing British films from a slavish competition
with American methods and establishing them with a character of
their own'.[12]

The campaign failed. In Harry Watt's version, the government
committee that was to decide their fate came and watched a selection of the Unit's films, which they thoroughly enjoyed. 'They told
Grierson he had obviously gathered around him a band of talented
and creative young people, went happily back to Whitehall, and
chopped us.'[13] Curiously, the chop was not fatal. Though the EMB
was officially closed down on 30 September 1933, Tallents had already
been asked by Sir Kingsley Wood – Clement Attlee's successor as
Postmaster General – to join the GPO's public relations department.
Tallents accepted the job, saying that he would come over all the
more happily if the EMB Film Unit and Library came with him.

Wood agreed, and almost overnight, the EMB Film Unit had become the GPO Film Unit.

*

The first days of the reborn Unit were glum; understandably so. To date, the only collaboration between Grierson's boys and the Post Office had been Stuart Legg's *The New Operator* and *Telephone Workers*: routine efforts, dull both to make and to watch, describing some technical aspect or other of the GPO's services. They feared that similarly uninspiring chores were all that the months and years ahead now held in store for them, and that their idealistic march towards great things just over the horizon had collided head-on with the brick wall of official dullness. (Had they been right in this, the history books would now be telling a very different story about film in the 1930s.) Thus far, Grierson's years of hard labour had yielded just two works of any enduring aesthetic quality, *Drifters* and *Industrial Britain*.

But for once, the gloom was misplaced. Thanks to a rare and happy conjunction of talented personalities and enlightened institutions, the Unit Jennings was soon to join was now entering on a period of unforeseen (and, in Britain at least, quite unprecedented) creative vitality. To the team's almost incredulous delight, the Post Office proved to be as generous and tolerant a patron of artistic innovation as any of them could have wished. Within just a few weeks of being adopted, the Unit had enjoyed three extremely welcome changes for the better.

The generosity of their new lords enabled them to rent greatly improved premises at 21 Soho Square in central London – an address which would remain their HQ until the end of the war. Next, they were given a small studio of their own, south of the Thames in Blackheath. For the first time, they had their own sound-making equipment – not very good equipment, true, but an essential weapon for their move back into commercial cinema. As Basil Wright recalled, the basic Blackheath gear consisted of a hand-held Debrie camera, left over from the EMB; a Vinten sound-film studio camera; the Newman-Sinclair camera that Flaherty had used; an Editola viewer; and a Vinten synchronizer. The sound equipment was British Visatone – a poor cousin of the American RCA and Western Electric systems.[14]

The final boon came in human form. Grierson's latest recruit to the Unit was an extravagantly talented Brazilian film-maker, Alberto Cavalcanti, soon to be known by all and sundry as 'Cav'. The last of these additions to the GPO Unit, Harry Watt wrote in his auto-biography, was 'by far the most important. I will categorically state that British documentary films would not have advanced the way they did without Cav's influence.'[15] As Watt expanded elsewhere:

> I believe fundamentally that the arrival of Cavalcanti in the G.P.O.
> Film Unit was the turning point of British documentary, because
> ... we really were pretty amateur and a lot of the films were
> second-rate, don't let's kid ourselves. It was only the newness of
> the idea of showing working men and so on that was making
> them successful. But Cavalcanti was a great professional . . .[16]

Nobody, Watt continued, had ever bothered to show him or his comrades the practicalities of directing a film – how to judge the appropriate length of a sequence, how to cut from a long shot to a close-up at the right moment, let alone the technical complexities of cutting sound: 'then this wonderful, sensitive, charming, hard-working fellow arrived on the scene, and he was my saviour. I would say again and again, if I've had any success in films I put it down to my training from Cavalcanti, and I think a lot of other people should say the same thing.'[17]

Who was this charming man and inspiring teacher? Alberto de Almeida Cavalcanti was born in Brazil in 1897. Something of a child prodigy, he became the youngest student enrolled at the University of Rio de Janeiro, where he read Law. Summarily expelled after mocking one of his professors and being caught in the act, he was sent to Europe by his father and told that he must neither study Law nor go into politics. He trained for a time as an architect in Geneva, and by the time he had turned eighteen was working as a draughtsman for an architectural firm in Paris. Short of money, he drifted into part-time work as an interior designer, and then moved into the French film industry as an art director. A fast learner, he made rapid progress, soon mastering the basic skills of editing and directing, and established his name as a director with two avant-garde silents, *Rien que les heures* (1926) and *En Rade* (1928) – both of which, as it happens, had been shown at the Film Society in London and seen by some of his British colleagues.

As he later recalled, the advent of sound caused him to be banished from the industry for a couple of years, because French studios shared the widespread superstition that silent directors were not capable of adapting to the talkies. But he bounced back by producing the French-language versions of American comedies for Paramount, and then a series of original French comedies. These were box-office hits, but their inanity bored Cavalcanti so much that he feigned illness and set off for London. Somehow or other – Cavalcanti supposed that it was probably through an introduction by his cameraman James Rogers – he found his way to Grierson and explained his position. Grierson, well aware that the Unit really could do with someone who under-stood how talkies worked, said, 'Oh well, come here for a month or two and amuse yourself at Blackheath.'

If Watt's recollections are accurate, Cav soon became the Unit's well-loved mentor – more of a mentor to some than to others, it's true, and most significantly of all, a mentor and protector to a young man who had yet to join the Unit: Humphrey Jennings.

*

According to a profile by 'George Pitman' written for the popular leftish periodical *Our Time*:

> One day in 1934 [Jennings] met Cavalcanti, the pioneer of the French documentary film, who had just come to this country to work for the newly-established G.P.O. Film Unit headed by John Grierson. Cavalcanti then knew no English, and Jennings was the first like-minded person here with whom he was able to converse freely and elaborately in French. As a result there came a speedy invitation [for Jennings] to join the Unit, nominally to train as a director, at what the impoverished Jennings thought the generous salary of £4 a week.[18]

Since 'Pitman', aka the journalist and print expert Allen Hutt, knew Jennings well, there is little reason to doubt that this is pretty much the way Jennings recalled the circumstances of his recruitment. It's a matter of record that Cavalcanti liked him very much: 'I got along very well with certain of the boys, which [*sic*] were brilliant boys . . . But the two important boys were Humphrey Jennings and Len Lye. Those were my favourite boys.'[19] Moreover, Cavalcanti immediately saw in Jennings something which few others – perhaps not even Jennings himself – guessed at the time: a strong intuition for the medium of cinema. 'It's funny that [Jennings and Lye] should have been painters to begin with. I've seen very few of Jennings's paintings, but I know that as soon as he touched films, he had a very acute sense, film sense . . .'[20]

Other accounts of Jennings's arrival at the GPO Film Unit differ slightly from the Pitman story. The film historian Elizabeth Sussex suggests, on the basis of an interview with Stuart Legg, that it was Legg who first invited Jennings to join.[21] If so, this may have been an old-school-tie invitation, since Jennings had been on friendly terms with Legg, Basil Wright and Arthur Elton at Cambridge. James Merralls's account appears to confirm Sussex's version: Jennings, he reports, 'joined the G.P.O. Film Unit in about 1934 through the good offices of Stuart Legg',[22] and most secondary sources have repeated or corroborated this. In anecdotal terms, the richest account of Jennings's cinematic debut was provided by his friend Gerald Noxon, who is vague as to the exact beginnings of his employment by the GPO, but precise about the curious events that brought him into film-making.

Late in 1933, at the time of the handover from EMB to GPO, Noxon had been briefly hired by Grierson to arrange a series of non-theatrical roadshows – organized screenings, in workplaces, schools and village halls – of the Unit's films. Noxon then quit the GPO to set up a film department for a London-based advertising agency, and was given the assignment to produce a short film for a major American oil company – the Socony-Vacuum Company, later rechristened Mobil – in time for the annual British motor show at Olympia in London. The company's advertising strategy was to alarm motorists about the dangers of a ghastly – and wholly mythological – substance called SLUM, which could inflict all kind of horrors on an innocent engine unless it was duly protected by the right brand of oil: 'Beware of SLUM in your crankcase,' ran the slogan.

By this time, the Jenningses were once again in serious financial difficulties: the legacy had all but run out, Humphrey was not selling any paintings (perhaps not even trying very hard) and there was, as usual, little prospect for steady employment. Noxon, knowing Humphrey well from Cambridge days, had a hunch that he might be the ideal man to tackle the SLUM project, especially since he would have

a well-trained and good-natured cameraman to show him the ropes of
directing. Still, Noxon hesitated. He was reluctant to ask a serious
artist, an artist of any kind, to undertake such a silly job as the SLUM
campaign.

> Of course, I should not have hesitated. I should have known that
> Humphrey's insatiable appetite for new experiences in communi-
> cation would make the proposition irresistible. He accepted
> instantly and in no time at all had made friends with the
> cameraman, written the script, charmed and amazed the oil
> company men, inspected the small rental studio on Marylebone
> Road where the film was to be shot, designed the set and worked
> out the lighting.[23]

This modest film was to consist of little more than shots of a cut-
away car engine – Jennings was characteristically delighted, 'almost
ecstatic', at the sight of his ingenious contraption – which would be
horribly polluted by SLUM. But there was a technical problem.
Though scouts had been dispatched to drain all the most repulsive
dregs from the most battered and shoddy vehicles on the Edgware
Road's used-car lots, the resulting fluids looked fairly innocuous on
camera, not much more offensive than black ink. Jennings next got his
men to mix these nasty liquids together and boil them up – 'a hideous
task which Humphrey insisted on attending to personally'[24] – but the
results were still disappointingly bland. Jennings would not admit
defeat. 'I'll fix it. I'll bloody well make some SLUM that will look like
SLUM.'

He went home to his studio and set about scraping together the
messy residues from his palettes and the left-over scraps from collages,
mixing them all together with varnish. The next day, he arrived at
the studio with an ample basinful of 'a concoction so horrible in its
glue-like consistency, so deadly menacing in its vague lumpiness, so
acutely threatening with its hints and glints of iron filings and ground
glass, that even the studio crew were appalled'.[25] Crew members
began to offer suggestions as to how this mess could be put to most
disgusting effect, but Jennings was intent on finding a method of his
own. He removed his tweed jacket, rolled up his sleeves, and declared
to his colleagues that 'SLUM is not a real substance. It is an idea, and
what is more it is essentially an emotional idea. Therefore its nature

must be demonstrated in a way which will produce a direct emotional response from the audience. There's no thinking needed here, boys.'[26] And he plunged his arms into the muck up to the elbows and squeezed and kneaded it vigorously, making it squirt and slurp nastily between his fingers. SLUM looked more satisfyingly vile than ever, and the film was greeted with enthusiasm by the oil men. Gerald Noxon concluded: 'Humphrey, it seemed, was from that moment destined to become involved with film work. It surprised both of us, for I'm sure that neither of us had thought of this odd film as anything other than a handy way of relieving a rather pressing financial situation.'[27]

Shortly after the SLUM episode, Jennings had signed on at the GPO Film Unit – though, as Noxon stressed, it is very unlikely that he was given any kind of long-term contract. In Noxon's memory, very few people had anything like permanent employment with Grierson at this time, and writers and directors in particular were usually hired on a project-by-project basis, being paid either by the week worked or with a single fee. 'Even if a full-time regular job had at that time been open to him,' Noxon adds, 'I doubt very much whether he would have taken it, for his whole approach to life and art was in many ways directly opposed to that of Grierson.'[28] The size and scope of Jennings's many private and freelance projects over the next few years must be attributed not only to his exceptional vitality but to the fact that his periods of paid employment continued to be sporadic until shortly before the war.

Whoever first issued the invitation, it is fairly certain that Jennings must have joined the Unit early in 1934. An undated letter sent to Cicely from his parents' house at 12 Holland St W8 says:

I don't know where to begin. The job, to begin with, is perfectly real – I have already begun work. I cashed a cheque and enclose £2 for the moment. I am staying here for tonight – after that I am not sure ... The hours are approximately 9 to 6 – or more like 10.30 to 6.30. Half day Saturday: Sunday off. They are taking me seriously enough – and are treating me as a 'director' at once.[29]

Another letter, probably written the following evening, added a few details of his new working life:

I have just had such a day: learning to 'cut' film, reading scripts, watching projections in the theatre, visiting the new GPO studios at Blackheath (very nice) – watching cameramen at work at the Wimpole St Sorting Office (a film about lost letters –) & so on. I am working immediately under Stuart [Legg]'s eye and to some extent 'with' Cavalcanti which all seems promising, & certainly it is very exhilarating stuff. Also not particularly strenuous & the people extremely pleasant.[30]

He was in luck: Grierson apart, the Unit appeared to be filled with kindred spirits. He seems to have relished the novelty of the work – that 'insatiable appetite for new experiences in communication', again – and the employment proved steady enough for him to be able to set up home with his wife and daughter. By the autumn of 1934, they were settled at 6 Brandram Road, Blackheath, conveniently close to the GPO studios. They were soon followed to the district by their Cambridge friends Charles Madge and Kathleen Raine, who did not want to be separated from the Jenningses.

The flavour of life and work at the GPO Film Unit around this time has been evoked by a number of witnesses and participants. Although written several years after Jennings's arrival and meant to apply to the documentary world in general, a satirical article for the *Cine-Technician* (September/October 1941) offers a lively caricature of the sort of company he was about to keep. Entitled 'How to Break into Documentary in One Easy Lesson', the squib was written by one Daniel Catling – he had worked in documentaries himself, for Gaumont British Instructional – who proposed:

The budding documentary director is sure of a job provided he can fulfil all of the following requirements, otherwise he hasn't a hope in hell.

He must:

A   Be a gentleman
B   Be a socialist
C   Have had a Varsity education
D   Have a private income
E   His own car
F   Long hair
G   Forswear bathing more than once a year

H   Have an adenoidal expression
I   Have made some sort of film on 16mm.

A well-developed case of H has been known to excuse the other
requirements (except A and B, of course).[31]

Naughty; and uncomfortably reminiscent of the (not always so
jocular) forms of class friction between 'creative' and 'technical' staff
in other, more recent, branches of the communications media. Still,
Mr Catling's cracks wouldn't have been deemed worthy of print unless
they had some sort of foundation in reality or, at least, in commonly
accepted stereotype, so one almost feels compelled to rush to the
defence of Jennings and company by pointing out that most of them
were quite as hard up as any of their working contemporaries, and not
conspicuously more adenoidal. A more affectionate, and no doubt
more accurate, evocation of the same milieu comes from the memoirs
of Harry Watt – himself decidedly not a 'Varsity' man:

> Our uniform was appalling flannel trousers, usually much too
> baggy, a not too clean check shirt, a stained pullover, and a
> dreadful tweed jacket, with bulging, sagging pockets and, more
> often than not, a tear somewhere. We were completely improvi-
> dent, spending what money we had on booze or girls. We were
> very politically conscious, and were fiercely anti-fascist and anti-
> Nazi . . .[32]

And in his autobiographical volume *Rain upon Godshill*, the novelist
and playwright J. B. Priestley admiringly recalled how much he had

> liked the enthusiasm of these rather solemn young men in high-
> necked sweaters. Most of them worked like demons for a few
> pounds a week . . . They were rapidly developing a fine technique
> of their own, so rapidly indeed that if you wanted to see what
> camera and sound really could do, you had to see some little film
> sponsored by the Post Office or the Gas Light and Coke Company
> . . . Grierson and his young men, with their contempt for easy big
> prizes and soft living, their taut social conscience, their rather
> Marxist sense of the contemporary scene, always seemed to me
> figures representative of a new world, at least a generation ahead
> of the dramatic film people . . .[33]

The earliest major GPO production on which Jennings was set to work was Cavalcanti's *Pett and Pott*. This, the Unit's first full-scale venture into sound film-making, was a whimsical tale of two suburban families, each with a limited amount of cash at their disposal, one of which is wise enough to install a Post Office telephone and so enjoys domestic bliss, while the other, foolish, snobbish and (it would appear) mildly decadent, indulges in the misguided one-upmanship game of hiring a feckless maid, instead. Result, predictable if not altogether plausible: the 'bohemian' Pott wife must toil home daily from the grocer's with loaded bags of provisions, and in agonizing slow-motion to boot, while the sensible Petts use their telephone to arrange regular home delivery; Pott's mousey husband starts to stay out at night carousing with showgirls and generally making whoopee, while Mr Pett keeps to the straight and narrow; and finally, on the fateful night of Friday the 13th – a ghostly chorus intones the fateful date in mournful, wobbly tones – the treacherous maid invites her burglar beau to the Pott household to do his worst. This dastardly act is foiled by the brave little Pett daughter, who telephones for the constabulary. (When they arrive, the police prove to be a rather timid singing troupe, presumably on loan from a Gilbert and Sullivan operetta.) The adventures end in court, where the judge delivers a homily on family values and – bearing the device of GPO sponsorship – makes a coy, not to say camp, allusion to the faint hints of a commercial message the audience may perhaps have detected in the preceding drama. *De minimis non curat lex.*

In its cheap-and-cheerful, unabashedly silly way, *Pett and Pott* is a highly entertaining trifle, and something of a showcase for experiments in both sound and vision: the scenes of bowler-hatted commuters travelling to work are set to a chanted, modernistically syncopated chorus of male voices, and there is at least one moment worthy of anything the Surrealists were getting up to across the Channel: a close-up of a sleeping suburban woman, alone in her bed, who (presumably dreaming of handsome lovers) snuggles up sexily to an anonymous male hand – the hand of a burglar. She wakes, panics, and opens her mouth: but what fills the soundtrack is not her voice, but the high-pitched howl of the commuter train's whistle (a device also used by Hitchcock in *The Thirty-Nine Steps*). Cavalcanti used Basil Wright and Stuart Legg as assistant directors, and asked Jennings not only to design the sets (his hand is most conspicuous in the skimpy, blatantly theatrical backgrounds for the courtroom scene) but to double up as a non-speaking actor – he played the Potts' jolly and assiduous grocer. According to Basil Wright, it was Cavalcanti's suggestion that they follow the technique of recording the sound first and shooting pictures to fit. Since everything was shot on the tiny Blackheath set, Jennings 'was very constricted, so he started to use false perspective in . . . a very ingenious manner'.[34]

He soon had the chance to play actor again in another, even more cheerfully daft romp, Cavalcanti's *The Glorious Sixth of June*. Here, he took the ingénu role of Albert Goodbody, a clean-cut and plucky young Post Office telegraph boy, who – despite the most knavish tricks of a gang of black-bearded foreign villains (one of them played, if that is the appropriate term for shameless mugging and hamming, by Basil Wright) who punch him, tie him to a tree, gag him and blow him up – still manages to bring the good news of reduced telegraph charges to Parliament, crashing through some stained-glass (in this case, paper) windows, black with smoke, and doughtily waving his message in the air. Cue for a clipped, terribly British shout of 'Hurrah!' from the chorus of MPs. Albert is duly rewarded, and goes home to tea with his devoted mum. It is fair to say that Jennings plays the role with gusto and a perfectly straight face, but beyond that gives no indication of how gifted a thespian he might have been.

By the end of 1934, Jennings had also edited two short films, the twenty-six-minute *Post Haste* and the twelve-minute *Story of the Wheel*. There is nothing shameful about either of these simple history lessons, and nothing very remarkable either, though it is possible to bring hindsight to bear on them and detect at least some embryonic traces of their *auteur*. *Post Haste*, for example, uses quotations from period documents in a manner which, one could contend if necessary, quietly anticipates his posthumous book *Pandæmonium*. A history of the development of the British postal service from the seventeenth to the early twentieth centuries, it touches on key stages of change and expansion: from the house of Sir Robert Bede in Lombard Street, the country's first sorting-office, via the advent of the mailcoach in 1784, the changeover from road to rail, Rowland Hill's introduction of the uniform penny postage and other technological innovations – to a triumphant concluding montage of contemporary Post Office activities, including the stirring sight of its trains, ships and planes.

The Story of the Wheel, as its title promises, takes an even longer historical view, starting in the Stone Age and leaping forward boldly to the Romans, the Middle Ages, and the sixteenth, seventeenth and eighteenth centuries before another rousing finale with the advent of the steam engine. By the end of 1934, Jennings had also earned his first credit as a director with the twenty-one-minute *Locomotives* – happily, railway engines had been a subject close to his heart since his earliest acquaintance with the Southwold railway, and were among the handful of key images that dominated his mature work. A good part of this short is taken up with close-up shots of the miniature engines in the Science Museum at South Kensington, edited to extracts from Schubert's 'Rosamunde'; like its two predecessors, it tells a simple tale of historical development, from the hissing of a kettle on the hob and the development of steam pumps in eighteenth-century mills and collieries to the birth of the railway steam engine and its subsequent conquest of the British landscape.

These slight instructional films, which continue to engage young children,[35] are modest to the point of invisibility, but, in addition to the pleasure he was no doubt taking in learning new crafts, Jennings would have had every reason to believe that greater things were in store for him. Unit morale was once again high, and artistic standards soaring. For the next year or two, hardly a couple of months could go by, it seemed, without the Unit producing some original, poetic piece of work – films whose qualities were immediately recognized by the more perceptive critics and which are now regarded as landmarks in cinema history, beginning with Basil Wright's lyrical *Song of Ceylon* (1934) and continuing in 1935 with three very different films: *BBC: Voice of Britain*, *Coal Face* and – the one GPO production everyone with an interest in cinema, railways or British social history is almost guaranteed to know – *Night Mail*, with its music by Benjamin Britten and poem-commentary by W. H. Auden. Jennings's own involvement with the first two films was fairly minimal. He probably directed one or two of the pithead sequences for *Coal Face*, and he took a minor acting part in the *BBC* film, playing one of the three witches from *Macbeth*; but he seems to have had nothing whatsoever to do with *Night Mail*. How often, though, popular memory attributes its authorship to Jennings – a misconception presumably founded in the assumption that the Unit's most famous director must have been the creator of its best-known work.

His later films, however, are clearly in debt to the technical and aesthetic advances made on these three films, and also, perhaps, to their content: the image of the anonymous, gently heroic team working in collective loneliness through the hours of sleep may well be one of the germs for the story of *Fires Were Started*, while the moving idea in films such as *Listen to Britain* and *A Diary for Timothy* of a nation listening in invisible unison to the BBC's broadcasts – an idea echoed and reinforced in stylistic terms by using radio soundtracks to bind together disparate images – is anticipated in *Voice of Britain*.

*

While Auden, Britten and co. were at work on their collaborations, Jennings was often busy freelancing elsewhere in the London film world, and was not to direct another GPO production until the ultra-modest short *Penny Journey* in 1938. The most remarkable of his works away from the Unit in these years was another advertising film, *Birth of the Robot*, produced and directed for the Shell Oil Company by his New Zealander friend, the extraordinary artist and abstract film-maker Len Lye (1901–80), who had come to London in 1926 on the good ship *Euripides*, having bought a drunken stoker's ticket for just £5. Lye was rapidly taken up by artistic circles, who knew him as the 'stoker-sculptor', and spent most of the next two years painstakingly making his wonderful abstract animation *Tusalava* (1929), just ten minutes long. His London years were dogged by poverty, and he found a measure of security only when Grierson recruited him to make a series of abstract colour films that, with a little judicious packaging, could be claimed to promote the services of the GPO. Lye and Jennings seem to have recognized each other as kindred spirits, and remained good friends until Lye emigrated to the USA after the Second World War.

On *Birth of the Robot*, Jennings is credited with 'Colour Direction and Production' – the process was Gasparcolor, a three-colour method which had been invented the previous year by the Hungarian Bela Gaspar. *Robot* is a strange seven-minute animated fantasy, which begins in the twinkling blue depths of outer space with Old Father Time turning a carousel on which the figures of Mercury, Venus, Mars and company twirl to the strains of 'Jupiter' from Holst's *Planets* suite; Venus plucks heavenly harmonies from her instrument, a lyre-like strung shell, or Shell. Down on earth, a reckless motorist is zooming blithely around the desert, up and down a pyramid and straight into a mighty sandstorm. The car's headlamp eyes roll up to heaven in plaintive supplication, but the sight of a service station ahead proves to be a mirage-garage (bad pun in original). Both car and man perish, choked with grit. The sun beats down on the bleached bones of the driver, until Venus takes mercy and plucks more notes from her lyre, which mutate into huge drops of oil as they fall to earth. When they rain down on the skeleton, it is transformed into a giant robot, much like a metallic lay figure, which then proceeds to cover the whole earth with machinery while a half-proud, half-ominous martial beat reaches its thunderous crescendo. It probably terrified small children, but – one criterion for a good commercial – it is hard to forget.

Despite his willing participation in this exercise, and at least three further ventures into colour film-making in the next few years, Jennings was far from convinced that colour was a suitable medium for serious cinema work. Some of his thoughts on the subject were published the following June in *World Film News* under the title 'Colour Won't Stand Dignity'; the occasion for his remarks was a Hollywood production, *The Trail of the Lonesome Pine*, starring Sylvia Sidney and Fred MacMurray:

> Colour is hopelessly revealing. It reveals not only new physical aspects and properties of objects, but becomes a devastatingly accurate index of the mentality of the film-maker, and of his approach to his material in the smallest details; and anything faked – faked sets or faked situations – shriek in colour where they could be got away with in black-and-white. This is because *Colour* and *Ideas* are fundamentally opposed; the black-and-white film has always lived on ideas; but colour depends upon *sensations*.[36]

In Noxon's memory, it was also around this time that Jennings became involved in a 'brief and implausible association' with the J. Arthur Rank organization. Up to this time, most of the Rank productions had been short Methodist tracts, but the company was now becoming interested in moving into feature-film production. Jennings was asked to come up with a shooting script for a feature based on Leo Walmsley's recent novel *Three Fevers*, a tale of North Sea fishermen with a highly uplifting moral tone. Jennings discussed his work on the screenplay several times and in great detail.[37] (The film was eventually brought to the screen, though Jennings's script was not used, under the title *The Turn of the Tide*; its editor was the man who would later be Jennings's most important producer at the Crown Film Unit, Ian Dalrymple.)

While Jennings was becoming more and more deeply involved in the world of film-making, an invitation from the poet Geoffrey Grigson gave him the opportunity to sum up his thoughts on the state of the contemporary theatre for a collection of essays, *The Arts Today*. (Born in 1905, Grigson was only two years older than his contributor.) Other contributors to the volume included Jennings's co-worker W. H. Auden and his boss, John Grierson. Jennings came up with an angry piece – charged, no doubt, with memories of his falling-out with Terence Gray at the Festival in Cambridge – which concluded:

> For a short period at the end of the sixteenth century and at the beginning of the seventeenth century Englishmen used 'the theatre' as they found it, for their own purposes of poetry and analysis of behaviour – *connaissance* – we have no word for it – naturally. That these [purposes] may still be constructed by Englishmen there seems just a possibility, but that they can or will use the theatre as a means is hardly possible since in one way or another it is precisely against these things (seeing in them its own downfall) that the present theatre's activity is directed (if one can use the word 'directed' of cottonwool) . . .[38]

To judge by his actions, Jennings's disgust was quite sincere: he never worked in the theatre again.[39] As for 'poetry and analysis of behaviour' – that's not a bad formulation for the distinctive qualities of his later films.

*

There is little record of the state of Jennings's family life at this period, save for one powerful piece of evidence suggestive of at least relative domestic contentment: the second of his two daughters, Charlotte, was born in August 1935. The place of birth was a nursing home on Shooter's Hill in South London run by a brace of food faddists who rejoiced in the names of Dr Pink and Dr White, both of whom were strict vegans and practised yoga. On one memorable occasion, Cicely, visiting Dr Pink for a consultation, was startled to find him standing on his head.

For a while, Cicely tried to enforce the same strict Truby King regime on Charlotte that she had on Marie-Louise, but Charlotte, a sickly child, was having none of it. Cicely had to spend hours manoeuvring spoonfuls of food into Charlotte's mouth, cooing 'one for Mummy', 'one for Daddy' and the like, with little success. When both girls were difficult over meals, Humphrey would apply moral pressure, reminding them that 'there are forty thousand starving children in Glasgow' – the 1930s precursor of later reminders of the unfed waifs in India, Biafra and other less amply supplied lands. Before long, Cicely abandoned her faith in Truby King and the Jenningses hired a uniformed nanny – a source of quiet satisfaction to Humphrey, who had a surprisingly old-fashioned pride in employing servants. At the same time, as though to underline their robustly bourgeois identity, he began to buy heavy Victorian furniture – then floundering in the lowest depths of unfashionability – and a set of 'Acropolis' china in green and cream, displaying classic pastoral views of shepherds, temples and cloudscapes.

The writer Ruthven Todd became friendly with Jennings around this time, and later sketched a lively verbal portrait of him in his late twenties: 'So far as I can recall I first met Humphrey in late 1935, introduced by Len Lye, on a train. I was 21 and he was rather older – seven years my senior and seven years then seemed like a generation.'[40] Elsewhere Todd expanded:

At our first meeting I thought him both brash and bumptious. 'There has only been one really good edition of anything that Shakespeare wrote,' he proclaimed modestly, 'and that is an edition of *Venus and Adonis* that I did myself, while at Cambridge' ... I think that Humphrey rather despised me then for my lack of a common culture.[41]

And again:

I was uncouth, ill-educated from [the Scottish public school] Fettes (although I spoke English without a Scottish burr), and ex-farm-labourer on Mull, and no equal for him ... at that time Humphrey – Perse School and Cambridge – was an overwhelming intellectual snob. We did not level out until 1940 when he found that I, self-educated, knew more about Blake than he did and was also informed in peculiar places where he had not thought to look about matters which were pertinent to *Pandæmonium* . . .

When I say that Humphrey was an intellectual snob, I do not mean that he was not a pleasant companion, but merely that I dared not venture an opinion on literature (pre – say – 1920) without a fear of being overwhelmed. His friendship with Len Lye is proof that he did not require intellectual companionship; Len is a 'natural' and writes in block letters . . .[42]

Unpromising as this early acquaintance must have seemed, Jennings and Todd soon became good friends – Todd says that he loved Humphrey '*dearly*', helped him to buy books:

Suddenly, I see Humphrey in that godawful tomato soup Harris tweed overcoat[43] waiting for me at the corner of Cecil Court (off the Charing Cross Road) where I have found some book which is not quite up my alley, but I think is right up his . . .

Humphrey would ask me to find some odd volume or half-forgotten pamphlet and I often found it for next to nothing. It probably was worth next to nothing in a box of mixed books, but put in among the books which were used for *Pandæmonium* it became a valuable book. So, on the whole, Humphrey wasn't as extravagant as he might have appeared. Humphrey *was*, admittedly, used to the bookshops of Cambridge, and their prices, but on the occasions that we went (probably three or four times) from Duton Hill to Cambridge, I could always find, in the cheap boxes, something which one or other of us wanted and of which we would have paid ten times the price. So, I'd guess, he paid much less for his library than anyone else at that time, and, alas, and of course, no one today, except a millionaire, could make the small but select libraries we both had.[44]

On another occasion, Todd recalled one of Jennings's minor eccentricities:

He was a paper-eater. He was always getting into trouble on the train to Blackheath from Charing Cross because, at the end of the journey, all he had to offer the ticket collector was a chewed ball of green cardboard. I recall once travelling down from Charing

Cross with him when he was full of theories which he was willing to expound even to an ignoramus such as myself who could not follow half of them. On this occasion he ignored his railway ticket but, engrossed in his expositions, he managed to devour nearly the whole of a rolled-up copy of the *Evening Standard* which he was carrying, and in those, pre-war days, the *Evening Standard* was physically, if not mentally, a paper of some substance.[45]

Perhaps mindful of his renewed responsibilities as a breadwinner, Jennings took a job for a number of months with the commercial film company Gasparcolor, who owned the rights to the process he had employed on *Birth of the Robot*. In the contributor's note for an issue of the literary magazine *Life and Letters Today*, to which he had contributed a strange prose-poem, 'The Space of Former Heaven', co-written with Charles Madge, Jennings described himself as a 'painter and film-director' who 'is at present working with the Gasparcolor group'.[46] At least one of the projects he began to develop for the company sounds extremely promising: on 10 January 1936, he wrote to the great political cartoonist David Low on Gasparcolor stationery, signing himself 'Production Manager': 'This company is proposing to produce a series of political or semi-political cartoon shorts in colour . . .' – and went on to suggest that Low might find the business of producing animated versions of his work rewarding both financially and artistically. 'I believe,' he concludes, 'that a very good opinion of this colour system and of the production standards of this company could be given you by, say, John Grierson or Stuart Legg or John Betjeman.'[47]

Low was sufficiently interested in the proposal to come up with some preliminary sketches, which still exist, but nothing seems to have come of the series. Nor is it clear how long Jennings remained employed at Gasparcolour; or – despite styling himself 'painter and film-director' – how committed he yet was to film-making, whether commercial or subsidized, as a medium of expression. Not very deeply, one suspects; for he was about to devote a great deal of time, emotion and energy to an artistic rebellion which, much as it loved the cinema, considered film as just one of many weapons in its devastating creative arsenal: Surrealism.

*

In the early months of 1936, Jennings was on the brink of becoming a major participant in the nascent British Surrealist movement, which by most accounts had its immediate origins – suitably enough, in view of the Surrealist faith in *hasard objectif* – in a chance encounter between the artist Roland Penrose and the young poet David Gascoyne on the rue de Tournon,[48] Paris, sometime in the late summer of 1935 or thereabouts. Interviewed in 1981, Penrose – by that time Sir Roland – began his recollection of British Surrealism by stressing the particular contribution of Jennings rather than Gascoyne to the movement's early days:

> When I came back to England in 1936 – I had left a lot of my friends in Paris and I had been away from London a long time, so it was a great excitement to me to find people like Humphrey Jennings here in London with whom I had once shared a great many ideas, hopes for the future and everything, and together we founded what became known as the Surrealist Group in London with Herbert Read, David Gascoyne and artists such as Henry Moore and Paul Nash and a great many others who came in because of the excitement that they felt about something of which they knew very little. Humphrey knew much more . . .
>
> Now Humphrey was an exception among all that group because he had something which was very fascinating – he had a life about him – a sparkle about him. A wit. A violence – which was perhaps almost a bit un-English. In fact it seemed to me very much to link up with the people I had known in Paris, my friends among the Surrealists in Paris, and that is why at once I found in Humphrey somebody that I not only liked as a friend but somebody who was full of inspiration in the right way . . .[49]

For Penrose, then, Jennings was the character most in tune with the essential spirit of Surrealism: not so much a willing junior recruit as a founding father.

But the standard, simplified version of British Surrealism as the offspring of Penrose and Gascoyne stands in need of other qualification. While it may be true that it was their Parisian street encounter which set the ball rolling, there had already been quite a number of isolated, uncoordinated outbreaks of Surrealist activity in Britain in the years before Penrose's return. To name just a few: notable exhibitions by

Picabia, Max Ernst, Miró and Arp at the Mayor Gallery (which was to emerge as one of the two or three most important centres of Surrealist art in the UK) in 1933; the publication, in October that year, of the first Surrealist poem in English, David Gascoyne's 'And the Seventh Dream is the Dream of Isis'; the publication, in July 1934, of extracts from Hugh Sykes Davies's Surrealist novel *Petron* in *The Criterion* (the completed text was issued in December 1935); Charles Madge's article on 'The Meaning of Surrealism' for the August 1934 issue of Grigson's *New Verse*; and the publication, in a French text, of Gascoyne's 'First English Manifesto of Surrealism' in *Cahiers d'Art*, in June 1935. Since, however, none of these had quite created the momentum to launch a full-bodied British movement by the mid-1930s, it would be fair to say that Surrealism had taken an unusually long time, well over a decade, to cross the Channel.

It is hard to give an exact date to the birth of the movement. Among a number of plausible contenders would be 1917, when the poet Guillaume Apollinaire coined the French word *surréalisme* to characterize the new sensibility he saw on display in Érik Satie's strange ballet *Parade*. Or perhaps it happened a year earlier, in February 1916, when a twenty-year-old poet and medical orderly in the French Army, André Breton, met a twenty-one-year-old soldier and former artist, Jacques Vaché, at the hospital in Nantes, and was enthralled by the older youth's astonishing originality of spirit, above all in the matter of what Vaché called *umour*, a term for which 'humour' or even ''umour' would be an altogether feeble translation (it has even been said that for Breton, the whole Surrealist enterprise was an attempt to preserve the memory of Vaché, who died young). Or maybe the decisive year was 1919, when the magazine *Littérature* published *Les Champs magnétiques*, a pioneering exercise in 'automatic writing' produced in collaboration by Breton and his fellow-poet Philippe Soupault.

Casting around for less proximate points of departure, 1914 might be seen as the crucial date, since without the obscene mass slaughter of the war the bright young Isaacs of Europe might not have taken such gleeful leave of sanity, as their Abrahamic elders defined it; or, more immediately, April 1916, when the German poet and philosopher Hugo Ball gave the name *Dada* to the wildly provocative words and actions he and his colleagues Tristan Tzara and others had been performing at the Cabaret Voltaire in Zürich, for without the scandalous precedent of the Dadaists, Surrealism might either have been stillborn or have grown up in very different ways.

A strong case could be made for any of these dates; but for the official inauguration of the Surrealist movement, rather than its antecedents and early intuitions, the crucial year is unquestionably 1924. This was the year that saw the publication of André Breton's first *Manifeste du surréalisme*, which famously if not altogether helpfully defined the phenomenon as 'pure psychic automatism, by which it is intended to express, verbally, in writing, or by other means, the real process of thought'. Nineteen twenty-four was also the year in which the 'bureau des recherches surréalistes' was founded, as was the journal *La Révolution surréaliste*, which replaced *Littérature* as the main organ of the Surrealist movement. Settling on a moment of origin does little, though, towards defining the nature of the movement.

Today, Surrealism is commonly thought of as mainly or exclusively a chapter in the history of the visual arts. Pressed to come up with the names of leading Surrealists, most laymen would probably mention Dali and Magritte rather than André Breton or René Crevel, and not without justice. It is, one must reluctantly concede, Dali's slick, coprophile grotesqueries and Magritte's deadpan businessmen in bowlers and eerie puns for the eye that have left the most enduring marks on the worlds of advertising, film-making and educated chatter, not the likes of Breton's visionary novel *Nadja* (1928) or Louis Aragon's haunting memoir-fiction-manifesto *Le Paysan de Paris* (*Paris Peasant*, 1926).

But such a narrowly art-historical identification is at once an insulting diminution and a distortion – to raise just one pedantic objection, it was writers rather than painters who brought Surrealism into the world. Surrealism was, or at various times aspired to be, not just another striking pictorial style or bag of arty tricks among the many tendencies cast up in the wake of Impressionism, but a dangerous conspiracy, a total revolution of mind and body, a vision of the miraculous, an utterly novel mode of sensibility, a programme of scientific and/or occult research, a quest for the Philosopher's Stone, a way of life, a delirium, a trance, a road to the infinite. (Julian Trevelyan was being mischievous, but came close to an important truth, when he had the word 'Surrealist' engraved on his military dog-tag as his

professed religion.⁵⁰) How far Surrealism managed to achieve any of
these exalted states is certainly wide open to dispute – sceptical
observers might say that the pettiness, silliness and childish spite of
much Surrealist activity are often more apparent than its visionary
heroism – but it is impossible to grasp the thrill of the phenomenon
for contemporaries without recognizing something of its proclaimed
ambition, its sheer audacity.

Hundreds of reference books have attempted to define the precise
nature of Surrealism; rather than simply regurgitate those definitions,
it might be more enlightening to come at the topic by evoking a few
typical Surrealist activities and crazes. At the broadest level, then, there
was a preoccupation with the realm of the unconscious mind, into
which the Surrealists would boldly venture by means of automatic
writing – an activity at once reminiscent and parodic of nineteenth-
century seances – mesmerism, sleeping fits (a sort of self-hypnosis or
profound meditative state) and drugs, and through the recording and
analysis of dreams. (Breton and company tended to revere Freud; the
father of psychoanalysis did not, to put it mildly, reciprocate their
admiration, though – disappointing to those with little time for the
opportunistic Spaniard – he had a certain amount of time for Dali.)
They were fascinated by the mechanisms of coincidence and chance
encounters, and – seldom being encumbered by the tiresome responsibilities of day jobs – would ramble for hours through the streets, parks
and markets of Paris in search of everyday manifestations of the
miraculous.

Allied with this taste for wandering and wondering was a fascination for all manifestations of the non-rational mind, or what might
(sometimes patronizingly) be seen as such: the low comedy of the
Mack Sennett movies, the writings and paintings of the insane and of
children, the tribal artefacts and fetishes that anthropologists were
bringing back in ever-increasing numbers from Africa and the Pacific.
(At least one of the leading Parisian Surrealists, Michel Leiris, was a
professional ethnologist.) Many, including Breton, were sympathetic
to both the orthodox and the unorthodox schools of the Western
Hermetic tradition, and often greatly learned in the occult sciences,
from astrology to voodoo. They were fond of constructing fanciful
lineages of proto-Surrealist antecedents: firstly in the nineteenth-
century Symbolist poets and their fellow-travellers – Rimbaud, Baude-

laire, Mallarmé and Lautréamont, from whose inchoate 'novel' or prose screed *Les Chants de Maldoror* they derived the most influential and frequently intoned of all Surrealist mottoes: 'Beautiful as the chance encounter on a dissecting table of a sewing machine and an umbrella'. Then, later, they sought imaginary grandmothers and grandfathers in such individuals as the Marquis de Sade and the Gothic novelists Ann Radcliffe (1764–1823), Matthew 'Monk' Lewis (1775–1818) and Horace Walpole.

The Surrealists were interested in the humour of cruelty, violence, bad taste and crazy leaps of illogic – something Breton, himself a rather sour man at times and almost totally devoid of a spontaneous sense of fun, had picked up from his friend Jacques Vaché's *umour*. They relished odd, eerie or witty juxtapositions of objects, phrases and ideas; one reason why collage was such a common and important technique for them, and why they spent hours playing the game *cadavre exquis*, 'Exquisite Corpse', a visual version of 'Consequences' in which a folded piece of paper was passed from hand to hand, each person adding some new lines in ignorance of what had preceded, so that the resulting image would be a metamorphic freak. They nurtured a fondness for the unrespectable, the unofficial, the detritus and rejected knowledge of Western civilization. They made a point of solemnly worshipping sex and all manifestations of the erotic drive (even though, again, Breton himself was somewhat prudish by nature, and disapproved both of homosexuality and of brothels).

Above all, they saw themselves as rebels: against the state, the Church (a classic image: the photograph of 'Benjamin Péret insulting a priest' in Breton's magazine *La Révolution surréaliste*), the academies, the values and tastes of the beastly bourgeoisie, and against the dominion of logic and lucidity. This posture of permanent rebellion led them along some strange paths, including some uneasy alliances first with the Communist Party and then, after some major internal quarrels, schisms and excommunications, with Trotsky and his followers.

This, then, was the heady brew which a largely unsuspecting Britain was about to swallow in quantity for the first time in the summer of 1936.

★

When and how had Jennings first encountered Surrealism? If we can trust his own – perhaps slightly boastful – account, he implies that he had read both *La Révolution surréaliste* and its more politically militant successor *Le Surréalisme au service de la révolution* on their first appearance; since the former was published from 1924 to 1929 and the latter from 1929 to 1933, it's conceivable that he was aware of Surrealist activities even as a schoolboy. (In the Surrealist *annus mirabilis* of 1924, he would have been seventeen – more than mature enough for a bright and polyglot lad to pick up on such things, either in print or on one of his regular visits to France.) It's almost certain that he had been aware of Breton and company as early as his undergraduate days with the *Experiment* group; Kathleen Raine certainly recalls that he was the first to introduce Surrealist art and ideas into their student circle. If so, he was not the only young Cambridge intellectual who had woken up to the new French revolution.

Though the earliest direct reference to the Surrealists in any English publication came in the December 1925 issue of Eliot's London-based *The Criterion*, Cambridge did not lag far behind. In October 1928, Anthony Blunt noted in *The Venture* that 'surrealisme ... is threatening to become serious'[51] – in subsequent years, the embryonic Soviet spy would become one of the most prominent opponents of Surrealism on the English Left – and Blunt's remark was soon followed by the first proper historical account of the movement in the *Cambridge Review*. In June 1930, the editor Eugène Jolas opened the pages of his magazine *transition* – a home for many forms of advanced literary experiments, including Surrealist efforts – to members of the *Experiment* group, and included a text by Jennings's close friend Julian Trevelyan. And the final, unlikely correspondence between Cambridge and Surrealism – one of the less well-trodden byways of cultural history – came in December 1932, when a French academic, Henri Fluchère, contributed an explanatory text on Surrealism to (of all unlikely journals) F. R. Leavis's severe *Scrutiny*.

Well-versed as he may have been in the theory and artistic manifestations of Surrealism throughout his early adulthood, Jennings showed little sign of adopting or adapting its methods until 1934 or so – the same year he began to work in film. There's a good chance that it was his new friendship with Cavalcanti, who had moved freely in Parisian avant-garde circles, that intensified or reawakened his interest;

or perhaps conversations with Madge and other ex-Cambridge friends were leading him irresistibly towards the example of Breton. At any rate, the first written evidence of Jennings's Surrealist inclinations is a prose-poem dated 1934 (though not published until 1936) – a paragraph-length 'Report', the (cod-)formal biographical account of an unnamed polymath: 'He was then resident, and afterwards envoy extraordinary at the Court of Tuscany. Music, painting, and statuary occupied him chiefly, and his unpublished catalogues, not less strikingly than his copious printed notes, show the care and assiduity of his research . . .'[52] A second such 'Report', dated 1935, has the same cool, slightly pedantic tone as the first, and reads like a fragment from an occult novel:

> The front windows on the ground floor were entirely closed with inside shutters and the premises appeared as if altogether deserted. In a minute the front door opened and Mr. Kellerman presented himself. His manner was extremely polite and graceful.
>
> His complexion was deeply sallow and his eyes large, black and rolling. He conducted me into a parlour with a window looking backward, and having locked the door and put the key in his pocket he desired me to be seated. The floor was covered with retorts, crucibles, alembics, bottles in various sizes, intermingled with old books piled one upon another. In a corner, somewhat shaded from the light, I beheld two heads, and entertained no doubt that among other fancies he was engaged in remaking the brazen speaking head of Roger Bacon and Albertus.[53]

According to David Gascoyne's memoir, it was also in 1935 that he and Jennings began to work on a series of translations from one of the most wilfully outrageous of the French Surrealists, Benjamin Péret (1899–1959); work that was eventually published in book form in Roger Roughton's Contemporary Poetry and Prose Editions in June 1936, first as *A Bunch of Carrots* and then, after being subjected to a rough act of censorship by his printer, which demolished two poems – 'The Chicago Eucharistic Congress' and 'Patriotic Ex-Serviceman's Hymn' – in an almost identical edition now entitled *Remove Your Hat*. The printer had mainly objected to Péret's blasphemous and anticlerical outbursts, such as 'The thing is god's been constipated for twenty centuries and so's had no foul messiah to fecundate the

terrestrial latrines . . .' Péret himself had proposed the revised title
Chapeau!, this being the traditional cry of protest aimed at ladies who
wore inconveniently large hats to the theatre during the *belle époque*;
'Remove Your Hat', Gascoyne recalls, was the best English equivalent
he and Jennings could devise. Of the twenty poems in this slender
volume – the second of only three published under Jennings's name in
his lifetime – nine were translated by him, including 'Four by Four',
'Nearly to a Millimetre' and 'The Good Old Days':

> The trumpet-shaped noses playing a funeral march
> and the four-leaved clovers
> announce the fine weather
> which has the brain of a child
> and the webbed feet of a duck
> as in the time of cherries
> when it snows
> fried eggs . . .[54]

Meanwhile, Jennings continued to produce his own original pieces
in a Surrealist vein. From June 1936 onwards, he began to contribute
these writings to the newly founded (mainly) Surrealist journal *Contemporary Poetry and Prose*, edited by the young Roger Roughton, at the
time a militant Communist, who, after a conversion to pacifism, was
to die by his own hand just five years later. Jennings's publications
here included both his poems and poetic prose 'Reports' as well as
further translations from the French, of poetry by the Belgian Surrealist
E. L. T. Mesens and Paul Éluard (later a courageous member of the
French Resistance, and now acknowledged as one of the major French
poets of the twentieth century). With the help of his fluent French,
Jennings soon became good friends with Éluard, who commemorated
their Surrealist friendship in appropriately oblique and cryptic style
with an unrhymed sonnet:

Humphrey Jennings

> Sous un ciel noir des maisons noires des tisons éteints
> Et toi la tête dure
> La bouche fléchissante
> La chevelure humide
> Des roses fortes dans le sang

Désespérant d'un jour infini blond et brun
Tu brises les couleurs gelées
Tu troubles le sillage du diamant
Une barque d'ambre à trois rames
Creuse la mare du désert
Le vent s'étale sur la mousse
Un soir entier soutient l'aurore
Le mouvement a des racines
L'immobile croît et fleurit.[55]

In David Gascoyne's translation:

Under a black sky black houses and burnt-out embers
And you with your hard head
Consenting mouth
Moist hair
Sturdy roses in your blood
Despairing of an endless fair dark day
You break the frozen colours
You stir up the diamond's track
An amber boat with three oars
Excavates the desert pond
The wind sprawls on the moss
An entire evening sustains the dawn
Movement has roots
Immobility grows and blossoms[56]

Meanwhile, Jennings began to adopt Surrealist techniques and preoccupations in his work. No longer confining himself to painting, he had begun to produce collages, poetic 'objects' and photographs. One of his most celebrated works from this period (c.1935) is a witty collage of a mountain and a Swiss roll – unlike his more enigmatic works, it relies on a buried verbal joke, about things that are typically Swiss – and he enjoyed the image so much that he later reworked it into a painting. Though one cannot make very large claims for Jennings's collage works in their own right – they do not begin to compare for mystery, wit and power with, say, Max Ernst's pictorial novel Une Semaine de bonté – the fundamental principle of collage, yoking together two or more unrelated objects or images so as to produce an entirely new set of meanings, is of the greatest consequence for the rest of his artistic career, both in his films and in his monumental text-collage *Pandæmonium*. But the bulk of that work was yet to come.

*

Far and away the most conspicuous and influential of all Jennings's Surrealist activities took place in the summer of 1936. With the critic Herbert Read, André Breton, Roland Penrose and others, he became a member of the organizing committee of the International Surrealist Exhibition, which opened at the New Burlington Galleries in London on 11 June. It is no exaggeration to say that this exhibition created an unprecedented popular sensation; a few months later, Jennings would write in jaundiced terms of the 'nauseating memory of the mixed atmosphere of cultural hysteria and amateur-theatricality which combined to make the Surrealist Exhibition of June so peculiar a "success"'. But that sour note is retrospective; there is every sign that he approached the task of staging the show in much higher spirits. There is a well-known photograph showing the inner quartet of E. L. T. Mesens, Penrose, Breton and Jennings; the last, smartly dressed in tie and flannels and holding a hat in his hand, looks directly into the camera with a boyishly cheerful, almost gleeful smile.

David Gascoyne had made a tentative announcement of the forthcoming exhibition at the end of his *Short Survey of Surrealism*, published in November 1935. In early January 1936, André Breton and Paul Éluard made plans to visit London with a view to organizing such an exhibition. Soon, Penrose and Herbert Read had formed their organizing committee, and on 6 April the first of eight planning sessions took place at Penrose's house, 21 Downshire Hill in Hampstead, with Rupert Lee as chairman; Paul Nash, Henry Moore and Hugh Sykes Davies were also present. Jennings joined the committee for the fourth meeting, as did the American photographer and painter Man Ray, David Gascoyne, Sheila Legge and, from time to time, S. W. Hayter and McKnight Kauffer. Eventually the committee also included Diana Brinton Lee and Mesens. (Besides Breton, Éluard and Man Ray, the French branch of the committee also included Georges Hugnet.) One of Jennings's personal jobs was to make contact with the London Film Society to arrange a series of related screenings.[57]

The organization was something of a nightmare. The exhibition had been hung, the items numbered and the catalogue printed when Breton swept in from Paris, declared the whole thing a travesty and ordered it completely rehung.[58] The published catalogue, therefore, is quite unreliable as a guide to the contents – though a handsome item in its own right, with a cover by Man Ray and articles by Breton and Herbert Read. Ruthven Todd provides a first-hand account of this hiccup:

> I became closer (but still inferior) to Humphrey with the Surrealist Exhibition of 1936, into which I had been introduced (but did not appear in the catalogue by Herbert Read) as assistant secretary – probably a good thing as we had hung the exhibition before André Breton arrived and had to rehang the whole thing the night before (and through) the opening and I was the only person with good enough visual memory to know where anything was to be found.[59]

The mishaps continued. On 10 June, the eve of the official opening, a packing case containing eight paintings by the Danish Surrealists Wilhelm Freddie and Leonor Fini was impounded by the Customs authorities and threatened with destruction on grounds of obscenity. After negotiations, six of the offending items were passed, and two (titled 'The Fallen in the World War' and 'Worship Exhibitionism') were shipped back to Copenhagen.

The event at the New Burlington Galleries had been well publicized in advance, and on the day of the opening, 11 June, the crowds held up the traffic in both Bond Street and Piccadilly. Before long, an estimated 1,150 people had crammed into the gallery, defying the sweltering temperature of this hottest day of an unusually hot summer. André Breton performed the opening ceremony, flamboyantly dressed in his favourite colour, green, and smoking a green pipe; Mme Breton's hair and nails had been dyed a matching shade of green for the occasion. A figure called the 'Surrealist Phantom' drifted through the proceedings – a young woman (Sheila Legge) dressed in a white satin gown and brilliant coral-coloured belt and shoes, her head wholly encased in a cage of roses, her forearms sheathed in rubber gloves, and carrying in one hand the life-size model of a human leg stuffed with roses and in the other a raw pork chop (eventually abandoned when the heat hastened its decay and it began to stink). The Phantom also drifted over to Trafalgar Square to feed the pigeons and alarm the populace. Back in the gallery Dylan Thomas made his way through the crowds offering teacups full of boiled string, and politely asking 'weak or strong?', while a Surrealist lecture was repeatedly interrupted by a loud electric bell.

The provocative antics did not die down after opening day. On 1 July, Salvador Dali delivered the most notorious lecture of his career – his subject was 'Authentic Paranoiac Phantoms', and seems to have concerned the improbable tale of a philosophy student who had eaten a wardrobe, piece by piece, over the course of six months. Dali was dressed in a deep-sea diving suit decorated with plasticine hands and a radiator cap, a jewelled sword hanging from his waist, and holding two borzois on leads. (According to Jennings family legend, it was Cicely Jennings who had hired the suit.) The wealthy dilettante Edward James, Dali's good friend and subsequent patron, used a highly decorated billiard cue as a pointer for the lecture's cryptic illustrations. After struggling manfully for a while to make himself intelligible from inside his diving helmet, Dali finally gave up and asked James to remove it. Unable to loosen the helmet's wing-nuts by hand, James tried to use his cue as a lever to work them loose; staggering, and tangled up in his borzois' leads, Dali ranted on and on until Ruthven Todd finally managed to remove the helmet and disentangle the poor bewildered dogs. Sadly, the latter half of the lecture proved barely more enlightening than the first, so heavily accented was Dali's French. Near to collapse from heat exhaustion, he was prised out of his rubber envelope and found to be so drenched with sweat that his expensive suit was ruined and his sea-boots filled to the brim with salty Dalinian fluid. His wife, Gala Dali, ran out to a nearby clothes store and bought him a complete new outfit, then treated Ruthven Todd to a big kiss for having saved her husband's life.

London's artistic *arrière-garde* also joined in the fun. William Walton, composer of the rousing march *Crown Imperial* and other patriotic works, came back to the gallery after lunch one day and fastened a kipper to the hook protruding from Miró's 'Object 228'. Miró pronounced himself delighted with the impromptu addition, but the increasingly pungent smell soon sent Walton's kipper the way of Miss Legge's pork chop; Paul Nash is credited with the disposal. An anonymous prankster smuggled a canvas into the gallery showing a woman with a (real) cigarette in her mouth and a small bird glued to her forehead; it was signed 'D. S. Windle'. Again, the exhibition committee declared that this was an entirely appropriate Surrealist action and allowed the rogue article to remain on show. There were other, more sober manifestations, including a variety of lectures: from Breton on 'Limits Not Frontiers of Surrealism', from Sykes Davies on 'Biology and Surrealism' and from Éluard on 'L'Évidence Poétique'. Éluard also read in French from his own work and the likes of Lautréamont, Jarry and Péret; translations, and original Surrealist verses in English, were read by Jennings, Gascoyne and George Reavey.[60]

Fuelled by extensive coverage in all sections of the national press and the Movietone News, the exhibition soon reigned supreme: well over twenty-six thousand people attended, the largest number ever to attend an art show in London up to that date. What visitors encountered there included some 360 (more or less) conventional works of art – paintings, sculptures, collages – as well as *objets trouvés* by Eileen Agar, Breton, Max Ernst, Read and Penrose, Surrealist objects by Mesens, Tanguy and others, some thirty African and Oceanic exhibits, and a variety of children's drawings: a total of sixty-nine named artists were represented, twenty-seven of them British.

Jennings put six pieces of his own work into the show: *In a Country Churchyard* (1933, oil painting), *Life and Death* (1934, collage), *Le Minotaure* (1934, collage), *Stereo* (1933, image-object), *Life and Death* (1934, image-object) and *Death at Work* (1934, image-object). *Le Minotaure* was a satirical swipe at Lord Kitchener, showing him wearing a fez with the miniature portrait of a child upside down on his chest. This provoked violent responses both from patriots and from a certain Mrs Tait, a member of the Royal Miniature Society, who claimed that Jennings had made unauthorized use of a colour reproduction of a painting she had made of her son, sixteen years earlier. Jennings replied rather loftily that he was not 'interested in other people's views' and that in any case he did not claim the painting as his own. 'To a surrealist, everything is anonymous and everything in the world is material to create imagery.'[61]

By and large, the press coverage tended to the jocular or the splenetic. Before the show had so much as opened, the *Manchester Evening News* was spluttering about 'meaninglessness for the sake of meaninglessness. A travesty of everything that's decent'. The *Daily Telegraph* sniffed about 'poor jokes, pointless indelicacies and relics of an outworn romanticism'; the *Evening News*, particularly put out by Meret Oppenheim's fur cup, bleated: 'It is not worth looking at. I don't mind it being meaningless, but it is horribly clumsy as well.' The *Daily Mirror* (headline: 'Needed Pork Chop – To Complete Dress'), the *Daily Herald* ('Here are Marx Brothers of Art') and other organs of the down-market press simply poked fun. Not even the high-brow publications kept an open mind: *The Studio* spoke of 'literal monstrosities and cheap horrors', while the *New English Weekly* wrote the whole show off as 'plastically worthless'.

To be sure, it is unseemly and myopic to deride the prejudices of earlier generations; still, it is worth recalling that the international team of artists being summarily dismissed by the gentlemen of the British press here included, among others, Arp, Brancusi, Calder, de' Chirico, Dali, Duchamp, Ernst, Giacometti, Klee, Magritte, Masson, Miró, Picabia, Picasso, Man Ray and Tanguy, as well as a home side including Henry Moore, Paul Nash and Graham Sutherland. Only two prominent journalists treated the show with intelligent sympathy: Cyril Connolly in *The Bystander* and (remarkably, in view of his later public persona as fogeyish teddy-bear and national treasure) John Betjeman for the *Evening Standard*. But if the fourth estate was blind to any merit in the Surrealist cause, the artists themselves were quick and generous in recognizing talent in each other, and made their admiration concrete in the most agreeable way by buying each other's work. Jennings bought one of the Magrittes, number 171 in the catalogue, *On the Threshold of Liberty* (1930),[62] and Éluard bought at least one picture by Jennings. As Roland Penrose recalled, the French Surrealists reacted warmly to what they saw as Jennings's unEnglish virtues:

> Humphrey combined the visual sense with his knowledge and that was something that was very rare. In England we are very apt not to have that visual sense sufficiently developed. But with Humphrey it was highly developed and he of course used it in various different ways. His painting was a thing which fascinated me because it was so very personal too. He painted rather in secret. He didn't exhibit, ever,[63] except when it came to the point of the great Exhibition and there he did exhibit several small

canvases. Very beautiful ones, and they were at once noticed by our Surrealist friends from abroad. Breton and Éluard at once spotted Humphrey Jennings as one of the painters who were of importance and of course liked him at once because they found a great deal in common with his knowledge of poetry, his sense of poetry and his sense of society . . .[64]

By the time the exhibition closed on 4 July, Surrealism had been firmly planted in the British national consciousness – not necessarily as a good thing, but definitely as a part of the modern world. Three days later, Penrose played host to a semi-official gathering: those present were Eileen Agar, Edward Burra, Hugh Sykes Davies, Merlyn Evans, David Gascoyne, Jennings, Rupert Lee, Sheila Legge, Len Lye, Henry Moore, Paul Nash, Penrose, Read, George Reavey, Roger Roughton, Ruthven Todd and Julian Trevelyan. The indispensable declaration was signed by all present, and was duly published by Anton Zwemmer that September as the fourth *Bulletin of Surrealism*. At long last, Britain had its own Surrealist Group.

*

Meanwhile, Jennings was also devoting his energies to forging other, less professional types of relationship. David Gascoyne, still only nineteen (he turned twenty in October 1936), began to write a journal in the wake of the exhibition. He later published sections from it, and his diaries offer us some of the most vivid first-hand accounts of Jennings's character and conduct. Jennings is present from the very outset; the first entry is for 22 September that year: 'Humphrey Jennings, who was at Emily's last Wednesday, seems to be having an increased influence on my ideas: there is no one like him, and I would sacrifice half-a-dozen acquaintances for his, though the feeling I have is entirely intellectual . . .'[65] At almost exactly the same time, Jennings had become a character in another intimate journal – that of the novelist Antonia White:

18 Sept   I had the feeling I like best – of flow and communication between people the other night, sitting up till 4.30 a.m. with [Humphrey] Jennings, [David] Gascoyne, Emily and [Samuel] Hoare. Jennings was amusing about his constant images – the horse, the electric light bulb, the train, Byron, the prism . . .[66]

Jennings helped Antonia White to publish, in *Contemporary Poetry and Prose*, her poem 'Epitaph', rejected by the *New Statesman* as 'too violent and emotional' – an episode which prompted her to remark: 'It is amusing to be called too violent and to appear for the first time in poetry among the revolutionary young. I feel much more at ease and stimulated among the young – [George] Barker, Jennings, Gascoyne than among the [Cyril] Connollys, [Peter] Quennells, [Raymond] Mortimers . . .'[67] (The emphasis on the youthfulness of these revolutionaries is slightly odd: born in 1899, Antonia White was only eight years older than Jennings, and Quennell only two.) On 13 October 1936, after a visit to Roland Penrose's house, Gascoyne wrote:

> I went up to dine in Hampstead. Herbert Read was there, talking with difficulty, not saying much. I tried hard to be a little animated, but it was like trying to push a wall over with one hand – the Lees, Hugh Sykes Davies and Humphrey Jennings came in afterwards, for a 'committee meeting'. Humphrey, as usual, was boiling over with energy and excitement; he brought a lot of photographs with him which he had just taken, one of which – a horse and an electric light-bulb – he gave to me. When the 'business' was over, I listened to him having a most animated discussion with Valentine Penrose, who had evidently taken to him. 'Voilà un vrai révolté!', she cried, turning to the room at large . . .[68]

Though, with one or two exceptions, British Surrealism was on the whole a far less sexually charged phenomenon than its French counterpart, there were obviously plenty of erotic energies in the air, and Jennings was among those animated by them. On 22 October, Gascoyne notes:

> Extraordinary news. Antonia tells me that Humphrey and Emily are wildly in love with one another. She says that Emily's behaviour is positively wild with elation, and that she threw her hat over Waterloo Bridge.
> Humphrey and Emily; Antonia and I. 'One each', I said. She laughed . . .[69]

The 'Emily' referred to by both Gascoyne and White was Emily Coleman.[70] This is the first record of Jennings's sexual infidelity; quite a few more such episodes were to follow, before, during and after the war, including, no doubt, some which have never been discovered and at least one which I have readily agreed not to make public while some of those involved are still alive.

Exhilarated as he seems to have been by his sudden love affair with Emily, Jennings had good reason to be depressed by other developments both at home, where he still lacked reliable employment, and overseas. In July, the long-threatened Civil War had finally broken out in Spain – a calamity widely viewed as the prelude to a more widespread conflict between Fascism and democracy. The English Surrealists, aligned (if awkwardly) with the British Left and internationalist in spirit, were among the many young intellectuals who felt obliged to join in the struggle against Franco in some way or other. Roland Penrose and his wife promptly joined the Independent Labour Party, affiliated to the anarchist Workers' Party of Marxist Unity, the POUM (in whose ranks George Orwell was to fight), and set off to Barcelona with David Gascoyne to assemble the basic materials for a propaganda camaign in support of the Republicans. Jennings's brother-in-law Edward was among those idealists who enlisted in the International Brigade; for a time, it seems, Jennings himself agonized about whether he too should join up, but was soon talked out of it. He was one of the eleven signatories of an incendiary 'Declaration on Spain' by the 'Surrealist Group in England', which was published in November 1936, and concluded:

we support the popular demand that the ban on the export of arms to the Spanish Government be lifted. We accuse our National Government of duplicity and anti-democratic intrigue, and call upon it to make at once the only possible reparation

ARMS
FOR THE PEOPLE OF SPAIN

Yet, happy as he no doubt was to add his name to this appeal, there are signs that Jennings was beginning to have his doubts about other aspects of the British Surrealist project. His growing sense of discomfort and disaffiliation was apparent in a combative, at times withering review he wrote for the December issue of *Contemporary Poetry and Prose* of the Faber & Faber book *Surrealism* – a dismayingly (as Jennings thought) sumptuous volume, edited by Herbert Read and with contributions from André Breton, Hugh Sykes Davies, Georges Hugnet and Paul Éluard. 'How,' Jennings began by asking, 'can one open this book, so expensive, so *well* produced, so conformistly printed . . . and compare it even for a moment with the passion, terror and excitement . . . which emanated from *La Révolution Surréaliste* and *Le Surréalisme au Service de la Révolution . . .*?'[71]

The general tendency of the Anglo-Saxon contributors to the volume, Jennings thought, was in effect to castrate Surrealism and render it respectable and utile, particularly to the growing industry of Public Relations. ('Our "advanced" poster designers and "emancipated" business men – what a gift Surrealism is to them when it is presented in the auras of "necessity", "culture" and "truth" with which Read and Sykes Davies invest it.'[72]) He was particularly offended by Herbert Read's suggestion that Surrealism was no more than the most modern phase of Romanticism, and used Breton's article in the book – which emphasized the importance to Surrealism of the coincidence – as the main cudgel with which to beat Read's argument. To define Surrealism as a mode of Romanticism, Jennings contended, was

> to cling to the apparition with its special 'haunt'. It is to look for ghosts only on battlements, and on battlements only for ghosts. 'Coincidences' have the infinite freedom of appearing anywhere, anytime, to anyone: in broad daylight to those whom we most despise in places we have most loathed: not even to *us* at all: probably least of all to petty seekers after mystery and poetry on deserted sea-shores and in misty junk-shops.[73]

It is a passage worth pondering. Many of Jennings's later collaborators would emphasize how much stock he placed on the role of what could reasonably be called *hasard objectif* – symbolic flukes, significant chance happenings, happy unplanned juxtapositions; though one should add that he was not always happy to tag these events with the precise term 'coincidence'. In his contribution to the memorial pamphlet published soon after Jennings's death, Ian Dalrymple would recall: 'Once when he went to shoot a cargo ship for a symbolic purpose he discovered, to his joy and amazement, that her name was BRITISH GENIUS. He rang up from the North with huge satisfaction just to tell me. I said "Oh Humphrey, you do have the luck." But he didn't think it was luck, or coincidence; it was the truth that won't be denied. Things like that were always happening to him . . .'

Jennings ended his review of Read's volume with the gloomy – and, at times, slightly cryptic – vision of a tepid, ersatz form of Surrealism, which would be an unintentional parody of 'the enduring statements of Picasso, early Chirico, Duchamp, Klee, Magritte, and of certain Dalis':

> so deadly agile is man's mind that it is possible, even easy to form a series of 'truths' and 'loyalties' which produce imitations of the creative powers of non-selectivity; forgetting that Surrealism is only a means and believing in the 'universal truth' of it . . . 'To the poet everything is the object of sensations and consequently of sentiments. Everything becomes food for his imagination' (Éluard, p. 174). But for the English to awaken from the sleep of selectivity, what a task. And to be *already* a 'painter', a 'writer', an 'artist', a 'surrealist', what a handicap.[74]

And yet, however grave his doubts in the last months of 1936, it can still be argued that the experience of Surrealism was crucial to Jennings's intellectual and artistic development; and however much he may have begun to consider it a disadvantage to work under a banner inscribed 'Surrealism', he continues to be listed in the more compendious dictionaries of the movement, and not merely because of a handful of poems and collages that happen to look the part. Some critics have argued that even his wartime films can only be fully appreciated in the light of Surrealist aesthetics.

In the course of the interview he gave to Kevin Daly in 1981, Roland Penrose made a number of perceptive points when trying to characterize the particular nature of Jennings's Surrealism, which managed to reconcile apparently contradictory commitments to revolutionary idealism and to conservative patriotism:

> . . . we felt that thing the Surrealists were always talking about: being *intégral* – that's to say not being just an artist, but being involved in society, in the needs of society; Humphrey felt [it] very strongly and [was] unlike the French surrealists who had really spat out all patriotism, spat out the idea of the State . . . for them that was something evil – 'open the prisons; disband the army . . .' were their sort of war cries. We appreciated that. But

we felt, I think, less revolutionary in that particular way . . . our attitude was more temperate than theirs . . .

Humphrey was very creative in all he did. His work in films particularly was . . . of great use in changing the ideas of society but also sustaining them to some degree, not breaking them down completely . . .

. . . there was this curious nationalist, patriotic side in Humphrey, which from the purely surrealist point of view was rather shocking. But from Humphrey's point of view it added certainly a genuine feeling of activity and a sort of solidarity between England, which he loved, and the whole revolutionary attitude which surrealism stood for. 'Change life' was certainly one of the war cries of all Surrealists, and Humphrey took notice of that very much. But his way of changing life was more tactful, was more constructive in a way than just an iconoclasm which would break up everything.

I don't mean to suggest that Humphrey was a patriot in the conventional way at all. His patriotism was far deeper than that. He was certainly anti-military. And anti-society when it became organized in an absurd way . . . But he had a great feeling for the construction of English society, English landscape and English way of living. And that's what comes out very strongly, I think, in his films. More and more so as they went on.[75]

Whatever his misgivings, Jennings was to remain actively involved with the Surrealists for at least another three or four years, participating as writer, editor, artist and fervent public speaker. 'Two American Poems', his last appearance in Surrealist pages, was published as late as March 1939, and he had some kind of status as an inactive member of the Surrealist Group in England until 1947. But he was loyal to the movement as he defined it, not necessarily as others might; and in the late months of 1936, Jennings's extracurricular interests had already begun to lead him out of a Surrealism conceived mainly as a matter of painting, poetry and photography, and into a quite different Surrealist practice: a form of 'domestic anthropology', soon to be widely known as Mass-Observation.

Five

1936 to 1939: From Mass-Observation to *Spare Time*

A singular glimpse into the daily routine of life *chez* the Jennings family of Blackheath, April 1937, composed by the man of the house:

> Woke up earlier or more easily than usual about 7.45. Got up at 8 exactly hearing front door bell to let in daily woman. Did this instead of C[icely] without difficulty. Someone has to do it every morning. Put on her dressing gown: warmer than mine. Agreed to have bath first this morning, and to turn on hers when I had done. Remembered that as I had got up first I must rake fire etc.: didn't want to. Did it however and then realised that I should have turned on bath first to save time and to have it ready. Did teeth while bath water was running: put too much mouth wash into mug: have a tendency to do this as too much produces a 'kick' like a neat spirit. Had bath, getting in water while water was still running: sat up and washed neck as there was not enough water to lie down in yet: usually lie down and soak first. Noticed sand on bottom of bath: M.L. [Mary-Lou] had played in sand-pit yesterday and M— had said that there would be sand in bath at night. Remembered this. On leaving bathroom just remembered to spread out bath towel; left bath mat untidy; noticed this but did nothing. Saw M.L. in her nursery for a moment – she had been crying but smiled at me. Came down to dress. C. had my dressing gown on: it looked old and shapeless. She reminded me to put on clean things (it being Monday.) This I did except for socks which I had changed the day before. . . .[1]

Not, to be sure, the most scintillating or cunningly modulated piece of prose Jennings would ever write; but then, it was never intended as a work of eloquence. Rather than a personal diary (he had seldom been in the habit of keeping such intimate journals, anyway), this somewhat plodding exercise in logging the unconsidered trifles of everyday life was a 'day report', written up in the pursuit of a new 'science of ourselves' – a 'science' partly created by Jennings himself: Mass-Observation. Before long, hundreds of other Mass-Observation recruits across the nation were busy filing similar day reports on the 12th of each month, and the most conscientious of them were striving to attain the same minute attention to the smallest details of their actions, feelings, thoughts and environments as Jennings was attempting in his exhaustive catalogue of morning bathroom procedures.

Far from being an occasional risk of the day-report method, the note of triviality – even to the point of tedium – was part of the exercise's point. In making a would-be objective attempt to find out exactly how people lived and what they believed, it was crucial for the recorder to have no hampering preconceptions about what might or might not count as a significant detail; and, whatever the other shortcomings of their method, the Mass-Observers were surely right in this refusal to discriminate. Today, for example, more than sixty years after that April morning, one of the unwitting revelations in Jennings's monthly report that strikes the reader is that middle-class English intellectuals of the 1930s felt a once-weekly change of clothes to be more than adequate. Another is that, chronically hard-up as they were – and Jennings mentions no daily occupation more remunerative than his volunteer work at Mass-Observation HQ (in less grand terms, 6 Grote's Buildings, Blackheath, London SE3, the house of his old Cambridge friends Charles Madge and Kathleen Raine, now a married couple) – the Jenningses were still somehow able to afford a daily help.

A closer reading of the 12 April report yields many more such minor insights, and the total body of thousands and thousands of Mass-Observation reports – now held in a large and much-visited archive at the University of Sussex – amounts to an unparalleled source of first-hand information about the mood, the texture, the smell, almost, of everyday British life in the late 1930s and early 1940s. Though it was criticized in its own time by journals of both the Left and the Right, and has sometimes been treated patronizingly in histories and memoirs of the period, few who have made an unprejudiced review of its accomplishments would disagree with the historian Tom Jeffrey's verdict that it was 'a decent and honourable organisation', as well as a highly instructive one. Its legacy has been far-reaching, and its full richness far from exhausted by the legions of historians, sociologists, literary scholars and other researchers who have used its archives. As one might have guessed, Jennings – never one of nature's joiners, and usually quick to develop heretical tendencies within any movement he did join – did not stay with Mass-Observation for very long. He quit after a series of angry confrontations with Tom Harrisson, early in 1938. Nonetheless, he was indisputably the movement's co-creator, and deserves a good measure of credit for what it achieved in its first exciting months.

*

Mass-Observation, by informed consent one of the defining cultural phenomena of Britain in the 1930s and already a household term throughout Britain by the time war came, had its modest origins in a series of private discussions between Jennings, Charles Madge, David Gascoyne and Stuart Legg at Madge's house in the autumn and winter of 1936[2] – talks prompted, in part, by the highly charged public reaction to the impending abdication of King Edward VIII, which had suggested (among other things) that despite all the social upheavals of the years since the Armistice, the royal family continued to enjoy an immense imaginative hold over the minds of the populace. To thoughtful watchers, the atmosphere of the time smacked of Shakespearean tragedy, with the disorder in the royal household seemingly echoed in omens and portents – above all, in the spectacular destruction by fire of the Crystal Palace[3] just before the scandalous news of Edward and Mrs Simpson was made public. 'That it was significant,' wrote the novelist Compton Mackenzie, 'the superstitious agreed; it was when they tried to interpret the significance that opinions differed.'[4]

Among the texts that gave point and direction to the Blackheath discussions were, first, an article on the place of 'myth' in national politics written by a progressive Cambridge schoolmaster, Geoffrey Pyke, in the *New Statesman* of 5 September, then his subsequent letter (12 December): 'There has been concentrated in the last ten days the reactions of the people of the British Empire to a sexual situation. Here, in a relatively limited form, is some of the material for that anthropological study of our own situation of which we stand in such desperate need.' Jennings, Madge and co. agreed with the general thrust of Pyke's analysis, and decided that they were the very men to get things started, regardless of their lack of formal – or even informal – training in anthropological methods. Thanks to a freak of *hasard objectif* which would delight their Surrealist sensibilities, that shortage of expertise was about to be remedied from a quite unexpected quarter.

*

Born in South America in 1911, the son of a former British Army general turned managing director of the Argentinian railway system, Tom Harrisson was an exceptionally charismatic, authoritarian, ferociously independent figure of the strong character type American sociologists would later term 'inner-directed'; at times, his contemporaries and countrymen would probably have favoured the term 'bloody-minded' or 'cantankerous'.[5] Like Richard Burton, T. E. Lawrence, George Orwell and other nonconformist English writer-travellers, Harrisson was part courageous man of action, part rigorous scholar, part adventurer and part bully. Educated at Harrow, he became a precociously accomplished ornithologist, and by his early twenties – already nationally respected by his peers and the author of two classic studies in the field – had taken part in naturalist expeditions to Lapland and St Kilda. After dropping out of undergraduate studies at Cambridge, where his best friend was Malcolm Lowry, he led a scientific expedition to Borneo, and then continued alone and on his own initiative to Malekula in the New Hebrides, where he lived for two years with a cannibal tribe until picked up (a typically unlikely Harrisson adventure) by the Hollywood star Douglas Fairbanks Sr, who just happened to be sailing around the world in search of exotic footage. Declining Fairbanks's generous offer to go and work in the American film industry as an expert on cannibals, Harrisson instead wrote up his tribal experiences in a book entitled *Savage Civilization* (first impression: January 1937), which became a minor best-seller for Victor Gollancz's recently founded Left Book Club, as well as for Knopf in the United States.

He decided to bring his personal quest for knowledge back home. As he later wrote, in a succinct if indelicately phrased summary of his intellectual development:

In my teens and twenties I was a biologist and was sent to various and remote places of the world to study birds and animals and later to study human beings . . . But it gradually became borne in upon me that what I was doing at great expense to various scientific bodies, as well as at considerable cost to my own time and health, could equally be done at home, within our own civilisation. The wilds of Lancashire or the mysteries of the East End of London were as little explored as the cannibal interior of the New Hebrides or the head-hunter hinterland of Borneo . . . In particular, my experiences living among cannibals in the New Hebrides . . . taught me the many common points between these wild-looking, fuzzy-haired, black, smelly people and our own, so when I came home from that expedition I determined to apply the same methods here in Britain.[6]

Harrisson duly set himself up in the Lancashire cotton town of Bolton, working by day in a variety of casual jobs (as lorry driver, ice-cream man, labourer), spending the evenings either in pubs, at political meetings or – via prodigious social somersaults – well-scrubbed and doused with cologne, hobnobbing at quite another level of Lancashire society with the Leverhulmes, wealthy owners of the Unilever Combine. As Harrisson later explained in a digressive passage of his war memoir, *World Within*:

The one and only thing which I could find that affected the lives of people in all the places I had been to everywhere in the world was the Unilever Combine. Even the cannibals in the mountains of Melanesia were touched by the tentacles of this colossus, buying copra, selling soap. Unilever stemmed directly from William Lever. He was born and started business in Bolton. So I followed there . . .[7]

Harrisson chanced across a letter by Charles Madge in the *New Statesman* for 2 January 1937 headed 'Anthropology at Home', while in the Bolton Public Library looking to see whether his poem 'Coconut Moon' – the one and only verse work of his entire literary career – had been published there. It had, and (enter *l'hasard objectif*) it was laid out immediately next to Madge's letter. Harrisson instantly saw the opportunity to turn a one-man project into a major research enterprise. He made contact with the Blackheath group, and took the train to London. As David Gascoyne recalled this meeting, 'Humphrey Jennings had a habit of talking with his elbow on the mantelpiece – and he was at one end of the mantelpiece talking at the top of his voice, and Harrisson was at the other end doing exactly the same thing, talking at the top of *his* voice.'[8] If Gascoyne's memory is accurate, it must have been obvious to everyone that a major clash of egos within the embryonic movement was going to prove all but inevitable. Any such misgivings were swept aside in the excitement of parturition, though, and within three weeks, Mass-Observation was a going concern.

On 30 January, the signatures of Jennings and Madge – by this time an intermittently active member of the Communist Party, working unhappily as a journalist on the *Daily Mirror* – were joined by that of Harrisson beneath another *New Statesman* letter. (Jennings, as it happened, had not seen the text of it, and was annoyed that his name had been added without his agreement.[9]) The manifesto-letter declared:

> Mass-Observation develops out of anthropology, psychology, and the sciences which study man – but it plans to work with a mass of observers. Already we have fifty observers at work on two sample problems. We are further working out a complete plan of campaign, which will be possible when we have not fifty but 5,000 observers. The following are a few examples of the problems that will arise:
>
>> Behaviour of people at war memorials
>> Shouts and gestures of motorists
>> The aspidistra cult
>> Anthropology of football pools
>> Bathroom behaviour
>> Beards, armpits, eyebrows
>> Anti-semitism
>> Distribution, diffusion and significance of the dirty joke
>> Funerals and undertakers
>> Female taboos about eating
>> The private lives of midwives

After this quaint list – which, as many have pointed out, itself reads somewhat like a Surrealist poem – the letter concluded that Mass-Observation does not set out in quest of truth or facts for their own sake, or for the sake of an intellectual minority, but aims at exposing them in simple terms to all observers, so that their environment may be understood and thus constantly transformed. Whatever the political methods called upon to effect the transformation, the knowledge of what has to be transformed is indispensable. The foisting on the mass of ideals or ideas developed by men apart from it, irrespective of its capacities, causes mass misery, intellectual despair and an international shambles.

The confident tone of this proclamation masked differences of intellectual interest and ambition that were almost guaranteed to split the movement into factions. At the simplest level, Mass-Observation was divided from the outset between two headquarters, with two distinct modes of operation. Its northern wing was an elaboration of Harrisson's existing one-man Bolton project, based in a small terraced house in Davenport Street (long since demolished, as I discovered in the summer of 2000). As recruits flooded in to join M-O, Harrisson ceased working as a Malinowski-style solo 'participant observer' and became more like a field general, sending his troops out on information raids: eavesdropping on conversations in pubs and stores, visiting fortune-tellers and football matches, compiling statistics on everything from the average time taken to consume a pint of bitter in the pub to the etiquette of queues. Some of the Observers, particularly the working-class locals, were paid small sums from Harrisson's own pocket; more were unpaid volunteers. Thanks to Harrisson's considerable powers of persuasion, a number of his recruits turned out to be remarkably talented. The embryonic politician Woodrow Wyatt, who was immediately captured for M-O when Harrisson went to address his Oxford literary society, recalls: 'I was deeply impressed by Tom Harrisson's vigour and denunciation of everyone else ... I thought everything he did was wonderful.'[10] As soon as term ended, Wyatt set out for Bolton – 'Worktown' as it soon became known in M-O literature and slang – and was hurled into an exhausting, exhilarating regime working sixteen hours a day and more, taking meals only when Harrisson's whim permitted:

[Harrisson] would rarely shave but would plunge out of bed unwashed into the front room and begin to write emphatic letters

and articles. One of my duties was to keep a portable gramophone
in the corner going as he liked to have a good background of
noise to his work. He had a weakness for George Formby and a
record we played again and again was 'Chinese Laundry Blues'
... Often we would wait until night-time before eating when
Tom would suddenly put on an overcoat and we would march
out to a fish-and-chip shop.[11]

Besides clever and impressionable undergraduates, the 'Worktown'
project attracted a number of artists who had already entered on their
careers, and Harrisson's cramped and grimy HQ produced some
substantial bodies of creative work as well as a store of sociological
data. The photographer Humphrey Spender started to pay flying visits
to Davenport Street when his work commitments for the *Daily Mirror*
allowed, and the images he made of Bolton at this time, until the
autumn of 1938 when he joined *Picture Post*, are still considered high
points of his artistic career. Julian Trevelyan took the narrow road to
the deep north, too, and was set to painting pictures and making
collages of street scenes. A brace of painters from the Euston Road
School, William Coldstream and Graham Bell, also joined up: Coldstream produced a well-known panoramic view of the town as seen
from the roof of the Public Library. Several young literary chaps, later
to become famous as writers and politicians, joined Harrisson's ranks
– Richard Crossman, Tom Driberg (aka 'William Hickey' of the *Daily
Express*) – while William Empson was assigned to take notes on the
contents of sweetshop windows. The assignments could be exciting,
an adventure, a lot of fun; but for most of these young men, the desire
to make contact with the hitherto unknown working classes was in
large part a question of duty, too. As Trevelyan wrote, 'I was aware,
not for the first time, of the gulf that separated me from these English
workers, the gulf of education, language, accent and social behaviour.
It was my constant desire during these years to bridge that gulf and
occasionally I succeeded.'[12]

Jennings was among those who made the journey to Bolton
whenever possible, and immediately set to work taking photographs
and painting townscapes. (Humphrey Spender recalls[13] having been in
the same room as Jennings for Harrisson's morning briefings, when
tasks for the day were issued, but, sadly, has no memory of ever

talking with him.) Some of Jennings's images, like other visual documents of Mass-Observation's sojourn in the town, are now preserved
in the Bolton Museum and Art Gallery, notably his 'Elephant Gate,
Bridson's Bleach Works', a photograph greatly admired by the critic
Michel Remy, a leading authority on British Surrealism, for its discovery of a fantastical element – a quasi-totemic elephant and castle
– in the most prosaic industrial surroundings. The profile of Jennings
in the journal by 'George Pitman' (Allen Hutt) suggests that, brief
as it was, Jennings's time in Bolton was the catalyst for his mature
work:

> At 5 a.m. on a summer day in the middle nineteen-thirties, a
> young man, with a Leica . . . over his shoulder, stepped out of the
> station at Bolton and took his first look at that typical Lancashire
> manufacturing town. He saw more than Bolton: the vision of
> mill-stacks and operatives' dwelling-boxes introduced him to an
> England he had not known before: the land of industry, of the
> factory and of the working class.
>
> That was perhaps the most important turning-point in the life
> of Humphrey Jennings, who is now someone quite special among
> our small band of film-directing aces. It explains, incidentally, the
> whole angle of his first piece of direction, the masterly *Spare Time*.
>
> Bolton, and the months he spent there working with Mass-
> Observation, living in an unemployed miner's house, and avidly
> attacking the classics like Engels' *Condition of the Working Class in
> England*, brought Jennings (as he himself says) from mediaevalism
> into modern times . . .[14]

'Months' must be either a dramatic exaggeration or a trick of
someone's memory, for Jennings simply did not have the freedom to
leave London for long periods at this time. Apart from heeding the
claims of family life, he also had his hands full organizing the other
wing of Mass-Observation from Blackheath with Charles Madge – that
is, recruiting volunteers to write day reports on the 12th of every
month, then, with the help of a new secretary, collecting and analysing
the results (for example, by producing statistics on the rates of beer
consumption).

This was one aspect of M-O activity. The other was the production
of field reports by M-O researchers who made notes on the everyday

lives of their fellow citizens in the spirit of a Malinowskian participant observer making notes on the activities of the Trobriand Islanders. It soon proved to be an overwhelmingly large task. In the early months of 1937, M-O recruited some five hundred Observers, and by the end of their first year of operation Madge's house was swamped with reportage; according to a newspaper report of the time,[15] some 2,300,000 words of day-report material had accumulated, creating a condition of 'infinite regress' – information streamed in far more quickly than M-O could ever hope to process it. (The practice of collecting day reports was largely given up in 1938, save for a few special occasions.)

The geographical gap within M-O mirrored an ideological divide. Where Harrisson regarded himself first and foremost as a social scientist, Madge and Jennings were a great deal more interested in what can be called the poetic side of Mass-Observation; indeed, they were persuaded that they were acting as midwives to an entirely new form of literature, and published joint articles justifying this belief in New Verse and Life and Letters Today.[16] Many of those who volunteered as Observers, perhaps thwarted in their literary ambitions, were attracted by the idea of seeing their words appear in print even if only anonymously. Some succeeded, the most conspicuous being the working-class novelist and playwright Bill Naughton, who would win fame as the author of Alfie. Others in the Blackheath circle agreed that the enterprise had roots much deeper than any merely documentary ambition. Looking back on these times from the perspective of the early 1970s, Kathleen Raine recalled:

> To Charles [Madge], who seemed at that time a man inspired, the idea of Mass-Observation was less sociology than a kind of poetry, akin to Surrealism. He saw the expression of the unconscious collective life of England, literally, in writings on the walls, telling of the hidden thoughts and dreams of the inarticulate masses. In these he read, as the augurs of antiquity read the entrails or the yarrow-stalks, those strange and ominous dreams of the years just before the second world war.[17]

She had – or, in retrospect, realized that she had suffered from – grave misgivings:

The strange spirits which were let loose upon our world made their entrance through 'possession' such as ours. Its English form seemed harmless enough; philanthropic, as Charles and his Marxist friends conceived it; yet our possession was akin not only to French *Surréalisme* but to the more violent upsurge of the irrational forces in Nazi Germany. None of those Surrealists or Mass-Observers at that time engaged in opening the dungeons of the unconscious and freeing energies imprisoned there had the wisdom to gauge, or the power to control or to transmute what came to light . . .

The poetic side of Mass-Observation captivated me; but the political side made me shrink and shudder. There was something in the faces, in the spiritual atmosphere, of some of Charles's Communist friends which I sensed as evil.[18]

Whether or not she was right to detect a whiff of brimstone in the enterprise, Kathleen Raine is certainly correct in emphasizing the degree to which it had political motives, albeit mixed ones. Madge was still a convinced if often dormant Communist; when anyone asked where he was, the inevitable reply was 'out chalking' – that is, writing slogans on walls.[19] Harrisson was, so his colleagues generally concluded, a sort of Liberal; and though the political temper of M-O was, as one might expect, broadly of the Left, a surprising number of Conservatives also took part.

Tom Jeffery's history of Mass-Observation usefully sums up the three fundamental concerns of its early years. First, and most obviously, that fascination with the role of myth and superstition in national life which had set the Observational ball rolling in the first place. Second, the no less important policy of principled antipathy towards, and suspicion of, Fleet Street – a suspicion brought to boiling point during the abdication crisis, when the national press followed the tight-lipped example of Chamberlain and willingly censored itself, giving none of the facts about the imminent abdication until the very last moment, and when foreign newspapers came under the censor's scissors before they were allowed to reach the news-stands. Lastly, as the unanimous testimony of those involved in the 'Worktown' expedition shows, the founders of Mass-Observation were determined to face up to an unpalatable fact: that there was a vast and all but unbridgeable gap of ignorance between the classes, which meant not only that the ruling and middle classes knew almost nothing of the frame of mind of the workers, but – a fact less often noted – that the workers found their rulers equally inscrutable. There had been a number of previous attempts to address these issues, and for a variety of motives. Market research and opinion-polling, for example, were both thriving businesses that had already achieved a fair degree of complexity by the late 1930s. Mass-Observation borrowed some investigative tools from these agencies, but its founders were determined that the information they gathered should be made democratically available to all.

As Jeffery puts it, M-O was to be 'a science of ourselves, for ourselves'.[20] In the last anxious years before the European war that everyone but the most self-deceiving knew was coming, there was no shortage of illuminating data to be gathered.

*

If Jennings needed any further reminder of the gathering storm[21] – unlikely, since, as M-O's soundings were starting to confirm, all levels of society were prey to swelling anxieties about an imminent European war – he need have looked no further than his in-laws. In February 1937, Cicely Jennings's brother Edward Cooper was killed fighting for the Republic in the Spanish Civil War. A young member of the Communist Party, he had become completely estranged from his father, who refused to speak either to him or of him. He had gone to Spain in the autumn of 1936 and 'simply disappeared'. His younger brother Arthur used to go along to the headquarters of the CP in King Street, Covent Garden, and ask if there had been any news, only to be told, 'Go away, little boy.' By the time that Edward's death was eventually confirmed, in August of that year, his father had also died. The CP's vile treatment of Arthur Cooper did not, however, prevent Jennings from feeling the attraction of Communist doctrines, and though he never joined the Party's ranks he often sympathized with its analyses at this time and became, as the 'Pitman' article suggests, a thoughtful student of the classical texts of Marx and Engels, as well as their elaborations by Lenin and others.

While the better part of his daily time and energy was now being devoted to Mass-Observation, Jennings did not yet abandon his Surrealist commitments, though not all of his works-in-progress came to fruition. *Contemporary Poetry and Prose* announced the imminent publication of '*Reports and Photographs* by Humphrey Jennings'; the volume never appeared. He remained fitfully active within the group at least until 1940, but there were frequent signs that he was chafing under the yoke. David Gascoyne's journal entry for 8 April 1937 records an unusually lively gathering of the London Surrealists at their usual venue, Roland Penrose's house in Hampstead:

> The surrealist meeting, at which all the boys were present except [Henry] Moore and Hugh [Sykes Davies], was gloriously funny. [Roger] Roughton and Jennings suggested that for various reasons the group should disband itself, which the group, presided over by a surprisingly astringent [Herbert] Read, indignantly refused to do. Abuse flew from corner to corner of Roland's polite, sumptuously decorated drawing room. 'I'm sorry, but all you've been saying is *absolute balls!*' Presently Humphrey, a very recent convert to the Party line ('And do you belong to the party, then?' he is asked. 'No,' he replies, 'I am not worthy!'), announced in tones of furious, long-tried patience: 'Well, now I'd like to read you a few lines of *Lenin* on the subject', and read a long passage from Lenin on dreams, implying that the dreams of those present were of the kind that fly off at a tangent and are of no service to the 'toiling masses of humanity' – a phrase which he continued to use every few minutes for the rest of the evening. Whereupon [Paul] Nash, who had been being most consistently futile ever since he arrived, completely losing the point, remarked that he entirely agreed with Lenin, and that he thought the passage quoted most applicable to the group; and then relapsed into an absorption with his little pocket asthma-apparatus. In the end R. [presumably Roughton, not Read] and J. resigned (much to everyone's relief) and we all went downstairs to drink beer and whiskey.[22]

Dramatic as it was, Jennings's resignation from the group was either withdrawn or tactfully forgotten on all sides, and Surrealism continued to colour his private experiments as well as his public career. As he mentions to himself in his 12 April day report,

> Crossing loggia noticed contrast of bicycles, old boxes and rubbish with sunny garden seen through round-headed arches. Nearly photographed one arch as I have experienced that in photograph-

ing from shadow through an arch into sunlight a curious optical
effect is produced . . . Wandered into churchyard to take photo of
tombs: as I was using filter I had to wait a long time for really
good sun. Shot no good in the end because while waiting for sun
I was afraid someone would come and complain of my photographing in churchyard. Walked again. Arrived about 2.30. As I
rang bell I thought 'I suppose photography has to get more and
more realistic as one gets older.'

His friends, not for the first time, wondered whether he might not
be spreading himself too thin as an artist and intellectual, or be in
danger of excitedly talking away into thin air more projects than he
tackled. Just a few days after the 12 April report, David Gascoyne used
his own (personal, non-M-O) diary to issue himself the stern reprimand:
'Warning: when you think you've got hold of a new idea or point
of view, don't dissipate all your enthusiasm by talking about it to
everyone you know. (This is what Humphrey Jennings does, though,
and it doesn't seem to do him any harm; or perhaps he would produce
more work if he could check the verbal flow a little more?)'[23] Perhaps
so. Still, even when he was not busy making money from freelance
work in the film industry, Jennings was being highly productive by
most people's standards. His poems, essays and other writings kept on
appearing in Surrealist journals – the spring 1937 issue of *Contemporary
Poetry and Prose* included his 'Report on the Industrial Revolution':

The material transformer of the world had just been born. It was
trotted out in its skeleton, to the music of a mineral train from
the black country, with heart and lungs and muscles exposed to
view in complex hideosity. It once ranged wild in the marshy
forests of the Netherlands, where the electrical phenomenon and
the pale blue eyes connected it with apparitions, demons, wizards
and divinities.

And in the midst of his other preoccupations, he was about to
create the most substantial of his literary works to be published in his
lifetime, which was also the weightiest legacy of his involvement
with Mass-Observation: his collage-documentary on the coronation of
George VI, *May the Twelfth: Mass-Observation Day-Survey 1937* (co-edited
with Charles Madge). With an alacrity that must inspire envy in those

used to the protracted mechanisms of publishing today, Faber & Faber would have this volume in the bookshops by September.

Having set off from Blackheath in the early morning of 12 May (his day report opens with a grumpy account of having slept through his 3 a.m. alarm, and so missing the first train into town at 3.45), Jennings spent the day photographing crowds in the Mall and writing detailed notes in longhand; not far from his spot, Henri Cartier-Bresson was doing almost exactly the same.[24] The day report that resulted, typed up on the 12th and 13th, runs to twenty pages of observations both public and intimate:

12. On the right the Abbey choir pours out across the Park. On the left the Marines' bugles blow in the barracks. Down the centre stream thousands of people. North country father to little girl: 'Ah! You'll have to forgo it for a bit – can you manage?'

12.20. Evening newspapers with pictures of the procession are on sale in Buckingham Palace Road: 'Haven't they got them all ready quick?'

At 12.40 at Hyde Park Corner the sound reproduction was definitely not good. The large numbers of wandering people distracted attention from the Crowning. On the words, 'His Majesty King George VI is acclaimed' there is a moment of indecision among the seat holders – whether to stand up or not – and by all whether to take off hats or not. The seat holders cheer first, then as the Abbey cheering comes through they stand up. About half the men in the general crowd raise or take off their hats. Two ice-cream boys push each other about in fun because one hasn't taken his cap off. Then the crowd in Hyde Park cheers and the first gun goes off. All this inside half a minute. Then someone up in Piccadilly gives a long single cheer and odd people near me laugh. As the organ swells up a periscope-seller lurches forward with an almost drunk mock-intonation. Coming away from Hyde Park Corner the guns continue and a little boy with his mouth full of ice-cream asks his father 'What they firing the guns for? What they firing the guns for?' . . .[25]

Jennings's report ends in that favoured locale for Mass-Observers, a pub, near Piccadilly Circus, where he eavesdrops on 'shop-girls' drinking port and champagne cocktails, and records fragments of their talk with the barest minimum of explanatory commentary:

> 6.10. 'We've had a marvellous day, Joe. Everything went as smooth as that.'
> Waiter: 'It was a fine spectacle. I wouldn't have missed it.'
> Girl: 'That service' (buffet service in store) 'was marvellous! It'll take them twenty-five years to get up that energy again.'
>   Other girls come in, and they all get rather drunk.
> '... who's afraid of Big Old Ginger?'
> She: 'I'll kiss you if you're not careful.'
> He: 'I feel scruffy.'
> She: 'So do we all.'
> 'I was sitting on the lavatory, and she. . . . . . .'
> 'Amami [shampoo] Night to-night!'[26]

Once all the reports came in – twelve main texts, written by 'professional' observers, eked out by a number of volunteer diaries – it fell to Jennings and Madge, with the help of (among others) Empson and Kathleen Raine, to cut and shape them into a narrative mosaic – as has been pointed out since the book first appeared, this was a collage or montage technique closely analogous to that of editing rushes, and *May the Twelfth* may be regarded, not too fancifully, as a prose documentary 'film'. According to David Pocock, who provided the afterword for the book's fiftieth anniversary reissue in 1987, Jennings consciously intended the book 'to carry on in prose the experiments being made with the documentary film'.[27] (Hence, too, the *New English Weekly*'s review: 'these notes, or reports, appear to have been treated as though they were so many film "shots", to be put together by a process of cutting, editing and effective juxtaposition, in short, by a process of *montage*'.[28]) Jennings left no record of his editorial labours in Blackheath, but Ruthven Todd recalls being dragged in at the very last moment before the manuscript was due for delivery:

> I never really knew what M.O. was about but, as the errand boy of poetry in the Thirties, I was willing to help out with anything my friends were concerned with ... I sorted papers for Charles [Madge], let Tom Harrisson steal my shoes and otherwise behaved myself. Then I found myself saddled with the job of making a

most complex index for Humphrey's *May the Twelfth* . . . I no longer have a copy of this, but my memory says there were at least two indexes, cross-referenced, and the job had to be done in three days! Well, damn it, I set to work and at 8 a.m. on the third day (during which period I had not slept a wink) I was drawing near to the typing of the horror. Enter Humphrey, kempt, shevelled and well-slept. He advanced to the fire and made it up from a few embers into a tidy blaze.

Then he came forward and picked up two or three sheets from the top of the pile of ts. [typescript] I had beside me. He looked at them casually and turned to me.

'Call this an index?' he asked, with the superior contempt of which he was capable in those days. 'Index? INDEX!'

I was tired, and bored, and fed up. I picked up the whole bundle of ts. and chucked it into the fire which Humphrey had just built up. I have never seen anyone scramble more quickly, and without regard to the fact that he was burning himself, than Humphrey did to pull two or three hundred pages out of the fire. Only a few edges of a few pages were actually burned. Humphrey tapped the whole into a neat heap and came and laid them upon the table upon which I had been working. 'Sorry,' he said and left the room.

I have paused here . . . because it suddenly appears to me that this was the moment upon which our relationship changed. I don't think that after that day in 1937, Humphrey ever treated me with disdain again. He had, I think, been forced to recognise that I was a human being too, with appetites and moods just the same as he had.[29]

Whatever hopes Madge and Jennings may have entertained for this edifice were short-lived. On the happy side, it was widely reviewed, M-O by now being one of the national press's favourite novelties. Less happily, most of the reviews of *May the Twelfth* were dismissive or worse. T. H. Marshall, Reader in Sociology at the University of London, wrote that it was 'so completely devoid of interest that even the most well-intentioned reviewer is at a loss to say anything about its contents'. In similar vein, the *Spectator* opined that 'Scientifically, they [the reports]'re about as valuable as a chimpanzee's tea-party at the zoo', and Evelyn Waugh, in other respects surprisingly friendly to the enterprise, found the book freighted with 'a great deal of pseudo-scientific showmanship'.[30] Perhaps Jennings's disappointment with the general response helped deepen his sense of disaffection with M-O; at any rate, as Charles Madge later observed, *May the Twelfth* 'was the first and last time Humphrey contributed to a Mass-Observation publication. Thereafter he shied away from what he felt to be a banal streak in Tom's expressionist quasi-anthropology.'[31] The book sold about eight hundred copies.

*

Not all of Jennings's energies in 1937 were devoted to artistic and intellectual pursuits. It was this year that he began a short-lived but eventful affair with the American heiress Peggy Guggenheim. Since many of her contemporaries took a dim view of Ms Guggenheim, and posterity has often concurred – she has been variously dismissed, condescended to or reviled as a spoiled brat, a dilettante, a chancer, an ignoramus and a nymphomaniac – it seems only fair to modify this prejudice a little from the outset. Whatever her lapses of taste and intelligence may have been, Peggy Guggenheim nonetheless went on to be one of the twentieth century's most influential and far-sighted patrons of art, a major champion of contemporary European artists from Mondrian and (one of her lovers) Yves Tanguy to Léger and (one of her husbands) Max Ernst, as well as a pioneering advocate of some of the leading American artists of the next generation, including Mark Rothko, Hans Hofmann, William Baziotes and Jackson Pollock. Far from being empty-headed, she was an ardent reader of Dostoevsky and Proust, and had long enjoyed the company of writers and intellectuals. As for the charge of nymphomania (a loaded, dubious insult that often says more about the accuser than the accused), while it is true that she went on to have 'a thousand'[32] lovers, the sum total of her erotic career before she met Jennings was fairly modest by all but the most monastic standards: one husband, two lovers and a one-night stand.

At the time that she became involved with Jennings, Peggy Guggenheim (1898–1979) was thirty-nine years old and undergoing what looks like a classic midlife crisis. For the last fifteen years she had done virtually nothing save try to play the complementary roles of dutiful wife, or wife-equivalent, to three men – her first husband,

Laurence Vail, then her lovers John Holms and Douglas Garman – and of conventional, nurturing mother to her children. But life had not treated her well. Holms, for whom she had left her husband, died while under anaesthetic for a minor operation, since his inner organs had been so damaged by drink; Garman, Holms's successor, had become a fanatical Communist and deserted her at Easter 1937 for a more suitable proletarian woman. Her children were away at school; her mother was in the final stages of a fatal illness, and, as she confided to her friend Emily Coleman, she feared that her own life was over. 'If you feel that way,' Emily replied, 'perhaps it is.'[33]

Instead of caving in to defeat or committing suicide, however, Peggy adopted the Surrealists' great maxim – taken over from the poet Rimbaud – and changed her life. A friend from New York, recognizing both the depths of Peggy's despair and the more cheering, if heartless, consideration that her mother's imminent death would shortly be bringing her an inheritance of some half a million dollars, suggested that she pull herself together and start a business that would at least get her out of the house and force her to meet people. Up to this point, Peggy had shown little interest in visual arts, and certainly not those of any period since the Italian Renaissance; but she resolved on the spot that she would follow the example of her Uncle Solomon, who in June 1937 had announced the establishment of the Solomon Guggenheim Foundation for Non-Objective Art. As her biographer Jacqueline Bogard Weld sums up with admirable terseness: 'Peggy knew nothing about starting an art gallery. She began by having an affair with a young English intellectual by the name of Humphrey Jennings.'[34]

They had met through his former lover Emily Coleman. Peggy Guggenheim's own account of their affair is more than slightly derisive and knockabout, beginning with her observation that Humphrey was 'a sort of genius, and looked like Donald Duck'.[35]

Humphrey came down to [Peggy's house at] Petersfield for the weekend. Emily was there, and as she was finished with him, she offered him to me as though he were a sort of object she no longer required, and I went in his room and took him in the same spirit. He had strange ideas about pleasures in life, and one was to spend the weekend in a millionaire yacht club. He never

achieved this ambition with me, as it was so far removed from
my normal taste. But he did follow me to Paris where I was
staying with my mother in the Hôtel Crillon. When Humphrey
came I took a room in a small hotel on the Rive Gauche. It was
filled with Napoleonic furniture and looked very formal.

Humphrey was very pleased with his ugly, emaciated body.
He kept jumping all over the bed saying, 'Look at me! Don't you
like me? Don't you think I'm beautiful?' I had no desire to spend
the weekend in bed. I insisted on going to the Paris Exposition
every time I could manage to get him out of the hotel. He wanted
to meet Marcel Duchamp, so I took him to see him, and in return
he took me to see André Breton in his little art gallery, Gradiva.
Breton looked like a lion pacing up and down in a cage.[36]

Her account goes on in much the same dismissively comical vein,
representing Humphrey both as a clinging nuisance and as an uncon-
trollable eccentric. He came out to Paris, she recalls, to visit her for a
second weekend, but this time she refused to leave the Crillon, so he
was forced to take a room on his own. Together they went to visit
Yves Tanguy, hoping to arrange a show of the artist's work in London; Humphrey had 'wild ideas' about the way in which Tanguy's
work might be exhibited – ideas which neither Peggy nor Tanguy
could follow, but to which the nonplussed painter made polite noises
of assent. Eventually, she felt obliged to give Humphrey his marching orders, pleading her undiminished love for Garman by way of
excuse. 'We were standing on one of the bridges of the Seine, and
I remember how Humphrey wept. I think he had hopes of some
kind of a wonderful life with me, surrounded by luxury, gaiety and
Surrealism.'[37]

But the emotional outburst appears to have been brief, and the
newly estranged lovers went on to have a good time at the exposition.
They seem to have remained on cordial terms for years to come;
certainly, in the late 1940s, Mary-Lou and Charlotte Jennings knew of
her by the more or less affectionate nickname 'Peg the Gugg'. Had he
been so inclined, Jennings could at least have consoled himself with
the reflection that his brief involvement with Peggy had put him in
unusually distinguished company. His immediate successor as Peggy's
mentor in artistic matters was Marcel Duchamp; his immediate succes-

sor in Peggy's bed was an obscure young Irish writer, known to Peggy as 'Oblomov' and to posterity as Samuel Beckett.

★

Unlucky as he may have been in illicit love, Jennings was once again thriving in yet another freelance career. In December 1937, he began what would be a short-lived but productive period as a writer and presenter of talks programmes for BBC radio. This was, it should be stressed, an experience that gave him a good deal more than just a platform and a fee. His wartime films are portraits of a world that lived by radio, whether the friendly BBC broadcasts of news, popular music and keep-fit classes of *Listen to Britain*, or the terrifying enemy broadcasts of *The Silent Village*. One of his favourite images was that of families listening to their wireless sets or – as at the start of *A Diary for Timothy* and throughout *Lili Marlene* – of professional broadcasters speaking into a studio microphone.

He made his debut on the BBC National Programme with a talk on 'Plagiarism in Poetry', which drew heavily on his abandoned Thomas Gray research. 'There are various dictionary definitions of plagiarism, which make it look like some sort of crime . . . Well – that takes a view of literature which is, I think, very narrow, and which is certainly not based on experience of poetry,'[38] the talk begins, before offering a somewhat simplified version of the arguments about Gray and poetic diction that he had submitted to Eliot at *The Criterion*. Judged by today's rather more timid editorial standards, it is moderately demanding stuff, but it evidently pleased his producers and editors at the Corporation, who commissioned several high-profile broadcasts on the subject of poetry over the next few months.

In February 1938, he gave a talk with the slightly misleading title 'The Disappearance of Ghosts', which, with the exception of what he admitted to be a 'terribly flat' spooky story by way of introduction, was actually about the decline of the ghost as a poetic symbol since the days of Homer:

> Now the *obvious* question is, 'What is the future of ghosts in poetry?' But I suggest that the proper question to ask is, 'What is the future of poetry without ghosts?' We have spent three hundred years or more in the position of Hamlet – increasingly

terrified of the possible impact of ghosts on existence. What our
poets have to do is to find the modern equivalent of the sword,
wine, water, flour and blood that Ulysses used to ask the *past*
about the future.[39]

This resonant question, and related questions about the nature of
contemporary poetry and its audience, were pursued and elaborated in
The Poet and the Public, a series broadcast between April and June 1938.
Some of the programmes were scripted talks, others were interviews
with the likes of C. Day Lewis, Herbert Read and the inspirational
people's poet, Patience Strong. Though this series has been all but
ignored by critics until quite recently, it is an exceptionally revealing
account of Jennings's views on the condition both of poetry and of the
other arts; and though it does not directly address questions of film-
making, it is the closest approximation to an artistic manifesto he ever
voiced.

A learned, imaginative and quirky history of the changing relationship between poets and the audience for poetry over the last four
hundred years or so, the whole run of *The Poet and the Public* is worthy
of attention; but it is the eighth and the tenth programmes which cast
most light on the development of Jennings's thought and on his future
practice.

Programme 8 considers the history of the poet laureateship, as a
re-examination of the original idea and a speculation about how it
might be adapted to make sense in the modern world. Citing Sir Philip
Sidney, Jennings recalls that laurels were originally given to poets in
honour of their triumphs in the literary sphere just as they were given
to generals for triumphs on the field of battle; then he points out that,
as is well known, Laureates have the task of celebrating royal events –
a task which has become more problematical in the last couple of
centuries since kings no longer lead their armies into battle. At the
same time, Jennings glosses that word 'Triumph' in a way that would
have been all too familiar to his contemporaries at college: 'triumph-
ing,' he explains, 'didn't just mean "victorious", it meant a real gala
show, with flags and music and prisoners and a crown and a chariot.
It was a Show – like a Lord Mayor's Show – and you could have a
triumph for any special figure: the triumph of Neptune or the triumph
of Love, for instance.'[40]

He suggests that the rot begins to set in to the institution of the laureateship with the Restoration, and continues into the eighteenth century, proposing that one reason for this is that the language of such official effusions became further and further removed from the realities of contemporary life – above all, because of the coming of industry – and, thus, more and more remote from the concerns of any broad audience for poetry. Nor, in Jennings's view, is it just the royally appointed poets who have succumbed to irrelevance. There have, he insists, been hardly any poets who have paid adequate attention to 'the mass of the people' or to 'individuals, in their idiosyncrasies', though T. S. Eliot earns honourable mention as a modern writer who – in early poems such as 'The Boston Evening Transcript' – has made noble attempts 'to talk about something fairly ordinary, fairly up-to-date, in a fairly straightforward way' (a verdict which will surely astonish every schoolchild who has had to wrestle with the allusive fragmentations of *The Waste Land*; which is not to say that Jennings is wrong).

No poetry produced by Laureates has so far managed to match Eliot in this regard, says Jennings. But other forms of communication have: the cinema, for example. He speaks of how moving he found newsreels of the funeral procession of George V. 'The film captured in a peculiar way the emotion of the people at the event, and re-presented it *to* the people.' He concludes:

Now, I don't suggest that the Poet Laureate should write a kind of newsreel. I suggest what he can do is to make an analysis of this emotion which the camera photographs, an analysis of the 'feel' of an event like the Coronation when people sat by their radio sets and burst into tears *and didn't know why* . . . The Poet Laureate's would be an analysis of a special emotion of a special Day, when the chariot reappears for a short time.

About thirteen months earlier, Jennings had been present at another Day when 'the chariot' reappeared – the coronation of George VI – and *May the Twelfth* had, of course, been an attempt at analysing the special emotions of that Day. Whether or not he had any inkling of the fact, this passage looks forward into the near future as well as back to the recent past: in wartime, he would become that self-appointed

cinematic Poet Laureate, that analyst of special emotions; and his films
would be Triumphs.

The tenth and last programme of the series is still more prophetic.
'Poetry and National Life' begins with a garden ritual from the
Trobriand Islands as recorded by Malinowski, then proceeds to a discussion of that celebrated passage in the *Ancient Mariner* where the
narrator, moved by the beauty of the water snakes, 'blessed them
unaware', and so, mysteriously, frees himself of the curse brought on
by his killing of the albatross that followed his ship. One of Jennings's
points is that there is something salutory in the very mysteriousness
of Coleridge's poem, and that it is the job of poetry in the modern
world to keep such mysteries alive – and alive in the face of a widespread suspicion that there is something faintly shameful about reading poetry.

> We've been so much brought up with the idea that with all our
> science we've conquered nature and grown into adults, and that
> now there's no necessity for us to indulge in any curious primitive
> practices such as the Trobriand Islanders talking to their ancestors,
> or to indulge in the sort of communication with the mysteries
> of existence that the poet brings up. And so we're ashamed of
> admitting that there are still bits of life that we don't understand.[41]

It is among the principal functions of poetry, Jennings proposes, to
remind us not to be so 'proud' – 'I mean by pride the way in which
the industrialization of the world has (so to speak) – hardened our
hearts' – and to remind us that there are still mysteries, 'and that these
mysteries reside in the humblest everyday things' (a sentiment which
chimes with his formulations on Surrealism and the 'marvellous').
He proceeds to cite instances of the juxtaposition of the everyday and
the marvellous in Hardy's poem 'Midnight on the Great Western'
and – though copyright restrictions prevent him from quoting directly
– in Eliot's *Waste Land*, where the 'inexplicable splendour' of a Wren
church, within earshot of pub revelries, serves as an ancestral presence
comparable to those of the 'grandfathers' of Trobriand ritual. Then
he comes to the nub of his case:

> You see, however industrialized we may be, we have ancestors
> whether we like them or not, and how they come in here is best

expressed by the French poet, Apollinaire, who said that unlike other men he didn't stand with his back to the past and face the future; on the contrary, he stood with his back to the future, because he was unable to see it, and with his face to the past, because it was in the past that he could discover who he was and how he had come to be him.

That idea of extracting an idea of 'what I am' from the past is a thing that the poet does for himself and especially it is a thing that he can do for the community; I mean he can try to tell them who they are. Now he can't tell the community who they are unless he does two things: unless he talks about the things that the community knows about, the things that they're interested in, and unless he also looks on the community's past – at the figures, the monuments, the achievements, the defeats, or whatever it may be, that have made the community what it is.[42]

Jennings adds one or two important riders to this declaration, above all the proposition that 'it's on a love of, a passionate attachment to the things round us, both the easy things and the inexplicable things, that poetry depends. It depends on it because this warmth, this attachment, is the only medium through which we can really get near either to things or to people; everything else is snobbery.'

Thus the poet, Jennings declares to the listening nation, has the task of reminding people of the mysteries of the everyday; keeps them in touch with their ancestors; relies on 'a passionate attachment' to, a powerful love for, the places he shares with them; tells them who they are, by reminding them who they have been. There could hardly be a more telling explanation of why Jennings's wartime films can be seen, should be seen, as major works of poetry.

★

But events would not call him to his unofficial laureateship for a while yet. In the wake of the excitement caused by the Surrealist exhibition, London was becoming unexpectedly alive to modern tendencies in art. Peggy Guggenheim had opened her gallery, Guggenheim Jeune, at 30 Cork Street. Together with the Mayor Gallery at number 19 Cork St and the London Gallery at number 28, these spaces made a 'united front' for the advancement of modernism: in May 1938, for example, Guggenheim Jeune showed the Dutch Expressionist Geer

Van Velde (introduced to the British public, not altogether seductively, by a text from the pen of Peggy's very own Oblomov, Samuel Beckett), while the Mayor showed Miró.

But it was the London Gallery that played the largest role in Jennings's life. Originally opened in October 1936, it had been taken over in April 1938 – apparently at the suggestion of Roland Penrose – by the Belgian Surrealist E. L. T. Mesens, who began his reign in triumphant style with the first full-scale British exhibition by his fellow-countryman René Magritte. Édouard Mesens (1903–71),[43] who would be a good friend to Jennings for the rest of his life, simultaneously launched a new magazine (described as 'a glorified catalogue' by one witness[44]), price one shilling, which would take over from Roughton's *Contemporary Poetry and Prose* as the most important local outlet for Surrealist texts: the *London Gallery Bulletin*, known after its second issue simply as *London Bulletin*. Jennings, Penrose and George Reavey would serve, in turn, as co-editors of subsequent issues. For its first issue – whose cover, drawn by Magritte, showed a man smoking a pipe, of which the bowl was a man smoking a pipe, of which the bowl . . . – Mesens commissioned Jennings to write an essay inspired by the Magritte show. He began: 'In Magritte's paintings beauty and terror meet. But their poetry is not necessarily derived from the known regions of romance – a plate of ham will become as frightening as a lion – a brick wall as mysterious as night. His painting is thus essentially *modern* in the sense required by Baudelaire . . .'

The *London Bulletin*, one of the most remarkable small magazines of a period rich in such inspired publications (the art critic David Sylvester[45] suggested that it was a work of genius), now became the principal arena for Jenning's literary work – including some reprints of pieces already published in *Contemporary Poetry and Prose* – until 1940, when it followed the example of the gallery itself by closing down. In May 1938, the *Bulletin* published his prose-poem 'As the Sun': 'The hat was over the forehead, the mouth and chin buried in the brown velvet collar of the greatcoat. I looked at him wondering if my grandfather's eyes had been like those . . .'[46] More importantly, in June it published in its third issue his essay 'The Iron Horse':

Machines are animals created by man. In recognition of this many machines have been given animals' names by him – 'mule', 'throstle', 'basilisk', 'puss-moth', 'taube', and so on. (Cp. also such phrases as 'donkey-engine', 'iron horse', and for an animal regarded as a machine at the time of the industrial revolution see Blake's *Tiger* . . .)[47]

A footnote informed readers: 'In July the London Gallery will present an exhibition of 19th Century Drawings and Engravings of Machines; also a complementary show of Cubist, Dadaist and Surrealist paintings.' In short, what subscribers to the *London Bulletin* were reading was Jennings's earliest prose sketch for the epic work that would become known as *Pandæmonium*; though the collage method of that book was more fully anticipated in 'Do Not Lean Out of the Window!', his major contribution to the next issue of the *London Bulletin*, which he also guest-edited. Here appeared six texts – from Blake's *Vala* (1797), Steele's *History of the L.N.W.R.* (c.1835),[48] Engels's *Condition of the Working Class in England* (1844), Samuel Smiles's *Industrial Autobiography* (1863), Ruskin's *Sesame and Lilies* (1865) and R. M. Ballantyne's *The Iron Horse* (1871) – prefixed by a note signed 'H.J.': 'The following texts are presented not in any sense as a picture of the development of Machinery itself, but to suggest rapidly some of the varying situations of MAN in this country in having to adapt himself rapidly to a world altered by the INDUSTRIAL REVOLUTION, and in particular to THE IMPACT OF MACHINES on everyday life.[49]

Interested readers could make their way to the London Gallery to see the eighty-seven exhibits displayed under the title 'The Impact of Machines': Jennings was the co-curator. It is reasonable to assume that, from this time onwards, he was engaged in the prodigious task of researching *Pandæmonium* whenever his many other projects were not claiming priority. Roland Penrose, reminiscing about his friendship with Jennings – 'brilliant and enthralling' – wrote: 'I remember meeting him more than once in the street, always immaculately dressed but carrying a heavy dilapidated suitcase. Asked what he had inside it, his brief answer was "Pandemonium" . . .'[50] Others have recalled that same case or one of its siblings – Nora Dawson, one of his assistants at the Crown Film Unit, remembered it as a case for sheet music – as one of Jennings's indispensable properties, as constant an element of his appearance as his trademark overcoat.

It was, they imply, his vade mecum, virtually until the hour of his death.

*

In the intervals of working for Mass-Observation, photographing, painting, writing, editing, curating and beginning to assemble his epic on the Industrial Revolution, Jennings also managed to make a handful of films. One of the best pieces of evidence we have for the chronology of his work as a freelance film director during this period is a press release issued on 5 October 1937, stating that he had just made or was about to make three films in Dufaycolor for the producer Adrian Klein:

> Work is practically complete on three short colour films. One of these will be named English Harvest . . . Another picture has been made of the last few top-sail schooners . . . A third film is promised in which an attempt is being made to break entirely new ground in rhythm and colour. The films are being directed by Mr Humphrey Jennings, whose work in recent colour films awakened considerable attention.[51]

Though the last remark is slightly puzzling – his brief period of employment at Gasparcolor does not seem to have added any further directorial credits to the Jennings filmography – this blurb helps clear up some questions of dating. Most reference books give 1939 as the release date for English Harvest, but it must have been shot in the autumn of 1937. The 'schooner' film, lost in the archives until very recently,[52] must be Farewell Topsails; and another short now attributed to Jennings, The Farm, was either made from English Harvest out-takes, or at one time was a much longer piece incorporating all or part of the harvest footage as an extended sequence. As to that ground-breaking third film: either it was never made (it sounds like the sort of thing Len Lye had been doing for Grierson) or it saw the light of day as Design for Spring, filmed during the winter of 1937–8, previewed as early as February 1938, but only released – under the title Making Fashion – in 1939.

This compact body of colour films is notable more for charm than for manifest genius. English Harvest is probably the best of the group: a slight but beguiling study of farm work at harvest time which is Jennings's most direct treatment in filmic terms of that potent set of pastoral images – horse, plough, rural labourers – to which he returned again and again in his paintings; some of its more ardent admirers have compared its warm, harmonious imagery to that of Constable, a verdict that may prompt more sympathy than agreement. It is set, unoriginally but not unpleasingly, to a full orchestral performance of Beethoven's *Pastoral* Symphony, and has a sparing commentary by A. G. Street, well known at the time as the BBC's 'Voice of the Country'. So lulling are its picture-postcard colours, so mellifluous its sounds, that the viewer may fail to notice the slightly harsher point it is making: that the countryside, seen by town-dwellers as a playground, is in fact an industrial zone potentially as unforgiving as any urban worksite, a place where hard labour never stops. Remembering that the man who made this superficially idyllic piece was deep in the study of Lenin, one might say that *English Harvest* is, so to speak, Jennings's sickle to the hammer of his later study of northern industry, *Heart of Britain*; though the film also hints that rural labour, based in tradition, might not be as alienated as the Communists would have people believe. 'Now for next year's harvest,' runs Street's voice-over, 'ploughing, the king of jobs, the most charming disguise that work can wear . . .'

By contrast, *English Harvest*'s sibling production *The Farm* is a negligible, not very pleasing thing, apparently admired in its day for the quality of its colour cinematography depicting 'cows with their calves, mares with leggy colts, and sows', but fatally marred by a hearty and would-be jocular voice-over. *Farewell Topsails*, a nine-minute short largely cut to the music of a sailor's jaunty accordion-playing – and shot, to judge by the brilliance of the sunshine, in the high summer of 1937 – is an elegiac treatment of a passage in industrial history, following one of the last voyages of a sailing ship bearing a cargo of extracted kaolin on her trip from Cornwall.

Design for Spring is a pleasant enough twenty-minute documentary cum commercial (or what would now be called an 'infomercial') about the fashion designer Norman Hartnell's new dresses for 1938, which begins in the designer's workshops during wintertime and concludes with a full-dress catwalk display of his creations. Hartnell had been one of Jennings's contemporaries at Cambridge. Sharp-eyed and well-briefed viewers can catch a glimpse of Cicely Jennings in the audience for one of these shows; and after a brief prelude spoken by an

abrasively plummy male voice comes the commentary, opening with
a reference to ancient seasonal myths – one of the few moments when
it is possible to guess at the director's identity.

By the summer of 1938, Jennings had returned both to black and
white (he did not touch colour again until his very last, unfinished,
film *The Good Life*) and to contract jobs for the GPO Film Unit. Two
rather slight GPO films date from this time: *Penny Journey*, which
follows the travels of a picture postcard from a little boy in Manchester
to his auntie in Graffham, Sussex, and is memorable mainly for its final
sequence in which the stoical village postman makes his leisurely way
by bicycle and on foot through dappled English countryside, bearing
the child's trifling message as earnestly as if it were a military dispatch;
and *Speaking from America*, which gives a detailed explanation of the
means by which radio signals can be transmitted from continent to
continent, and is memorable – if at all – for its finale, a cameo
appearance by President Roosevelt addressing a college commence-
ment, which, for those who lack a taste for elementary physics, offers
a welcome relief after some ten minutes of unadulterated lecture-room
material.

Perhaps the single most striking thing about Jennings's film work
at this time – especially in the light of his later productions – is that it
seems almost hermetically sealed both from his private intellectual
concerns and from the topics that were obsessing everyone else.
Fashion shows, bucolic idylls, white sails against the brilliant summer
sky, the faithful English postman on his beat: the most charitable
reading of these images is that they amount to a last glimpse of the
peaceful world that is about to be bombed into oblivion.

*

September 1938 was the month of the Munich crisis: a time of dread,
anger, relief and profound humiliation – emotions well documented
in Mass-Observation's *Britain*, published as a Penguin Special early in
1939 and an understandable best-seller. By now Jennings can hardly
have been immune to the general sense of catastrophe narrowly and
shamefully averted, and the national atmosphere must have tainted
the pride he would otherwise have taken in a notable personal
achievement. Thanks to Mesens, in October 1938 he was given his first
one-man show, containing twenty-six exhibits,[53] at the London Gallery;

the only one of its kind during his lifetime. Sadly, it did not create much of a stir. Those not too stunned by developments on the continent to neglect art entirely flooded, instead, to the exhibition of Picasso's *Guernica*, first at the New Burlington Galleries (4–29 October) and then at the Whitechapel, where some twelve thousand visitors saw the anguished canvas in the course of just a fortnight. It is likely that Jennings was among them, since he and Cicely had already seen the painting once, when they (like so many others at the time) visited Picasso in his studio on the quai des Grands Augustins in Paris.

That same month, Jennings published an essay entitled 'Who Does That Remind You Of?' in the *London Bulletin*; again, he was pondering some of the implications of photography, and (again) it appears that he was as much preoccupied with the world of subjective fantasy as with the public nightmares of Europe. This time, his authority was Freud rather than Lenin.

> Photography itself – 'photogenic drawing' – began simply as the mechanisation of realism, and it remains *the* system with which the people can be pictured by the people for the people: simple to operate, results capable of mass reproduction and circulation, effects generally considered truthful ('the camera cannot lie') and so on. But intellectually the importance of the camera lies clearly in the way in which it deals with problems of choice – choice and avoidance of choice. Freud (*Psychopathology of Everyday Life*, Chapter 12) says that the feeling of Déjà Vu ('Who does that remind you of?') 'corresponds to the memory of an unconscious fantasy'. The camera is precisely an instrument for recording the object or image that prompted that memory. Hence the rush to see 'how they came out'.[54]

This was the last piece of speculative prose Jennings was to publish for the better part of a decade. The times were increasingly ill-suited to leisurely ruminations; and they were certainly unpropitious for major projects of historical research. Nonetheless, in January 1939 – the month when Barcelona fell to Franco's forces, and Hitler's armies occupied Czechoslovakia – Jennings felt sanguine enough about the future to write to the economic historian H. J. Beales, who worked for Pelican Books, with an outline for a book that he had suggested just before Christmas:

I enclose a rough memo. of what I think it should contain, and also a series of proposed excerpts, which should suggest the type of material which I have been collecting.

But I do not think that either the memo, or the passages suggest the final effect – which would lie as much as anything in the exact order of presentation – the effects of juxtaposition and so on. The introduction would also be less abstract than it sounds since it would be possible to refer to the passages themselves – and also to two or three other Pelican or Penguin books – notably [Freud's] 'Totem and Taboo' . . .

I am working all the time at the problems of collection and synthesis which this programme entails – but it would be a great spur to me to be able to imagine publication.

Beales's reply, when it finally arrived some months later, was encouraging, though nothing like a firm contract:

Who knows what, if anything, will be publishable when Adolf has done with us? But it may serve as a stimulus to know that we are favourable to the idea of the book. If you care to continue without a definite commitment, we shall be glad & I do not believe you will be disappointed.

The probable length should be estimated rather less than we originally had in mind. Paper difficulties must be met by shortening. Say, 50,000; a little ± won't matter.

In the event, Beales was the one to be 'disappointed': the manuscript of *Pandæmonium* grew and grew, never to be finished in Jennings's lifetime, and was finally published thirty-five years after his death.

*

Early in 1939, Jennings abandoned his freelance status and rejoined the GPO in earnest: with the world so uncertain, a little more stability of income would no doubt have been comforting. So began the longest period of regular employment of his life. At the same time, he and his family moved from Blackheath to 19 St James's Gardens, London W11. In March and April, he travelled to the North of England and to Wales to shoot his most important assignment to date – a documentary about the leisure activities of working-class people. This project was intended as one of two films to be made for exhibition at the forthcoming New

Frank and Mildred Jennings, Humphrey's parents

Humphrey Jennings and an unidentified friend, sometimes said to be
the young George Orwell

Left. Cicely Cooper

Below.
Cicely and Humphrey
in Cambridge

Jennings acting as one of the Weird Sisters in *Macbeth* for the GPO Film Unit's production for the BBC – *The Voice of Britain* (1935)

Making *Fires Were Started* (1942)

Directing villagers in *The Silent Village* in Cwmgeidd (1943)

Directing *A Diary for Timothy* (1944)

Making *A Diary for Timothy* (circa 1944). Photograph by Walter Bird

Humphrey Jennings working on *Pandæmonium* (circa 1946). Photograph by Beiny

Above. One of Jennings'
photomontages, using his
own photographs of
Coronation Day 1937

Right. One of Jennings'
oil paintings, *Horse's Head*
(circa 1937–8)

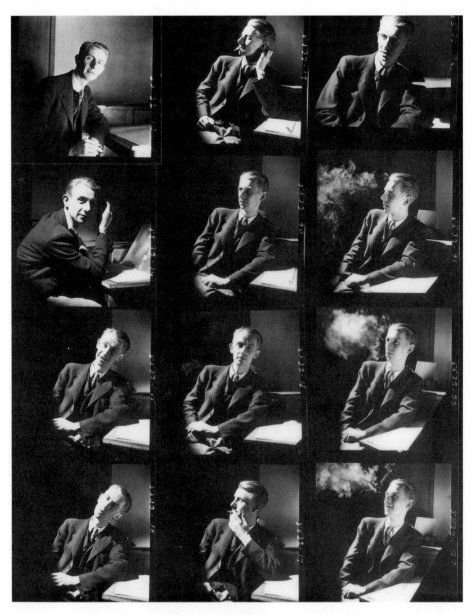

A contact sheet from Lee Miller's photoshoot for *Vogue* (1944)

York World's Fair under the joint title *British Workers*; one film would deal with life in the workplace, the other with recreational activities. Now largely forgotten, the former film was directed by George Pearson as *British Made* (1939). The second was to prove far more enduring. An internal memorandum at the GPO Unit says of this project; 'The general purpose . . . is to show that workers of all grades have a secondary life, over and above their working life, in which colliers may become musicians, musicians may become engineers, engineers may become dog-fanciers and so on.'[55]

In the earliest stages it was suggested that the film might best be made by a team of directors, each assigned a particular sequence to be shot under the close supervision of a producer – presumably Cavalcanti: lists of possible candidates included J. B. Holmes, Norman McLaren, Jack Chambers, Richard Massingham, Gerry Bryant and Pat Jackson – though not Jennings, who was still freelancing at the time. Various people chipped in with suggestions, anecdotes and observations that might help flesh out the film: what about competitive leek-growing? Pigeon-fancying? Works bands? Amateur dramatics? One note in particular provided a fertile seed: 'A strange phenomenon of North East England is the popularity of kazoo bands for children. The children dress up in costume and competitions are arranged'; an additional comment, crossed out but still legible: 'This recreation is rather pathetic.'[56]

Later draft plans show these ideas becoming refined, probably under Jennings's own hand. 'The film will be shot in three locations, and will represent the personal lives of the people who depend on three main industries – cotton, steel and coal . . . It cannot be scripted in detail, since it depends on what the director finds in the locations.' (If that last remark does not come from Jennings, it is at least a very fair indication of his characteristic working method. Directing, for Jennings, was typically a matter of discovery – of people, places and things – and of imaginative, sympathetic collaboration with what he discovered.) 'The general tone of the film will be bright. Without being in any sense unfaithful to the truth, it will attempt to show the natural gaiety of working people, and the varied expression which it finds. . . .'[57] The plan was that the film should end with the rousing spectacle of a Cup Final – an ambition soon abandoned when it was learned that the commercial newsreel companies owned the rights to coverage of such events.

Reasonably clear by now as to what they were after, Jennings and his crew – including the fine cameraman Chick Fowle, who would go on to shoot several of Jennings's best films, including *Listen to Britain* and *The Silent Village* – began to film in south-east Lancashire (Manchester, Salford and his old Mass-Observation stamping ground, Bolton), Sheffield and South Wales (Pontypridd and other towns). Despite his eye-opening experiences with the Harrisson group, Jennings was still dismayed by some of the industrial landscapes he saw on his travels. He wrote to his wife:

> Cotton seems to produce a desolation greater – more extended – than any other industry. From Stockport it is really all streets through Manchester, Bolton, Preston – almost to the sea at Blackpool – about 60 miles. The desolation – the peculiar kind of human misery which it expresses comes I think from the fact that 'Cotton' simply means *work*: Spinning what is produced or grown elsewhere in America or India. Coal and Steel at least suggest something produced on the spot. At Manchester there was a sort of thin wet sunlight which made it look pathetic. It has a grim sort of fantasy. And a certain dignity of its own from being connected with certain events in history.

One of the 'certain events' Jennings had in mind must have been the Peterloo Massacre of 1819 – an atrocity to which several important passages in *Pandæmonium* would be dedicated.

The film that Jennings eventually made from the footage shot during this latter-day Cobbettian journey through northern England and Wales marked a wholly new stage in his career. It was called *Spare Time*. Not surprisingly, given its interest in the minutiae of working-class life, this GPO Film Unit production has often been identified as a documentary made for or by Mass-Observation. But this was far from the case. Jennings had by this time already quit the movement, partly because of fierce personal disputes with Tom Harrisson, and it is doubtful that he would have felt comfortable about meeting Harrisson again when the schedule took his unit to Bolton. Julian Trevelyan came closer to the truth about this new film in his autobiography *Indigo Days*, where he describes *Spare Time* as the director's 'surrealist vision of Industrial England; the cotton workers of Bolton were the descendants of Stephenson and Watt, the dwellers in Blake's dark satanic mills reborn in the world of greyhound racing and Marks & Spencer'.[58]

The commentary for *Spare Time* was read by a new recruit to the Unit, Laurie Lee, today best known as the author of *Cider with Rosie*. Itself spare to the point of terseness, the script nonetheless contains some quietly suggestive phrases: 'As things are, spare time is a time when we have a chance to do what we like, a chance to be most ourselves.' That apparently innocuous modifier 'As things are' insinuates that social matters might, perhaps, be ordered very differently. Otherwise, though, the commentary adds little in the way of reflection to the film; neither does it lead the images, for the most part serving simply as a way of identifying locations so that the viewer shall not feel lost. In short, Jennings is now beginning to move away from the 'lantern lecture' approach of his recent films and towards the more associative, purely visual and musical structures of *Listen to Britain*.

In its eighteen minutes, *Spare Time* encompasses a considerable variety of activities, arranged – as the research documents proposed from the outset – into three principal sections. First – 'Steel – there are three shifts, so spare time can be morning or afternoon,' announces Lee's voice-over. We are shown a brass band rehearsing, intercut with images of factories, steel mills, houses and domestic interiors; a housewife serves up a pie to her family. Out of doors, a man takes his lurchers for a run, another sees to his pigeons, boys fiddle with their bicycles and a cycling club trundles through the countryside, stopping at a pub. The steel sequence concludes with a football match, cross-cut with advertisements for football pools and men queuing for postal orders.

Next, Cotton: the kazoo band, dressed in shiny, flimsy, pyjama-like costumes and floppy hats, parades in what seems like chilly weather on an exceptionally desolate wasteground, razzing away at 'If You Knew Susie', a tune that's sustained through images of house exteriors, a mother with her child, children drawing on the pavement, a man wrapping a parcel and a woman watering plants in a greenhouse. Cut back to the kazoo band, who now present a sort of cod-Elizabethan tableau, in which a young girl dressed as Britannia is hoisted shoulder-high on her makeshift throne while the band buzzes and trills its way through a jazzy version of 'Rule Britannia'. The kazoo melody is sustained through a montage of Manchester's Belle Vue amusement park – a tiger, lions in cages – and a wrestling match. Another surprise leap to a rehearsal of a Restoration comedy, and then to ballroom dancers swaying round the floor to the tune of 'The Bells of St Mary's'.

Finally – Coal: and shots of the pitheads in the dark landscape, with rows of terraced houses. Cut to a choir rehearsal where a woman plays the piano as male singers begin to gather around her; she does not falter for a second in her playing as one of them helps her off with her coat from behind. They begin to sing Handel's 'Largo', and once again the music continues to sound through a montage – shop windows, a pub interior and card-players, a puppet show (depicting a Welsh flax spinner and harpist), more shops and pedestrians, and a long tracking shot past more brightly lit shop windows; boys playing a ball game; and another domestic interior, with a mother serving a meal while her husband reads the paper. Then the finale starts to take us back into the world of work – we see the next shift coming on duty, the cage full of miners descending into the pit, chimneys outlined against the evening sky. 'As things are . . .,' muses the voice of Laurie Lee. *Finis*.

By this stage of Jennings's career, abbreviated summary becomes more and more inadequate as a means of recording what it is like to watch such material. The editing of *Spare Time* – usually credited to Stewart McAllister – is more supple, more subtle, than anything in his previous work; the bizarre wit of the juxtapositions (Britannia/big cats/wrestlers . . .) more surprising; the content of the images either more cryptic or more charged with significance. After a fitful apprenticeship, Jennings has finally begun to find his identity as a director, and *Spare Time* is his first film with claims on the attention of posterity.

The art historian David Mellor has argued that *Spare Time* 'offered perhaps the strongest concentration of pop iconography in any work by a British artist' before the conscious formulation of the Pop Art aesthetic by the Independent Group at the ICA in the mid-1950s – a quality that points not only to Jennings's recent passage through Mass-Observation but also to his affinities with that other eloquent connoisseur of boys' comics, dirty postcards, pub life and other manifestations of democratic industrial folkways, George Orwell. And the overall organization of the film – again, associative rather than narrative – is a good deal more complex than anything Jennings had so far tackled. The editor and film critic Dai Vaughan has made the ingenious suggestion that the unseen world of work is hinted at in a series of understated, not to say subliminal, metaphors: the Sheffield sequence concentrates on metallic objects such as brass instruments, bicycles and a kitchen range; the Manchester sequence emphasizes fabrics – ball gowns, theatrical costumes; while the coal-mining town in Wales is shown almost wholly by night, and is filled with dark, heavy objects.

It was these very qualities of complexity and ambiguity admired by subsequent generations of viewers that provoked intense dislike of the film in some parts of the documentary world – a dislike which, if anything, deepened with the years and became something of an orthodoxy in some circles. Above all, it was that 'rather pathetic' kazoo band sequence that really stirred up resentments. 'The feeling,' Basil Wright told Elizabeth Sussex many years later, 'was that Humphrey seemed to show, in our opinion, a patronizing, sometimes almost sneering attitude towards the efforts of the lower-income groups to entertain themselves', and elsewhere he wrote of the 'cold disgust' which lay beneath this 'brilliantly presented' scene. In his *History of the Cinema*, Eric Rhodes says the sequence is 'filled with revulsion'.

It is hard to counter such objections on a shot-by-shot basis except in negative terms, by pointing out that Jennings presents these activities about as neutrally as might be imagined, with no distorting angles, no sarcastic cut-aways, no obvious accentuation of the (supposed) pathos of the scene – in short, with none of the editorializing devices that are part of the repertoire even of relatively inexperienced directors. And it is this very policy of abstention, one suspects, that makes viewers uncomfortable, since it presents them with a smooth surface in which they are able to see, not Jennings's preconceptions, but a reflection of their own. Today, more than sixty years after the event, some audiences are inclined to smile at the film's quaintness, but a smile is not the same as a sneer or a shudder of disgust. And others, more in tune with the general drift of *Spare Time*, have found in it a melancholic mood akin 'to that found in early Fellini – the day after the carnival in *I Vitelloni*, perhaps, or the religious procession in *La Strada*'.[59] Jennings's real offence here, it has forcefully been said, was not so much a matter of having unwittingly displayed his own social snobbery as his refusal to adhere to the unstated law within the documentary movement that there were only two permissible ways of showing working people: as noble heroes of labour or as dignified victims of capitalism – 'appropriately heroic in adversity', as Edgar Anstey, the director of *Housing*

Problems and other exposés of grim social conditions, later put it in mildly self-mocking terms.

One can sympathize with both sides: faced with the urgent task of raising concern for injustice, the socially engaged film-maker can seldom afford the luxury of ambiguities, digressions and complex emotions. But *Spare Time* is not – or not directly – a work of social propaganda. It is the earliest piece of film-making by Jennings that can plausibly be referred to as 'poetic'; and it remains today a fascinating, living piece of cinema when Anstey's *Housing Problems* and *Enough to Eat?* are little more than period documents.

Whatever misgivings his colleagues may have voiced, either to his face or behind his back, Jennings seems to have been justifiably proud of the film. Many years later, Cicely remembered that 'Humphrey liked to pretend that he was a painter and was only in films "for the money" – but I remember going with him to see "*Spare Time*", his first really personal, individual film, and he was so excited that he sat on the edge of his seat in the cinema like a small boy!'[60]

*

The constraints of regular employment did not prevent him from pursuing his other intellectual concerns. In May 1939, with his experience of the industrial North still fresh in his mind, Jennings gave a talk on James Nasmyth for the BBC programme *Science Review*; this would be his last broadcast on domestic BBC services save for a talk about his film *The Silent Village* four years later, in May 1943. Nasmyth was the inventor of the steam-hammer; a writer of the 1860s declared: 'It is not too much to say that without Nasmyth's steam-hammer we must have stopped short in many of those gigantic engineering works which but for the decay of wonder in all of us, would be the perpetual wonder of the age, and would have enabled our modern engineers to take rank above the gods of all mythologies.' Part of Jennings's intent was to show that Nasmyth was closer to the 'gods of all mythologies' than he might appear. This, after all, was a man who had drunk a toast to Thor ('the Scandinavian Vulcan', as Nasmyth called him) on a visit to Uppsala, who had thrown the business card of his Bridgewater Foundry into the mouth of Vesuvius by way of homage to the original Vulcan, and who spent *his* spare time gazing at the moon through his telescope and producing a series of sentimental etchings of fairies.

Nasmyth would also put in a first-person appearance in *Pandæmonium*, describing the Black Country in terms that may have suggested to Jennings his Miltonic title:

> I lingered among the blast furnaces, seeing the flood of molten iron run out from time to time, and remained there until it was late. When it became dark the scene was still more impressive. The workmen within seemed to be running about amidst the flames as in a pandemonium; while around and outside the horizon was a glowing belt of fire, making even the stars look pale and feeble.

★

With post-production on *Spare Time* complete, Jennings was given a fresh GPO assignment. In July, he travelled to the Mediterranean to make a film about the final voyage[61] of a merchant navy vessel, S.S. *Ionian* (slightly different versions of this film were issued under the titles of *Her Last Trip* and *Cargoes*). He and Cicely made plans to meet up in Marseille on his return trip to England several weeks later, but there is no evidence that they managed this brief holiday. In artistic terms, *S.S. Ionian* is something of a step backwards after the great leap forward of *Spare Time*. It's a fairly negligible piece, at best polished rather than inspired, and there is little in the work to identify it as Jennings's save for a trademark reference to ancient myth comparable to that which opens *Design for Spring*. 'Once upon a time,' the commentary begins, 'a Greek sailor got lost on his way home and sailed out of the Aegean Sea westward, past Malta and Gibraltar . . . the Greek was Ulysses and his voyage the *Odyssey* . . . Today we've turned the tables. Now it's the Northerners who are running their vessels South by East.'

The structure of the film is dictated by the order of the voyage it depicts, starting in Gibraltar, where the *Ionian*, under her skipper Captain William Smith, takes on a cargo of steel, explosives, corrugated iron, cement, aircraft spares . . . and beer. Two and a half days at sea take the *Ionian* to Malta, where a British battleship is also near port; the commentary explains that when a merchant ship passes a vessel of the Royal Navy, both ships dip their ensigns to acknowledge the time-honoured relationship between the two services. The *Ionian* then sails

on to 'Alex' – Alexandria – which is another three and a half days
away. There, she encounters both a British sea plane and another RN
battleship, the *Malaya* – 'oil burning, armed to the teeth, 1150 men'. In
dock, the sailors unload explosives and parts for 'the RAF depot at
Aboukir Bay, where Nelson smashed Napoleon's navy over a hundred
years ago'. After unloading, the *Ionian* puts back to sea for another day
and reaches Haifa, where, to the tune of the Barcarolle from *The Tales
of Hoffmann* (supposedly emanating from a gramophone played by Jim,
the apprentice), a group of RN destroyers, 'fast as whippets', sail past
in convoy. From Haifa to Cyprus, where the *Ionian* unloads the last of
her outgoing cargo and then reloads with a cargo of oil, wine, locust
beans; and 'the last port is Stavros, where once upon a time stood the
groves and temple of Venus'. Then it's back to Alexandria for further
supplies, and so – to the strains of 'Pomp and Circumstance' – for the
journey back to Britain, past the *Antaeus*, past the *Malaya* again, past
the *Warspite* . . . and, just in case the viewer is slow on the uptake, the
commentary points out: 'Throughout this voyage, the *Ionian* has met
with ships of the Mediterranean Fleet . . . North is where the Home
Fleet guards the way.' Finally, after passing the white cliffs of Dover,
the *Ionian* sails up the Thames to London, where she unloads at
Butlers Wharf – 'her cargo brought safely from Cyprus and Alexandria
under the protection of the British Navy, the greatest Navy in the
world'. The film ends with moonlight over the Thames, and further
rousing words.

By now, even the most sluggish-witted members of the audience
will have grasped that this short film which purports to be about the
commercial activities of the merchant navy is in fact a reassurance
that the Mediterranean is bristling with His Majesty's warships, all of
them ready, willing and able to take on any nasty surprises the region
has in store. Yet there is also a strange, and no doubt unintended,
note of whistling in the dark about these robust assurances. What the
viewer actually takes away from the film is the ominous implication
that all this peace, all this picturesque sea and landscape, is about to be
shattered by the unnamed enemy.

*

In the late autumn of 1939, back in England, Jennings wrote a brief,
sombre prose-poem:

A derelict cart with dead grass entwined in its great wheels: plants and grasses which had climbed up in the spring-time and been upheld by the spokes, flowered in the summer and now died in October. The cart unmoved all the year round – the wheels unmoved and unmoving – lit and unlit with the daily light of the great sun . . .

The sombre note was appropriate. A month earlier, war had been declared.

Six

The War Years – 1939 to 1942:
From *First Days* to *Fires Were Started*

The story of those first eerily uneventful months of the conflict – the period which became known as 'the phoney war' – has been told many times. It was a curiously unreal as well as an anxious period, in which rumours about the imminence of a Nazi invasion of Britain, the near-certainty of mass civilian slaughter in London and other major cities by the Luftwaffe's bombs, infiltration by enemy agents and saboteurs and the likelihood of social collapse on an apocalyptic scale were offset by the day-to-day recognition that nothing very disastrous was actually happening just yet. Famously, the air-raid sirens went off just minutes after Chamberlain made his grim monotone announcement that the country was at war with Germany; famously, it was a false alarm. As the weeks passed, many of the early emergency precautions began to seem unduly cautious: for example, many of the cinemas which had been closed in anticipation of major bombing raids (at the suggestion of Sir Joseph Ball of the Ministry of Information, soon to be replaced by Kenneth Clark) were reopened. If the GPO boys were going to carry on making films, at least they would have somewhere to show them.

And they were determined that they would go on making films, at least until someone came and told them to do otherwise. One of the most vivid mementoes of that ominous time, especially since it was not unduly infected in the making by the spirit of hindsight, is the short film Jennings put together in collaboration with Harry Watt and Pat Jackson, *The First Days* (1939). It was largely an improvised piece. Frustrated by the apparent shortage of worthwhile work to do or coherent direction from above, the Unit took the initiative, and went out simply to make a visual record of the earliest effects of war on Britain. As Pat Jackson has written,

Cavalcanti and Watt decided that we would record, as far as we were able, the day-to-day observations of England reacting to war: the filling of sandbags in the London parks; the new air raid wardens collecting their tin helmets, helping police direct traffic; the arrival of the balloon barrage [*sic*]; sandbagging and reinforcing hospital wards; children being evacuated and settling down in the country; girls in uniform looking longingly at glamorous evening dresses in shop windows.[1]

Jackson evokes the resulting film fairly accurately. Just twenty-three minutes long, *The First Days* provides a compendious view of a country (or at any rate, its capital city) preparing for conflict. While the tone is necessarily upbeat and resolute, it does not lack in more chastened and reflective notes, starting with its very first sequence, of boys playing on the disused First World War cannon outside the Imperial War Museum, while the narrator, Robert Sinclair, intones the words 'Twenty years' – by which he means the two decades of tentative peace enjoyed by Britain since the Armistice. Then the events of 3 September 1939 are recalled and, tactfully, restaged: Chamberlain's voice – '. . . I have to tell you that no such undertaking [to withdraw the German invasion force from Poland] has been received, and that consequently this country is at war with Germany . . .'; then the sirens, and the rush for the shelters. An archetypally indomitable cockney quips, 'Old 'Itler didn't take very long, did 'e?', and is obliquely answered by the voice-over: 'People joked, but in their hearts was devastation.' There follows a long sequence of trenches being dug, sandbags being filled, ARP men on patrol, civilians pitching in with a will. Here, the commentary introduces a major theme that will come to echo in British propaganda films for the next few years and beyond – the idea that, in the face of a common threat, Britain's ancient and notorious class structure is now dissolving like dew in the sunlight:

the hardening of London's face, the growing ruggedness of the streets, meant a warming of the heart and a quickening of the sympathies . . . The thousands of classes [*sic*] of London, some from their damp basements and some from their luxury flats, came to work for the public good . . . They did indispensable work, which no leader could have ordered and no money could have bought.

It would be easy to be cynical about the reality of this spontaneous mutual embrace of the classes; and yet, after more than six decades, Sinclair's rhetoric of democratic unity still rings surprisingly true rather than sounding merely wishful. To say that *The First Days* is playing its part here in forging a powerful wartime myth is not to dispute or sneer at the accuracy of its reportage, and there is abundant evidence that the experience of total war did in some measure ease the chronic tensions of class war (though, as Angus Calder and others have persuasively shown,[2] there were also circumstances that exacerbated them).

We now move from the civilians to the fledgling troops and airmen. The commentary provides a refreshingly intelligent balance of historical awareness and topical exhortation: 'A remarkable thing: a generation of young men, born in the last war, and brought up in contempt of militarism and the fruitless romance of the battlefield, went into uniform willingly and with clear understanding . . . These were London's children. Now they carry on, but they are still our children.' Then come more general shots of London's overnight transformation into a giant fortress: hospitals and schools being evacuated; army convoys in the streets, barrage balloons, drills and training, the emotional farewells of young lovers; trains and troopships; the empty walls of the National Gallery (Sir Kenneth Clark had supervised the shipping of its treasures to safe stores in Wales), the West End and the East End. Last in this sequence comes an interesting digression on the local refugees and other Londoners of foreign origin – 'A hundred thousand people of many lands. They are part of London . . .'

The First Days is a patriotic work, but it is wonderfully free of narrow jingoism. Decades before 'multiculturalism' would become a wooden rallying-call, or a hoarse jibe, Jennings and co. quietly emphasized that one of the things that made Britain most worth defending was its – fragile, often embattled – liberal traditions of tolerance and pluralism. (The fact that the Unit's boss was a gay Brazilian may have helped keep this thought to the forefront.)

A mildly surreal editing trick, in which a cat appears to be responding quizzically to the flight of a barrage balloon, introduces the sorrowful reminder that many of London's pets were killed painlessly by their owners to spare them the fate of painful death by bomb and fire; then come those window-shopping, haute-couture-hungry ATS girls of Pat Jackson's recollection, followed by more general shots of troops departing. Night starts to fall, and the West End theatres are closed: 'Locked for the first time since the Puritans closed them nearly three hundred years ago' (one suspects the touch of Jennings the inveterate cultural historian, here) '. . . but no one has ever stopped the cockney voice of London.' Factories, hospitals and searchlight crews work through the night, until the coming of dawn prompts the commentary to obvious but rousing metaphor: 'This is not twilight that has come to England, it is dawn.' Further shots of troops, sentries and balloons lead to Buckingham Palace, where the King and Queen look up to the heavens as a barrage balloon rises – literal uplift to evoke emotional uplift.

As even this brisk summary should make clear, *The First Days* is essentially a decent and well-crafted propaganda film which once in a while rises to a slightly more thoughtful and inspired plane. Not a great work, it can nonetheless be watched today with pleasure, and even found moving – no mean achievement for a film made on the hoof, and at a time when there was little more than dark rumour and fear for even the most reflective minds to work on.

At the same time that Jennings, like other good Londoners, was pitching in on a collective effort, he had a solo project of his own to develop. *Spring Offensive* (1940) adds an urgent contemporary note to the pastoral matter of the two short colour films about farming he had made in the 1930s. Once again, A. G. Street provided the commentary. Shot almost entirely in Jennings's native territory of Suffolk, it explains in dramatized form – acted, not altogether expertly, by real-life farmers and their families – how British agricultural workers were meeting the challenge of feeding a country whose international supply lines, the same ones shown in *S.S. Ionian*, were now threatened by the German navy. (It's worth noting that this was the first time Jennings had directed actors before the camera; he does not yet seem to have learned the trick of coaxing natural behaviour from non-professionals.) By way of a reminder about the other important wartime use of the British countryside, it also shows how Ken, a young London lad newly evacuated, rapidly adapts to farm life and comes to idolize a resourceful countryman – 'Bob, the tiller driver'. The other principal characters are Fred Martin, a farmer at Shottisham; his wife; members of the local War Agricultural Committee; and the 'Land Girls' being trained to operate tractors: 'many colts have joined up, so the fillies come to the rescue', in the arch words of Street's voice-over. As the film demonstrates, a large part of the rural war effort involved reclaiming many of those farmlands (in this case, a place called Grove Farm) which fell into disuse during and after the First World War – a sorry state of abandonment due to the fact that so many young men from farming districts perished in the mud of France. It ends with a stern moral:

> Remember – we've looked after the land properly only during periods of war. In September 1939 you asked the countryside to provide you with a safe refuge for your children and security against famine. Both these things it has given you. Now the countryside asks you to do something in return. When peace comes, don't forget the land and its people again.

Ostensibly aimed at the urban viewer who has taken too little heed of what his country cousins have been doing, these words also sound a clear note of social criticism directed at the British governing elite; a note easy enough to miss if you are listening only to its official message of town and country coming together for the common good, but a distinct anticipation, in the first wartime months, of that more sustained and anguished meditation on the cruelty and missed opportunities of the past at the finale of *A Diary for Timothy*, which Jennings would compose half a decade later in the final months of war.

*

One of those who worked closely with him in the early days of the hostilities was a lad called Joe Mendoza – today a retired hotelier, living in Cornwall – who had joined the GPO Film Unit in January 1940 as an assistant editor and general dogsbody. Joe was just nineteen, and was training as a radio operator for the merchant navy, having graduated from a two-year course at the Regent Street School of Kinematography in July 1939. He first met Jennings when the director was at work on *Spring Offensive*.

> He was shooting a sequence in our studio of a little boy from London being evacuated to Suffolk. It was a dialogue sequence, and the continuity girl was ill, and Humphrey said, 'I've got to

have continuity!' Because Humphrey quite frankly had never done lefts and rights and eye-lines and all that sort of stuff. So he said, 'I'll have Joey!' And I said, 'But I don't know anything about continuity!' And Humphrey said, 'Look, just keep a note of everything we shoot. You've got to get the focus distance and the lens, and if we're tracking in, however long the track is. Just keep checking with the camera crew.'

Mendoza tried his best, scribbling out every detail he could in longhand, and somehow 'it all went off quite happily'.[3]

They did not work closely together again until *Listen to Britain*, though Mendoza was also called in on a couple of other projects, including Jennings's next short contribution to the war effort, *Welfare of the Workers*. 'It was so boring I used to fall asleep watching the rough cuts,' Mendoza recalls. 'But a great number of the audience shots for the Flanagan and Allen concert scene in *Listen to Britain* are from *Welfare of the Workers*. Just about everything that Humphrey shot would end up reappearing in some other film.'

Welfare of the Workers (1940), if not quite as soporific as Joe Mendoza suggests, is certainly not a major jewel in the Jennings canon. Ten minutes long, it recalls – through a commentary by Richie Calder, read over images of factories and a working-class family listening to the radio – the long history of skilled workers organizing into trades unions and struggling for their rights. 'Then war came,' Calder continues. '. . . On the continent, Hitler had destroyed the trade unions . . . To resist such tyranny, the British worker was asked to surrender some of his hard-won rights, to give up by choice what Hitler takes by force.' In short, the propaganda is pitched in terms that are wholly, and surprisingly, friendly to a socialist version of history.

After this scene-setting flourish, the film settles down to a more routine exercise in spreading cheery enlightenment, and shows a girl leaving home on being recruited for factory work, moving to another part of the country, being resettled by the Women's Voluntary Service, being favourably impressed by the bright, clean conditions of her spanking new factory, then chivvied into all manner of healthy leisure activities in the countryside. The film ends, somewhat abruptly, with canteen shots of lunchtime entertainments – some of them, as Mendoza says, ultimately destined for recycling in *Listen to Britain* –

and a lightning appearance by Ernest Bevin himself, then Minister of Labour, telling the cheering workers: 'We can not only work and fight, but we can be cheerful doing it as well.' The nation was soon to grow used to hearing rather more sublime and sonorous rhetoric than Bevin's.

*

While Jennings and the rest of the GPO Film Unit were busy improvising their most appropriate response to the first months of war, major changes were taking place behind the scenes in Westminster – changes which would soon put the Unit's work on an entirely new footing. In April 1940, Sir John Reith reorganized the Film Division of the Ministry of Information, appointing Jack Beddington head as a replacement for Sir Kenneth Clark, who had been occupying the post since 1939. Beddington, who would remain in charge until 1946, was to be advised by Sidney Bernstein – later to be one of the founders of Granada Television. (Clark was promoted to Controller of Home Publicity, then to head of Planning, but would be moved out of the MOI entirely in August 1941 when Brendan Bracken became Minister.) Then, in May 1940, Churchill came to power. One of his first initiatives was to appoint Duff Cooper as Minister of Information, with Harold Nicolson as Cooper's parliamentary secretary. The MOI's headquarters was at the Senate House of the University of London – later to serve as the architectural original for the Ministry of Truth in Orwell's *Nineteen Eighty-Four*.

It was not easy to predict how these changes would affect Jennings and his colleagues. On the face of it Beddington's appointment, for example, looked like good news for documentarists. A Balliol man, he had been in charge of the film unit at Shell, where his appointees included Jennings's friend and fellow film-maker Arthur Elton; indeed, Beddington had been ultimately responsible for commissioning *The Birth of the Robot*. But Duff Cooper's short-lived period as Minister has seldom been warmly judged by anyone, including Cooper himself, who felt that the MOI was an unworkable chaos – 'too few ordinary civil servants in it, and too many brilliant amateurs' – and that Churchill was not interested in giving him the support he needed: '[Churchill] knew that propaganda was not going to win the war.'[4] An uncompromising intellectual snob, Cooper was hopeless at wooing the press, and his regime is chiefly recalled for the unpopular measure of recruiting a group of Mass-Observation-style investigators who became known as 'Cooper's Snoopers'.

It was Cooper who decided that the GPO Film Unit should come under the direct control of the Ministry of Information; the body was also to be rechristened with the less commercial, more patriotically resonant title of the Crown Film Unit.[5] The move was not quite as encouraging a signal as it may sound. There were dark mutterings that the Ministry was seriously considering the option of disbanding the Unit altogether. Sadly, Cavalcanti was persuaded that it was in everyone's best interests that he should leave the Unit – a proposal, his colleagues felt, almost certainly tainted by xenophobia or still more illiberal sentiments. In Joe Mendoza's memory: 'Well, Cav being a Brazilian and an ex-communist and a surrealist and a homosexual, they thought, "We can't have a *British* film unit run by someone like this", so Cav was very gently eased out. And Michael Balcon at Ealing was trying to get hold of Cav anyway. So he left us and we got Ian Dalrymple.'

Clearly philosophical about this brush-off, Cavalcanti went on to play his own distinguished and distinctive part in the artistic war effort as a director: his dramatic tale of Nazi spies infiltrating a quiet English village, *Went the Day Well?*, is a classic of its kind, and there is little doubt that he would have been a fine and well-liked leader for Crown had he been allowed to stay. Jennings in particular must have been sad to see his mentor go.

But Cav's successor, Dalrymple, while not perhaps in Cavalcanti's league as a creative artist in his own right, was, if anything, a still more brilliant cultivator and champion of the talents of others. Ian Dalrymple (1903–89) is one of the less commonly acclaimed figures in British documentary history, so it seems only fair to cite a generous but just assessment of his work by one impartial source: 'Under [Dalrymple's] patient, highly professional, yet sensitive guidance, the Crown Film Unit produced a matchless series of films, the best of which, in the tradition of Renaissance art, elevated good propaganda of the moment into lasting works of art.'[6] And another, from a thoroughly partial source, Pat Jackson:

He was going to make sure that we would not be bothered and bewildered by niggling little minutes from the Films Division of

the Ministry of Information and other bureaucratic bodies. He
was our shining knight who was to protect us from all the clap-
trap – and what's more, he did . . . Never before or since has any
group of film people enjoyed such creative freedom, and this is
the debt that we owe him . . .[7]

Dalrymple's Crown appointment began on 12 August 1940. Yet
another Cambridge graduate – he had edited the university's best-
known literary magazine, *Granta* – he had previously worked in the
commercial sector, writing screenplays for Gaumont-British before
being recruited by Alexander Korda to make *The Lion Has Wings*, a
drama-documentary about the RAF which had proved an unexpected
box-office hit. His decision to accept the post was wholly idealistic in
material terms – it involved giving up, as he ruefully noted himself,
'five-sixths' of his previous income – but not without its spiritual
rewards. Dalrymple considered it an 'honour' to work with the Unit's
fervent young men, and later said that he thought his years with
Crown 'the best time of my life'. His temperament was ideally suited
to the task in hand: intransigent, stern and ferociously protective when
dealing with the Ministry (who soon noted with dismay that their new
appointee was 'taking the bit between his teeth'), he was also thoughtful, compassionate, patient and diplomatic with his own team. Pat
Jackson found him 'shy';[8] almost everyone considered him a gentle
man, and a gentleman. Best of all, he had a sharp eye for talent and
creative notions about how best to develop it. And his favourite talent
at the Unit was Humphrey Jennings.
    Besides becoming Jennings's regular producer, 'Dal' became his
friend, his kindly uncle-figure and his landlord. It can hardly be a
matter of chance that all of Jennings's major films were made with his
support. Theirs was, Joe Mendoza believes, an ideal creative partnership. 'Dal was marvellous because he understood Humphrey at once.
Dal was a highly literate, very well-educated guy, as Humphrey was,
whereas all the rest of the unit was a bit of a mix-up.'[9] And Jennings,
seldom quick to bow to the opinions of others, developed an untypical
reliance on Dal as an arbiter of taste. Denis Forman, who saw the two
of them working together after the war, noticed how often Jennings
fell back on Dalrymple's authority: Jennings 'regarded him as a
touchstone of good judgement and common sense. Was this idea too

wild? Refer it to Dal. Did this sequence work or didn't it? Refer it to Dal . . .'[10] Few major artists at any period of history have made their way without some form of patron. Though he probably did not realize it, Jennings had now met his.

★

In September 1940, Cicely Jennings left for the United States with Mary-Lou and Charlotte. The reasons for their abandoning Britain, rather than simply evacuating to the countryside as most families chose to do, are not altogether clear. Mary-Lou Legg suspects that chronic marital difficulties played their part, but, at the age of six, was still far too young to grasp the complexities of such things. 'I do remember him saying goodbye to us, on the platform at Euston. I was seven a week later. He came to the platform and there was an air raid. The whole platform went dark, and that was the last I saw of him for four years.'[11]

Cicely took her daughters to New York. They stayed for a while with relatives in an apartment on Park Avenue, then, in 1941, moved to a modest apartment of their own at 791 Lexington Avenue, where their downstairs neighbours were old friends from Cambridge, David Reeves (brother of the poet James) and his wife Robin. Before long, Cicely had managed to find a decent job – essential to keep her young family afloat, but also, one suspects, satisfying in its own right. She worked, first, for the British Purchasing Commission, and then for a branch of the Special Operations Executive (SOE) called British Security Co-Ordination, headed by the Canadian Sir William Stephenson. Her work was in the department which dealt with those refugees from Occupied Europe who were judged to have a valuable part to play in the war effort; after initial recruitment, they were sent off for special training in London, Ontario, and then smuggled back into their native countries to join various underground resistance movements. On Saturdays, Cicely would sometimes bring Mary-Lou along to the SOE offices on the thirty-third floor of the Rockefeller Center, and the young English girl was duly impressed by the all-American modernity of the set-up: Cicely's personal glass-walled office next to the huge typing pool, complete with water-cooler and paper cups. Mary-Lou was allowed to help with the filing, a colour-coded index system, and remembers how good the exercise was for her knowledge of the

alphabet and visual memory. At the time, she recalls, hundreds and
hundreds of these cards dealt with Polish émigrés. Both Mary-Lou and
Charlotte came to love their time in the United States, and rapidly
learned to speak with American accents.

Another circumstance of Jennings's great war films, then, is that he
made them when he was once again a single man. In many ways, he
surely missed his family. His letters to Cicely and the girls are frequent
and warm; he took a fond interest in the way the girls' characters were
developing, and did his best to make them feel that their father was
still a benign and active presence in their lives; and there is no overt
reference or even veiled hint in the transatlantic correspondence to the
possibility that the marital rupture might be permanent. On the other
hand, he may well have been quietly relieved to be free of all the
wearying petty distractions of family life at a time when his film work
was perforce to become all-absorbing. And as a man who had already
strayed from strict marital fidelity at least twice already, it is likely that
he would also have welcomed the mood of greater sexual freedom
that was – so spicy handed-down folklore and sober social historians
agree – one notable feature of wartime Britain. Some of his affairs may
have passed unknown even by his colleagues, and others remain
conjectural. This need be no grave matter for regret, since none of
these liaisons was serious enough ever to fracture the marriage for
good, or to change the set course of Jennings's career.

In fact, it borders on irrelevancy even to evoke the idea of a 'love
life' for Jennings in the period from 1940 to 1945: the demands of
wartime film-making were so intense, the working hours so long, the
deadlines so pressing that his film-making career largely *was* his life. As
he wrote to Cicely in November 1940: 'life is pretty hand to mouth &
we hardly let up at all: so anything private gets a very second look
in . . .'. There were a few brief intervals of respite from all-absorbing
artistic, patriotic and political mission: a little reading, a little painting,
a few scribbled letters, the occasional night out at the music hall . . .
the odd discreet affair. To be sure, he changed profoundly in those
five years: he grew from a fascinating minor figure, a protean jack-of-
all-skills, into a major artist. But the story of that change is one that
takes place, so to speak, in plain view; it is a story which, for the most
part, can be understood simply by watching his films. His upbringing,
his stringent formal education and still more intensive self-education,

his diverse experiences of writing and painting and ideas – all of this now looks like a long apprenticeship for a task that, had European history been less disastrous, might never have come his way. It was war – the urgencies, the dangers, the intensity and the sudden warm comradeships – that forced him into greatness.

*

One cause of wartime promiscuity, it is widely agreed, was the widespread mood of *carpe diem* induced by the possibility of sudden death. September 1940, the month the Jennings family went its separate ways, was also the month in which the Luftwaffe carried out their first night raids against London: the Blitz had begun, and it was as terrible as people had always feared. Joe Mendoza recalls being in Kent at the time of that first raid, making a film about the police, and seeing the entire night sky lit up red as London blazed. Stewart McAllister and others responded by going out with cameras, and filming the destruction. Jennings himself almost died; as his brother Rodney recalls, a bomb struck and destroyed the house next door to their parents' home in Kensington.[12] Had the bomber pressed his switch just a hair's breadth of a second later, the name of Humphrey Jennings would now be little more than a footnote to the 1930s.

Hardly surprisingly, his next film, again made with Harry Watt, came out of London's first experience of massive enemy air raids. *London Can Take it* (1940; known in the UK in a slightly shorter but otherwise identical cut, *Britain Can Take It*) is a fine, richly stirring tribute to what became known as the Spirit of the Blitz, and while not the most accomplished, it is perhaps the most influential work he ever made – one of the few films that have played some small part in changing the course of history. Joe Mendoza:

> The idea was that the GPO would take all the footage of the Blitz that had been shot by the newsreel people and make a film about the bombing of London. So Harry Watt and I went down to Lime Grove [the BBC headquarters] and sat for hour after hour looking at all this material. Harry was very depressed. He said, 'It's a lot of shit, isn't it? Let's shoot our own film.' So he went to Cav and Cav said, 'All right, let's have a go.'
>
> The film was in two parts. The first part Harry directed, and

the second part Humphrey and McAllister directed. We worked
at it continuously for ten days and ten nights, sleeping on the
cutting-room floor. It was designed for [the famous American
journalist and broadcaster] Quentin Reynolds, who was due to go
to New York in a fortnight. The idea was that he would take it to
New York under his arm, and this is what happened. And the
film, when it was shown in New York, was such a success that
the MOI thought, we've got something here which is much more
significant than we reckoned – it's not just making advertising
films for the Post Office. Because the general feeling was that
Britain really wouldn't last two or three weeks after the Blitz
began, that London was being destroyed and we were pretty
much finished – that was the feeling the Germans were trying to
put over. So *London Can Take It* was really quite an important
piece of propaganda. I think Quentin actually showed the film to
Roosevelt himself, he was that kind of guy.

After its private screening for the President, the film was put out
on general release in the United States, and soon caught the imagination of the public in that still-neutral nation. (On 25 October 1940,
for example, Harold Nicolson, parliamentary secretary to the Minister
of Information, noted in his diary that *London Can Take It* had been
a 'wild success' in the United States, and had already taken the very
respectable sum of £11,180 at the American box office.) It is easy to
see why the film had such an impact, and a good deal of the credit
must go to Quentin Reynolds for his pungent, tough-guy commentary,
which, with its mixture of world-weariness about the vile tricks of the
bad guys and warm admiration for the courage of the good guys,
might easily have come from the mouth of one of Humphrey Bogart's
taciturn anti-Fascist characters.

Following hard on a shot of Jennings's beloved St Paul's, Reynolds
introduces himself – 'I'm speaking from London. It's late afternoon
and the people of London are preparing for the night' – over a series
of shots of commuters hurrying home in the rush hour: 'the greatest
civilian army ever assembled', Reynolds calls them, before laconically
pointing out that the bombers tonight will 'destroy a few buildings and kill a few people, probably some of the people you're
watching now'. Further shots show preparations for the raids –
shelters, wardens, ambulance men – until suddenly a hand reaches

out to move a siren switch from OFF to WARNING: ''And there's the wail of the banshee!'

The German bombers are audible in the distance. Searchlights come on, and rake the clouds; then the anti-aircraft units start firing. Bombs crash down. Inside the shelters, an elderly couple slumber, men play darts, families curl up like hibernating animals. Above ground, a church takes fire, a house explodes, and fire crews rush in to fight the blaze. Reynolds: 'Now the people's army swings into action. Bombs have started fires. When a bomber starts a fire, he immediately returns and uses it as a target and drops more bombs ... yet the people's army ignores the bombs ... brokers, clerks, peddlers and merchants by day, they are heroes by night ...'

Comes, at long last, the dawn, and the sirens sound the 'All clear.' 'London raises her head, shakes the debris of the night from her hair, and takes stock of the damage done.' Shots of rubble, shattered glass – a woman kicks some shards aside as she collects the milk from her doorstep – demolished blocks of flats. Then the morning commuters set out on their journeys, though not always by the usual means – while a double-decker bus stands up-ended against a ruined house, smartly dressed civilians hitch a ride on the back of a horse-drawn cart; and a woman enters a shop via the space where its window has been blown away. (Had Mendoza not already confirmed that the second half of the film belonged to McAllister and Jennings, one might have guessed it from the sharp-eyed, edgy surrealism of some of these images.)

Now bombed-out families start to gather up their possessions; the Queen and King move gracefully through the desolation, chatting with the workers. Reynolds waxes ferocious, sardonic: 'Doctor Paul Josef Goebbels said recently that the nightly air raids had had a terrific effect on the morale of the people of London.' Meaningful pause. 'The good doctor was absolutely right. Today the morale of the people is higher than ever before. They know that thousands of them will die, but they would rather stand and face death than kneel down and face the kind of existence the conqueror would impose upon them.' More shots of damaged buildings and the great civilian clear-up. 'I am a neutral reporter. I have watched the people of London live and die ... I can assure you, there is no panic, no fear, no despair in London town.' (A nice touch of romance in that mildly archaic 'London town'.)

The mood switches from defence to attack. A newspaper-seller writes 'BERLIN BOMBED' on his board; RAF men load a bomber; our planes set off in the direction from which the enemy came. It's true, Reynolds stoically concedes, the Nazis will be back again tonight, and the night after, and the night after that, and they'll kill thousands of people and destroy hundreds of buildings: 'But a bomb has its limitations: it can only destroy buildings and kill people. It cannot kill the unconquerable spirit and courage of the people of London.' Cue the cheekily insouciant figure of a Civil Defence man – obviously a cockney – cadging a light from a taxi driver and swaggering away from the camera with his tin hat at a raffish angle. Finale, over a shot of the statue of Richard I flourishing his sword outside the bomb-stricken Palace of Westminster: 'London Can Take it!'

Irresistible. You can hardly believe that Roosevelt did not declare war the second the lights went up. *London Can Take It* is splendidly vigorous and timely propaganda; it has also proved an endless fertile resource for subsequent documentary-makers wanting footage of the Blitz, and virtually everyone who has seen such a film on television will have seen chunks of the Jennings/Watt/Reynolds collaboration. Valuable as it is, though, it does not have quite those uniquely poetic, humanist qualities for which Jennings has become known and admired. His next two short films began to move in that direction; he was rapidly learning how to be the director he would ultimately be.

*

Recognizing the real danger that Crown could easily be obliterated by the air raids, the Ministry of Information decided that it was time for the Unit to be evacuated from Soho and Blackheath. It took over Britain's largest film studios, Pinewood (opened in 1926 by J. Arthur Rank) and moved the Crown Unit there along with the film units of the three services, and some commercial film-makers.

It was a clash of two very different, and mutually suspicious worlds, each of which entertained a hostile caricature of the other. To the commercial-features crowd, the documentarists were bolshy, scruffy and technically incompetent. To the Crown faction, the features people were frivolous, pampered and morally corrupt – McAllister, for example, used to refer to them as 'lice'. But, according to other accounts, the strange bedfellows soon began to learn a little grudging

respect for each other's ways, and even to borrow from each other –
the feature-makers began to find out more about location shooting
and the achievement of verisimilitude, while the documentarists,
previously starved of all but the most basic studio equipment, 'grabbed
with joy at the elaborate film-making facilities there'.[13] Jennings was
among those who would eventually come to enjoy these resources, as
well as shoulder some new occupational burdens. Like other members
of Crown, he was obliged to join the Pinewood unit of the Home
Guard. 'He was a very *bad* member of the Home Guard,' Mary-Lou
Legg recalls. 'He went out on a march and got wasps or something
down his boots. Then he pitched his tent somewhere where a river
ran through it, so the only way that he could get to sleep was to slope
off to the local pub and get drunk on port. He was absolutely useless.'
For the next year or so, he would spend far more time shooting on
location than in the studio.

By October 1940, Jennings had begun work on *Heart of Britain*,
intended as a sort of northern counterpart to *London Can Take It* and
showing how doughty the spirit of that region's industrial workers
could be, though he initially described it rather misleadingly in a letter
to Cicely as 'a kind of *Spare Time* assignment'. As Joe Mendoza put it,
'There was a feeling that London isn't England, we've got to make a
film about the rest of England, so Humphrey made *Heart of Britain* . . .'
His wartime letters to Cicely and others now begin to take on an
entirely new tone: simpler, more urgent, and often rhetorically heightened – at times, almost to Churchillian levels. In these letters he
conveys the British response to the Blitz in stirring, eloquent terms –
terms which are the first hint anywhere in his writings, private or
public, of that sense of a nation transfigured in adversity which
animates his wartime films:

> Everybody is in good spirits: after one's first bit of bombing
> one is all right. Some of the damage in London is pretty heart-
> breaking – but what an effect it has all had on the people! What
> warmth – what courage! What determination. People sternly
> encouraging each other by explaining that when you hear a
> bomb whistle it means it has missed you! People in the North
> singing in public shelters: 'One man went to mow – went to
> mow a meadow.'[14] WVS girls serving hot drinks to firefighters

during raids explaining that they really are 'terribly afraid all the time!' People going back to London for a night or two to remind themselves what it's like.

Everybody absolutely determined: secretly delighted with the *privilege* of holding up Hitler. Certain of beating him: a certainty which no amount of bombing can weaken: only strengthen. A kind of slow-burning white-heat of hatred for the Jerries and a glowing warmth of red flame of love and comradeship for each other which *cannot* be defeated: which has ceased to think of anything except *attack*.

Maybe by the time you get this one or two more 18th cent. churches will be smashed up in London: some civilians killed: some personal loves and treasures wrecked – but it means nothing:[15] a curious kind of unselfishness is developing which can stand all that & any amount more. We have found ourselves on the right side and on the right track at last![16]

It is a wonderfully ardent piece of prose, and perhaps the closest Jennings ever came to articulating in words alone the spirit that animates his wartime films. Revisionist historians have been inclined in recent years to argue that this was not at all the way most people regarded the war – there was looting and corpse-robbing, defeatism and despair, hatred of the war in general and Churchill in particular – and it is plainly important not to take one artist's impassioned vision as a sober record of the quotidian reality of Britain under siege. On the other hand, it would be mean-spirited to discount such flights as nothing more than the self-indulgence of an overimaginative romantic; for Jennings was surely not wrong in believing that the same British citizens could and did act, think and feel in just the ways he describes.

Although he managed to find time in late October and early November 1940 for a couple of visits to Kathleen Raine, who was now living near Ullswater in the Lake District, *Heart of Britain* was a busy, eventful shoot, and at times a dangerous one: 'The whole unit escaped by about eight hours being wiped out in [the mass bombing of] Coventry,' Mendoza remembers. But Jennings's spirits were good. On 3 November he wrote to Cicely: 'And the war? well we feel we aren't doing too badly: in fact there is a kind of secret exultation. You know I have always said the war was a moral problem for the English.'

The best moments of the resulting film – particularly in its use of music – rise to a visual eloquence which is as new to Jennings's film work as the note of defiant exultation was to his letters.

Beginning with the sturdy gravity of a symphonic work by Elgar, *Heart of Britain* (the American version was called *This is England*) dwells on the wild, timeless landscapes of Yorkshire, Derbyshire and the Lake District – the vistas, since the main body of the film will concentrate on industrial, city life, providing a subdued metaphor: the English people we are about to meet are an ancient race, calm and reliable as rock. Or, as Jack Holmes's commentary (rather gratingly patrician to a modern ear – the American version of the film, otherwise exactly the same, is more comfortable for today's audiences) puts it:

> The winds of war blow across the hills and moorlands of Yorkshire and Derbyshire. They stir the grasses in the sheep valleys of Cumberland, ruffle the clear surface of Ullswater. They sing in the cathedral towers of Durham . . . in the spires of Coventry. But the heart of Britain remains unmoved and unchangeable.

The first of these unmoved, unchangeable folk who are England's true heart is a Sheffield furnace worker, George Good, seen coming away from his labours before confronting the camera. He has one of those knobbly, gentle faces Orwell thought so endearingly English, and addresses us in friendly, if slightly stilted tones: 'Well, I reckon I've had a rough shift today. Never mind, got a good dinner to go home to. After that, I'm going on the ARP [Air Raid Precautions] bit.' Then, as in *Spare Time*, we travel from steel to cotton – Lancashire, with ARP teams, and rooms full of women typing up addresses and the like – before the commentary introduces the threat of daytime bombing raids and quick runs for the shelter. The film's first set-piece – heavy-handed, true, but charming – shows a group of mill girls in a shelter: 'Just look at these Lancashire lassies cowering before the Luftwaffe.' Needless to say, they are doing no such thing, but playing a noisy and slightly suggestive game involving a balloon; the explosion, when it comes, is not a German bomb but the sound of the balloon bursting as the loser sits down on it to the ribald shrieks of her pals. 'These are the folk,' says the narrator as if pitying the poor fools in the Nazi High Command, 'whom Field Marshal Goering hopes to bomb into capitulation.'

Jennings – for the sentiment sounds very much like his – now introduces a more sober thought: sober, and almost astonishingly civilized in this piece of militant wartime propaganda. We see Malcolm Sargent conducting the Hallé Orchestra in a performance of Beethoven's Fifth. 'But in Manchester today they still respect the genius of Germany – the genius of the Germany that was.' Beethoven's titanic music continues to mourn and thunder throughout a sequence depicting the fresh ruins of Coventry. It is a devastatingly powerful passage, somehow thrilling despite its bleakness: Jennings's earliest, and also one of his greatest, realizations of what emotional peaks may be reached when the right music is married to the right image.

But the film is not quite over. Now we meet Mrs Patterson, a plump, slightly posh middle-aged lady who talks directly into the camera about her work with the WVS, making tea for the emergency services. At first brisk and cheery, she seems a little silly, a little comic . . . until her face grows more sombre and her voice more hesitant as she speaks of the sense of futility she often feels when standing in a bomb crater, in the darkness, surrounded by the dead and the barely living. (Her words would draw tears from the toughest audience.) But then she rallies herself, smiles again, remembering the grateful words of the men as they wash down the dust and the blood with those cups of tea.

And now comes the film's finale, another grimly majestic wedding of music and image – and words. The Huddersfield Choral Society launch into a splendidly full-lunged rendition of the 'Hallelujah Chorus' – and their voices carry the film home. 'People who can sing like that in times like these,' our narrator assures us, 'cannot be beaten. These people are slow to anger, not easily roused. Now they and their mates, their wives and their children, have been subjected to the most savage ordeal ever inflicted upon human beings. But these people have the power to hit back. And they are going to hit back . . .' Cut to an aircraft factory, and workers constructing bombers: then, over the final peroration, a completed bomber being wheeled out of the hangar and setting off on its mission. 'And the Nazis will learn – once and for all – that no one with impunity troubles the heart of Britain.' The bomber rises into the night sky, borne on its vengeful way by the final swell of 'Hallelujah!'. Unlike much of Jennings's work, essentially humane in its implications, this finale is ferociously powerful warmongering.

*

By December 1940, Jennings had moved to Ian Dalrymple's cottage on the common at Chorley Wood, Hertfordshire. His stay began as little more than a weekend visit, to rest after the weeks of intensive work on *Heart of Britain*. But it stretched on and on for the better part of two years, and the Dalrymple cottage would be his main home base until early in 1943, though he would sometimes stay for brief periods at the Étoile Hotel in Charlotte Street in London, or with his brother Rodney, or – when he was fire-watching – at the shelter in Soho Square:

> Almost everyone does fire-watching now. It's a boring job mostly – and sleeping in your clothes is not so pleasant but one gets used to it. The blitz is [a] queer thing: it's not the danger itself that bothers one – but the mess afterwards – the smell of death and ruin and ambiguity meeting the daylight again. The gaps in the landscape. The smoking horror. The next morning.[17]

To while away the long watches, Jennings began to compose a series of 'Specimen Nights' about the Blitz, in imitation of Walt Whitman's *Specimen Days*; he had been reading Whitman in the Nonesuch edition. These texts have not survived, though his letters to Cicely no doubt echoed their phrases from time to time.

Out at Chorley Wood, life was much more agreeable than it had been for many months. The Dalrymples were generous with their space. Earlier in the war, they had taken on no fewer than six evacuee children, and adult house guests came and went for the rest of those six years. Jennings wrote enthusiastically: 'I have a lovely semi-circular "study" overlooking the (enormous) garden and endless woods and valleys – very high up – and at night over the tree-tops you can see the gunfire in London.'[18] Jennings's arrival was dramatic: 'He fainted on the doorstep,'[19] said Ian Dalrymple's wife Megan. But the reason for this untypical failure of robustness soon became apparent: 'He was just exhausted, he'd had a such a bad night . . . they'd had a pretty good going-over [from German bombers] in London.' Once over the initial shock, Megan reported that Humphrey turned out to be

> quite a good house guest. He didn't mind our children, though he didn't care for the children on April Fool's Day very much – my step-son woke him up very early in the morning, probably

after he'd been up working late, and that wasn't quite his cup of tea . . . but he did his best to fit in. In the evenings, after they came back from work, we would sometimes play cards. He could get rather snappy if the cards didn't go his way. Quite often he would go straight upstairs and start painting, though only for half an hour or so. I think he found painting relaxing.

She remembers, particularly, Humphrey working on a large Surrealist work and a smaller study of a cow.

He also tried to do his bit in the local community, and once joined Megan Dalrymple as a volunteer worker in a NAAFI-style canteen in Chorley Wood, though, as she recalls, his dexterity in passing out food was somewhat impaired by his refusal to put down the copy of Shakespeare he held in one hand – 'he felt he was wasting his time unless he was doing something like that [i.e., studying texts]'. Not surprisingly, he never volunteered for that job again. Thanks to the generosity of the Dalrymples, though, he not only had a roof over his head but a comfortable place to relax, a friendly and encouraging atmosphere and even a surrogate family. Relieved of petty domestic responsibilities, he was all the more free to focus on the task at hand.[20] In the brief lull between finishing *Heart of Britain* and starting his next major assignment, he even, remarkably, had time for one or two extramural projects.

On 10 February 1941, he wrote to Cicely to say that he was finally on the point of selling his 'Industrial Revolution book': 'The book [the future *Pandæmonium*] really does promise well – the ancient and bitter problems of art and Marxism, and working-class poetry and poetry and science – but I promise you not as awful and dull as that sounds.' Nothing came of these negotiations, however, and though Jennings continued to work at the manuscript, he shelved the idea of publishing it for the duration.

He also found time to pick up the threads of his career as a radio broadcaster. On 23 February he wrote and presented a five-minute talk, 'Pourquoi j'aime la France', on the BBC French service: 'Souvenez-vous, la France a toujours été un foyer international de la culture. C'est pour ça que j'aime la France, et que je ne peux qu'attendre le jour où nous serions tous libres de retrouver les choses que maintenant je ne goût qu'en image.'[21] 'After nine months of "not thinking about

France", ' he wrote to Cicely after recording the talk, 'it was good to take a deep breath and think of the France of Corot and Renoir and "The Man with a Knife and a Glass of Wine". The war makes one think not of peace but of well-being: the riches of the earth and the warmth of the sun.'[22]

And, though he had pretty much left Mass-Observation behind, he disciplined himself to write an M-O-style day report on the events of Saturday 8 March, a 'pretty astonishing day', which began with recording music with the London Philharmonic for a proposed film about the raid on the Lofoten Islands off the coast of Norway, and which reached its climax in one of the most terrible air raids London had seen – the notorious raid in which the Café de Paris was bombed:

> There were two Canadians who come and say 'Where are all the people killed?' And we tell them and they take their coats off and go across and bring out more dead on stretchers. We watch one body carried across right to an ambulance and another left put into a side street – and Mac [McAllister] says 'Do they put any labels on them?' After a bit it gets really too grim and we move along to Lyons [Lyon's Corner House, a popular, inexpensive restaurant chain], but inside on the unused tables there are wounded lying with their heads tied up and rescue squad men in white tin hats getting them food and drink . . .[23]

It was also in the early months of 1941 that Jennings wrote what has come to be his single best-known and most frequently cited poem, 'I See London':

> I see London
> I see the dome of Saint Paul's like the forehead of Darwin
> I see London stretching away North and North-East, along
>   dockside roads and balloon-haunted allotments . . .

Though full of obvious Surrealist touches – the unexpected juxta-positions now brought about by the disruptions of war rather than by the metaphor-forging appetites of the poet's mind – it is a far simpler, more straightforward piece than the cryptic prose-poems that had been his principal contribution to the *London Bulletin* and other publications of the British Surrealist movement. And contrived as it may sound – the line 'I see the green leaves of Lincolnshire carried through London on the wrecked body of an aircraft', with its hint of laurels and procession, seems to fit just a shade too patly into Jennings's private mythology of Triumphs – there is no reason to doubt that the poem is substantially autobiographical, and that the Whitmanish brag of vision may be taken at face value.[24] Here is the third and final stanza, part of it drawing freely on the events recorded in his day report for 8 March:

> I see a thousand strange sights in the streets of London
> I see the clock on Bow Church burning in daytime
> I see a one-legged man crossing the fire on crutches
> I see three negroes and a woman with white face-powder reading
>   music at half-past three in the morning
> I see an ambulance girl with her arms full of roses
> I see the burnt drums of the Philharmonic
> I see the green leaves of Lincolnshire carried through London on
>   the wrecked body of an aircraft.

*

At some time in late 1940 or early 1941, Jennings befriended the Austrian scriptwriter Wolfgang Wilhelm, with whom he started work on a project intended to juxtapose Britain's preparations for an invasion in 1941 with the period in which the country was waiting for Napoleon to invade – an idea that soon proved too complicated and expensive to pursue past the planning stage. At about the same time, Jennings proposed that a film might be made showing how Hitler had betrayed the German ideal – that true genius of Germany mentioned in *Heart of Britain* – as expressed by the writings of Goethe and Heine; nothing came of this proposal, either. He then decided, instead, to make a film about the British army: another unrealized project, but one which gave him the starting-point for his next film – the first of his most intensely personal series of war films, *Words for Battle*.

While working on the British army project, Mendoza recalls, 'the first thing [Humphrey] did was to film the Unknown Soldier's tomb in Westminster Abbey, and he also photographed Handel as well, because he had a thing about Handel'. Handel does indeed seem to have been very much on his mind at the time, perhaps as a result of the concerts he had been to in the course of his travels – 'people are singing Handel and listening to Beethoven as never before', he wrote to Cicely on 25 January. His decision to end *Heart of England* with the 'Hallelujah Chorus' had proved offensive to some of his more aggressively secular colleagues, though: 'I have just been accused here of "going religious" for putting the Hallelujah Chorus at the end of *This is England*. This of course from [Paul] Rotha and other of Grierson's little boys who are still talking as loudly as possible about "pure documentary" and "realism" and other such systems of self-advertisement.'[25]

By Easter 1941 his ideas for *Words for Battle* (known in its earliest stages as *In England Now*) had become clear; they were anything but Griersonian. On 9 April he reported to Cicely that he was busy making 'a film which Mary-Lou would like about the Lincoln statue in Parliament Square'[26] – a curious way of summarizing *Words for Battle*, a short anthology film in which a series of poems or heightened prose works evoke the many virtues of Britain (and, in a strategic but nonetheless inspiring afterthought, of her as yet neutral cousin across the Atlantic), particularly of Britain as an embodiment of the spirit of Liberty. Images of the present conflict – some specially shot, others taken from library sources, a few intensely beautiful – are set against extracts from Camden's *Description of Britain* of 1586, Milton's *Areopagitica*, Blake's 'Jerusalem' (that is, the famous short lyric 'And did those feet . . .?' generally known by that name, which is actually a verse preface to his epic poem *Milton*), Browning's 'Home-Thoughts, from the Sea', Kipling's 'The Beginnings', Churchill's sonorous 'We shall fight on the beaches' speech of 4 June 1940, and the Gettsyburg Address: '. . . that the government of the people, by the people, and for the people, shall not perish from the earth'. Laurence Olivier reads the passages; magnificently.

The earliest draft treatments[27] of this miniature gem are reasonably close to the finished version save in two particulars: an opening commentary and a central sequence are both missing from the latter. The former deletion is no great loss, since the commentary is needless, and at least in one draft slightly condescending too: 'Among the most precious memorials of England, now nightly threatened by fire-bombs, is Westminster Abbey. Here lie the tombs of Kings and Queens . . . and here too the much humbler shrines of English poetry. You may think of the poet as a dreamer and not a man of action, but they too were stirred by the events of their day . . .' And so on. The disappearance of a passage of poetry from the film's midpoint is more regrettable: it came from Shelley's *The Mask of Anarchy*:

> Men of England, heirs of Glory,
> Heroes of unwritten story,
> Nursling of one mighty Mother,
> Hopes of her, and one another;
> Rise like lions after slumber
> In unvanquishable number,
> Shake your chains to earth like dew
> Which in sleep had fall'n on you –
> Ye are many – they are few.

Shelley's lines were a direct response to hearing news of the Peterloo Massacre. Jennings, fascinated by that atrocity and by other scenes of class conflict, included a long section from *The Mask of Anarchy* in *Pandæmonium*, and it seems curious that he would pass up the opportunity to incorporate one of his private obsessions into a public film. Perhaps the exhortation 'Ye are many – they are few' was simply too stubbornly revolutionary in spirit to be press-ganged into a different kind of patriotic meaning, for while it was fair enough to suggest that the British were 'many', it was all too plain that the enemy could not convincingly or usefully be described as 'few'.

But *Words for Battle* was a triumph – in the critical sense, as well as in the terms of Jennings's critical vocabulary of Triumphs. Part of its strength derives from the unexpected ways in which the images, as it were, speak to each other, so that the film does not merely raise contemporary events to the level of timeless epic by dressing them in noble words, but also serves to reanimate these familiar words by showing them, literally, in new lights. Milton's grand evocation of 'a mighty and puissant nation rousing herself like a strong man after sleep ... an eagle mewing her mighty youth' takes on quite startling new power when set against, first, shots of young RAF recruits and their planes; while his reference to 'the whole noise of timorous and flocking birds, with those also that love the twilight' is suddenly transformed into a bitingly apt commentary on those strange birds Hitler and Goering and Mussolini. Conversely, the visionary intensity of Blake's lyric is shown to embrace the lamb of children at play as well as the tiger of martial struggle; shots of London's evacuated boys and girls enjoying the English countryside hint at that transfigured, postwar Albion for which the most idealistic were struggling. And so on, through evocations of the Royal Navy in the Mediterranean for the Browning passage, and a chilling portrayal of bomb damage which explains why, in the new war as in Kipling's day, 'The English began to hate.'

Then Jennings shelves his anthology of classic poems in favour of a modern oration that has the simple gravity and grace of classic poetry:

> . . . we shall fight on the beaches;
> we shall fight on the landing grounds;
> we shall fight in the fields and in the streets;
> we shall fight in the hills;
> we shall never surrender.

Olivier almost accomplishes the impossible in his reading of these words; he almost makes you forget the majestically irritable growl and snap of the original. For its final sequence, Jennings's film takes up Churchill's broad if well-mannered hint to our friends in America ('the New World with all its power and might') that a little help might be welcome, and shows armoured cars and uniformed souls passing the statue of Lincoln in Westminster, while Olivier reads words from the Gettysburg Address which, again, have a pertinence unforeseen by their author: '. . . we here highly resolve that the dead shall not have died in vain, that the nation shall, under God, have a new birth of freedom, and that the government of the people, by the people and for the people, shall not perish from the earth'.

Several months later, after *Words for Battle* had been on general release for a while, Jennings wrote to Cicely that it 'sounds very highbrow and queer but although it might have been we chucked ourselves into it pretty deep and the result turned everybody's stomach's [*sic*] over and was a huge and quite unexpected success in theatres here . . .'[28] That power has not been dimmed by the passage of years.

★

With May came the end of the Blitz. London suffered its last serious raid on the night of the 10th. During that day, Jennings had written to

Cicely, in response to her latest letter: 'Your remarks about Wellington
and Waterloo and the last twenty years very good. Excellent analysis of the same thing in George Orwell's *Lion and the Unicorn*: still
quite a bunch of "intellectuals" here who are afraid of becoming
"patriots" . . .'[29] Jennings, manifestly, felt no such fear. To be sure, his
patriotism was an idiosyncratic thing, not the kind churned out for
editorials. But it was sincere, deep and passionate, founded on – among
other things – an unbreakable attachment to specific places (the
landscapes of Suffolk, the dome of St Paul's), an exceptional knowledge
of English history, literature, art, music and architecture, and – now –
a respectful familiarity with British working people and their cultures.
It was a familiarity which, while not yet as fully developed as it would
become over the next year or two, was already greater and warmer
than that of most intellectuals of his generation.

For almost two years now, all of the things Jennings most valued
had been at risk of subjugation, mutilation or destruction. No wonder
they had started to seem newly precious as well as newly fragile. No
wonder, now that the British people had apparently withstood the
worst the enemy could do (and at best, withstood it with compassion,
humour and quiet pride), now that the future course of the war
seemed at least a little more hopeful,[30] that an artist like Jennings
should feel moved to celebrate a revivified vision of Britain and
Britishness. He set about doing so, and the result is an unrivalled
masterpiece: *Listen to Britain*.

It was a film that changed and grew dramatically in the making.
Originally it was to have been little more than a portrait of one of
Myra Hess's famous lunchtime concerts at the National Gallery, in
which she played Mozart's Piano Concerto in G Major, K453. There
is an earlier treatment entitled 'National Gallery',[31] which suggests
that this film would have been much like the existing finale of *Listen
to Britain*, which also features Myra Hess playing Mozart. (A later
treatment, dated August 1941, refers to the work-in-progress by the
title of 'Tin Hat Concerto'; fortunately, good taste prevailed.) As Joe
Mendoza recalls:

> We shot the Myra Hess sequence, and then the Unit broke up for
> a holiday. Humphrey and McAllister went away on holiday
> together to Scotland, and when they came back, Humphrey said

to me, 'We're going to make a completely different picture. It's not just going to be about the National Gallery, it's going to be about music and sound.'

They went on to film in Manchester, Blackpool and the Lake District, as well as reshooting the Mozart performance.

Mendoza's job usually involved his travelling a day or so ahead of the crew to make arrangements for them, but he did have the chance to see Jennings at work as a director on several occasions. One day, the Unit was in a school yard, filming children dancing something called the 'Clapping Polka'.

> We had a feature camera operator that day, and we did our shots, and he said, 'I suppose you'll want to go again.' So Humphrey said, 'Why?' And he said, 'Well, that little girl stumbled and made a mistake, don't you want to do it again?' 'No,' said Humphrey. You see, the conventional film people would have done it again until it was perfect, but for Humphrey it was real life, you see. That was to a certain extent a part of the whole Surrealist idea, you know? You let extraordinary things come together, and their coming together is another thing.
>
> The only thing that was shot which was never used – Humphrey had this thing about having the human voice in it, and we shot a sequence of a woman reading to a little boy in bed, and of course, being Humphrey she was reading about Captain Oates going into the snow . . .

Mendoza was impressed by what he saw of Jennings now: the young tyrant and prima donna that many at Blackheath had dreaded working with had mellowed greatly in the last few years, and had developed a gift for management:

> Humphrey was terribly good, you see. He never pushed himself, he never behaved like a film director. He was not modest, but he knew how to handle people. Although he was weird and wonderful and eccentric and had terrible green teeth, he had a kind of warmth and tenderness about him as a personality. He always made instant communication with people – very ordinary working-class sort of people – but they didn't ever think that he was terribly clever and above them, because he always managed to

make this contact just by his manner. He was never patronizing in any sense of the word. I think it was because he was a *complete* person . . .

Jennings himself left relatively few records of this period of film-ing, which was more or less complete by the beginning of December 1941 (at which point, immune system worn down by months of over-work, he promptly succumbed to flu). He first mentions the making of *Listen to Britain* to Cicely on 15 June: 'I seem to have been busier than ever in the last few weeks: mainly photographing the lunch-hour concerts in the National Gallery including Myra Hess – tremendous screen personality and of course enormous audiences – and then . . . the Queen! All part of a film about music in wartime: quite a possible subject.' But he returns to the subject only once or twice in the next few months. Instead, he prefers to talk about nature ('It is a great year for lupins'), gossip about other film-makers ('You have probably heard of *Target for Tonight*, Harry Watt's new film about the crew of a Wellington: terrific technically – a bit soul-less'), his bits and pieces of bedtime reading ('Turgenev – Lawrence's poems . . .') and the progress of the war. He was tremendously cheered by the Soviet Union's entry into the war in June 1941, and felt that his fellow-countrymen were rapidly learning that the great ogre to the east was not quite as thoroughly wicked as the British press had been telling everyone:

> The break-up of the Russian-bogey illusion and the years of trickery and dishonesty which produced it are now becoming really clear to the nation here as a whole and producing a new kind – or several new kinds – of people who wish the USSR well. People who cannot be bothered with politics and who regard newspapers as rubbish and arguments as propaganda are yet tremendously impressed by Russian newsreels and by the simple fact of Russian resistance – one of these days this is going to come back on the people who have misled everybody.[32]

It's worth remembering that Jennings was not now and never had been a member of the Communist Party. Still, like many other intellectuals of the Left, he continued to 'wish the USSR well' through-out the war. With the benefit of half a century's hindsight, generations brought up in full knowledge of Stalin's murderous tyranny may consider this attitude – at best – naïve. Perhaps it was; there were certainly British intellectuals who had been horrified by, among other nightmares and betrayals, the forced collectivizations of 1929–33, the Great Purge trials of 1936–8 and Russia's grotesquely cynical pact with Hitler which held until the German invasion of 1941. 'The sin of nearly all leftwingers from 1933 onwards,' Orwell once wrote, 'is that they have wanted to be anti-fascist without being anti-totalitarian.'[33]

One can rally to the defence in a number of ways: by pointing out, for example, that Jennings was generally quite as antipathetic towards the Spender–Auden type of parlour Communist as Orwell ever was; by pointing out that he was far from being the only humane and intelligent West European whose proper scepticism about the honesty of the capitalist press was not adequately balanced by an awareness of the gross mendacity of the other camp; by insisting – which is important – that his brand of socialism was humane and thoroughly grounded in daily reality, utterly unlike the power-hungry brand that Orwell diagnosed in his peers.

Rather than defend his attitude in our own, retrospective terms, however, let us concede that he, like many other people of goodwill, was gravely misguided about the Russian political system. And then let us immediately recall that he also recognized something essential about the Russian people, and the Russian armed forces, that has not been tainted by hindsight; a recognition which imposes a duty of awareness on posterity every bit as great as the duty to recall the show trials, the mass murders and the great betrayals carried out in the name of Soviet socialism: 'I do not think it has been sufficiently appreciated publicly – but in our hearts we know now that not only have the Russians saved us from the Nazis, but also that they are beating them for us all. I hope and trust we shall not forget.'[34] Now that Hollywood is firmly in charge of popular historical awareness in the Western world, those words are sadder and more pertinent than ever.

On a lighter note, one should also bear in mind that Jennings was, at heart, far too much the idiosyncratic aesthete to be anyone's political stooge. The theme most typical of his correspondence with Cicely from the summer and autumn of 1941 is one of defiant refusal to be swamped by current events:

What a game also politics & economics & the rest: but I don't
find that the war makes me take a greater interest in them really:
on the contrary. I agree our foreign policy is a joke and our home
organization a cruel farce; but I still think that the real world is
the world of Mozart and Uccello.[35]

Why those particular Old Masters? Probably because they both
contribute to the texture of *Listen to Britain*: Uccello's *Rout of San
Romano* – or a large-scale reproduction of that work – is clearly visible
in the National Gallery sequence, for the film sets out to embrace
cultural manifestations of all sorts and conditions, and the works of
those creators now become beautiful fragments in a fresh work of
genius. It can plausibly be argued (and has been) that *Listen to Britain*
is one of the greatest humanist works that the cinema has produced:
an exquisitely articulated sequence of sounds and images, often warm
and even playful in tone but with emotional depths and complexities
that have seldom been rivalled; simple, sensuous and passionate
enough to move all but the most callow or cynical viewer, yet complex
enough to hold and yield mysteries even for those who have seen it
dozens, even hundreds, of times. I watched it again while revising
these passages: it never fails to move and astonish me.

Summary alone cannot hope to do it justice, but it may lay the
groundwork for an attempt to justify some of these high claims.
Wholly free of commentary, the film simply (not so simply – the
cutting is remarkably complex) ranges over the life of the nation from
late afternoon, through the watches of the night and into the next day,
concentrating on the performance of music – in a ballroom, on the
radio, played and sung by a solo pianist, blared out by a military band
– but also, rather in the spirit of later avant-garde composers, making
a kind of *musique concrète* from other sounds: steam engines heaving
into motion, bells and whistles, snatches of half-heard conversation,
the clopping of horses' hooves, metal being beaten in furnaces. You
could think of it as a single tune made out of many individual tunes (a
pleasing metaphor for a nation united in a common cause), and the
tune goes something like this:

Afternoon in the countryside; corn waving in the breeze. Spitfires
zoom overhead, while Land Girls and the Observer Corps work below.
The hour for putting up the blackout curtains falls, and the BBC six

o'clock news comes on the radio. The light thickens, and helmeted men on night duty look out at the sea, waiting for signs of invasion. In the Tower Ballroom in Blackpool, hundreds of servicemen steer their partners round the dance floor to the cheerful strains of 'Roll Out the Barrel' and other popular hits of the day. Cut to a pithead, and the night shift going underground. Elsewhere, Canadian servicemen are whiling away their stalled railway journey by crooning along to 'Home on the Range', until the line is cleared and their train pulls away into the darkness.

More vignettes of the night: a bomber factory; a plane taking off; women volunteers in an ambulance station listen to the high-pitched voice of one of their number singing and playing the old folksong 'The Ash-Grove'. Big Ben chimes, and the BBC Overseas Service, cued by the 'British Grenadiers' march, broadcasts in countless languages to listeners around the world. Come the dawn – the old sound of birdsong and the mildly comical new sound of a BBC fitness instructor, Coleman Smith, waking the nation to vigorous efforts with his trademark PT song. A housewife watches children dancing to the 'Clapping Polka' in a nearby playground; we guess from the photograph at her side that her husband is fighting overseas. (Perhaps he is already dead?) Bren-gun carriers trundle and grind through the half-timbered streets of a village; a little girl watches and giggles.

Another radio cue – the bugle call announcing the popular BBC show *Music While You Work*. In a razor-blade factory, the girls on the production line grin and sway and sing mischievously along to 'Yes, My Darling Daughter'. Soldiers mass on a station platform; canteens serve rescue squads; a painter dresses up a factory in camouflage. The sound of a familiar male voice singing a sentimental ditty proves to be a lunchtime concert in a workers' canteen by the music hall favourites, Flanagan and Allen, singing 'Round the Back of the Arches' while the appreciative crowd whistles along. The final sustained note of the song merges seamlessly into the same note, now played by the RAF Orchestra as part of a driving rendition of Mozart's Piano Concerto in G major. Close-up on the matronly form of Myra Hess as her hands, powerful but precise, take up the piano part; multiple cuts to the National Gallery audience, including a wounded soldier, a languidly elegant young woman and, next to Kenneth Clark, the bravely fixed, approving smile of Her Majesty the Queen.

Beyond the gallery, still suffused with glorious Mozart, the nation quietly and determinedly goes about the business of war. Factories produce tanks; the noise of heavy industry drowns Mozart, but is itself drowned by a Royal Marines band playing 'A Life on the Ocean Wave'. Back to the demonic world of industry, where arms are being forged for the struggle; over the hellish blaze of furnaces rises the angelic sound of an unseen choir, singing the final bars of 'Rule Britannia'. This patriotic anthem runs throughout the final sequence of landscape montage and aerial shots, while, in the words of the Unit post-production script, 'The fire in the heart of our people, the music in their voices, swells into the air, out of the factories, over the fields of grain, and up over the land.' High among the clouds, the camera lifts gently upwards in an almost subliminal flourish of Triumph.

Why do those of us who love this twenty-minute film consider it so extraordinary? There are many possible answers: one of them is to do with it being a *Gesamtkunstwerk*, a total work of art in which each of Jennings's pre-war apprenticeships reached its fullest flower. Shot by shot, sequence by sequence, it has an intense visual beauty, albeit a beauty of the kind that previous centuries could not have seen: the legacy of Jennings's years as a painter (and equal respect due to his abundantly gifted cameraman, Chick Fowle). It is full of surprising juxtapositions of subject-matter, strange quirks and accidents – the little boy stumbling, an old man caught surreptitiously spitting, an art gallery full of empty frames, uniformed British servicemen solemnly playing 'German' music: the heritage of Surrealism (and credit also to Stewart McAllister, who created many of these effects). It pays respectful attention to people of all classes and to music of all genres: the spirit of Mass-Observation. It contains moments of curious emotional ambiguity, comparable to those found in the sixteenth- and seventeenth-century poetry that had obsessed Jennings as a student and scholar.

All true enough, but all far too formalist to account for the film's unique potency, either now or then. One comes nearer the heart of the matter if one considers what it meant to its first audiences. During the war, Lady Forman (aka Miss Helen de Mouilpied) worked for the Ministry of Information's 16mm-film distribution wing. Thirty years later, she remembered:

One of the non-theatrical films under the heading of 'general' in our jargon which was liked and applauded was Humphrey Jennings's magical *Listen to Britain*. All sorts of audiences felt it to be a distillation and also a magnification of their own experience on the home front. Especially factory audiences. I remember one show in a factory in the Midlands where about 800 workers clapped and stamped approval. Films got very short shrift if they touched any area of people's experience and did not ring true.[36]

'Distillation and magnification' is an admirably exact phrase. Nor was it just factory workers who were moved by the film on its first showings. Jennings reported to his wife: 'I hear *Listen* was well thought of in Hollywood – also among the troops in the Middle East. A toughish Commando officer was raving about [*Words for Battle* and *Listen to Britain*] yesterday – which was really very gratifying – shows it's worth taking trouble and not underrating people.'[37]

Jennings knew perfectly well that the film might be considered too complex for its audience (and he was right to have misgivings: some of his colleagues in the documentary movement not only hated the film, but thought it a disaster in propaganda terms).[38] His pleasure at its glowing reception by the people he most wanted to reach was, among other things, the pleasure of vindication. Like the hypothetical modern Laureate he had imagined in his pre-war radio broadcasts, he had shown the people who they were and who they had been. It was a heightened, idealized portrait, but they recognized it and took it to heart. With *Listen to Britain*, Jennings had become his nation's unofficial cinematic Poet Laureate.

And like the works of earlier poets, the film has become part of the past we need to know about. It has often been remarked – usually in tones of surprise – how singularly lacking in conventional notes of propaganda it is, even by Jennings's standards. Not once does it whip up hatred or resentment for the unseen enemy: there are hardly any shots of the wounded, no lingering over bomb damage as in *Heart of Britain*, no tragic fires. Nor, still more remarkably, is there any of the idealizing rhetoric that is the all but inevitable hallmark of the propaganda film: in place of the Stakhanovite worker, the grizzled old man quietly spitting on the floor; in place of highly orchestrated shots of the Great Leader addressing the adoring masses, an almost throwaway shot of the Queen, a nice middle-aged lady enjoying her lunchtime music just like all the other Londoners. *Listen to Britain* does, of course, idealize the British, but it does so in a deep and subtle way: it shows their eccentricity, their individuality, their humour and their capacity to create and enjoy beauty in all its forms. Jennings shows the strength of this humanity, but also hints at its fragility. Just off-screen are the bombers, the storm troopers, the Panzer divisions and the destroyers: to turn an almost exactly contemporary phrase of Auden's, the nightmare of the dark.

In case this account smacks of complacent national partiality, it seems fitting to offer the last word to a non-English writer, the French film critic Jacques Rancière, who in 1997 wrote:

> Que fait donc ce film militant pour attester de la mission historique d'un peuple résistant? Il nous présente l'extraordinaire de sa guerre exactement semblable à l'ordinaire de son existence pacifique. L'équivalent en images, si l'on veut, de l'oraison funèbre de Périclès, l'éternel discours d'Athènes la civilisée face à Sparte la guerrière: 'Notre manière de nous préparer à la guerre, c'est notre existence sans contraintes.'

> What does this militant film do, then, to bear witness to the historic mission of a resisting people? It shows us the extraordinary aspect of war as being exactly the same as the ordinary life of peacetime. It's the equivalent in images, if you will, of the funeral oration of Pericles, the eternal claim of civilized Athens confronted by warlike Sparta: 'Our way of preparing ourselves for war is our life of freedom.'

Listen to Britain, in short, at once fulfilled and transcended its official function of propaganda, and became Jennings's first unblemished masterpiece. What's more, he was about to equal, or even surpass it.

*

Though final post-production work on *Listen to Britain* was not completed until early January 1942, Jennings found time to start work on treatments for his next major project as early as the previous October. A draft text titled 'N.F.S.' – 'National Fire Service' – is dated '25.10.41'. Over the next few months, in the course of which the project's working title changed to 'Counter-Attack', 'The Bells Went Down!', then 'To Be A Fireman', Jennings worked out the characters, situation and plot of this first full-scale venture into drama: a story about the heroic work of the regular and auxiliary fire services during the worst nights of the Blitz in the winter and spring of 1940/1 – before the Government established a unified National Fire Service in August 1941. One of the basic components of the firemen's story was there from the very first sentence: 'The film might begin with a fireman feeding some rabbits, and talking to the rabbits and he would be the man who was going to get killed in the film.'[39]

So *Fires Were Started*[40] – the quietly haunting, Blakean name by which the finished film is now generally known, though some sticklers for detail prefer *I Was a Fireman* – was always intended to be a film that would culminate in one man's death; a human sacrifice, as some have seen it.[41] And it was always intended that the various characters in the film would be played by actual firemen, some of whom would later complain that the task of making the film was just as hazardous as genuine fire-fighting, sometimes more so. 'Most of us had been through the Blitz with hardly a scratch – but in this job we all got burned, and so did Humphrey and his assistants . . .'[42]

By 27 January 1942, by which time he had also done a good deal of first-hand research at a fire station in Cheyne Place, Chelsea, Jennings had written – in occasional collaboration with the novelist Maurice Richardson[43] – a long and detailed treatment which not only minutely described each of the film's principal scenes but sketched out sample passages of dialogue. Tempting as it would be, then, to believe the much-told stories that Jennings directed the entire film from notes scribbled on a single piece of paper, or simply made most of it up as he went along, the archives show that the film was as meticulously preplanned as anything in his career save his last film, *Family Portrait*. To be sure, his day-to-day working methods allowed plenty of room for improvised dialogue, for the telling expansion of character detail and for the odd scene created on the spur of the moment – including two memorable segments with music: one very short scene showing a man blowing into a penny whistle, and a more substantial one in which a piano player busks a rhumba-type tune to which his friends dance a comic jig. Also, Jennings was delighted by the speech rhythms and turns of phrase of his predominantly cockney performers, and would try to work some of his favourites into the action. Observers were impressed by this ability to create on the hoof, and to capitalize on what the location gave him: 'Humphrey could be likened to an obsessive insect with antennae always alert and instantly sensitively selective, without human hum and ha, of what was needed.'[44] But this improvised quality of *Fires Were Started* should not be overstated. In most other respects it was thoroughly planned on paper before a foot of film was exposed.

The idea for a film about the fire services had first been floated by the Public Relations Committee of Civil Defence almost a year before Jennings started work, in January 1941, but such a film had seemed difficult if not impossible to make while the country was still taking heavy bombing. By the summer, as Ian Dalrymple explained, matters had started to look up: 'The Germans had taken all of their aeroplanes to go and hit the Russians, and after May 1941 we were more or less at peace so that one could take many more risks in the blackout and that kind of thing, and it was suggested that a film should be made about the National Fire Service.'[45]

It was Harry Watt – usually no great fan of Jennings – who suggested to Dalrymple that Humphrey might be the man for the job, a fact that has prompted the speculation of malice on Watt's part, and his expectation that the two ex-Cambridge men would make a mess of such an action-based film. True or not, Dalrymple later confessed that he had his own, benevolent motives for assigning Jennings to the Fire Service project:

He had the artist's gift of setting up his camera at what might be called the *angle juste*; but his films until now had tended to be a series of static images of places and persons, their effect depending upon symbolic, enigmatic and sometimes epigrammatic juxtaposition of image and sound, worked out by himself and [McAllister] in the cutting-room. It was Harry Watt who got me to allot him an action-subject, for the good of Humphrey's soul and the widening of his scope. With qualms I followed his advice: and when the chance came to devote a feature-length film to the Auxiliary Fire Service, I offered it to Jennings. The result was *Fires Were Started* which, despite arguments over the final ending to meet the distributor's views, emerged as a happy blend of realism with poetry. And it proved that Humphrey, who was a marvellously well-organised person, was as able to handle the active as he was the static.[46]

Shooting on *Fires Were Started* began in February and ran till the beginning of June, mostly on location in Stepney and Wapping, with additional studio scenes shot at Pinewood. As well as being dangerous, it was an arduous and eventful shoot, which occasionally ran into unexpected trouble. As Fred Griffiths, one of Jennings's firemen/actors, later recalled:

> We had a deputation come down with a letter about [how] we were Fifth Columnists who were lighting up the sky for the Germans to come and bomb us. Well, that same night they come over, right, and they dropped a couple. Coz the hooters gone and I'm flying up the hill to go down the shelter and this old girl shouts out as she goes up the hill, 'You'll get the bloody lot of us killed one night, you will!'[47]

On 12 April, taking advantage of a brief hiatus, Jennings wrote to Cicely for the first time in many weeks and explained exactly what had been going on. It is one of his finest and most self-revealing statements, as well as an evocative résumé of work in progress:

> We have more or less taken over a small district, roped off streets, organized the locals and so on. It has been exceptionally hard and tiring work. A difficult film anyway, then a lot of camera trouble and no Chick [Fowle, his usual cameraman] and everything – film, petrol, supplies of all sorts very short. But of course the place and the people illuminating beyond everything. The river, the wharves and shipping, the bridge in Wapping Lane smelling permanently of cinnamon, the remains of Chinatown, the *Prospect of Whitby* and another wonderful pub called *The Artichoke* which is our field Headquarters . . .
>
> For the last two months we have been working down there for twelve hours a day six days a week: we are now roughly half way through and pretty exhausted: the results peculiar and very unlike anything I have had to do with before: popular, exciting, funny – mixture of slapstick and macabre blitz reconstruction.

Then, after some news of family and friends, and remarks about the critical and public response to *Listen to Britain*, now showing at the Gaumont, Haymarket ('a success and very popular'):

> To continue: it has now become 14 hours a day – living in Stepney the whole time – really have never worked so hard at anything or I think thrown myself into anything so completely. Whatever the results it is definitely an advance in film making for me – really beginning to understand people and not just looking at them and lecturing or pitying them. Another general effect of the war. Also should make me personally more bearable.
>   ... Life concerned with a burning roof – smoke fire water – men's faces and thoughts: a tangle of hose, orders shouted in the dark – falling walls, brilliant moonlight – dust, mud tiredness until nobody is quite sure where the film ends and the conditions of making it begin: a real fire could not be more tiring and certainly less trouble. But what one learns at midnight with tired firemen . . .[48]

Other gifted writers and speakers left their own memoirs of making the film. The successful novelist William Sansom, who played the major role of the new man Barrett and, like his fellow leading actors, was himself an auxiliary fireman, wrote a detailed recollection of *Fires Were Started* and its unorthodox director:

> He gave little of his own personal life away, he talked little of himself and only of work. He worked obsessed with the job in hand – and because he never spared himself he endeared himself to his employees, though he showed few of the usual endearing qualities, and certainly neither flattery nor histrionics. He was a man of medium height, tow-haired, with sharp blue eyes, inwards-pointing teeth and the shaped but blubbery lips of a Hollander, and his neck was so straight it pushed his head forward and often to one side. He shouted awesomely, and often smiled – but with the quick fade of one who has really no time for it.[49]

An admirably balanced account, considering that in one scene, where Barrett goes up to join his new mates on the blazing warehouse roof, Jennings had almost killed him:

To avoid trouble an assistant was told to empty a bucket of water over me before I went up. Unfortunately, he chose the bucket of paraffin standing about for feeding the fire. With all the smoke-smell about nobody noticed. And so I ascended through the fire drenched with fire-lighting fluid. By some miracle of flash-points – or perhaps a last exudation of Humphrey's forceful will – that lively little living torch never went up.[50]

Other versions of this anecdote have Jennings deliberately soaking Sansom in oil; one suspects that these yarns have grown more exaggerated with the years. On the whole, though, Sansom corroborates the impression Jennings gives of good on-set morale: 'He dealt well. Democracy the rule, Christian names all round, discussion and beer together after work – he gave us the impression of making the film *with* him instead of *for* him.'[51]

We were all glad to be away from station routine, all rebellious that we were not paid extra for these expert duties. Humphrey thus had to deal with an enthusiastic lot who had a convenient grudge whenever necessary – ideal constituents for the British temper . . .

The only revolt occurred over the funeral episode. Some of the men had already attended the real funerals of burned-up friends. They refused to carry this false coffin. Beneath this, I suspected deeper superstitions: they did not like acting in the old weed-grown churchyard, on holy ground, and among the symbols of death. They were, in fact, shocked.[52]

Otherwise, Sansom reports, the cast would do anything he asked of them – 'because it was Jennings who asked it, and we had developed by then a kind of hero-worship of him . . . a personal passion, an obsessive drive, and the knowledge that he was a thoroughly intelligent tough aesthete carried him way above the ordinary run.'[53]

For Joe Mendoza, in Jennings's company for long stretches again now that the busily itinerant shooting of *Listen to Britain* was over and done, the weeks spent in the East End were an important phase of his education:

Working with Humphrey was a perpetual seminar. We would walk around London for hours and hours and hours and hours, talking

– that is, he did the talking, I did the listening. *For Whom the Bell Tolls* was published then, and I said, what does 'For whom the bell tolls' mean? And he said, it's by Donne, and I said, who's Donne? so I had a marvellous lecture on the [metaphysical] poets. And he would talk to me about Blake, and Stubbs – he was mad about Stubbs. What fascinated him about Stubbs was the way he used to take horses to pieces in his studio. And he had this thing about the Industrial Revolution, he was always working on *Pandæmonium*.

Out of all this apparent confusion – the fire and smoke, the fatigue, the near-fatal accidents, the off-the-cuff inventions and buskings, the hours of grumbling or of inspired talk – Jennings crafted a film of classical balance and grace.

Fires Were Started is very nearly as complex as *Listen to Britain* in emotional terms, but its plot is – or appears – entirely straightforward and linear. The film begins as the day begins, with members of Heavy Unit One leaving their homes and turning up for work at Auxiliary Fire Station 14Y in the East End, near the docks. One by one, we meet the leading characters. Sub-Officer Dykes, or 'Sub' (played by Commanding Officer George Gravett), chats at the dockside; Johnny Daniels (Fred Griffiths) spars with his little boy, who deals him a big punch from which he pretends to reel; Brown (T. P. Smith) and Vallance (John Barker) meet each other on the street; S. H. 'Jacko' Jackson (Johnny Houghton) leaves his newsagent's shop – 'Don't do nothing silly, will you, Sid?' begs his wife – and mounts his bicycle; Walters (Philip Wilson-Dickson) comes out of his front door; Rumbold, jocularly referred to as 'the Colonel' (Loris Rey), looks up at the Limehouse Church clock.

We are almost complete, but today a new boy is joining the crew – Barrett (William Sansom): he asks his way to 14Y from a local Chinese civilian. (This is, after all, Limehouse, London's oldest Chinatown.) By the time he arrives, the team – known affectionately as the 'Crazy Gang' by the station's firewomen – is busy at work. Unlike the other men, Barrett is plainly a bit of a young toff, but Johnny Daniels, a true-blue cockney, treats him with gruff kindness and introduces him around. After routine cleaning and other chores are finished, the men carry out a full-scale hook-ladder drill; then, after lunch and some banter about their civvy street jobs (Johnny was a taxi driver, Barrett an advertising man), Johnny shows the rookie around the district they have to protect, drawing particular attention to a ship being loaded with guns and ammunition, and a sunken barge containing some ten thousand gallons of potentially life-saving water.

The day's routine work done, the men relax and wait for nightfall. Already, a few people have commented grimly that tonight will be a full moon, the usual cue for heavy bombing. In the interval, though, the men are almost determinedly cheerful: they play games, drink beer, take the mickey out of each other. Barrett, egged on by Jacko, sits down at the station's old upright piano and improvises a rhumba theme. Cut away to shots of the river at night, the munitions ship and the warehouses; then back to Brown and Johnny doing an improvised comic dance to Barrett's tune. A firewoman comes in to tell them that they are now on standby, and they head back to their beds to put on their fire-fighting equipment.

Barrett, the first to emerge dressed, returns to the piano and starts to play the rollicking old folksong 'One Man Went To Mow', doing appropriate comic variations on the theme as each of the team – Rumbold, Walters, Jacko, Joe Vallance, Brown and 'Sub' – makes his entrance. Their knockabout fun is suddenly pierced by the distant fateful wail of an air raid siren – like the arrival of a spectre at the feast. Rendered solemn for just a second, they pull themselves together and finish the song with full-lunged gusto.

From this point on, the mood of the film changes: from daytime to night; from drab, cosy reality to the realm of archetypal myth. Soon, our pack of clowns will have to play the part of heroes. Outside: darkness, mud, the all-too-vulnerable munitions ship, anti-aircraft fire. Inside, Rumbold reads lugubriously from Sir Walter Raleigh:

> O eloquent, just and mighty Death! whom none could advise, thou hast persuaded; what none hath dared, thou hast done; and whom all the world hath flattered, thou hast cast out of the world and despised. Thou hast drawn together all the pride, cruelty and ambition of man, and covered it over with these two narrow words: *hic jacet* [here lies].

It is chilling, morbid: no wonder Sub brusquely breaks the mood by chipping in, 'Righto, Colonel, we'll set that to music – when we get back.'

Cut to the Observer Post Control, from where the night's action will be coordinated; cut back to the station, where the blokes are singing, or bellowing, the anti-sentimental popular song 'Please Don't Talk about Me When I'm Gone'. The bombing intensifies, comes closer; crews are sent out; finally Heavy Unit One gets the call and is dispatched to Trinidad Street, Johnny singing lustily as they go to check out the warehouse, where a fire is already burning on the top floor. The crew hunts for a hydrant: Sub, Jacko and Rumbold break into the warehouse and head up to the roof; as the bombs continue to fall all around, they haul a hose up and prepare to fight the flames. Sub comes back down, and telephones Control to warn them that the fire is coming close to the munitions ship and that they urgently need at least ten more pumps. At Control, the hard-pressed officer in command tells his people that all he can spare is five.

Barrett and Vallance bring a second hose up to the roof. Finally, the water begins to spurt: Jacko and Rumbold control one hose, Barrett and Vallance the second, and Sub rejoins them. But the water is already running low, and Johnny sends Barrett off in search of another supply. As he runs down the street, past a man leading a terrified horse, the water gives out completely. Eventually he relocates the sunken barge Johnny had shown him, and tells an incoming fire engine to prepare a link-up. The flames lick ever closer to the ammunition ship, but, after an agonizing wait, the water from the barge starts to flow copiously. Back at Control, a firewoman is on the phone to HQ as a bomb hits the building. Cut to HQ; cut back to Control, where the young woman, bleeding from a cut on her forehead, climbs back up to the phone and, unfazed, apologizes politely for the interruption.[54] Montage of firewomen at phones, the urgent search for back-up.

By now the warehouse fire is raging. Johnny and Barrett work the pump below; Sub, Rumbold and Jacko remain on the roof. Sub sends Rumbold down the flaming staircase to pass a message to the new Chief who has just arrived at the pump; the Chief tries to shout to the men and tell them to come down, because a turntable ladder is on its way. But they can't hear him, so Barrett races up the stairs with their orders: 'District Officer says you've got to get off the roof, sir.' Sub: 'How the hell does he think we're going to get down there?'

A bomb hits. Sub falls into the flames. Barrett pulls him out. The turntable ladder arrives and they prepare to lower Sub to the ground on a line. 'Give me that line, I know what to do with it. You get down!' Jacko shouts to Barrett. The younger man hesitates, then goes. Thanks to Jacko's firm grip on the line, Sub reaches the ground safely. Back on the roof, Jacko fights the flames alone. Then the burning roof gives way beneath his foot. The hose falls; Jacko falls. Johnny watches in horror, shouts Jacko's name. There is a tremendous explosion from inside the warehouse.

Back to the switchboard: a hundred additional pumps have been ordered into the area. New firemen start to arrive, and join the remaining members of the team in their fight to contain the flames. Gradually, they are starting to win. Sub, already in a hospital bed, is rueful. At last, Observer Post tells Control that the fire has been successfully contained. Comes the dawn: the sound of the 'All Clear', sooty faces, smouldering ruins. Barrett winks tiredly at Johnny. A mobile canteen arrives and a pretty, smiling girl hands out cups of tea. A man greets Brown and Vallance and, noting their gloom, innocently ribs them:

> 'What's the matter, can't you take it, chum?'
> 'You 'eard?'
> 'No, what?'
> 'Jacko's copped it.'
> 'Copped it bad?'
> (Angrily). 'He's copped it, I tell you!'

The long and weary process of packing up begins. The mood is glum, until Johnny responds to a man who sympathetically remarks 'Bad night' with the robust words: 'Bad night? You wanna go down the road. There's a boat down there, good as new, she ain't got a scratch on 'er. A sight for sore eyes!' It's true; and the soundtrack music underscores their sense of victory. Back in Jacko's shop, his new widow is listening to the impassive voice of the BBC morning news summing up the night's events: 'It does not appear that casualties are likely to be heavy ... in one district the attacks were heavy and several large fires were started. These, however, were successfully prevented from spreading...' Wordless, she brushes a lock of hair from her face.

Back at the station, exhaustion and anticlimax. Rumbold reads a curiously bitter, misanthropic passage from *Macbeth*:

Ay, in the catalogue ye go for men;
As hounds and greyhounds, mongrels, spaniels, curs,
Shoughs, water-rugs, and demi-wolves, are clept [called]
All by the name of dogs . . .

A firewoman passes out six mugs of tea: she affectionately addresses Barrett, no longer the new boy, as 'Bill', and he calls her 'Mum'. Jacko's unmentioned, unmentionable absence is obviously weighing heavily on all. Finally, Brown explodes angrily: 'Come on, chums, snap out of it!' And so to the final scene: Jacko's funeral in Whitechapel Church, his coffin borne by his six mates. Their procession is intercut with the ship that they have saved, sailing up the Thames; and the film ends with its bow proudly cutting the waters.

*

A simple tale, then. But as Lindsay Anderson wrote in 'Only Connect', the most important essay ever published on Jennings:

> . . . in treatment [*Fires Were Started*] is of the greatest subtlety, richly poetic in feeling, intense with tenderness and admiration for the unassuming heroes whom it honours.
> . . . No other British film made during the war, documentary or feature, achieved such a continuous and poignant truthfulness, or treated the subject of men at war with such a sense of its incidental glories and its essential tragedy.

There are many qualities worthy of praise in the film. Here, following Anderson, are four: poetry, subtlety, tenderness, truth.

Poetry: where *Listen to Britain* is a densely crafted lyric, *Fires Were Started* (though barely more than an hour in length) is an epic: and those wonderfully vivid flashes of characterful faces in the former expand and blossom into full-blooded life in the second.

Subtlety: the film teems with images, phrases and moods from farce to morbidity to deep mystery, that – though by now we expect this of Jennings – might seem to have no place in a propaganda film. Think of the startled horse running from the explosions, or the evocation of Raleigh, or the firemen's eccentric little rhumba, or the unforgettably odd penny-whistle player, like some character on loan from *The Waste Land*. Jennings was, as his writings show, fascinated by Eliot, and there are many muffled echoes of Eliot's London in Jennings's London: the great churches, the cockney banter, the snatches of popular song, the allusions to Shakespeare, the image of a city in flames ... Material here for a thesis, perhaps, especially when one recalls the argument that, like *The Waste Land*, *Fires Were Started* draws heavily on the traditional imagery of the Tarot deck, especially the Chariot and the alchemical image of the Maison-Dieu, or burning house.[55] Indeed, if one takes seriously the hint that, at its deepest level, the film is all about a man who must be killed and replaced by a new man, then there is even a faint rumble of Eliot's vegetation myths, Jessie Weston's *From Ritual to Romance* and *The Golden Bough*. Not that it greatly matters whether this is precisely so or not: what is important is to feel the complexity of the film's journey from the everyday to the timeless and back again.

Tenderness and admiration: the main reason why the film is deeply moving is that Jennings had himself been deeply moved by the 'unassuming' heroism and other humane virtues he had seen all around him in the war, and possessed the artistic means to make his emotion public. As he wrote to Cicely:

> In any case my (I say my[,] but) firemen have certainly proved one thing to me, but proved it in practice – that all these distinctions of understanding and level and other such are total rubbish and worse – invented by people to mislead. And not merely the distinctions made by the famous upper-classes but also those made [by] the grubby documentary boys who try and give a hand to what they call emerging humanity, the common man and so on.[56]

But even if we did not have such written accounts of the magnificence achieved by ordinary people – the term seems more grotesque than ever – under fire, the film would be more than eloquent testimony of his respect. As with his other films, but in a way accentuated by the requirements and gifts of narrative, *Fires Were Started* seizes on the feeling that the war has done away with the idiocies of class distinction in Britain, and amplifies it. In the 1930s, as Professor Jeffrey Richards has pointed out, it was rare for working-class characters to be shown in British feature films as anything other than figures of fun. In *Fires Were Started*, almost everyone is shown in some comic light or is the target of a joke or two, but no one is seriously mocked, and everyone – even Barrett, who seems a languid and effete toff when he first comes into view – is a potential hero. For a respectful sense of democracy, of essential human equality, shapes the story as well as the mood: the film's 'hero' is not Jacko, who gives his life to save others, but the whole unit, any one of whom (we feel) might have done the same. And what is true of the unit is, by extension, true of the other units who come to their help, and of the people at HQ, of Jacko's unweeping widow, of the smiling canteen girl, of the Chinese pedestrian and the penny-whistle player. In short, the hero of *Fires Were Started* is the British people.

Truth: as with Jennings's other war films, *Fires Were Started* conveys a sense of large general truth that can withstand any amount of revisionist history writing, scepticism or sneering. Using real-life firemen as his performers had its risks, and there are moments in the film when their lack of training as actors shows through: lines thrown away or muted, slightly unnatural rhythms of speech and movement. But these were a small price to pay for the film's mood of complete authenticity, since it is also trying to tell a local, specific truth about the wartime Fire Service. According to those who knew best, it succeeded. William Sansom:

> the film was true to life in every respect. Not a false note – if you make the usual allowances for the absence of foul language which was in everybody's mouth all the time. It may be thought that, working with the men on the spot, such truth would be an inevitable result. I don't believe it. Romanticism, tricks for tricks' sake, false patriotism, militant smartness, intrusive humour and many another nugget of Director's Delight could have crept in. But this director kept it clean, and infused the meat of realism with his own passion and intellect to make of it all a poetic work of art.[57]

And, introducing a screening of *Fires Were Started* at the National Film Theatre in the 1950s, Fred Griffiths said: 'In the audience tonight I've brought along a couple of my mates who were in the Fire Service with me, and – well, I shall live, and they will live those nights over again when they see this picture. And I tell you this: that as you see it depicted here, so it was, and sometimes far worse.'

Critical consensus has gone along with the verdict of Messrs Sansom and Griffiths. One brief testament may stand for many. In 1969, Daniel Millar wrote in the magazine *Sight and Sound*: 'Fires Were Started ... seems to me the highest achievement of British cinema; and Jennings is not only the greatest documentarist but also, counting Chaplin and Hitchcock as American, the greatest film-maker that this country has produced.' But the last word should go to Fred Griffiths, who paid handsome tribute to Jennings at the end of his speech at the NFT: 'If just a little bit of that man's greatness brushed off on me as he passed by, I should be very happy.'

Seven

The War Years – 1942 to 1945:
From *The Silent Village* to
A Diary for Timothy

On 28 July 1942, as the exhausting work on *Fires Were Started* finally wound down and he began to think about his next major project, Jennings wrote to his wife in more than usually contemplative mode:

> I am finding more than ever that the chief problem in all times is to fit in all the worlds that exist together. The world of the day to day war – the world of the past (Suffolk, Cambridge) – the great landscapes of the USSR and the USA – the rich nostalgia of France and Italy – the constant struggle of poetry and economics – the alternate claims of man and nature – the sudden long-term reminders from Greece and China – how to fit all in ... – To shift rapidly and easily from Tobruk to Courbet – from the monumental shaft of six o'clock sunlight to the local politics of the Welsh valleys – Handel, Moscow, Vermont ... you alone combine and do not separate ...
>
> I should theoretically be very tired at the end of a picture but I don't think I do [*sic*] – at any rate everybody, including your mother, says how well I'm looking. On the other hand, I only have to lay my head on the pillow to fall fast asleep. I don't think it's work – so much as war: one just hasn't as much energy. Or maybe it's middle-age[1] – but I don't feel middle-aged, on the contrary – younger than ever. There is nothing so exhilarating as seeing even a few ideas one has had coming into being on screen.

His next potential source of exhilaration came from a wholly unexpected quarter. A few weeks earlier, on 10 June, in reprisal for the assassination of Reinhard Heydrich, second-in-command of the SS, the

Germans had massacred the people of Lidice, a village in Czechoslo-vakia. About a month later, Jennings received a single page of a typed letter from a Mr Viktor Fischl, an émigré poet who worked for the Czech Ministry of Information in London. It was headed: 'A village in Bohemia: the first draft of a synopsis for a short film on Lidice', and it began with the words 'This is the small village of Lidice somewhere in Czechoslovakia, and this is the village of X in Wales. It is not so long since these two villages were exactly like one another . . .' The docu-ment went on to outline the ways in which parallels between them could be illustrated. Jennings, as he recalled a year later in a talk for the BBC Home Service, thought it 'really one of the most brilliant ideas for a short film that we'd ever come across'.[2] The Ministry of Information agreed with him, and the Lidice film was immediately given the green light.

After brief discussion with his colleagues, two principles were established. First, Fischl's dramatic idea was radically simplified: instead of cutting between a real Welsh mining community and a faked-up Lidice, the film would be, so to speak, a hypothetical drama set in just one village – it would be a story that would show in frighteningly realistic detail how life might have been for the Welsh if the Nazis had successfully invaded Britain as they had occupied Czechoslovakia. Second, it was soon realized there was no point in trying to dream up the details of Welsh village life from committee rooms in London: they would have to find a village that corresponded to Lidice in most essential physical and social respects, and to enlist the cooperation of the whole community for filming. So Jennings, on the advice of his friend Allen Hutt, contacted Mr Arthur Horner, the President of the South Wales Miners' Federation, who in turn advised him to steer clear of the traditional heartland of the Welsh mining industry in the Rhondda and to head instead for the anthracite end of the western Welsh coalfield in the valleys towards Swansea, where the population still had strong farming roots and where Welsh was still quite widely spoken. (The district, as I discovered when I went there in the early months of 2000, was also well known, even notorious, for its staunch left-wing politics. One miner's son, now in his seventies, told me that when he was a small boy his father had made him read the *Daily Worker* instead of the *Beano* or *Dandy*; and some people still refer to the area, not altogether in fun, as 'Little Moscow'.)

More specifically, Arthur Horner put Jennings in touch with Mr
D. D. Evans – 'Dai Dan' – the miners' agent for a small village called
Ystradgynlais. Dai Evans, in Jennings's recollection, was 'a person of
great enthusiasm and tremendous physical strength – sort of a Tolstoyan figure of a man – used to play rugger for Swansea at one
period, and with all the blue in his face that shows a man has been
cutting coal all his life – little bits of coal that fly off and embed
themselves in the skin'.[3] After a brief discussion about the general idea
of the film, Evans sent them off to prospect several villages in the
general direction of Swansea, assuring them that they'd be bound to
find a suitable location before long. Within a minute or so of leaving
him, Jennings went into the nearest stationer's to buy a notebook and
noticed a postcard of an extraordinarily picturesque village, embla-
zoned with its name: CWMGIEDD. When he asked the shopkeeper
where this Cwmgiedd (approximate pronunciation for non-Welsh
speakers: Cum-ge-eth) might be, he was told that it was just a quarter
of a mile away. Jennings and his team footed it there, looked around –
at the straight high street of small stone terraced houses climbing up
into the hills, the mountain stream running parallel to the street, the
white Methodist chapel with its graveyard, the grocer's shop owned
by Mr Tom Powell, the village school – and realized that luck had
guided them to their perfect Lidice.

Slightly shamefaced at having picked his spot so quickly, Jennings
went back to Mr Evans, who gave him a lightning social history of the
area, which in the last war had been called 'the neutral country'
because not a single inhabitant had volunteered for the war – under
the influence of a local self-taught philosopher, they had all become
confirmed pacifists.

Jennings returned to London to enthuse about the success of his
recce, only to discover that he had almost been overtaken by a letter
from the chairman of the newly created 'Provisional Film Committee'
of Cwmgiedd, expressing the villagers' sense of deep honour at having
been chosen to re-enact the story of the Czech people's heroic
resistance. 'If you don't go back to Wales,' an MOI official told
Jennings, 'they'll be making a film without you.' So he raced back to
Cwmgiedd in time to find Dai Evans handing out a circular inviting
people to a public meeting to explain the nature of the project.

On 21 August 1942, about a hundred representatives from local villages gathered in the Welfare Hall at Ystradgynlais to hear what Jennings required of them. 'I said that we were going to be a nuisance; I said that we were going to turn their houses upside down; that they might think that it was going to be very exciting to be on the films to begin with, but by the time we had been down there four or five months, they'd begin to regret it.'[4] Undaunted by his sobering words, the meeting passed a vote of confidence and a film commitee of twelve local representatives was appointed. It would help the Crown Film Unit in all practical ways, but also monitor the progress of the film and give editorial criticism as to its authenticity. This last point became more crucial to Jennings as the months went by: as he grew to love Cwmgiedd and its people, his ideas for the film underwent a subtle change. In addition to bringing home the horror of Lidice, the film must also, he thought, be a tribute to the traditions of Wales and to the politics and culture of its working people. As he later summed it up:

> in this picture you see not only the reconstruction of the Lidice story, but also the clash of two types of culture: the ancient, Welsh, liberty-loving culture which has been going on in these valleys way, way back into the days of King Arthur and beyond, still alive in the Welsh language and in the traditions of the valleys; and this new-fangled, loudspeaker, blaring culture invented by Dr. Goebbels and his satellites. And it's through the clash of these two cultures that the mechanism of the film, so to speak, is presented and not simply as a blood-and-thunder story of some people marching into a village.[5]

So, for the next six months, the film went ahead much as Jennings had outlined, with the people of Cwmgiedd, Ystradgynlais and nearby villages playing themselves. *The Silent Village* (as the Lidice film would eventually be called) worked its way into almost every aspect of village life: 'we were down in Cwmgiedd and in those valleys from August until January: we came down in the marvellous weather, with leaves on the trees and bright sunlight, and we left in the middle of snow and rain and floods'.[6] By the end of September, Jennings and his assistants had been joined by the rest of the crew:

> There are no hotels of any kind there; we – the whole unit, up to twelve or thirteen people – lived in the miners' cottages and lived

with them. And I think that on both sides it was a great success, because, for example, some of our chaps from the Unit – one of the electricians and one of the camera men – were allowed to bring their wives and families down to live with the miners' wives and families, and I think that these people were genuinely sorry to see us go.[7]

This does not seem to have been mere wishful thinking. Today, more than half a century later, the making of the film continues to be remembered vividly by the local community, since many of those who acted in the film as children – as well as one or two adults – still live there, and recall the oddity and excitement of having a film unit descend into their midst like a visitation from another world. Everyone who knew them still speaks of the Unit, particularly 'Mr Jennings' and his assistant Diana Pine, 'Di', with warmth and regard; almost every-one there of mature years has seen *The Silent Village* at some time or another, knows at least something about Jennings's subsequent career and early death, and regards the film as one of the most remarkable things ever to have happened in the area. The general impression of the film's director is perhaps most succinctly summed up in the words of Mr Dai Roberts, a former miner who played one of the resistance fighters in the film, and who was two weeks away from his ninetieth birthday when I interviewed him in May 2000: 'Mr Jennings was a *gentleman*' – meaning not that he was a typical representative of the English upper classes, but that he always treated everyone with consideration and kindness (a verdict, to be sure, that might have astonished some of his fellow-workers in the CFU).

Jennings's letters of the time confirm that his experience in Wales consolidated the final stage of a sentimental and political educa-tion that had begun for him in the making of *Fires Were Started*. On 10 September, he wrote to Cicely:

Down here I am working on a reconstruction of the Lidice story in a mining community – but more important really than that is being close to the community itself and living & working inside it, for what it is every day. I really never thought to live to see the honest Christian and Communist principles daily acted on as a matter of course by a large number of British – I won't say English – people living together. Not merely honesty, culture, manners, practical socialism, but real love: with passion and tenderness and comradeship & heartiness all combined. From these people one can really understand Cromwell's New Model Army and the defenders of many places at the beginning of the Industrial Revolution. The people here are really Tolstoyan figures – or it is a place where Turgenev's 'Lear of the Steppes' could have taken place –

Well we are photographing them as honestly as possible – neither like *How Green* [*Was My Valley*] – too theatrical – or *The Grapes of Wrath* – too poverty-stricken. No one seems to have emphasised yet the *double* image of wicked conditions and real zest for life – parallel perhaps to town & country – worker & peasant – hammer & sickle.

Jennings was staying in the house of Mr and Mrs Dave Hopkins, and in one letter to Cicely expressed his gratitude for the care they had given him during a bout of ill health: he had been bedridden with a 'combination of abscess from a tooth and general cold in the face and overwork hastened by working in the coldest and draughtiest places in a coal-mine here'. He was both astonished and dismayed by the superhuman energy and discipline shown by Mrs Hopkins in her day-to-day labours as a collier's wife, from five in the morning until late at night. As his letter suggests, Jennings was working hard enough himself, but the effort paid off handsomely. *The Silent Village* is not often mentioned in the short-list of his four or five major achievements, but it should be: it's a wonderful film.

*

For much of its first reel, *The Silent Village* might easily be mistaken for an unusually well-composed travelogue sponsored by the Welsh Tourist Board. Though shown to be based on one of the most dangerous and brutal of all industries, coal-mining, Cwmgiedd looks like an earthly paradise of peace, order and goodwill, set amidst the beauties of nature and music. Chick Fowle's fine camerawork shows off the place at its best, from the glittering stream that runs through the village to the snug, modest domestic interiors. Not that life here is without its bitterness and conflict – we eavesdrop on a miners' meeting, where the issue of silicosis is under debate – yet it is, no less plainly, a place of quiet happiness. Villagers sing, lustily and tunefully, in the chapel; children listen attentively to their teacher instructing them about the planets, in Welsh; housewives do the washing, the grocer serves customers, and the shift coming off duty celebrates the end of the working day with a communal shower and more hearty song. Night falls: miners bàth at home and have their evening meals; at the cinema, children laugh at a Donald Duck cartoon; a young woman has her wedding dress fitted.

Abruptly, the tranquillity is shattered. The tinny noise of a military band issues from a loudspeaker mounted on top of a black car bearing the swastika, growing louder as the car trundles into the village and comes to a halt. Music gives way to the barking of orders: 'Achtung! Achtung! . . . Attention! Attention! To the population of Cwmgiedd . . .' People break off from their daily routines to listen. 'Deputy Reich Protector S.S. Obergruppenführer Heydrich calls upon all classes of the people to give their loyal cooperation in the rebirth of your homeland . . . Put your trust in the Führer!'

Almost immediately, a campaign of active resistance begins. The miners vote to strike, an underground movement is hastily improvised . . . and violently suppressed. Machine-gun fire; the bloody corpses of villagers in a barn; mournful singing in the chapel; the village school-teacher sadly instructing her pupils not to forget their Welsh, even though it has now been outlawed.

But in the hills nearby, in the ruins of a castle, the resistance movement is gathering strength. The fighters print an underground newspaper urging go-slows at work, acts of sabotage. To the lilting sound of 'All Through the Night', a lone sniper, eyes gleaming in his coal-darkened face, crawls slowly and carefully into position and shoots a Nazi trooper (one of the rare moments in the film when the occupying forces are visible – for the most part they are a menacing off-screen presence, heard rather than seen). Saboteurs set fuses, blow up machinery. Speaking in English, the schoolteacher explains to her children about the invasion of Wales by the armies of William the First . . . she does not need to spell out the historical parallel.

Another shock announcement, this time from the radio. There has been an attempt on the life of Heydrich, and the hunt is on for the would-be killers. Daily life in Cwmgiedd becomes still more regimented, and all citizens are made to line up and give their personal details to the authorities; one of them is our sniper. The radio broadcasts details of young men who have been shot for openly expressing their approval of the assassination attempt ... then announces that Heydrich has died. The assassins must be delivered into the hands of the secret police by midnight.

The villagers, knowing full well the consequences of their decision, hold their peace. To the noise of marching feet and shouted German orders, the women and children of Cwmgiedd are gathered together and sent off to detention camps. The men of the village, young and old alike, are backed up against the churchyard wall, solemnly defiant, singing a patriotic Welsh tune. An unseen commander barks out the fatal order to his firing squad. Cut to a shot of the graveyard; a volley of gunfire. Silence. Then the rich, triumphal sound of Wagner welling up on the soundtrack as the camera passes over the sparkling waters of the river, then treasured household possessions burning in the rubble. An intertitle explains that the events we have just seen did indeed take place – not in Cwmgiedd, but in Lidice.

Back to the peace of real-life Cwmgiedd, to the idyll we saw in the opening reel. A woman reads out the news, and the Nazi boast of having obliterated Lidice. A miners' leader replies: 'No, comrades, the Nazis are wrong. The name of the community has not been obliterated: the name of the community lives on! ... It lives in the hearts of miners the world over ... Lidice shall live again!'

*

Heart-warming as it was to make the film, it was also an arduous process, and Jennings's life was made no easier by the news that he would now have to worry not only about the film he was currently making but about the one he thought he had satisfactorily delivered. About three weeks before Christmas 1942, while he was bedridden in Wales with a swollen face (his CFU colleague Stewart McAllister was also ill, and 'much more bad tempered than me even!'), a major row blew up back in London over the running time of *Fires Were Started*. As Jennings explained to Cicely in a long letter, the problem was that, though almost everyone connected with the MOI who had seen the film had enthused over it, the commercial distributors in Wardour Street were unhappy, feeling that it was far too slow – expecially at the beginning – and too long for their proposed programming schedules. Jennings was, he claimed, happy enough to trim the film a little in compliance with these objections, but the dispute suddenly took an angry momentum of its own, as he reports in his letter:

> All sorts of people – official and otherwise who had not had the courage to speak out before suddenly discovered that that was what they had thought all along – that the picture was *much* too long and slow and that really instead of its being the finest picture we had produced (which was the general opinion till then) it was a hopeless muddle which could only be 'saved' by being cut right down and so on. Well of course one expects that from spineless well-known modern novelists and poets who have somehow got into the propaganda business – who have no technical knowledge and no sense of solidarity or moral courage. But worse – the opinion of people at Pinewood began to change – Ian [Dalrymple] of all people suddenly demanded what amounted to a massacre of the film – all this arising out of the criticisms of one or two people in Wardour Street – who had other irons in the fire anyway and who fight every inch against us trespassing on what they pretend is their field. In the meantime [the influential film critic C. A.] Lejeune of the *Observer* had seen it and said that it was easily the finest documentary ever made and that to touch it would be like cutting up Beethoven!

Jennings was right about Caroline Lejeune's support. In a private communication to Jack Beddington, head of the MOI Film Division, that she wrote at the suggestion of Ian Dalrymple, she had elaborated on her verdict:

> In my opinion this is a film on which a stand must and ought to be made. It should be shown quickly, it should be shown widely, and it should be shown in its present form. Apart from a few small criticisms, which I have made to Crown, I think it is one of the finest documentaries we have ever made. I am quite sure it will bring prestige to the unit and to British films generally. I can guarantee that what I may call 'my' public will like it, and I have enough faith in the good heart of the wider public to believe that they will like it too. I have never known a film as honest and human as this one fail to get its message through.[8]

Angered, even disgusted, by these unforeseen setbacks, Jennings was seriously tempted to quit the Crown Film Unit, and thought once again about whether or not he should join up:

> Well, for some time it looked as though the only thing to do was to get out of the unit – particularly as there were other pieces of stupidity (or so they seemed to me) which [we] were letting pass. But against that there was the fate of the Lidice picture – by now far more important to me than the Fire one – and important not just to me or to the unit but for the miners in South Wales and as a real handshake with the working-class which we have not achieved before. Further there was money and the eternal problem of uniform [whether to join one of the armed forces] or not and so on . . .
>
> . . . well, after a really desperate fortnight or so around Christmas I had to go back to Wales for some final shots and I went down feeling very sick at heart and as we came into our beloved valleys and villages there it really was nauseating to compare the two Nations (as Disraeli called them) and to feel that precisely what had happened to the Fire film was only too likely to happen to the Lidice one – if not worse . . .

Since he had been trying throughout the filming in Wales to be as honest and straightforward as possible with the local people, he felt obliged to be equally open with them about what was happening to his previous film and what might well happen to the one that had played so large a part in their lives for the last six months. In particular, he wrote a long letter to Dai Evans. When he called at Dai's house to discuss the matter, he found that the miners' agent was away, but he had left him a letter full of advice, analysis and encouragement – 'the most astonishing and magnificent document . . .'

It is not hard to see why Jennings was so impressed. Dai's letter ran, in part, thus:

> I always kick off on the following basis – 'Propaganda knows neither truth nor falsehood, it only knows what it wants.' If the dominant section of the ruling class of this country knew clearly what it wanted, then we would know Capitalist Society for what it really is.
>
> As miners we have known this from experience for the best

part of a century. We have seen the product of our labour produced in the most haphazard manner, lending to the miner no desire to develop pride of craft. We have seen mother earth hitting back at us with relentless precision, killing and maiming a small army of men in a few years. The result is that we have no interest in the final outcome of our collective labours, but rather in the standard of life we are able to wrench from our masters. Whilst our very work develops in us a grandeur seldom found in men in other industries, our beings are completely divorced from the product – COAL.

Not so, with your industry. You not only work for wages or salaries – you produce a thing that can express your own personalities. You have a very deep interest in the final product of your collective labours, but in the main [these are] the ideas of one or at the outside two individuals, hence your strong personal feeling when that work is to be mutilated, and Mac's [Stewart McAllister's] strong objections to doing the mauling of your creative effort. Perhaps, even that could be made much more effective, if the whole Unit was to be made to feel that the finished article was a part of them to a greater degree than they do at present . . .

This frustration is no new thing. You will find it in every aspect of the productive, social and aesthetic relations in this Society. What of the thousands of scientific workers that meet it at every corner? What of the hundreds of artists that meet it in the same way? In fact, every man meets it in some form or other in his particular mode of expressing himself. Strangely enough, the people that grow most in stature are those that meet it on the greatest number of occasions.

Therefore, Humphrey, whatever your intensity of feelings on the matter you should not leave Pinewood. You would only be leaving the scene of battle, only to pick up another job, and sooner or later come up against the same thing in your new tasks. It would be as if the people in the occupied countries looked for their salvation by emigration from their homes. It would be just abandoning the struggle, leaving, quite possibly, weaker men to face up to it.

I know that this is not your make-up. It is only a question of getting the matter in its proper perspective. Shedding the subjective attitude for the more objective one. There will be many another Lidice to be filmed by Film Units. It is quite possible that Directors would endeavour to cut out altogether films that tend to show this old world as it is, but despite their heavy hand of censorship, men will express their creative ability, just as working-class women make miniature palaces of hovels. As long as the means obtains, man will strive for a higher situation in life. Therefore, pause and reflect on the situation. Look for the weaknesses in your armour, strengthen them by any means at your disposal, ready for the final blow that is to be delivered by tortured humanity for its final liberation.[9]

Cheered and strengthened by Dai Dan's fraternal, visionary words, Jennings returned to London, entered into arguments with those demanding swingeing cuts and managed to achieve a compromise – 'a sort of minimum re-cut which is at least not the massacre it was before'. The film that had been given a sneak preview in Preston, Lancashire, on 4 December 1942 under the title *I Was a Fireman* had eight minutes trimmed from its running time and, at sixty-three minutes, was released to the general public as – a far better name – *Fires Were Started*.

★

Early in January, a difficult month for Jennings made grimmer by yet another bout of flu, he finally moved out of Ian Dalrymple's house. Despite their recent wrangles over *Fires Were Started*, this was not an angry separation. In fact, Jennings wrote a warm and conciliatory letter to his producer and friend, expressing gratitude – 'I owe you in the office and Megan at South Cottage more than I can thank you for' – and resolving to settle their immediate working disputes in an amicable manner: 'In the meantime Ian, please try and put up with me and I will try and be reasonable.'[10] He now moved back into the place that had been his occasional London base during the period he had been living with the Dalrymples: a small but pleasant room on the top floor of the Étoile, at 30 Charlotte Street, London W1 – in the raffish district, popular with artists and writers, north of Oxford Street and west of Tottenham Court Road, sometimes known as Fitzrovia after one of its most popular pubs, the Fitzroy Tavern. He was no doubt aware that the Étoile had

been a gathering point for Wyndham Lewis and the Vorticists before
the First World War, though one of his friends suggests that his choice
of lodgings owed a good deal more to the modest hotel's excellent
French cuisine than to its artistic associations.

From January to May 1943, he was mainly at work with Stewart
McAllister editing *The Silent Village*. At the same time – a wholly
unexpected by-product of his period in Wales – he was once again
looking at the collection of documents on the coming of the Machine
that he had first begun to assemble as early as 1937. He wrote to
Cicely:

> I have got out again as a result of talking to Dai the material
> assembled years back on the Industrial Revolution and he has
> asked me to go down to the Swansea valley and give a series of
> talks to the miners on poetry and the Industrial Rev. which really
> is a golden opportunity – so doing some work on that I have got
> as far once again of thinking of it as a book and looking for a
> publisher and so on. Masses of new material – but again no time
> or very little.

Soon afterwards, he took up Dai Evans's invitation and went back
to Wales to give a series of readings from the work-in-progress, which
'went down astonishingly well'. Newly enthused, he finally managed
to put together an acceptable proposal and – largely thanks to Herbert
Read's energetic support for the project inside the publishing company
– signed a contract on 11 March with George Routledge & Sons for
a book to be entitled *Pandæmonium*. He was to receive a royalty of
10 per cent on the first five thousand copies sold, and 15 per cent
thereafter, with an advance of £50 on receipt of the manuscript, which
was not to exceed 150,000 words.[11] The manuscript was due for
delivery that June, for likely publication in the early autumn. In the
event, it would not be published for another forty-two years.

At the end of March, the recut *Fires Were Started* opened at the
Tivoli and New Gallery cinemas in London, and went on national
release from 12 April. Reviews were on the whole extremely favourable – 'a tremendous press', Jennings told Cicely with understandable
pride – with only a few dissenting voices, of which the sourest was
that of Campbell Dixon in the *Daily Telegraph*, who complained that
the film took 'an unconscionable time to get started' and that, even

when the action finally begins, 'the spectacle is disappointing'. Otherwise, it was laurel wreaths all the way. The *Daily Express* (27 March) said: 'This picture will thrill millions of people whose minds are still scorched by the blitz of 1940–41 and the blazing times we lived through then . . . You must certainly see this picture. You will never forget it.' The *New Statesman and Nation* (3 April), rebuking the dismissive *Telegraph* review, proposed that 'Humphrey Jennings builds up, without either hurry or failure, a drama that could not well be surpassed in excitement and intensity . . . *Fires Were Started* creates its own tempo, which quite rightly is not that of the dramatic feature film – and brilliantly justifies it.' The *Daily Mirror* called it 'inspiring and dramatic'; the *Star*, 'magnificent, stirring and often deeply moving'; the *Daily Mail*, 'a noble and convincing tribute to the firemen'; the *News Chronicle*, 'thrilling and admirably made'; while the *Sunday Times* stated that 'the scenes, largely reconstructed, have an authenticity which is moving and terrifying, and the acting and presentation seem to me to set a new standard in this kind of documentary'.

Jennings had every right to feel vindicated. On 26 May, he gave a talk on the BBC Home Service about the making of *The Silent Village*. In the same week, he went back to Cwmgiedd to show the completed film to the miners and their families in the Welfare Hall – its 'World Premiere', as he called it. He told Cicely of the experience:

a blindingly moving final week-end in the Swansea valley: really, I think, achieving the thing long-wished-for – that of showing the people on the screen to the same people themselves – and being able to say 'Look we have done it for you' – 'We have not betrayed you' and getting their real agreement to this. Difficult to say good-bye to this mixture of coal-dust and clean brass – warm hearts and grim faces.[12]

His spirits had improved enormously, as – for a short time at least – had his working relations with the Ministry, which despite his forebodings had not imposed any substantial cuts or distortions on his Welsh film. He wrote to his wife and children:

I am feeling especially well and happy and energetic – at the moment everything seems to be going very well – people say I look thin but I think I always did. Someone said yesterday – 'Do

you direct films – you look too thin for that – you look like an
assistant!' I suppose directors are always supposed to be fat like
cooks. We have had a few air-raids lately – on clear moonlight
nights – but nothing much: a tremendous noise from our guns
banging but very few bombs. From making my book I have
collected here all sorts of funny books about machines and about
English history – which I shall keep so when Mary-Lou has done
with the Greek gods and goddesses and the Chinese emperors
and philosophers she can learn about the English inventors who
had even more wisdom than Minerva and cheated even worse
than Juno. I have also been thinking of doing some more painting
but it is difficult to fit it all in with work and fire-watching and
home-guarding and all![13]

The Silent Village went on general release in early June. Again, the
reviews were good, and Jennings was particularly moved by Allen
Hutt's pseudonymous notice in *Our Time*: he wrote to give Hutt his
thanks 'not for the personal write-up but for two things':

1. Because Allen you are really the one person from whom such
statements are precious in this country . . .

2. Even more important the surge of comradeship that comes
from this final meeting of intellectual and worker. It was to begin
with – do I have to tell you? – the greatest privilege as well as
pleasure to work with the people in Wales; it was the greatest
ratification of hopes and promises to have their acceptance of the
thing finished . . . I wonder if they realize what that means to one
of the artist tribe – so long, all of us, in ivory towers. Now your
words complete the circle of intellectual–workers–intellectual and
take the energy latent in one little film towards the future. You
talk about moving to action – but that is what their acceptance
and your words do. Sorry to be so pompous, but so moved . . .[14]

The reaction to *The Silent Village* was equally warm within the film
industry. Michael Balcon wrote from his office at Ealing Studios on
22 May 1943:

Dear Mr. Jennings,
    I have just seen THE SILENT VILLAGE (our people, as you
know, are distributing it). Apart from being wonderful cinema it

is one of the most important pictures I have ever seen and incomparably the best anti-Nazi propaganda yet projected. I congratulate you most sincerely . . .

Alberto Cavalcanti, also based at Ealing now, saluted his former protégé:

Dear Humphrey,
    I seem to do little else but send you letters of congratulation – this one is to offer you my felicitations on 'LIDICE', which we saw down here and which impressed Mick [Balcon] and all who saw it . . .
    Please congratulate Fowle on his side of the job, which I thought was magnificent, too.

The film received a particularly helpful publicity boost when the popular illustrated magazine *Picture Post* ran three pages about the production in its issue of 3 July: 'A Welsh Village Makes a Film in Honour of Czech Lidice'.[15] Among the villagers featured were Chris Evans, the collier; Mr T. Powell, the grocer, and his wife; Harry Williams, the retired miner crippled by silicosis, shown being helped along to the premiere by Diana Pine; Edith Williams, wearing her real-life bridal gown (she had been married just a few weeks before Jennings asked her to be a bride again for the cameras); and, on the last page, a smiling Jennings, swamped by his baggy old suit and with his white shirt open at the collar, standing among a group of school-children. Jennings was never exactly a household name outside literary, cinematic and artistic circles, but in the last years of the war he began to receive a fair share of publicity. His youthful dreams of fame came closest to being realized in the early to middle 1940s.

*

The curse, or the blessing, of working for the Crown Film Unit was that a new project always followed hard on the heels of the last one. By June 1943, Jennings was already at work on a treatment for a film about the history of the Royal Marines. Various scraps of documents give some suggestion of the sort of thing he had in mind, of which the most revealing is a hastily typed couple of paragraphs, breaking off abruptly at the end, and alternating between black and red ribbon for emphasis:

My idea is to avoid at all costs making *another ruddy documentary service picture*; but at the same time not to fall back on a fictional story with actors as the only alternative – because it isn't. What I propose is something both simpler and more original. To take the theme at its face-value: *the story of the Royal Marine Forces and especially their part in the coming offensive*. As I see it parts of this tremendous story are documentary – parts fictional – but all of it basically fact – history – *already* dramatic, thrilling, human, box-office and so on.

There are certain basic *ideas* in the story – *tradition* – *pride of corps* – *utter disregard of danger* – *historical knowledge of combined ops*: *etc.* These ideas are far stronger dramatically than any single hypothetical incident à la Nine Men [made by Balcon's Ealing Studios] or Fires Were Started. I therefore propose to disregard the usual unities of space and time and use flash-backs – historical and even in costume – to illustrate the central theme. This is *that in a global war of combined ops the Royal Marines have been the original commandos . . .*[16]

A few other fragments help flesh out this idea. There are to be three main characters, each representing one type of the Eternal Marine across the centuries: one of about thirty-five to forty, very much the traditional, disciplined soldier; one of about thirty, rough, handsome, rebellious (and seen being press-ganged in one historical sequence); and one in his early twenties, physically more delicate, an imaginative run-away-to-sea type. There would also be a number of female characters in the film, especially in the scenes set in 1747 (a 'female warrior' pub sequence), 1770 (Captain Cook in the South Seas), 1885 (Florence Nightingale's angels), 1914–18 (WRNS) and the present day, on the eve of 'Operation X'. And so on.

But Jennings's work on the historical development of the Marines was suddenly interrupted by a 'special mission' involving the present-day Marines: he was ordered to film the imminent invasion of Sicily.

He was away on this mission for about six weeks, filming first commando training in Scotland and then the actual invasion. 'The chaps themselves . . . were really tremendous,' he wrote to Cicely (still in New York) a few months later, on 3 September:

Young and on their toes – not at all the popular conception of Commandos as rough-necks. The officers principally ex-intellectuals

– a landscape painter, a writer, a man with the Oxford Book [of English Verse] in his pocket – chaps extraordinarily like the old GPO boys. The imagination of the type said seriously to be better when it comes to it than the military order-obeying mind, the men violently anti-propaganda ('flannel' they call it). Small wiry fellows mostly, with very strong unit-sense. Everyone including Brigadier under 40 – mostly under 30.

Jennings and his cameraman Jonah Jones found themselves mostly idle for the convoy both out and back, Jennings seeming to occupy himself mainly by filling exercise books with page after page of careful notes. They enjoyed the good Navy food despite the mild nausea caused by their antimalarial drugs, bronzed their bodies and bleached their hair in the Mediterranean sunlight, and saw almost nothing of the enemy save for a few Focke-Wulfs and some bombers on the route back to Britain via Algiers, Oran and Gibraltar. This was the one time in the whole war when Jennings was sent into a combat zone, and though he understandably played down a little the hazardousness of the enterprise when telling his wife about it, it seems that he was at once stimulated and frustrated by his experience of filming a major military action:

> We did some pretty good shooting I think – but as ever the most exciting and moving stuff quite unphotographable – as the night landing itself (very dangerous, as it had been blowing a gale all day and the sea was swamping landing-craft), as the last night in port – the chaps singing 'Goodbye ladies' and – astonishingly enough – 'Who killed cock-robin' and a miraculous little song beginning 'Ohhhh! the little humming-bird . . .' Then the church parade held simultaneously by the whole convoy – including lessons from the Revelation – the vision of the White Horse.[17]

By the time he got back from filming, around the end of August, his ideas about the Royal Marines film had changed radically, and he abandoned the project. On his return he also found a letter from Mr V. Cunard of the Political Intelligence Department of the Foreign Office, with whom he had held discussions a few months earlier, proposing a film about the life of an unusual war hero – a Mr Picchi, an employee of the Savoy Hotel, who had volunteered to be dropped over Italy by parachute and was subsequently, despite being a British national, captured and executed as a traitor to Italy. Cunard liked the idea very much, and thought that Jennings was just the man for the job, having deeply admired his last two films: 'They both seem to me quite flawless and extremely moving. It is so refreshing to see films which are free from all the over-statement and vulgarity which one associates with Hollywood, and which are directed with real imagination and sense of poetry . . .'[18] But nothing ever came of the Picchi proposal, either.

By now, Ian Dalrymple had left the Crown Film Unit to go and work in the commercial sector with Alexander Korda. His place was taken by another CFU veteran, Jack Holmes, to Jennings' considerable gloom – he thought Holmes 'hardly a producer', and in a letter to Cicely he lamented the passing of the old GPO Unit ethos in the new age of proliferating bureaucracy:

> Not a good situation and I doubt if the group will survive it. Seriously, the old GPO group and sense has practically disappeared – the whole thing has become too big and too mechanized and official and actually less efficient. I wonder very much what to do and think of resigning at least once a week. Theoretically I have nothing to complain of – certainly nothing they can understand. It is a pity – a great pity – the unit has been a remarkable institution – a really democratic and anti-bureaucratic group with great influence and still greater possibilities – but it needs a Dal [rymple] or Cav[alcanti] or a Grierson to lead it. Then again as the war becomes clearer so do the true colours of the people in it and particularly the people with whom one has been collaborating. Ah well . . .[19]

Even so, there were some reasons for cheer. About this time, he had further direct evidence that his reputation as a director was spreading well beyond the CFU. He bumped into the American director Frank Capra, already famous for such films as It Happened One Night, Mr Deeds Goes to Town, Lost Horizon and Mr Smith Goes to Washington, though still a few years away from his most widely loved creation, It's a Wonderful Life (1947). Capra, who was in London to discuss a collaboration between the UK and the USA on a film about the North Africa campaign,[20] told Jennings how much he liked Listen *to Britain* and *The Silent Village*: high praise, and expert praise, too, since Capra had immersed himself in the study of wartime propaganda films when he was recruited to the 834th Signal Service Photographic Detachment as executive producer of America's powerful (and occasionally xenophobic) series of inspirational films for the troops and the home front, *Why We Fight*.

Jennings's letters of the time (this next, also to Cicely) are marked by their tempered optimism and their sense of resolution both in personal matters and with regard to the society emerging from the war:

I am still under the roof of the Étoile – very cluttered up with books but very comfy and well looked after. We took a packet of bombing in London once upon a time – but at the end of four years we are extraordinarily lucky – compared to anywhere in Europe itself. What happens in German (and Italian) cities I do not like to imagine. I suppose we shall sort it out sometime. Do not, dearest, in the next year as things get confused and rougher, forget me or let me get further away: the confidence we have got must be there when the fighting stops – sententious as that may sound. No, but I say that because England has[,] you will find, changed a great deal: not so much any one person is different but the young coming up are pretty determined – and people in general if they have the same character have had a good think. The man and woman in the particular job – the ploughman and the coal-cutter and the commando – are very definite as to what was wrong five years ago. The present resilience of Russia – the sheer performance – from Stalingrad to Kharkov and beyond has had an effect I think even greater on us than the original heroic resistance and scorched earth. We ourselves were good at taking a beating. But with all due respect to our great 8th Army – the dazzling Russian advances of this summer: done by mere sheer military means – invoking neither winter nor mud nor snow nor heat nor terrain nor poor allies nor internal collapse – but by the art of war – this has really opened our mouths. I do not think it has been sufficiently appreciated publicly – but in our hearts we know now that not only have the Russians saved us from the Nazis, but also that they are beating them for us all. I hope and trust we shall not forget.

The sense that an Allied victory was now within sight is warmly expressed in Jennings's next film, which not only serves as an oblique tribute to 'our great 8th Army' but, in its relaxed and sometimes even slightly whimsical tone, breathes a new kind of confidence. *True Story of Lili Marlene* isn't one of his major films, but it is an interesting and highly watchable experiment, combining well-staged reconstructions with power ful archive footage, and ending with a mildly Utopian sequence of the way life will be when the lights go back on in Britain. The basic idea is simple, but – as far as I am aware – quite novel for its day:[21] it traces the way in which the haunting German song about the girl waiting outside the barracks gate became a nostalgic hit among German troops on their far-flung battle fronts, and was then captured and adopted as a musical trophy by the Eighth Army during the North Africa campaign.

The film begins with Jennings's old Perse friend Marius Goring speaking to camera: what follows for the next few minutes is essentially an illustrated talk, explaining that the song 'Lili Marlene' dates back 'to the year 1923, when the men of the Eighth Army were still children' (against the word 'children', Jennings sets a shot from his 1939 film *The First Days* of youngsters messing about on cannon outside the Imperial War Museum). Newsreel shots flesh out Goring's thumbnail history of German hyperinflation and the rise of Hitler: 'In the North, and particularly Hamburg, they stuck to democracy . . . Hamburg was the last German stronghold to fall before Hitler's attack . . . and it was in Hamburg, then the largest port in the world, that Lili Marlene was born.'

Cut to a set – a clean, well-lighted garret studio with an artistic-looking young man working at a typewriter. He is Hans Leip, a minor poet and painter of the day, and author of *Die Kleine Hafen-Orgel* ('The Little Dockside Barrel-Organ'), a slim volume of verses which included the poem fated to be turned into a song lyric:

> Vor dem Kaserne
> Vor dem Grossen Tor
> Stand eine Laterne
> Und steht sie noch davor
> So wollen wir uns da wiedersehen
> Bei der Laterne wollen wir stehen
>   Wie einst Lilli Marlen
>   Wie einst Lilli Marlen.

which, translated (approximately):

> In the dark of evening
> Where you stand and wait
> Hangs a lantern gleaming
> By the barrack gate,
> We'll meet again by lantern shine,
> As we did once upon a time,
> We two, Lily Marlene,
> We two, Lily Marlene.

In the film, Hans Leip is played by a tall, striking, blond-haired chap with sharply defined features and prominent ears, who speaks German with a clear voice and a good accent: one Humphrey Jennings, Esq. The story continues: 'Lilli Marlene' was set to music in 1938 (in fact, though the film doesn't mention it, by a Nazi Tin Pan Alley merchant called Norbert Shultze), and first sung in a nightclub by a Swedish girl, Lalli Andersen (played by a professional cabaret singer, Pat Hughes). No one paid much attention to the song at first: the Nazis were scoring their triumphs in France, and forming the Afrika Korps with its marching song 'Panzers Advance into Africa'. It was only in the spring of 1941 that the song's fortunes changed. Here, beginning with newsreel and then moving on to dramatizations, Jennings depicts the invasion of Yugoslavia and the armed takeover of Belgrade radio station by a *Propagandakompanie*. At the end of the first transmission, the Nazi broadcaster reaches out for a gramophone record by way of play-out, and just happens to choose 'Lilli Marlene'.

Almost overnight, the song becomes a smash hit with German forces on fronts from Africa to the USSR, and forms the basis for regular 'messages from home' programmes. Lalli Andersen has become a star and performs (with barely disguised reluctance) for nightclubs full of Wehrmacht officers. So popular is the song that even Frau Emmy Goering performs it at the Berlin State Opera House ... Cut back to North Africa, the Eighth Army, and the grizzled BBC news correspondent Denis Johnston, telling the next part of the story to the camera in terse, dramatic terms that must almost certainly have been scripted but have a convincing air of spontaneity: British forces, bored and underemployed, used to tune into the German radio broadcasts after the

British news was done, and would start to whistle along with the catchy tune.

Violent explosions in the night sky introduce the battle of El Alamein. Denis Johnston continues his story: 'The Eighth Army swept on to Agheila, capturing on its way eight hundred miles of desert, seventy-five thousand prisoners . . . and a famous enemy song.' Marius Goring picks up the commentary, and introduces a scene of BBC men at a monitoring unit, carefully analysing the song; clips from the battle of Stalingrad, and the surrender of Paulus; the pitiful sight of Lalli Andersen behind the wires of a concentration camp (she had been caught sending a message home to Sweden – 'All I want to do is get out of this terrible country'); and we witness the BBC's attempt to turn Lilli Marlene into an agent for the Allies. Backed by a BBC studio orchestra, the actress and singer Lucie Mannheim (in private life, Mrs Marius Goring) sings newly composed, bitterly sardonic words to the famous tune; and Jennings intercuts shots of German corpses in the snow and other images of defeat.

A bridging passage of a cockney soldier talking about the way the troops have adopted, adapted and improved the song as their own leads to the finale – a long tracking shot across a street market and into a snug domestic scene. 'Now,' says Goring, 'look into the future. Come to the London docks on a Saturday night in peacetime . . .' The camera shows a child looking at a photograph of his dad in uniform; his mother takes it from him and hangs it up on the wall. A candle burns next to a Union flag. 'The lights of London are relit. The shining domes of Stalingrad have been rebuilt. Then the true people and the real joys of life will come together again, and the famous tune of Lilli Marlene will linger in the hearts of the Eighth Army as a trophy of victory and as a memory of the last war. To remind us all to sweep fascism off the face of the earth, and to make it really – the *last* war.'

*

Shooting on *Lilli Marlene* was finished by the very end of the year. It left Jennings exhausted:

> [the production] has really kept me up night and day for three months . . . I have been working without a producer and very much on my own (except for Chick [Fowle] – thank goodness) and

have felt rather out of my depth – with professional actors and so forth and a very *theatrical* story. The book [*Pandæmonium*] still staggers on – but too slowly really. I need a 48-hour day or two pairs of eyes or hands or something.

All the same, for the first time in all this I have begun to feel like having something to say – both in print and film – instead of being merely a reporter. The work on the book has opened my eyes very wide about history and the reception of *Silent Village* has made me think inevitably about personal style and ideas and so on. One gets to the moment of having if possible to *be* something more than *promising* –

The winter of 1943–4 was a hard one: 'flu and cold and misery – that wet penetrating cold so typical . . .' At the end of January, Jennings moved out of the Étoile and into three rooms of the ground floor of 8 Regent's Park Terrace – 'just by the Primrose Hill railway cutting – rather noisy at times but extremely romantic'. This was the home of his friend Allen Hutt, who had first put him in touch with the Welsh miners. The new arrangement proved a great success – 'You can't think how lovely it is to have all of my books and papers and paintings together in a house of my own again' – and Regent's Park Terrace would be his home for much of the remaining six years of his life.

In April 1944, *Vogue* magazine ran an interesting, conspicuously literate article about 'The True Story of Lilli Marlene' by the journalist Lesley Blanch,[22] copiously illustrated with production stills and with a portrait shot of Jennings by his good friend Lee Miller, who had visited the set. Though the article concentrated far more on the story of the song than the film, it left no doubt in the reader's mind about the talent of Jennings ('all Humphrey Jennings' work as a director is distinguished') or the value of the film: 'I hope you will be able to see the film. I hope it will not go the way of so many first-class interest pictures which, because they have no big star, or glitter, are dropped flat by a conspiracy of commercial cinema managements who act in a most high-handed and prejudiced manner, in entire defiance of public wishes. For shame.'[23]

From March to June, Jennings was seconded from the Crown Film Unit to the independent company Two Cities, to write a treatment and a script for a film about twenty-four hours in the life of London and New York, which he had originally proposed as early as 13 January.

There have been quite a number of films made about the life of a single city [his first treatment ran]. They have usually been vivid, symphonic or generalised studies, but there is no doubt that it was found difficult to get drama into them without bringing in a story in an unnatural way. But to make a film about two cities and give each of these cities its representative (its ambassador, so to speak) in the other one, and any human story that you like to play around each of these characters will appear perfectly natural . . . [was it perhaps the thought of his wife in New York that prompted this idea of 'ambassadors'?]

Jennings was pleased with the completed script, but the film was never made, and on 1 July he returned to Pinewood, 'where I have been given more responsibility for actual supervision than before & have had to work harder than ever'. In the same month, the first flying bombs started to fall on London. Jennings went filming on location in the South of England, documenting the effects of this new and terrible form of attack in a more or less straightforward piece of reportage – a fourteen-minute film called *The Eighty Days*, mainly concentrating on the activities of the coastal anti-aircraft gunners who were trying to shoot the V-1s out of the sky before they could reach their targets. The distinguished American broadcaster Ed Murrow supplied a commentary. This film was later re-edited into a slightly shorter (ten-minute) form for overseas use, given a new commentary and retitled *The V-1*.

*

A poem of the time by Jennings: 'Bedford Square, 5 July 1944':

> As the syrens [*sic*] were sounding
> The children were singing
> 'Run along little Tishy run along'
> As the syrens were sounding
> The eyes were brimming
> As by the Square railings
> A woman was walking
> In a black cloak and black bonnet
> And black scarf waving
> As the syrens were sounding
> As the eyes were brimming

> And the children laughing
> 'Run along little Tishy run along'

★

The True Story of Lili Marlene went on general release in the late summer. The ever loyal C. A. Lejeune gave it an enthusiastic review and it enjoyed a healthy box office, especially in working-class districts,

> but [Jennings lamented] everyone else including many 'intelligent' friends of mine sat hard on it and complained – between them – of almost everything in it. They have for years criticized me for being high-brow and over people's heads – now the fault is apparently the opposite. I confess to being upset, particularly as when we finished making it I was tired out and could not 'see' it any longer and was prone to think them right . . .[24]

Still, the wave of publicity which had begun with the *Picture Post* feature and continued in *Vogue* was still swelling. The high point, at least in personal terms, came when 'George Pitman' (Allen Hutt's usual pseudonym) wrote a lengthy profile for *Our Time* magazine, 'Men of Our Time No. 8: Humphrey Jennings' – the first substantial critical assessment of his career and personality to be published. It is a fine piece of journalism: lively in expression but thoughtfully constructed, and written with the easy authority of a man who not only knows his subject well but (though he does not confess as much) actually lives under the same roof. Much of the biographical material it rehearses is familiar enough, though it frequently throws an original, unexpected light on the story. It begins, for example, with the image of a young man arriving at Bolton station at five o'clock one summer morning with a Leica slung over his shoulder, and surveying a landscape he has never known before: 'the land of industry, of the factory and of the working class'. This, the beginning of his Mass-Observation work, was, Pitman suggests, the most important turning-point in the life of Humphrey Jennings, 'who is now someone quite special among our small band of film directing aces'.

In some respects, Pitman's assessment of why Jennings was 'quite special' has never been bettered – though some of his emphases now seem a little beside the point – and the passages in his article that read most compellingly are those in which he attempts to sum up the rare qualities that define Jennings's character and talents:

he was affected artistically by contact with the Surrealists (he was never of them,[25] but, as he says, they had at any rate the notion that somehow or other painting and life were related), politically by the war in Spain, and theoretically by reading Darwin. That last was a suggestion by his Cambridge friend, Charles Madge, and Jennings lays great stress on its importance for his own development; the point being, I think, that it was his first mature comprehension of the scientific approach and method.

East Anglia . . . Bolton . . . Darwin: perhaps these three are the main formative factors in Jennings' make-up. Put them differently . . . the Land . . . Industry . . . Science. The history of these things is certainly the key to his own remarkable, and passionately cultivated, library, where the eighteenth-century Annals of Agriculture jostle with the Reports of the Poor Law Commissioners and the History of the Royal Society is a neighbour of the lives of Brunel or [William] Fairbairn or the outpourings of [the scientist] Andrew Ure.

All this can be put, if you like, in the simplest way by saying that Jennings, both in his thinking and in his doing, is a many-sided character. He paints, he snatches a rare book from an obscure shop's darkest recess, he ploughs a sprawling furrow along the historical byways of the Industrial Revolution (and therein lies a book which will sooner or later see the light of day) with the same talkative energy, the same confidence and enthusiasm, that he brings to film directing. Indeed, he repudiates the notion that a film director can be in any sense a narrow specialist: to him painting, writing and so forth line up and make one whole with the specific technique of film-making.

Here, I feel, is the explanation of the richness which has marked his treatments from the first; which, for example, made *Fires Were Started* the supreme example of the horror and heroism of the London blitz. But not the whole explanation. For what has been growing and deepening in Jennings has been his feeling for people, for ordinary people, for the plain, blunt working men and women of our country. Bolton began it. Cwmgiedd added the final touch . . .

Pitman concludes:

Here, then, are some sidelights on a man who, in his middle thirties, is moving on from documentary to the big-time feature field. I confess I am unmoved by the one or two plaintive snivels that have come from arty and sectarian old ladies from the back of the hall. Indeed I see only one danger ahead – one possible danger – for Jennings: the encyclopaedism that he extols and seeks to express in himself might conceivably degenerate into eclecticism – that still too common English fault. And since Humphrey Jennings is English to his marrow, that is something he will need to watch out for.[26]

★

In the autumn of 1944, Jennings began location work on his last great film of the war – his last great film – *A Diary for Timothy*. Once again, the basic idea was simple: find a child born on the fifth anniversary of Britain's entry into the war, and then put together a portrait of the last months of the conflict, 'explaining' to the infant what was happening and why. To be sure, the end product is a good deal more complex than this germ of an idea suggests, not least because Jennings was in no position to guess exactly how the final act of the war would play out; but the initial conception survives into the finished film. The thought of communicating to children ought to have been much on Jennings's mind at this season, since, after months of correspondence about the wisdom of the move, Cicely left New York and brought Mary-Lou and Charlotte back to England in November. As Mary-Lou Legg recalls:

My mother had tried to come back earlier in 1944, but because my uncles were working in the security services here, and knew about D-Day, I think she got the message not to come back until later in the year . . .

I know that when I saw [my father] again, I was struck by how odd he was, and how unfamiliar – almost, was I related to this person? The first thing that surprised me – and he was nothing but a surprise – was when we got back to England he was working on *A Diary for Timothy*, somewhere in Wales I think, and so a message had to be got to him that we'd come back. We went to my grandmother's house in Oxfordshire, and he came there about a day or two later. My mother and Charlotte and I went to meet him off the train, and we stood on the platform, and suddenly there was this man dressed as a soldier. In fact, he was wearing either War Correspondent uniform or Home Guard uniform.

Cicely Jennings and her daughters stayed at the Oxfordshire house, the Grange at Duns Tew, for about six months: London was still under bombardment from V-2s, and there was, anyway – as *Diary for Timothy* reports – a terrible housing shortage in the wake of the Blitz.

> We didn't move until about February or March of 1945, when we went to live in a rented cottage in Clavering in Essex, and stayed there until we were evicted. The reason that we were evicted was that my parents ran a committee room for the Labour Party in the election of 1945, and we put up posters, and I went around on my bicycle giving out leaflets.

Just as work on *The Silent Village* had had to begin with a hunt for an appropriate Welsh mining community, so *Diary* had to find its baby. The unsuspecting mother of that baby, Mrs Betty Jenkins, later recalled her first encounter with Jennings as a chilly affair:

> Two days after Timothy was born about eight people came to the nursing home. They didn't explain what it was all about at all. Then a very serious-looking man who afterwards I was told was Humphrey Jennings walked round my bed, looked me up and down – and Timothy – and eventually after several minutes said 'I'm quite satisfied, are you?' to [his assistant] Diana Pine, and she said 'Yes, oh perfectly!' It wasn't until after he decided he wanted to do it or not that they told me what it was all about.[27]

Not one of Jennings's finest hours as a sensitive handler of people's feelings; the most charitable interpretation would be that he was so carried away by his inner vision of the film in prospect that he forgot common civility. There was certainly no element of class condescension or snobbery here. Mrs Jenkins was thoroughly middle-class.

Jennings continued to work on *A Diary for Timothy* until about April. It was decided that the diary form of the film called for something he had largely, and justifiably, shunned for most of his war work: a narration, and a narration of a highly personal kind. Jack Beddington, head of the MOI Film Division, suggested that this should be written by either Max Beerbohm or E. M. Forster; his CFU colleague Basil Wright, fearing that 'Beerbohm would satirize it too much', plumped for Forster. The commentary was to be spoken by Jennings's old Cambridge associate Michael Redgrave. And in addition to the infant Timothy, the film would keep tabs on what was happening to four other real-life 'characters': a Welsh coalminer, Goronwy (echoes of *The Silent Village*); Bill, an engine driver (back to Jennings's beloved locomotives); Alan, a middle-aged Suffolk farmer who has spent much of the war reclaiming land (echoes of *Spring Offensive*); and a young fighter pilot, Peter, whose plane crashed in France and who is now convalescing in hospital, waiting to be sent back into action.

So much of the structure was planned in advance: the rest was in the hands of the gods, the generals and the elements, and one of the excitements of the film is the realization that no one making it had any precise idea of the nature of the events it would be including. Although almost everyone in Britain now believed that the war would be won by the Allies, no one could predict when or how, and the film is punctuated by some drastic setbacks.

It begins in a BBC radio studio, on Sunday 3 September 1944, the fifth anniversary of Britain's entry into the war, as the newsreader broadcasts an early-morning bulletin about the progress of hostilities. Dissolve to the tranquil English countryside, and eventually to baby Tim. Redgrave's voice – deep, resonant, rather patrician (and at times almost hectoring) – picks up the significance of the date: 'And it was on the third of September 1944 that you were born . . . in a nursing home near Oxford, England. Very comfortable . . .' Barely minutes old, poor Tim is already being preached at: 'If you had been born in wartime Holland, or Poland, or a Liverpool or Glasgow slum, this would be a very different picture . . . All the same, you're in danger . . . around you is being fought the worst war ever known.' Dissolve to a military band – a shot that will be familiar to viewers of *Listen to Britain* – and then to children walking purposefully through a cityscape devastated by bombs. Back to Tim being weighed, and then, as Redgrave explains the concept of 'total war', involving every member of the population, we travel around the country meeting our principal adults. Pitheads, a miner's cage: Goronwy. Farmlands, a man examining hay: Alan. Smokestacks, an engine yard, a cabin: Bill. A hospital ward, and a man in bed with his leg in plaster: Peter. 'All these people were fighting for you . . . though they didn't exactly know it.' His cast firmly established, Jennings proceeds to tell the month-by-month story of 'your first days on earth, the start of your life, the end of our war in Europe'.

September 1944. In the wake of the Normandy invasions, there is a widespread hope that the war may be over – fateful phrase – by Christmas. And as Timothy is brought home for the first time, on 17 September, the First Allied Airborne Army lands in Holland. For the first time in five years, the blackout is slightly lifted, and replaced by a mere 'dim-out'. Bill and his wife settle comfortably at home; Alan shows his family home movies of clearing previously uncultivated land on the farm, so as to squeeze wartime crops from every last possible square yard of earth at the start of the war; his film ends with a tree stump being blown up in a controlled explosion. Back in London, the wail of an air-raid siren alerts the public to an incoming V-1. ('I hope you'll never have to hear that sound, Tim,' says Redgrave.) Bill and his wife dive under the table, sheltering from the uncontrolled explosion . . .

October. Bill in his driver's cab, Alan on his farm, Peter bantering, a little stiffly, with his nurse; Timothy's mother studying demobilization tables and wondering when her husband might come home. But the news from Holland is grim. Gathered round their radios, our cast listen to the Canadian war correspondent at Arnhem, Stanley Maxted, giving a commentary on the siege of the Allied forces, now fighting grimly against the advancing German army with almost no rations or other resources. 'Luckily, or unluckily, it rained, and they caught the water in capes and drank that . . . Give them some Germans to kill and even one chance in ten and they'd get along somehow.' The sombre beauty of Beethoven's 'Appassionata' overlaps this news: Myra Hess is playing the piano at one of her morale-boosting concerts, as in *Listen to Britain*, and she continues as rain pours down on the streets of London, as the roofs of damaged houses are slowly repaired, as Maxted's final phrases are repeated. Redgrave's voice, at its most plummily patronizing: 'Did you like the music that lady was playing? Some of us think it is the greatest music in the world, yet it's *German* music, and we're fighting the Germans. There's something you'll have to think over later on.'

Rain is universal: it even trickles down into the mine where Goronwy is working. Mrs Jenkins writes a postcard to her husband overseas; Bill drives his engine, Alan studies his accounts, and the rain is still falling on the day of Timothy's baptism, complete with choir. In the hospital, Peter, on crutches, is slowly managing to walk again.

In the coalfields, a cage brings up a wounded miner – Goronwy. He is taken away to hospital: 'It's pretty shocking that this sort of thing should be happening every day, though we've been cutting coal for five hundred years. Something else for you to think over . . .'

November. Soldiers clear mines from Britain's beaches: a loud explosion, and then cut to London, where men are digging in their allotments – the 'victory gardens' – while the dome of St Paul's looms in the background. At the Haymarket Theatre, John Gielgud is playing the graveyard scene from *Hamlet*: 'Why was he sent into England?' The Clown replies: 'Why, because he was mad; he shall recover his wits there, or, if he do not, 'tis no great matter there.' Gales of laughter from the audience; three and a half centuries after Shakespeare wrote the lines, the English still love hearing jokes against themselves. In a canteen, an ARP man talks about the aerodynamics of missiles, ending with a question to his friend; cut back to Hamlet, whose lines apear to respond to that question – 'Nay, I know not'; cut back to the canteen, where for a second an explosion makes everyone jump; cut back to Hamlet contemplating Yorick's skull ('Let her paint an inch thick . . .'); cut to ARP men carrying out a rescue mission in the rubble. In the Underground, Londoners sleep in makeshift bunks as a train enters the station, and the attendant calls out, 'All change!'

December. At last the country feels safe enough to stand down the Home Guard, who march in a final parade. (Private Jennings was among those relieved of duties.) Peter, much improved, is having his leg massaged. Though the war is still, obviously, far from over, the country nonetheless prepares for Christmas festivities: the postman brings a card from overseas for Master Timothy Jenkins, ATS girls sing 'Good King Wenceslas' in a barracks, window-shoppers enjoy the – still rather austere – fashion displays. But '. . . in those days before Christmas, the news was bad and the weather was foul'. Fog everywhere: in London, where news comes in of a massive German counter-offensive; in the countryside, and across the tracks where Bill is driving his engine.

> Death and darkness, death and fog, death across those few
>   miles of water . . . and death came by telegram to many
>   of us on Christmas Eve . . .
> Until, out of the fog, dawned . . .

Loveliness.
Whiteness.
Christmas Day.

Exquisite close-up of frost-covered grasses by still water; a choirboy's high, pure voice sings the ancient hymn 'Adeste Fideles' – 'O come let us adore him, Christ the Lord' – Timothy's face, despite his copious dribbling, becomes, briefly, a local surrogate for the holy infant sought by the Magi. Across the nation, in the accents of all classes, glasses are raised to 'Absent Friends'; as he does so, Bill winks affectionately at his wife. A man's voice reads from the card Timothy's father has sent him: 'My dear son, a very merry Christmas to you . . . May you always be happy and truly content with this life you have been given.' The solemn note gives way to festivities: a New Year's Eve party, and 'Auld Lang Syne'.

The New Year: final section. Bill returns to work, but, as Redgrave explains, the grim winter has left everyone in the dark as to what is going to happen next. 'But about the middle of January, we began to see something was coming: something tremendous.' Dramatic music. BBC announcer: 'Marshal Stalin has announced a great offensive . . .' Alan in the field, Goronwy now recovering in hospital. Over domestic shots – buses, men and women buying coal – comes word of the Red Army's spectacular advances, and then the rousing sound of an orchestral rendition of Chopin's 'Polonaise Militaire', followed – as a tribute to our Russian allies – by the Soviet anthem. BBC: 'The Russians are twenty miles inside Germany . . .' Peter and his fellow-patients are being put through their healing paces by a tough but humorous keep-fit instructor. News of a massive American bombing raid on Berlin. But now the triumphal rhythm and tone of the last few minutes give way to a more reflective note.

First, over shots of Tim being weighed and houses being rebuilt, Michael Redgrave again: 'Life is going to become more dangerous than before, oddly enough . . . because now we have the power to choose and the right to criticize . . . We're free men. We have to decide for ourselves, and part of your bother, Tim, will be learning to grow up free.' And then, after news of the Big Three and their conference, cut to Goronwy, gazing at the baroque painted ceiling of his 'hospital' – clearly, in peacetime a stately home – and his private musings: 'That afternoon I was sitting thinking about the past. The last war . . . The unemployed, broken homes, scattered families. And I thought, has all this really got to happen again?' More of his thoughts, then bracketing shots of an English children's choir singing a jolly song in praise of the USSR – 'You must study your Marx and your Lenin! . . .' – Alan on his farm, and Goronwy's wife with a ration book: 'I remember people going to hospital on flat carts . . . now we've got our own ambulance, nursing service, hospitals . . . Surely, if we can do that thing during that period, nothing at all will stop us after this war.'

Now cut to fighter pilot Peter, chatting with clumsy flirtatiousness to a girl at a dance: when the war is done, he says, he thinks he'll take off to the Pacific and go in for beachcombing – 'I can sit in the sun and do absolutely nothing.' The band strikes up, and it becomes obvious, as he and his partner take the floor, that Peter is well again. Redgrave: 'So Peter goes back to his plane, and Goronwy goes back to his mine – back to everyday life and everyday danger . . .' Goronwy's radio gives news that the British Second Army and the American Ninth, under the command of Montgomery, are crossing the Rhine. Titanic music on the soundtrack, shots of bombs raining down on Germany, the devastation intercut with Tim being fed from a bottle by his mother. Safely back in his cot, the baby becomes the target of Redgrave's final homily:

> Well, dear Tim, that's what's been happening around you . . . and you see it's only by chance that you're safe and sound. Up to now, we've done the talking, but before long you'll sit up and take notice. What are you going to say about it and what are you going to do? You heard what Goronwy was thinking – unemployment after the war, and then another war and then more unemployed.
>
> Will it be like that again? Are you going to have greed for money and power ousting decency from the world as they have in the past? Or are you going to make the world a different place – you and all the other babies?

Extreme close-up of Tim's face (and, in some versions of the film, a superimposed shot of celebrating Britons dancing round a victory bonfire). The background music – composed by Richard Addinsell (1904–77) – has been swelling throughout from a single violin theme

to a thunderous orchestral chord; and then the solo violin, fragile and
forebodingly sad, returns as the end titles appear and the film fades to
black.

*

If this has seemed a slightly disenchanted sketch of Jennings's film, it
should be stressed at once that, for all its flaws of tone and execution,
A Diary for Timothy remains profoundly moving – to some viewers,
especially those born at around the same time as Timothy, almost
unbearably moving – and at times very beautiful. When it touches on
moments of Allied advance and victory, it is wonderfully stirring (the
Chopin extracts are at once noble and thrilling);[28] and it has all the
Jennings grace notes of wit and strangeness and charm: Gielgud's
Hamlet, the lyrical visions of snow and ice, a po-faced pianist apparently bored stiff with pounding the keyboard for the dancers – until
her face suddenly breaks into a wicked grin.

But the film's deepest emotion is sadness. It aches with melancholy,
not just in the obviously downbeat passages of the Arnhem siege or
the winter fogs or the devastated houses, but above all in its finale,
which looks forward in deep anxiety. At the very moment of recording
absolute military victory abroad, Jennings dwells on the likelihood of
imminent social defeat at home, as if all the paradoxical moral advances
of the war – the solidarity, courage and kindness his earlier war films
had celebrated so eloquently – were about to be snatched away. One
reason why grown men and women sometimes weep at the end of
the film is that they know, or at any rate suspect, that Jennings was
right to be full of misgiving in 1945: though the forces of 'decency'
achieved much in the postwar years, they can hardly be said to have
triumphed over the lusters after money and power. On a more local
and personal note, Jennings may also have intuited that he was about
to be robbed of his ideal subject – war – and his clear vision of what
he could do in and with his films was being inevitably clouded. Here,
too, some apprehension would have been justified: rightly or wrongly,
A Diary for Timothy is often referred to as his last important film.

Important it certainly is, both as a work of art and as a social
document. It has sometimes been described as the best evocation,
in film or any other medium, of the reasons why the country 'went
Labour' at the 1945 elections. Compared to Listen to Britain or Fires

Were Started, though, it is certainly flawed, and in two respects above all.

The first is that, thanks to an internal wrangle at the Crown Film Unit, Jennings's invaluable collaborator Stewart McAllister was sacked from the project at an early stage, and the job of editing handed over to an extremely junior recruit – Jenny Hutt, the daughter of Jennings's good friend Allen. (The film's credits name Alan Osbiston as Supervising Editor and Jenny Hutt as Cutter.) Jenny Hutt, now Jenny Stein, recalls being confronted with such an overwhelming pile of rushes that she burst into tears and had to be taken out for a lavish dinner by Jennings before she could summon up the courage to go on with the task. In fact, her work on the film is of a high order, but it does lack the fluency and quirky brilliance that McAllister brought to Jennings's films, a contribution that Jennings was the first to acknowledge, even though the two of them often fought like Kilkenny cats during the actual process of cutting. As Sir Denis Forman recalls,

> Humphrey used to speak of Mac as if he was a sort of burden he had to carry . . . But he also knew, of course, that the strength lay in the combination of the two of them. The fact is, the two together were very much more than either working separately with another person: because Mac recognised Humphrey's abilities and the genuineness of his perceptions, and respected them; and Humphrey respected the fact that, in the end, Mac would make a better picture than he could, when it came to putting the material together. He wasn't a vain person at all, Humphrey. In fact he was quite oblivious of his own ego when he was making a picture – in a way that *very* few film-makers are.[29]

The other, and more serious, area in which *A Diary for Timothy* is compromised is – fairly obviously – its commentary. As I've suggested above, it was precisely in eschewing the 'lantern lecture' approach to documentary, in which the pictures serve merely or largely to illustrate verbal points, that Jennings had grown and shone as a film-maker; and though the images do not stand in such a subservient relationship to words in this last film of the war years as they did in his earliest, the effect of pictures and sounds being harnessed to a didactic narration is at least cramping; at worst, bathetic. Spoken, albeit with consummate professionalism, in the accents of the English ruling classes (as *Heart of*

Britain had been), the tone of the commentary, as already noted, is at best 'patronizing', and though this stance may be justified by the dramatic logic of an adult addressing a newborn baby, there can be few viewers who do not feel that they, too, are being patted on the head by this know-it-all uncle. (I have heard one viewer say, not wholly in jest, that she found listening to all those finger-wagging rebukes and reminders directed at poor Tim tantamount to witnessing child abuse.) Small wonder that in the early 1960s, when the bright young satirists of *Beyond the Fringe* set themselves to mocking the myths of Britain at War, they targeted *A Diary for Timothy*'s pious little homily on 'German music'.[30] There are times, too, when the commentary is horribly precious (Redgrave shamelessly milks his delivery of 'out of the fog dawned ... *loveliness*') or simply mendacious: when Timothy is informed that life in Britain is, 'oddly enough', going to be more dangerous now that the bombs have stopped dropping, poetic licence is licensing nonsense.

Oddly enough, E. M. Forster said, when he saw its final assembly just before he agreed to supply the commentary, that he was unhappy with the film. In a lengthy letter to Basil Wright dated 15 May 1945, he wrote to Crown saying that though he was sympathetic to the general idea of the film and admired its 'fine sensitive details', he was troubled that

> the film comes out with a social slant and suggests that Britain ought to be kept right for this one class of baby and not got right for babies in general. True, Tim must be someone, and why shouldn't he be born in a rectory and have a lovely choral baptism instead of being an industrialist baby [*sic*] at a registry office? But this does establish the slant, and I submit it hasn't been sufficiently corrected.

It was he who proposed that Tim should be reminded that 'he might have been born in a Liverpool slum' – a sentiment, and a place-name, that duly ended up in the final script. Forster had other objections, too: he didn't like the absence of 'gloomy or cynical' remarks, and felt that the film offered 'much too simple and smug a picture of wartime England'. Nor did he like the Soviet Youth song near the end, but he expected that this would have to be cut anyway 'for political reasons'. Otherwise, he said, he found each part of the film, in itself, 'delightful and moving', and had particular praise for the man at the screening who had supplied the trial commentary: 'I forgot to ask whether, if I did attempt the job, you wanted me to talk the commentary as well as to write it ... I liked Mr Jennings's speaking immensely, and don't really know why you call in anyone else.'[31]

Whether or not one agrees with them, these are all sensible and even acute points, and Forster's particular sensitivity to what he saw as the film's middle-class bias makes it all the more surprising, and disappointing, that the words he eventually supplied for Crown should themselves be so vulnerable to accusations of smugness, insensitivity and unwitting class arrogance. Perhaps his best point was his last; perhaps, if the film needed a commentary, the best person to supply it would have been Mr Jennings.

Everyone who watches the film is bound, at some point, to wonder: what became of Timothy James Jenkins? Though he was diffident about his connection with the film, it caught up with him at least twice.

On 7 September 1960, Granada Television broadcast a programme entitled *Timothy's Second Diary*, which replayed the original film and then descended on its main players: Alan had given up his farm and started a plant nursery; Goronwy, still a miner, was suffering from pneumoconiosis; Bill had retired; and Peter had emigrated to Canada and become a psychiatrist. Timothy, by this time, was a shy schoolboy. Half a lifetime later, in 1995, a journalist for the *New Statesman* repeated the exercise, and discovered that, after a period as a scooter-crazy Mod in the 1960s, he had settled down and become a comprehensive school teacher. Not such a bad choice of life for anyone who, instead of lusting for money and power, wants to work towards making the world a better place. When, in the summer of 2000, the director Kevin Macdonald and I were working on the Channel 4 documentary *Humphrey Jennings: The Man Who Listened to Britain*, we decided – after a good deal of discussion, to respect Mr Jenkins's privacy and did not try to contact him. By sad chance, just a few days before the film was due for transmission on 23 December that year, I heard that Timothy Jenkins had died, and immediately reached for the phone. Channel 4 added a short obituary title to the broadcast.

*

In May 1945, the Allied armies met in Berlin, Hitler killed himself in his bunker, and Germany surrendered. Jennings, as noted, was able to use a shot of jubilant, flag-waving crowds dancing around a VE night bonfire for one version of the final reel of *Timothy* – a shot, though, which does nothing to compromise its downbeat note, so powerful is the tug of mournful emotion by this point in the film. Weeks later, the USAAF dropped the atomic bombs 'Fat Man' and 'Little Boy' on Hiroshima and Nagasaki, Emperor Hirohito surrendered, and 'the greatest war the world had ever known' was, finally, over. Jennings's unique career as Britain's Martial Laureate was over, too. Many – most – of his admirers believe that none of his work would ever achieve the same brilliance, lyricism or emotional power again; had he died at the completion of the editing of *Timothy*, his reputation as a film-maker would not be diminished in the slightest. But the conventional wisdom that the last five years of his life were a period of sorry anticlimax is greatly overstated, and if they were thin years in terms of projects completed, they were rich in new possibilities for his art and thought.

It was in the postwar period that he made his first attempt to move into the world of commercial features; discovered the riches of a great civilization quite new to him in the Far East; began to develop some potentially fascinating (unrealized) ventures, from a book on Edward Lear to a film series about the British Empire to a poetic autobiography. Released from the wartime routine of fourteen-hour working days and urgent deadlines, Jennings was once again – to his immense pleasure – able to apply himself to his first artistic passion, painting. And with a settled domestic life, he could seriously contemplate gathering the thousand fragments of *Pandæmonium* into complete form. Far from being a disappointing coda to his years of greatness, the late 1940s may be seen as a time in which he was hard at the fascinating work of reinventing himself, exploring ways in which his protean talents could tell as profoundly in peacetime as they had in war.

Eight

1945 to 1950: From *A Defeated People* to *Family Portrait*

Most people who have watched *A Diary for Timothy* with care will understand the force of that much-repeated observation that it helps explain why Britain 'went Labour' at the 1945 General Election. But another quality of the film, much less commonly discussed, is the way in which its underlying melancholia is also, in its way, prophetic of the gloomy state of national morale in the immediate postwar period, once the euphoria of VE and VJ days was over. By and large, memoirs of the years immediately following the war describe them as a grey, drab, depressing time for Britain: an 'Age of Austerity', many histories of the times call it, with the material deprivations of the war years dragging on – and some even growing worse – but with none of the wartime sense of national unity in righteous struggle by way of emotional compensation.

Postwar England certainly struck the young Misses Marie-Louise and Charlotte Jennings as a wretched time and place: cold, dark, shabby and altogether lacking in the modern facilities they had come to love in their American schools. Both of them had strong American accents, which were laughed at by the children of Oxfordshire and Essex, and which they soon learned to lose. Half a century later, Mary-Lou recalled: 'I came back when I was eleven, but I couldn't pass the 11-plus, or Common Entrance, because I'd never done Latin. So I went to a succession of crummy schools. We, my sister Charlotte and I, were sent to a convent in Bishop's Stortford for a couple of years.' Charlotte remembers that the journey to school was so slow and awkward that they had to be up at 5.30 in the morning and were often not back until 5.30 p.m.; Cicely arranged for them to be excused some of their homework to ease the burden slightly; though, as Mary-Lou recalls, being home was hardly more attractive than being in class: 'In

the winter of 1945–46 we lived in Tilty Hill [a house near the small
town of Thaxted in Essex which had belonged to the Surrealist painter
John Armstrong; one of the rooms, usually kept locked, was crammed
with his canvases], which was miserable. It was freezing cold and
surrounded by mud, and my father wasn't there . . . I pined to be back
in New York, back in America.'[1]

The reason for their father's having left just at the point when they
should all have been learning to live together again as a family was
that he had been sent off on his first postwar assignment to Germany
– a nation now vastly worse off, even, than dismal, exhausted Britain
– to film a report on the aftermath of war. Jennings spent September
and October in Germany with Fred Gamage as his principal cameraman, mostly in Hamburg and Düsseldorf, shooting the material that
was later edited into *A Defeated People*. Early in his visit, he ran into the
poet Stephen Spender. As might have been predicted from Jennings's
rather scathing attitude towards W. H. Auden and his poetic coterie,
the two English intellectuals did not hit it off. In his journal for 10
September 1945, Spender wrote:

> Everything about Humphrey Jennings irritates me, beginning
> with his Adam's apple, his flapping ears, his pin-head face, and
> his bumptious expression, which looks odd in a man who now
> has white hair. He talks an appalling kind of Anglo-American
> film-world slang in which he mixes up Americanisms such as
> 'oh boy oh boy' with Cockney slang such as 'Bob's yer uncle'.
> He combines the gestures of a GI with those of a stage
> Frenchman . . .[2]

They argued about the Germans, Jennings taking the harsher and
more vengeful line on German culpability; and when one compares
Spender's report of their row with the phrasing in some of Jennings's
letters home to Cicely, it's clear that Spender is a fairly accurate
reporter. He concludes his account of their unhappy evening: 'his
attitude that everyone except the director of his film unit is a bloody
fool annoys me. All the same he is a live wire and part of my irritation
arises from jealousy and competitiveness. Went to bed still thinking
of the Düsseldorf Orchestra, and depressed by Düsseldorf and the
cocksureness of Jennings.' With the benefit of hindsight, Spender's
assessment became still more even-handed. In the published version

of his journals, he adds a footnote explaining that 'The impression I formed of him does him less than justice. See Peggy Guggenheim's *Out of This Century: Confessions of an Art Addict.*'[3] And however peeved he had been by Jennings's views on the Germans, he seems to have been willing enough to have dinner with him again a couple of weeks later, on 5 October. 'He was ebullient. "Boy, what a day. Gee, what shots. I've never seen anything like it." A Belgian joined us and Jennings got going in a corresponding kind of French version of his Hollywood English. With every other sentence he banged the table and exclaimed "Je suis foutu." '[4]

Ebullience and cocksureness are not, however, the most obvious feature of Jennings's letters home to Cicely.

> In Essen they still fetch their water from stand-pipes and firehose in the streets and the sewers rush roaring and stinking open to the eye and the nose – seep into blitzed houses into cellars where people still live. Look down a deserted street which has a winding path only trodden in the rubble – above, the shapes of windows and balconies lean and threaten – below by the front-door now choked with bricks you will see scrawled in chalk 'IM KELLER WOHNEN . . .' [We live in the basement] and the names of the families who have taken over the underground passages where there is no light (or once I saw one bulb crawling with bees – they too must live through this winter in Essen), no water – no gas – a ray of daylight from the pavement's level airhole – and down here they have brought a cooking stove which has a flue of its own whose wisp of smoke indicates to the stranger that there is life still in this city – beds (very clean – all the clothes and linen exceptionally clean – washed mostly in the street at the water-points) – and a few bits of furniture. The Life Force is certainly strong . . .[5]

The more he saw of the defeated enemy, the less respect he felt. For those who admire what has been called the 'cleanness' of Jennings's work as a propagandist – its refusal to play the ancient game of pretending that your adversary is subhuman, and to be despised as well as feared – it is at times quite shocking to see how his new-found scorn for the Germans curdled into disgust. Our times are more sensitive than his to the vocabularies of ethnic hate, quicker to seek offence, and it is all too easy to wax priggish about the shameful attitudes of our forebears. Yet Jennings is otherwise so free of what we now call 'racism' that his talk here of a 'biological problem' is far more dismaying than it would be in most of his contemporaries. Nietzsche – hardly a liberal – warned against struggling with monsters, lest we become monsters; and Jennings's dismissive words about the Germans echo eerily with the chill rhetoric of the recently slain monster:

> Have I think been getting nearer the problem of the German character and nation – and a grey, dust-swept character it is: seeing, watching, working with the Germans en masse – terrified, rabbit-eyed, over-willing, too-friendly, without an inch of what we would call character among a thousand. Purely biological problem – almost every attribute that we strive to make grow, cultivate, has been bred or burnt out of them, exiled, thrown into gas-chambers, frightened, until you have a nation of near-zombies with all the parts of human beings but really no soul – no oneness of personality to hold the parts together and shine out of the eyes. The eyes indeed are the worst the most telltale part – no shine, often no focus – the mouth drawn down with overwork and over-determination – to do what? Terrified of the Russians – cringing to us . . .

There is nothing else in Jennings's writings even remotely like this; and the film that resulted from his trip through the ruins was a good deal more balanced in tone.

*

A Defeated People was released in 1946. After the Columbia Pictures logo – the only visible sign of Hollywood in any of Jennings's films – the credit sequence shows a map of the British Zone of Occupied Germany. As the title music fades, a sound montage of English voices, male and female, expresses a variety of opinions, variously vengeful and compassionate, about the condition of the former enemy: 'Life in Germany must be terrible . . .' – 'Well, they asked for it, they got it . . .' – 'Yes, but we can't let them starve . . .' – 'I don't know about that, I've got a son out there. As far as I can see, it would be a good thing if some of them *did* die . . .' The film's commentary, apparently scripted by Jennings himself, promptly picks up on the imaginary

conversation – 'Well, a lot of Germany *is* dead . . .' – and sets about
replying to these remarks in a number of ways. The commentary is
spoken by William Hartnell, a reliable English character actor of the
day, often cast as a shrewd NCO figure, who went on in the early
1960s to become well known as the first avatar of BBC television's
most successful science-fiction hero, Dr Who.

His words balance due moral indignation about German guilt for
the war with reasoned explanation of why the German people can't
simply be allowed to stew in their own juice. Many of the arguments
are wholly pragmatic, and appeal to British self-interest: if we allow its
demoralized people to starve, die and rot among their ruins, Germany
will soon be the breeding ground for epidemic diseases that will sweep
across Europe. Moreover, left to rebuild their country alone, without
supervision, the Germans might well be at risk of succumbing to a
new strain of Nazism, and the seeds of a new war sown. This easy
rhetorical move from literal to figurative disease is repeated at intervals
throughout *A Defeated People*.

The film proper begins with images of flowing water: a river
running through the remains of a bridge destroyed by the last waves
of Allied bombing. It then proceeds through shots of lost and wandering civilians – 'searching, looking for food, looking for their homes,
looking for each other' – and of handwritten notices pinned to boards,
plaintively asking for news of missing husbands, wives, sons. Of the
seventy million German survivors, some thirty million are displaced or
lost: 'They are stunned by what hit them, but' – and here the
commentary picks up the Shavian term Jennings used in his letters
home – 'the Life Force is beginning to stir again . . . We can't afford
to let that new life flow in any direction it wants.' After a quick visit
to the British Control Commission ('Our military government – that
is, your husbands and sons – have to talk the Germans into putting
their house in order'), we reach the first plain statement of the film's
essential burden: 'We have an interest in Germany that is purely
selfish. We cannot live next door to a disease-ridden neighbour.' And
then, for those viewers slow to catch on that there is more than one
kind of disease in question here: 'Diseases of the mind, new brands of
fascism, come springing up.'

From this point on, the film becomes a lightning tour of the
new German wasteland: rubble, collapsed buildings, trenches, squalor,

apparent lifelessness. And yet, 'underneath the rubble, there are people living . . . living with the stench of corpses and sewage but still . . . with the will to live'. The camera reveals smoke rising from a pipe, an open-sided kitchen cum living room three stories up, assorted *hausfrauen* and old women trying to scratch together the rudiments of hygiene and diet. We go on to Essen, where the output of the Ruhr coalfields is ordered and distributed (though 'Germans aren't allowed to have coal, and must scavenge for wood' – and so they do, hacking and sawing at felled trees). We see trains overspilling with people under the suspicious scrutiny of the British Military Police; military courts presided over – the camera pans down from a Union Jack – by British judges; the cautious remaking of a German police force (the German policeman 'has to understand that he is the servant of the public and not its master'); British doctors carrying out medical tests on the population, to make sure its minimal food intake of 1,000–1,200 calories per day isn't creating illness; children playing in the rubble – a dream playground, Hartnell's voice points out, before grimly reminding us that with every passing day 'they are growing up and getting more like their fathers'.

When we reach Berlin, the film breaks away from its moralizing travelogue format for a brief historical digression. Jennings pans closely across a group portrait of the industrialist Krupp family, while the commentary gives us a swift résumé of their key role in German militarism: 'They are just as responsible . . . as Hitler and Goering. By killing they grew rich. This time, their war plants have been left a mass of twisted girders' – as we can see for ourselves. Then the tour resumes with scenes of ex-Wehrmacht soldiers ('the master race of men') being stripped, de-loused and numbered. Reprising the metaphorical link between physical and moral contamination, Jennings cuts to the different kind of de-lousing being carried out at a de-Nazification centre, where we meet a 'meek little man who looks like a clerk or a grocer' but proves to be a recent Luftwaffe pilot. Other men are searched for the SS insignia tattooed beneath the left armpit, cross-examined about their war records and, in one case, identified as potentially dangerous: 'Rejected – back to the cage'.

Night falls over Germany, the sirens sound the curfew. Hartnell's voice is stern: the point of the siren is to remind them that 'they lost the war of their own making . . . to remind them . . . that, much as we hate it, we shall stay in Germany until we have real guarantees that the next generation will grow up sane and Christian again'. The tone softens, the mood modulates to the happier vision of a hypothetical Germany of the future, a 'Germany of light, life and freedom. A Germany that respects truth and tolerance and justice' – optimistic words accompanied by the sight of little girls dancing, hand in hand, in the sunlight. The film ends with an intercut sequence: a line of earnest-looking, newly recruited and duly de-Nazified judges being sworn in to uphold democratic law, 'So help me God!' – and the small girls once more, dancing in a ring. This final note of uplift is not altogether reassuring, and does little to dispel the prevailing grimness of the piece.

*

Jennings's next assignment followed soon afterwards, and, on the face of it, should have been an ideal subject for his talents. In March 1946 he went to Workington in Cumberland, to direct a film about the modernization of the mining industry – recently nationalized by the Labour Government. Though Jennings was still an employee of the Crown Film Unit, this production was to be made for the Ministry of Fuel and Power, with the active cooperation of the United Steel Companies and the National Union of Mineworkers. For many other directors the prospect of going down the pit might have been unspeakably dreary, but Jennings would have brought to his new project the warm personal associations of his time with the miners of Cwmgiedd when making *The Silent Village* and, more recently, of filming the 'Goronwy' sequences for *A Diary for Timothy*.

Besides these personal and political associations, he also had an intellectual fascination with the technology of mining to rival that of the machine-crazy young W. H. Auden. A great many of the *Pandæmonium* extracts are about the growth of the mining industry, and particularly about mining disasters. There is an extraordinary authorial note in the published version:

In the fantastic symphony of the Industrial Revolution from the beginnings up to today – yes, today – the dull subterranean explosions of the great and horrible pit disasters return (precisely like the periodic activities of a volcano) like a Fate theme, like

reminders from the unconscious (as in dreams) of this work
that goes on, out of sight, day and night. Yet these 'accidents'
are unnecessary, and the idea that they are due to 'Fate' is a
conception à la Calvin to depress the people. And with each
explosion, the reverberations drown for a time all the petty
squabbles on the surface – Felling (1812), Wallsend (1829), Haslam
(1844), Risca (1862), Gresford (1934).[6]

The Cumberland Story was to add to this sombre litany the name of
another disaster: Workington, 1837. Jennings decided to dramatize this
historic catastrophe as part of the film about postwar modernization.

Jennings had no qualms that his task might be tiresome; but,
surprisingly, his interest in the subject was not enough to elevate the
project above the mundane – indeed, it seems to have faded rapidly as
filming went on. Only a few of his letters home from the shoot have
survived, and these are unremarkable – gripes about the climate ('The
weather here is appalling'), the accommodation ('The food here is
dreadful') and the working hours ('I am really just getting up, working
and falling asleep every day').[7] There's not a hint of the emotional
involvement and sense of revelation so evident in his letters on the
making of Fires Were Started.

The end product was certainly uninspired. The Cumberland Story is
quite the most boring long film Jennings ever made, and by far the
most flawed of his mature career: plodding in exposition, unconvinc-
ingly acted and – even though the splendid Chick Fowle wielded the
camera – on the whole visually unremarkable, save for a terse sequence
of historical reconstruction which ends with a short, brilliantly convincing dramatization of the underground flood in Lady Pit, Workington,
in which thirty-six men and boys drowned with their horses. Briefly,
The Cumberland Story takes the form of a history of the new machines
and working methods brought to the pit town during the war years
by a Mr Nimmo, the manager of a group of collieries along that north-
west coast. The film begins with his arrival in Cumberland shortly
after the outbreak of war; he tours the pits, notes the suspicious
attitudes of the working men and, after exploring the pits and
examining the charts and records, concludes that the only way forward
is to drill out beneath the sea from Lady Pit – a plan first drawn up
more than a century earlier by one Mr Buddle, whose notes survive.

Drinking in a local pub, Nimmo sees a memorial with the names of the colliers drowned in Lady Pit – the cue for the historical reconstruction, voiced by a man with a local accent: 'On 28 July 1837, the whole neighbourhood was appalled by the breaking in of the sea. Thirty-six men and boys, with as many horses – and machinery – irrevocably destroyed . . .' The powerful sequence of panic and disaster concludes with a sombre shot of water lapping in the pit. The reconstruction over, Nimmo takes up his account again and brings us forward to 1940/1, when he had drawn up his plans for new tunnellings during nights of fire-watching. But, he explains, for the redevelopment to proceed he had to win the confidence of the local miners' union, who tended to suspect that every form of technical advance introduced to their industry would have the likely effect of lowering their wages, putting them out of work and generally enfeebling their cause: here, cue some poorly staged confrontations with the union representative Mr Stephenson, and a brief history of local labour struggles, including a flashback to the hunger marches of 1934.

In a series of expository scenes that would tax the patience of all but the most charitable or committed viewer, Nimmo explains about the underground surveying that had to be done, a wages negotiation with the union, the introduction of new drills and other forms of mining technology . . . and so on. Eventually, agreements are struck, work on the new tunnel begins, and Main Bend is successfully reached. Over shots showing how modern mines operate, the film's moral is drawn, none too subtly, in a speech by Stephenson to his union comrades: 'In the past, battles with coal owners tended to divide the miner from the mining engineer . . . now, the miner himself can become a modern craftsman . . . now our battle with the coal owners is ended, and the pits belong to us all . . .' The film ends with a bang: the detonation of a controlled explosion underground. Even less stimulating than this bare synopsis makes it sound, The Cumberland Story is best left to rest, unwatched, in the obscurity of film reference books.

*

By August 1946 or thereabouts, Jennings's wife and daughters had left their house in Essex and come to live in London, at 8 Regent's Park Terrace – the address where Jennings had been living, on and off, since

January 1944 with Allen and Shena Hutt. Mary-Lou was sent to King
Alfred's School in Golders Green, a coeducational institution with a
reputation for being 'progressive'; Charlotte was sent to the single-sex
South Hampstead High, which maintained very high educational
standards. (Today, Charlotte thinks this a very odd choice on her
parents' part, since 'Mary-Lou turned out to be much more the
academic than myself'.) Cicely was greatly relieved to be back in
London – 'she loved the bright lights, she loved the cinema,' Charlotte
recalls; 'she had *hated* the country where she had no friends.' Unfortunately, little else changed for the better, and she was often 'desperately
unhappy'.

For Charlotte and Mary-Lou, though, the Camden flat offered their
first real experience of living with their father, since he had been no
more than a frequent visitor to the country houses in which they had
lived since 1944. For Charlotte, the younger child, he remained a
somewhat remote and chilly presence: she has no memories of playing
with him, or being cuddled or affectionately treated in any way. 'I
remember that one day my Uncle Jos [Cooper] came to stay with us
at the house in Oxford, and he immediately put me on his knee and
said, "Now, which book shall we read?", and I thought, oh, I *like*
this . . .' Mary-Lou, two years older, found it easier to communicate
with Jennings on something like an adult level, but also recalls that he
was often stern and even somewhat alarming.[8]

The family would continue to live in the Camden apartment for
the rest of Jennings's life. Today, after a wave of gentrification which
began in the Sixties and was given a degree of literary glamour by
some of the writers and intellectuals who took a leading part in the
revival (above all, perhaps, by Alan Bennett), Regent's Park Terrace is
one of the most desirable addresses in London, but it all seemed very
different in the 1940s, and life for the family, as Mary-Lou Legg recalls,
was both physically and emotionally confined:

> We had the top two floors of a five-storey house. The sitting-
> room and my parents' bedroom were on the lower, and on the
> top floor were the kitchen, where we ate, a bathroom and a
> bedroom which Charlotte and I shared. This would have been a
> tight fit at the best of times, especially as Charlotte and I were
> now adolescent, but for the first three years my father worked

at home. He wrote and painted in the sitting-room and was extremely intolerant of any noise made by us above him. He would appear out of the sitting-room and roar up at us, 'Be quiet!' if we made even the most reasonable noise . . .

The kitchen arrangements were exiguous: a butler's sink in the corner with a wooden draining-board, a gas stove and a minute refrigerator. We ate on the kitchen table. Despite these problems and the difficulties of rationing, which was more severe after the war, my mother managed to cook and my father paid tribute to her skill with the impossible ingredients.

The great problem of Regent's Park Terrace was the dirt, and the noise. Across from the Terrace and the other side of Oval Road was the main line out of Euston to Scotland. Throughout the day and night, trains picked up speed and roared north, pouring soot and smoke over the neighbouring houses. The windows needed cleaning constantly and the house shook . . . My father spent time carefully removing his seventeenth-century leather-bound books from the shelves and dusting them with a special brush. But we got used to the noise, and I missed it when we left. Whenever I hear the noise of the shunting goods train in *Listen to Britain* I remember hearing the same noise in bed at home. And I remember the noise of the horses galloping up the cobbles of Oval Road, pulling empty goods carts on their way to the depot at the top.

It was fraught with problems – they ran the boiler down in the basement, and there was always a crisis with hot water upstairs. To this day, I can't bear seeing people run hot water taps, because I'm convinced that the supply is going to run dry. My mother and Shena had monumental rows over this, and the provision of dustbins and coal. We had a cast-iron stove in the sitting-room, and all coal had to be carried upstairs from the coalholes in the basement area and all rubbish carried down-stairs to the dustbins.

One of the legacies of my childhood was that we could never afford anything. My parents never owned a property, they always lived in rented flats, and there was always a sense of insecurity and dissatisfaction with where we lived. For people of my mother's class, it was absolutely unthinkable that you should live somewhere so crummy [as Regent's Park Terrace].

Still, the gloom of Camden life was not unrelieved, and – territorial disputes over coal and dustbins notwithstanding – by and large the Hutts and the Jenningses got on fairly well, particularly since Allen was such a benign presence:

I liked Allen. He was an amusing, studious man whose passion was the history of print and the development of the Industrial Revolution. Every morning, all the daily newspapers were delivered to him, and I would sit reading them on the hall floor. Occasionally I would help him to paint the vast staircase, when we would talk companionably. His wife, Shena, was a different matter. She was a tough Scot (I believe Glaswegian) who taught English at the Soviet Trade Mission in Highgate. Unlike Allen, who was not a proselytizer, she would take every opportunity to denounce capitalism and preach politics. They occasionally had parties, to which my parents were invited. I suppose I saw all the postwar CP apparatchiks at these occasions. Allen and Shena had two children, Sam and Elena. I don't know what happened to Elena, but Sam, who I first saw aged six sitting on a potty, is now Hank Wangford [the world's most eminent Country and Western singing gynaecologist].

It was within the confines of the upper two storeys of the house that life could really be difficult.

The atmosphere was not good, it was ghastly. There were constant rows, and depressions. My mother would slam doors, my father would slam doors – it was almost like the Carlyles. But the children had to be quiet, we couldn't practise musical instruments, and I couldn't have friends home to tea, because we had this giant Magritte painting, called *Au Seuil de la Liberté*, which my father had bought from Magritte at the International Surrealist exhibition. It depicted a room with a cannon in it, and a woman with bare breasts, and I felt very embarrassed – a thirteen-year-old would feel very diffident about bringing home her friends to that room, never knowing what mood my father was going to be in, and with that picture there. It was eventually sold, in 1948, for about £120, to pay for having my teeth straightened.

Another source of domestic tension was Humphrey's spendthrift attitude. Even though they were constantly short of ready cash, he would rarely stint himself on the luxuries he considered necessities. Charlotte: 'He was always impeccably dressed. He had bought real leather shoes in the middle of the war, he bought the best canvases from Roberson's in Parkway [Camden], the best paints, the best brushes, the best turps, the best linseed oil . . . and he was always augmenting his library, with rare and out-of-print editions.' Mary-Lou again: 'There were lots of books in the house and he took tremendous care of them. He had a lot of good bindings – he had all the early transactions of the Royal Society leather-bound, and would polish them . . . If you wanted to look at one, he'd ask, "Are your hands clean?" But he would scribble in their margins with a pencil.'

A portrait photograph by Beiny taken at about this time appears to show him doing just that – inscribing a note at the side of a page of some thick volume with his left hand, a faint smile on his face. Though obviously posed, it has an agreeably spontaneous air, and captures more clearly than any other portrait the gentler and more unworldly aspect of Jennings's nature – one of the aspects that could make him loved even by some of those he could also irritate beyond measure.

Uncomfortable as these material circumstances were, outsiders might reasonably have concluded that the Jenningses were going up in the world. While still at work on *The Cumberland Story*, Jennings became entitled to add the letters 'OBE' to his signature, for the Birthday Honours List for 18 June 1946 admitted 'Frank Humphrey Sinkler Jennings, Esq., Director, Crown Film Unit, Ministry of Information' to the Order of the British Empire. 'Everyone has been very charming about the Honours List I must say,' he had written to Cicely, still in Thaxted, at the beginning of July '– the Unit seems to realize it included them.' But not all his associates were quite so charming, or charmed. The surviving members of the English Surrealist Group issued a *Déclaration du groupe surréaliste en Angleterre* in the catalogue of the International Surrealist Exhibition held at the Galerie Maeght in Paris; their *Déclaration* announced the formal expulsion of Jennings from the Surrealist movement for having accepted the imperialist honour. If Jennings was at all hurt by this excommunication, he could at least console himself with the thought that he was in excellent company. His fellow-expulsees included Henry Moore ('for making sacerdotal ornaments'), Herbert Read for eclecticism and David Gascoyne 'for mystification'.[9]

It was soon time for Jennings to say goodbye to another institution, too. Once post-production on *The Cumberland Story* was complete, he finally resigned from the Crown Film Unit – his truest home for more than twelve years, the years of his greatest achievement – and joined Ian Dalrymple's newly formed production company Wessex Films. Jennings's reasons for this move to the commercial sector aren't altogether clear, though the possibilities of an increase in salary and warm personal loyalty to Dalrymple were no doubt among them. Still more attractive for a man young in ambition was the strong possibility of working on a full-length dramatic feature. Before long, though, he may have had cause to doubt the wisdom of his move from Crown, since the next two years were mainly given over to research and development on projects that never went before the cameras – the old, old story that many British (and other) directors could tell. His first main job was to produce a treatment for a documentary version of R. J. Cruickshank's recent book *Roaring Century*, a study of the years 1846–1946 – a subject highly congenial, of course, to the author of the perpetually unfinished book on the Industrial Revolution, *Pandæmonium*.

Since it soon became clear that money for the *Roaring Century* film was not immediately forthcoming, Jennings also began work on an adaptation of a best-selling novel, H. E. Bates's *The Purple Plain*, about the struggles of an airman shot down in the Burmese jungle. It was an ambitious subject for a fledgling company to undertake, but was evidently considered a realistic proposition, since Wessex agreed to co-finance a lengthy reconnaissance trip to the country in conjunction with the MOI, who were interested in making something more along the lines of a dramatized documentary about contemporary Burmese life. Apart from scouting for locations, recruiting possible local actors and generally enquiring into the logistical practicalities of making the Bates film, Jennings was also asked to come up with ideas and story lines for another film about life in contemporary Burma. With plans for *Roaring Century* still up in the air, he set off to the Far East.

He arrived in Rangoon on 2 February 1947 for what turned out to be a three-month stay. During that time, he travelled extensively: northwards to the Shan States, to the wolfram mines of Morchi (today, Mawkma:), to the old former capital Mandalay, up to the Chinese border and, finally, to the Irrawaddy delta zone. Burma, poor and chaotic after the withdrawal of the Japanese occupying forces, was building up to a general election in May, and voices on almost all sides were agitating for withdrawal from the British Empire. Nonetheless, Jennings was treated with great courtesy, as a visiting dignitary suitable for invitations to weddings, official receptions and other ceremonies, and he made contact with at least one local politician who looked favourably on the idea of reaching some accommodation with Britain and remaining within the Empire: Aung San, the leader of the Anti-Fascist People's Freedom League (and father of Aung San Suu Kyi, the leader of the present-day National League for Democracy).

It did not take long for Jennings to be enraptured by the place; and though his very first letter home to Cicely, dated 2 February 1947, dwells on the poverty and discomfort of central Rangoon – complaints about the constant heat and humidity must have read wryly back in Britain, which was suffering a bitterly cold and protracted winter, one of the worst since records began – the note of affection for this country and its people is already clear:

I am writing this lying under the mosquito netting at 11.30 at night – the distant dogs barking, the cicadas chirping – everything else quiet. I am in an English family's house 5 miles out of Rangoon. One of a number of semi-European villas very comfortable with an Indian cook and a Chinese servant – surrounded by quiet farming country with rickety mat houses, stalls full of fine white oxen, beds of delicate flowers which are grown for the market and above us on a little dusty hill a tiny Buddhist monastery with shaven monks in yellow-orange robes who this evening were watering their garden next to a small but delicious pagoda – all rather dilapidated but with clay models of the reclining and meditating Buddha recently set into the niches.

The town of Rangoon is partly like any newsreel of the East – big Western banks and offices – rather blitzed some of them – Indian and Chinese slum quarters – very smelly and lively – and on all roads leading out of town lines of mat houses with Burmese shops and families. Wretched in one way – Eastern pre-fabs – but preferable I should say to the squalor of the big streets. The river wide and dirty – lined with docks and shipping – some wrecked, some converted landing-craft – some looking just like the Thames or the Clyde. Perhaps a third of the men in some sort of uniform.

Trucks, jeeps, barbed wire. Political slogans. Strike notices. The
dockers are on strike, so are the University students, so are the
school children! In the papers intense political activity. Bright sun
– just bearably hot. Above all the newly gilded dome and spire of
the Great Pagoda.

So far our discussions have been with Burmese and English
[and] are going on well. Everyone very charming and helpful. If
there is anything sinister behind it hasn't shown up yet . . .

Of course all this is not really Burma. We hope to get up-
country in a few days, depending on discussions with Aung San
and the Governor-General. Everywhere an extraordinary mixture
of violence and delicacy. Lorries of police with tommy-guns, train
robberies, tear-gas and at the same time nearly every Burmese
woman exquisitely dressed with gay skirts and flowers, all-night
dance festivals . . .

His stay is richly documented in both words and images. Though
he wrote only half a dozen letters home to Cicely and to Ian
Dalrymple, these communications are long, full of detail and anecdote,
and supplemented by many pages of typed or scribbled notes – story
ideas for the film about contemporary life, accounts (half reportage,
half prose-poetry) of the sights and ceremonies he had witnessed. And,
quite apart from their intrinsic interest, the Burmese letters deserve
attention as the last major body of correspondence he ever wrote.
The inadvertent autobiography he began with his love letters to Cicely
in his last year as an undergraduate during 1928–9 was now almost
complete.

To Cicely Jennings, 15 February 1947:

The Burmese are really first-class: friendly and bright and very
intelligent. Very French in many ways. We haven't yet left
Rangoon owing to shortage of transport, but hope to leave on
Wednesday the 19th to go up to the Shan States (up towards
Mandalay nearer to China) for a meeting of the Shan chiefs who
are holding a big PWE. The Pwe is a kind of semi-serious semi-
clown pantomime. Partly traditional stories and dancing and
costumes plus slapstick and patter. Cross between a mediaeval
mystery play and Itma.[10] They are played in the open, at night
and all night! They begin as soon as it gets dark, hot up about

midnight and continue till near dawn. In any case there is no transport home for most of the audience until about 5 or 6 in the morning – so they camp out: smoking cigars and chewing betel and talking and sleeping. The whole family very often – squatting on rush matting plus a rug or shawl. The acting equally is pretty stylized and partly music hall. The orchestra carry on a sort of jam session – continuously. We walked out about ten o'clock the other night across a piece of waste land called 'Pineapple Jungle' to see a rather rough Pwe which had been sponsored by AFPL (Anti-Fascist People's League: Aung San's party). It was held in the grounds of a ruined house built by a maniac Chinaman (Citizen Kane style) with paintings inside by Dod Proctor. It is mentioned in Collis's *Trials in Burma*. Now deserted. The stage was made of matting and bamboo raised on empty oil drums, and the audience sat in a sort of encampment with mat-walls. Outside the encampment in the night tea tables, candy and cigar stalls and so on. Horses tethered. Fires burning with big cooking pots. The stage decorated with canvas curtains and hangings – partly painted Burmese style – partly European. Some backcloths very beautiful. We couldn't follow a word of the dialogue of course or the songs. But we sat among the people on the matting until about 2 in the morning and got into the same mood: just paying attention when we wanted to. Some very exciting murder scenes. Bits of stylized dancing and then a sort of Eddie Cantor [the American comedian and singer] character who had the audiences howling with laughter. The dialogue taken at great speed – the timing really remarkable. The actors also talking to the audience on the side like Groucho Marx. It was lovely . . .

. . . since Aung San's return most political papers have been very critical of his not having demanded complete independence as promised. So now there are demonstrations of anti-AFPL parties including communists – with processions, loudspeaker vans and all. Of course the elections come off in April – which will settle Aung San's position more or less – so everybody is pretty restless. It doesn't stop them being gay however and individually very friendly. Once again it is like France: tremendous political activity – recriminations, bribes, hatred of the police and so on – but at the same time an extraordinarily unified everyday culture: partly due to Buddhism which pervades everything (there are

strike flags and committees sitting in the great Shwe Dagon
pagoda) and partly that relatively life is easy here – food is
abundant compared to India – the country is enormously rich in
materials – and these two together have allowed them to develop
a real art of living. It hasn't produced Beethoven or Tolstoy – but
exists as in France in their dress and cooking and love of flowers
and children and theatricals and so on. They have a natural sense
of style. And of course as with the Indians and Chinese those who
have been to England or America have come back with an
amazing grasp of another culture . . .

To Ian Dalrymple, 1 March:

I have . . . just returned to Rangoon from a trip five hundred
miles or so up country – into the Shan Hills (described in Collis's
'Lords of the Sunset'). In a week or so I am expecting to go on a
second trip up into the Arakan [in the west of the country, along
the Bay of Bengal] and across to Mandalay. But superficial as of
course any such voyaging is, certain things become clear enough
for me to write to you. Well, first of all there is fantastic film
material here – I am not just thinking of the 'mystic east' but of
the peculiar classless aristocratic sense of life, simultaneously
sophisticated and naive, which appears to be proper to Burma. Of
course, there are troubles – political dishonesty, disinclination to
get down to a national job of work, serious dacoity (bands of a
hundred armed with Bren guns). I will omit for the moment
descriptions of the living folk-lore that nightly produces in the
Pwes the lion-throne at Mandalay fringed with the purest crazy-
gang clowning.[11] Or the liquid depths of their drum-music. The
fact is that the picture I was sent out to prepare *a* would have
first-class backing from the Burmese on an Executive Council or
an Interim Government level, *b* must be made in colour, *c* cannot
be made by the present resources of CFU, COI or any such
collection, *d* needs a long period of preparation with a writer of
the order of Collis and therefore *e* could not be started in under
15 months from now – if that. But what a picture of a compact
ancient culture facing the atomic-bomb world on its own feet,
could be made.

I mention the incapacity of CFU principally because I see
more clearly from this distance than in London how little they

would measure up to the organizational problems of such an expedition as would be necessary . . .

Now I trust and pray that 'Roaring Century' is still on the map, because whatever happens, Ian, I should return in early May and report to Tritton etc. precisely what I outlined above. Even supposing they agreed to a long delay, the expense and trouble of colour and so on, I still do not propose to sit about doing nothing in the meantime. Moreover I am exceptionally sick of their day to day incompetence – example: correspondence dealing with regulations for accommodation in first and second-class hotels – when of course there are no hotels in Burma at all!

However if it still holds I am hoping and indeed longing to come to you say June 1st to crack into 'Roaring Century' . . .

To Cicely, 25 March:

I am now back in Rangoon again after a trip up the Arakan coast . . .

The journey back [from a short trip to the famous Buddhist shrine at Mahamuni to their temporary base in the village of Kyautaw, on the River Keladan] in the ox-cart taught me more about Burma than any other thing we have done . . . It was so uncomfortable it didn't matter. The sun was dropping fortunately – we lumbered through little villages where the women were pounding the rice, passed lines of similar carts jolting home at the same philosophical speed – two–three m.p.h. The "chico" [lad] beside me sang Burmese songs imitating the drum-parts of the orchestra in between the words – we met files of Chin women carrying large bundles of rushes on their heads, cooked some ducks' eggs and a calabash at a tiny farm – just bamboo & rushes – rather like Rembrandt's etchings of a poverty-stricken countryside. Saw the hand-loom, and the rice store, and the fishing tackle and then bumped on again throwing up illuminated dust behind us. Fell into thought about the whole world and saw how a contemplative religion like Buddhism holds the mind out here. At that pace, in that landscape, and in that sun, everything – the wheel of the cart, the oxen, the cry of the driver with the pagoda tattoed on his back, even the shadows we cast – could in a moment become symbols . . .

. . . we have been annoying some of the local British for 'frat-

ernizing' with the Burmese too easily – treating servants too well
and so on. There are two very definite British types out here –
(1) the adventurous soldiers – an Irish colonel of the Chin Rifles
called Flanagan who spoke Chin to all his own officers – or the
present Governor who was on Mountbatten's staff – or come to
that Mountbatten himself who as far as one can see is almost
solely responsible for the relative quietness of Burma (I mean
compared to Indo-China) – this type speaks the language, mixes
with the Burmese and everybody, is business-like and straightforward. He has nothing to be dishonest about. Then (2) there
is still a percentage of old-world Adminstrators – super Civil
Servants who would be intolerable in England and are doubly
so here – even when they are graciously condescending to
'Johnny Burman'. They spend their time informing us that 'oh
but it's different out here' and always have nasty little tales
about Burmese individuals. The 'Passage to India' mentality but
applied to a small, cultured, sensitive people, with an acute perception of manners and motives. Of course the result has been
disastrous. The Burmese have (compared to us) a peculiarly classless society and (compared to India) an extraordinary religious
unity. Anyway there's no stopping them now, which is something. In a year's time there won't be any British administrators
to speak of . . .

On 11 April he wrote Cicely a long letter from Maymyo, Upper
Burma, describing his travels from Rangoon up to the Chinese border,
and including two major set-pieces – an account of Mandalay and his
futile hunt there for what might be left of the legendary Lion Throne
('where reigned Thibau and Mindon and to which Alaungpaya
returned from Siam in triumph . . . But, you know, there was nothing
left . . .'), and a still more detailed portrait of the funeral of a Buddhist
monk, in which he spotted one of his favourite images, a triumphal
chariot: 'the first thing we saw was a squad of PVOs drilling in front
of a bamboo and paper pavilion. In front of it also there was a great
triumphal chariot for the coffin constructed on a motor lorry but representing simultaneously a triple pagoda and a mythological creature
with the beaked head of a bird and the tail of a dragon or fish . . .'
But the grandeur of the first part of the ceremony, he reports, had
given way to grimmer sights:

Then the lorry shorn of its pagoda-spires lest they catch on the trees – minus the singing girls – minus the procession – now just a motor lorry carrying a gilt coffin bumps along the dusty road and swings over the bridge to the place of death.

Once again a dusky turbaned figure stripped to the waist takes charge and with a big *dah* (knife-axe) unscrews the coffin lid. Now all the lustre has left the ceremony. Inside the coffin there is a tin box in which the body has been embalmed in a black powder. All this is opened up and exhibited in the cruel light of the sun. The cemetery workers tie handkerchiefs across their mouths and light the fire. Kids scramble for a ride back on the lorry. Through the rising flames and smoke one can just perceive a sordid shape that was once human. The gorge rises.

That evening back in Maymyo the sun which had guarded its strength inside my head since two o'clock struck me a violent blow. I awoke the next morning to hear the bells of the Church of England calling the people to rejoice. It was Easter Sunday.

Since then we have been up to China, taken part in the Water festival, but I think seen nothing that so clearly pictured the contrasts, the sense of life and death, past & present in Burma, as the few days described in haste above . . .

*

Jennings arrived back in England in June. Neither he nor anyone involved with Wessex was ever to make *The Purple Plain*, though it was eventually filmed in 1954 by an American director, Robert Parrish, with Gregory Peck in the lead role. But his contract with Wessex was renewed, and he now set to work on adapting another novel – a highly suitable one, given the production company's name: Thomas Hardy's *Far from the Madding Crowd*.

Many people who met Jennings at this time noticed a change in him; it was assumed that he had been greatly affected by his months in Burma. Mary-Lou Legg recalls his obvious affection for the Burmese: 'this sophisticated people, but not sophisticated by machinery, leading a rural life even in the large cities. He said that they were so elegant and so educated . . . he really liked the Burmese, he liked the world they lived in, the ethic and the spirituality, and I think he felt he'd really discovered something there.' Kathleen Raine, in particular, felt that it had been something in the nature of a spiritual awakening for him. In the second volume of her autobiography, *The Land Unknown*, she writes:

> most and last, he was moved by Burma, where he found the human society which to him seemed to come nearest to an ideal perfection: a traditional Buddhist society, where all took its meaning from its orientation towards a spiritual vision. All, as he explained, from the weaving of the basket in which men carried their vegetables to market, to the burial of the dead, was done according to that philosophy which holds in a single thought the impermanence of all things and the existential mystery of the here and now. Years before he had talked of Lao Tze; and now he had found a society which cared nothing for the permanence of things made, because the *Tao* is inexhaustible: 'work it, and more comes out'. He had been present at the cremation of a Buddhist monk, and had, perhaps for the only time in his life, there understood what it is when an entire society is informed by a sublime metaphysical vision; something lost, or all but lost, from the modern West.[12]

While in Burma, Jennings took about two hundred black-and-white photographs: the negatives have been lost, but many contact prints survive in good condition. Though this set of images has no public standing – it has never been exhibited or published – it can be considered an artistic project in its own right: a major documentary in still images, Jennings's only full-scale venture into the photographic essay. Besides its intrinsic beauty, it is a fascinating portrait of a world that was soon to disappear. (In 1947, Aung San, who had been successful in his campaigning and was made Prime Minister in April, fell victim to an assassin.) Perhaps it will be published one day; perhaps, by then, Burma (Myanmar) will no longer be the nightmarish police state it has become since Jennings was enchanted by its gentle, artistic, profoundly civilized people.

*

On Sunday 17 August 1947, Jennings composed a Mass-Observation-style day report, prompted by three dramatic events. Once again, the 'fantastic symphony' of the Industrial Revolution had claimed the lives of British miners: 'the William Pit disaster – at Whitehaven – in which one hundred and eleven miners working in the Six-quarters out under the Solway Firth were trapped – crushed – suffocated by a tremendous explosion'. Already shaken by this news, the nation had also to come to terms with an economic crisis, as 'the last remains of the vaunted American loan which had been designed to last us till 1951 – were being drawn day after day ... Other banks in other countries suddenly appeared to take away from us the very means of buying food.' And from the Indian sub-continent came word of 'the mobbing of Mountbatten – the raising of the two flags of Pakistan and India ... Aeroplanes in the night sky writing Jai – Jai Hind – Victory'. Jennings summed up:

> Ah! if this story has been rightly told how clearly will these three events stand linked together. Not as cause and effect – the links of History are subtler than that – but as a final statement of our problems – industrial – financial – Imperial.
> The Cabinet huddles together to halt the drain on dollars – to plan at long last that we in this Island shall try to grow the food we eat – the rescue squad hacks its way through a hundred yards of fallen rock – the troopship roars out 'Bless 'Em All' as the engines begin to race. From now on – we are all – all of us – on our own.[13]

In the more leisured circumstances of peacetime Britain, Jennings now found time to write his first substantial piece of critical prose for almost a decade. The December 1947 issue of *Our Time* ran an article by him entitled 'Colorado Claro' and subtitled 'Thoughts on the "Cleaned Pictures"' – those, that is, at one of his best-loved haunts, the National Gallery. Perhaps the most revealing part of this publication was the caption biography of its author – drafted by a subeditor, no doubt, but bearing the distinct stamp of the man himself: 'Aged 40, Humphrey Jennings is a film director and painter. He was with the GPO and Crown Film Units from 1934 to 1947, and is now working for Wessex Film Productions. He has also painted continuously since 1930. Home ground: East Anglia. Politics: those of William Cobbett.'

I asked Mary-Lou Legg whether politics were much discussed at home:

Oh, constantly, constantly. Not between my parents so much
as between my father and people who came for meals, or
when he went out for meals. My father felt very passionately,
but he became very alienated, I think, from certain aspects
of the Labour Party. I remember him getting very angry when
the canals were nationalized, and all the boats were painted over,
so that all the little castles and flowers and other decorations –
decorations painted by the owners, as they sailed up and down
the canals [– were blotted out]. He felt that personal expression,
art and tradition were being wiped out by this bureaucracy.

Jennings strongly approved of the effect wrought by the cleaning
of the Old Masters – approved as loudly as the Old Guard, such as
the critic for the *Daily Telegraph*, had been horrified by it: 'They are
men defending vested interests,' Jennings claimed. To the reactionary
charge that the removal of glass, dirt and yellow varnish has ruined
the 'mystery' of works by Poussin, Velázquez and others, he triumphantly assents, replying for the defence: 'if we approve that the
cleaners of the National Gallery under enlightened direction have
cleared away so much fake mystery, we must say also that what they
have revealed is a thousand times more marvellous, more poetic, and
in another sense mysterious'.[14] After noting that the 'new' Velázquez,
for one, is a far greater artist than the one seen through the comfortable fug of dirt and glass, indeed a visionary of Blakean dimensions,
Jennings brings his argument home with a resonant final paragraph:

> We are used to hearing that such and such a modern artist is
> really 'in the tradition'. This Exhibition illuminates the path of
> tradition the other way round. In it we see the Old Masters
> as youthful, visionary creators, whose pictures do indeed look as
> though they 'have been painted today', who, like Renoir and
> Degas and Van Gogh enjoyed life, savoured it with passion, and
> who (no less than more 'political' names) can teach us to trans-
> form it.[15]

The word 'transform' has slightly Marxist tones, but the pay-off line
also echoes, and more importantly, the old Rimbaud maxim, adored
and adopted by the Surrealists: *changez la vie*. 'Colorado Claro', one
of the most stimulating pieces Jennings ever wrote on art, is also evidence that the mere technicality of expulsion from the Surrealist circle

had done nothing to dampen his ardour for its most enlivening promises; that he was still, at heart, the man in whom Valentine Penrose
had recognized *un vrai révolté*.

For Jennings, one of the greatest pleasures of renewed peace was
that he was once again able to look regularly at paintings:

> He went to exhibitions a lot [said Mary-Lou Legg], mainly at the
> National Gallery; there were two or three really superb loan
> exhibitions just after the war, of paintings from Austria and
> Munich, and I know that he had a season ticket to them and
> went to them a lot. I think that something people haven't
> thought about enough is the way in which he kept looking at
> things, reinforcing his vision. I think he used to go to the
> National Gallery at least once a week.

He had only ever tried to give more public form to this passion on
odd occasions, writing about painting and the other visual arts in odd
corners here and there from *Experiment* back in his Cambridge days
to the Surrealist *London Bulletin*, but now he was thinking of writing
at considerably greater length on an English artist in whom he had
long been keenly interested: Edward Lear.

At about this time he painted a large imaginary portrait of Lear,
and he was busy collecting extracts from the artist's letters, travel
journals and poems for a small book, provisionally entitled 'The Road
to San Remo; or, The Pilgrimage of Edward Lear'. Mary-Lou Legg
recalls: 'The book on Lear was never finished – a pity because he was
well before everyone else [in taking a serious rather than an amused
or affectionately condescending interest in the nonsense writer.] He
had a lot of Lear's engravings in big books; I think what interested
him was the language, partly.' Lear's eccentric and proto-Surrealist
use of language, yes; but also his significance as a representative of
modern sensibility – a man who needed to escape from industrialized
England both in mind and in body, as many intelligent and sensitive
people of his time did, but who was always clear-sighted and unsen-
timental about why such escapism might be necessary.

Jennings's draft introduction to the unfinished book also makes
clear his belief that Lear can not be adequately understood if we slice
his activities up into hermetically sealed compartments – that his
real significance only becomes apparent if and when we start to see

the unity of his concerns. Once again, the ruling sentiment is 'Only Connect':

> I am aware that nothing is more boring than explaining jokes or rationalising mysteries. And I can promise the reader absolutely that this book contains no psycho-analytical interpretations either of Lear's character or of his writings. Its purpose is simple – to suggest – with the maximum of quotations from Lear and the minimum of comment – that we should cease to regard him as a not very successful landscape artist who wrote children's books in his spare time, which grown ups also find amusing and to which some people would go so far as to give the name 'poetry' ... In place of this picture I see the life of Lear as a whole – the so-called Nonsense poetry filling an increasing part in it as he got older and being increasingly absolutely an expression of himself ...
>
> Lear was a pilgrim – his writings – Journals, Letters and Poems – all describe 'the days of his pilgrimage' and the visions he saw in them – romantic scenes, human curiosities, moments of intense nostalgia, 'dream-landscapes', the horrors of reality ... An escapist, certainly ... but one whose wishes and regrets are never far from our own ... A minor poet? ... but one full of self-knowledge – who escaped from the world of Victorian England as far as he was able – but who was less guilty of self-deception than any ... of us. (Hypocrite lecteur mon semblable mon frère ...)

(The last, biting phrase is from Baudelaire's poem 'Au Lecteur'; it had become famous again in the early twentieth century when Eliot used it as the culminating line of *The Waste Land*, Book One.) True to his avowed intent, Jennings put the book together almost entirely from Lear's own words, punctuated occasionally by memoirs from his friends. Such critical annotation as does occur often looks more like Jennings reminding himself about something than giving lessons to the reader – 'Note that in the Ionian and I think Abruzzi travels L. often uses the word *Poussinesque* – to our ears perhaps a cliché – a variant on picturesque – but remember that at Knowsley Hall L. would have seen – have lived with one of the great Poussin landscapes *Les Cendres de Phocion*.'

(Knowsley Hall was the seat of Lear's close friend the Earl of Derby, the principal dedicatee of *A Book of Nonsense*.) The completed book – and though on the short side at no more than about a hundred pages, the typescript Jennings left lacks only a little polishing to be ready for the presses – would almost certainly have been no more than sparingly annotated.

A number of the passages Jennings extracted for 'The Road to San Remo' also found their way into the working papers for *Pandæmonium*. Recognizing the prominent place that Lear held in her father's attention towards the end of his life, Mary-Lou included several passages from the author in the published version, and reading these few extracts gives something of the flavour of Jennings's abandoned work. A couple of them are deliberately amusing, notably a letter from Lear to Lady Waldegrave dated 4 November 1852: 'I went into the city today, to put the £125 I got for the "Book of Nonsense" into the funds. It is doubtless a very unusual thing for an artist to put by money, for the whole way from Temple Bar to the Bank was *crowded* with carriages and people, – so immense a sensation did this occurrence make. And all the way back it was the same, which was very gratifying.' And there is an episode from the summer of 1867 (in the published version – the 'San Remo' draft gives the autumn of 1866), in which Lear describes riding in a railway carriage and hearing an irate and stubborn old man explaining to his family, all keen readers of the *Nonsense* book, that its true author is the Earl of Derby – 'Lear' being an obvious anagram for 'Earl' – and that there is no such man as 'Edward Lear'. When he can stand no more, Lear shows the old fellow several letters addressed to him and the name written on his cane and in his hat. Collapse of opinionated party.

Pandæmonium also includes a letter, in hexameters, from Lear to Lord Carlingford, of 9 July 1859:

> Washing my rosecolored flesh and brushing my hair with a
>   hairbrush, –
> – Breakfast of tea, bread and butter, at nine o'clock in the
>   morning,
> Sending my carpet-bag onward I reached the Twickenham
>   station . . .

And finally, in a much more sober vein, there is another letter to Lady Waldegrave, dated 11 December 1866, referring to a recent debate within (and outside) the Church of England over some unorthodox views expressed by John William Colenso, the Bishop of Natal, and full of anticlerical spleen.

A broader creed, – a better form of worship – the cessation of nonsense and curses – and a recognition of a new state of manners brought about by centuries, science, destiny or what not – will assuredly be demanded and come to pass whether Bishops and priests welcome the changes or resist them. Not those who believe that God the Creator is greater than a Book, and that millions unborn are to look up to higher thoughts than those stereotyped by ancient legends, gross ignorance and hideous bigotry – not those are the Infidels – but those same screamy ganders of the church, who put darkness forward and insist that it is light.

It is in passages like this that one glimpses why it was that Lear began to seem important to Jennings. Did he share Lear's need to escape, that hunger which sent Lear scuttling off round the countries of the south, from Albania to Egypt, and off into worlds of his own imagining? If so, one of the main things from which he seems to have wanted to escape was married life with Cicely.

*

Working on these more private projects may also have been a way of compensating for the frustration of labouring on so many uncompleted ones. Whatever the irritations of working for Crown, Jennings had at least never been short of films to make: for most of the war, he had been able to move on from film to film with very few wasted weeks. With Wessex it had so far been different, but now his luck changed. By the early summer of 1948, he was well into work on a treatment for a short film provisionally entitled 'Awful Old England'. This time, at last, something came of his preparations: 'Awful Old England' was the first of his Wessex films to reach the screens, though it changed title en route, to *The Dim Little Island*. A treatment dated 10 June 1948 shows that Jennings's thoughts on the film were already quite far advanced. The original idea was to make it a gentle riposte to the voice of Kipling's disgruntled, disillusioned and displaced old soldier:

> Me that 'ave been what I've been –
> Me that 'ave gone where I've gone –
> Me that 'ave seen what I've seen –
>   'Ow can I ever take on
> With awful old England again . . .

The sentiments of Kipling's veteran Tommy were newly pertinent again in the depressive mood of late 1940s England; Jennings originally planned to underline that pertinence by ending the poem with 'flashes from the XIVth Army – the face of the soldier in the jungle – the bouquets of flowers and kisses for the liberators of 1944–45'. The rest of the film would hand over the task of replying to four notable Englishmen who would explain to Mr Thomas Atkins that the old place wasn't really quite so awful as he thought.

Jennings's musings about the state of the nation, and more gener-ally about the nature of 'awful old England', were brought into sharper focus by his commission to review a book entitled *The Character of England* for the *Times Literary Supplement*. The review, published on 7 August, is one of his most carefully crafted pieces of prose (a hint, with 'Colorado Claro', that he was starting to flex some long-neglected muscles as a literary stylist, and may have been pondering a rather more active additional career as a writer or journalist than he had been able to contemplate for years). As one would hope, it is full of original insights and quite lacking in nostalgia: 'There is only one occasion when admiration for past deeds may be given full rein, and that is in an epitaph. It is a dangerous tendency for the living. Narcissus was very beautiful and quite rightly spent a very long time admiring himself; but he died of it.'[16] He treads a fascinating line between rapturous admiration for English achievements and bleak acknowledge-ment of English failings ('their great unwillingness to admit facts, their power of pretending that things are not so'[17]); not for him the received idea that the English are the nation of the stiff upper lip and fair play:

> The English are in fact a violent, savage race, passionately artistic, enormously addicted to pattern, with a faculty beyond all other people of ignoring their neighbours, their surroundings, or in the

last resort, themselves. They have a power of poetry which is the
despair of all the rest of the world . . .'[18]

The piece ends, possibly to the bafflement of many contemporary
readers, with a flight of rhetoric which, in its curious mingling of the
cryptic and the apocalyptic, echoes the mood of his 'day report' of
the previous August: 'These quick, tremendous, inventive, bold people
are to be tested once more. They will have to move suddenly from
the period of Racine to the period of Villon. One of the great epics
of the world is to be played out before us, and played out now.'[19]

The Dim Little Island (for many years, even the most reputable
filmographies left out the title's definite article), released in 1949, was
a great improvement on its pedestrian predecessor of two years earlier,
The Cumberland Story. Though barely eleven minutes long, it manages
to touch lightly on a wide range of ideas and tones; and despite the
fact that it purports to be no more than a humble platform for other
men's opinions, it marks the clear return of a personal note to
Jennings's film-making. The film's brief is simple: it's meant to be a
pep talk, a morale-booster, a reassurance to the British people that life
after the war need be neither as drab nor as glum as they may have
come to believe. The four men given the task of bucking up the battle-
weary troops are, in order of appearance, the cartoonist Osbert
Lancaster, the industrialist John Ormston of Armstrong Vickers, the
naturalist James Fisher and the composer Ralph Vaughan Williams: a
curious quartet, with some unexpected points to make.

Lancaster, his superbly moustached face glimpsed in a mirror as he
chain-smokes and draws, claims the right to open the proceedings: 'In
ancient times,' he declares in off-hand patrician tones, while deftly
inking in a drawing of a traditional bladder-on-a-stick court jester and
a brace of shocked aristocrats, 'the licensed fool was allowed to speak
while the others held their peace. So perhaps I, as an avowedly comic
artist, may be allowed to speak first.' He goes on to explain that the
essence of his job is to 'remind the public of what they really look like,
and to destroy their happy illusions of dignity and beauty'. A rostrum
shot nicely illustrates his point, showing a frightful collection of
Lancaster's contemporary British grotesques queuing beneath advertising hoardings full of beautiful smiling faces and svelte figures.

His initial joke made, Lancaster moves rapidly on to slightly more philosophical points about the contrast between illusion and reality, and suggests that, whatever inflated ideas his countrymen may have about the beauty of their persons, they tend to deceive themselves in quite the opposite direction when they muse on the country itself. 'There are many other illusions. For instance, the illusion that compared to the romance and mystery of High Tibet, or the rolling prairies and limitless expanse of the Golden West' – cut-aways to his artwork illustrate these fancied landscapes – 'Great Britain is rather a dim little island . . . that now, of course, as always, the country is going to the dogs . . . "Ichabod, Ichabod, thy glory is departed." '

Lancaster's commentary now moves to a set of images so close to Jennings's *Pandæmonium* concerns that it is hard to believe the director did not have a hand in the scripting. The cartoonist reminds us of Ford Madox Brown's painting *The Last of England*, and muses on the dramatic contrast between the received idea of the early 1850s as a Golden Age ('a time of optimism, of expansion and the Great Exhibition') and the mood of fear and misgiving etched into the faces of Brown's departing emigrants: 'To them, England was the land of the twelve-hour day, still suffering the effects of the Hungry Forties [a calamity to which Jennings also alludes in his next film, *Family Portrait*], its faith undermined by Mr Darwin . . .' And his commentary concludes: 'Many of these things were indeed realities: the illusion was that they would result in the collapse of Britain.'

The remaining nine minutes or so of *The Dim Little Island* seek out some of the more optimistic realities of contemporary Britain: the prospect that its shipbuilding industry might soon revive (a hope which from the perspective of the early twenty-first century can only be pondered on ruefully or with bitterness); the wealth and variety of its wildlife and scenery, and the care which is now going into their preservation; and the peculiar genius of English music. Not the most obvious trio of reasons to be cheerful, and yet each of the short sermons is touchingly expressed and at points even persuasive. John Ormston speaks briefly of the rise, fall and rise again of the Tyneside shipyards, James Fisher takes up the wildlife theme – 'Wild nature in Britain – what's the use of it? I'll tell you: it's interesting, we learn from it; it's beautiful, and you refresh your soul with it; it's fun, you can take pleasure in it' – and Ralph Vaughan Williams lectures on the history of English music, from the sweetly mournful folksong 'Dives

and Lazarus' to the twentieth-century flowering of English composition
in the works of Elgar, Bax, Britten and, of course, Vaughan Williams.
Then Jennings begins to intercut and orchestrate contributions from
all four of his guests.

In the film's last movement, each of them concludes with some
note of reassurance or defiance, albeit tempered with misgiving.
The men of science and technology are downbeat. Fisher: 'If we don't
go on learning about [nature], we'll hurt it.' Ormston: 'If we can get
supplies, if we don't take things too easily – two very big 'if's – we can
still compete.' The two artists are more robust. Lancaster: 'Doubtless,
were we a rational race, the spectacle of our present position would
overwhelm us . . .' But 'we remain deaf to appeals to reason. We're
convinced that the experts are invariably wrong. And at Dunkirk,
which was the illusion and which the reality?'

The screen explodes into a brief, horribly magnificent sequence of
buildings ablaze from *Fires Were Started*. Vaughan Williams picks up
the waiting metaphor: 'So – the fire is ready. Does it require a match
to relight it? Some great upheaval of national consciousness and
emotion?' Jennings intercuts shots of the Blitz with sixteenth-century
engravings of lutenists. Vaughan Williams continues: 'The Elizabethans
experienced this, and as a result they produced poetry and music that
has never been surpassed. Have we not also experienced lately such a
national upheaval?' And he goes on to recall how, during the war,
people from all walks of life had begun to take music seriously for the
first time, and to crowd the concert halls. Parting shot: 'Today our
music, which so long had seemed without life, is being born again.'
The music swells, Osbert Lancaster asks, 'Who can talk of an end,
when we're scarcely at a beginning?', and *The Dim Little Island*
concludes with a shot of *The Last of England*.

Rather as in the final minutes of *A Diary for Timothy* – though the
note is less one of foreboding than of a rather sweet English melancholy – the film's official belief in a bright future is compromised,
indeed all but contradicted, by the grimness of Ford Madox Brown's
painting and the elegiac tug of Vaughan Williams's score. The effect
isn't cynical, and doesn't provoke cynicism. (In public screenings, I
have often expected to hear people giggle at Ormston's *Boy's Own
Paper* observation: 'There's one very big thing in our favour – that we
are good sailors . . .' But they never do.) On the contrary: *The Dim*

Little Island is moving in precisely the same way that the reflective and retrospective passages of *A Diary for Timothy* are moving. Once again, Jennings proves himself most eloquent in the contemplation of things that he values and that are – whatever the boys at the Central Office of Information might be saying – in danger of being lost or destroyed. Little prized by most critics, *The Dim Little Island* is a fine film, and might have been an elegant coda to Jennings's career. But he had one more film in him, and – though this view has often been disputed – a very remarkable one. Before he could make it, however, there were a couple of other projects in store, one of which followed naturally on from the investigation of music he had undertaken with Vaughan Williams.

*

After completing *The Dim Little Island*, Jennings spent several months researching and preparing a documentary about the London Symphony Orchestra. Though it was never made, an edited version of the copious notes he took in the course of his research, covering the period from 6 December 1948 to 10 May 1949, was published four years after his death under the title *Working Sketches of an Orchestra*. Charlotte Jennings remembers occasionally accompanying her father on his visits to rehearsals in a bitterly cold Albert Hall, and the sight of Kathleen Ferrier bundled up in a fur coat trying to keep warm. Perhaps it was that first morning, 6 December 1948, when the orchestra were rehearsing Mahler's *Kindertotenlieder*:

> Kathleen Ferrier comes in in large hat and heavy coat – gets chair from up behind 'cellos – orchestra have given slight applause on music-stands at her entry – she begins singing sitting – ends without hat, coat and standing. At emotional moment Krips [Josef Krips, the conductor] says 'wait – wait' to orchestra – leans over to soloist as though to pull the notes out of her mouth . . .[20]

The other great unrealized film project of the postwar period was a highly ambitious history of the British Empire, to be made as a series of a dozen episodes. (It is not clear whether it was intended for cinemas or for BBC television.) Jennings put a great deal of hard work into researching and planning this work, and his surviving notes run to many hundreds of pages, some bearing little more than a single typed or scribbled phrase, others filled with long passages of carefully revised exposition and commentary.

Roughly half of the notes are devoted to primary research – lists of dates and book references, but also long verbatim extracts from contemporary documents by Johnson, Burke, Wellington, Cobbett, Macaulay and other notable agents and opponents of Empire. In this, the notes closely resemble (and in some cases neatly overlap with) the work he was doing on *Pandæmonium*. A good part of the remainder is made up of essays or rough commentaries by Jennings, outlining the kinds of argument that each episode would advance. With very few exceptions, there are no hints as to how his adventurous ideas would be translated into visual language; in fact there is only one document, outlining a possible beginning for the first film, that even begins to suggest that he was thinking in terms of a shooting script.

The Union Jack.

The Union Jack fluttering against a hard winter sky.

Then the bells begin to toll in the snow-covered belfries of the Meeting-houses – muffled peals as though for one dead.

Then the flag begins to drop from the mast-head to half-mast.

Next a table with wine-glasses and backgammon. The back-gammon boxes are swathed in crepe . . .

This proves to be a trick opening: we are not in Britain, but in New England on 1 November 1765, the day on which the Stamp Tax, much hated by the colonists, was about to go into effect; and the funeral solemnities are not for a recently deceased person but for the death of 'LIBERTY – AGED 145 YEARS . . .'

There is nothing else anywhere in the notes to rival this sequence, save perhaps for some drafts for a ruminative monologue, written in the voice of a fictitious present-day English lieutenant-colonel, who at the age of thirty-five finds himself retired from active service in Burma and shipped back to England, where he takes to mooching around his native Suffolk – the area near Walberswick, to be precise – and musing both on its history and its timelessness in recognizably Jenningsesque terms. Much that he sees has been the same since the sixteenth century; and perhaps the Burma he knows so well can be seen as entering its own Elizabethan age . . .

The absence of any other documents in this cinematic vein is a fairly clear sign that 'The Decline and Fall of the British Empire' (Jennings's proposed title) was abandoned well before the pre-production phase. If visual details are sparse, though, the overall structure and general argumentative drift had reached quite an advanced stage by the time it was dropped:

THE PATTERN OF THE DRAMA

1. [Deleted: 'The Loss of the first Empire'] How to lose an Empire and the statement of principles. (The Declaration of Independence. Burke on America and Canada.)

2. [Deleted: 'The Island'] The Nation of Shopkeepers – its survival. (Napoleonic ways. Sea power. Food and trade problems.)

3. The Liberals. (The education of India. The Reform Bill. Anti-slavery and so on. Macaulay.)

4. The Emigrants. (The Hungry 40s. The Development of the new 'colonies'. The Englishman abroad.)

5. The dream of 1851. (The first Exhibition: the futures of the Earth – the possibilities of man. Prince Albert, Charles Darwin, Brunel.)

6. The realities of the world. (The Crimea. The Mutiny. – The use of force.)

7. [Deleted: 'Imperialism'] By Jingo! (The Suez Canal. 'Empress of India'. 'By Jingo . . .')

8. 'Lest We Forget'. (The South African war. The voice of Kipling.)

9. The Liberals again. (Campbell-Bannerman.)

10. Survival again and the Return movement. (The Empire 1914–18.)

11. The Statute of Westminster.

12. [Deleted: 'The "Loss" of the Second Empire'] The final Decline and Fall. (The liberation of India. The justification of Burke. Food and trade: full circle.)

Jennings had also worked out a reasonably clear standpoint for the whole series.

I am not at this point concerned with *history* at all. Much more important to my mind to get clear the point of view from which the picture is made and to establish *who* is the hero (who is it about?) and to indicate the shape of the drama. It is made from the British point of view. It is about *us*. But that does not mean explicit self-congratulation by any means. *We* have many sides, impulses, voices. We are motivated by self-interest and also by conscience – in other words we as a people behave very much as an individual does. At the opening we are clearly divided into three clearly defined camps. Later the different points of view and interests are never again so clear. Much of the drama lies in this. But in the end we may say that the best in us does come out. That is the point of the picture.

Other papers in the 'British Empire' file imply that what Jennings meant by 'the best in us does come out' is that the latter-day retreat from Empire was, on balance, a humane and dignified policy which showed that Britain had learned from its earlier mistakes.

Since he did not expose so much as a foot of film on the series, it is hard to say how far Jennings might have succeeded in bringing his ideas to the screen. There are tantalizing hints of the ways in which he hoped to make his rather abstract concerns spring to life: every episode, for example, was going to have some key musical theme or song – 'The World Turned Upside Down', 'All Around My Hat', 'We Are Fred Karno's Army' and 'Bless 'em All'. And, as a throwaway line explains – 'the Church bells are of course the basic sound link of all' – Jennings had assiduously researched the deeper mysteries of campanology (one of his sources was *Nine Tailors*, an East Anglian thriller by Dorothy L. Sayers), and had unearthed some fascinating lore, at least some of which could have supplied matter for commentary.

As one would expect, the working materials for 'British Empire' sometimes flash with the kind of inspired leaps of imagination that make *Pandæmonium* so fascinating, and even if Jennings had bungled its development into film, it would have been – at the very least – a stimulating and provocative enterprise. The likelihood is that it would have been far too expensive to bring off in the Britain of the late 1940s; series of this kind, from Sir Kenneth Clark's *Civilization* onwards, were a good twenty years into the future. Jennings's ghost must have looked down from the Empyrean more than a little wryly to note that one of the 'landmark' series of this kind, *The Ascent of Man*, was written and presented by his old Cambridge friend and *Experiment* colleague, Jacob Bronowski.

★

Sometime in 1949, another old Cambridge friend, Charles Madge, lent Jennings a room in which, loosed from the constraints and annoyances of family life, he could at long last paint freely again at all hours, as he had been able to in his youth. It could hardly have been more conveniently sited – at 2 Regent's Park Terrace, just seconds away from his front door *chez* Hutt.

Even before this small liberation, Jennings had been finding the time to paint a good deal more regularly than at any period since the late 1930s. This postwar work varies greatly both in scale and in accomplishment, but, since most of the canvases are at the moment hidden away in various store rooms, it is hard to make reliable or informative generalizations about them. One day, with luck, a sympathetic art historian will track down all of the *oeuvre*, some of which has gone as far afield as Australia and the United States, and show exactly how it developed. For the time being, though, it's worth noting some of the preliminary conclusions that could be drawn from the Mayor Gallery's sizeable Jennings exhibition of November 1993.

In brief, the overwhelming impression made by Jennings's paintings of the postwar years was of a return to the mainly pastoral and rural sights of his boyhood – studies of farming and farm implements, work horses, Suffolk churches (especially the magnificent church at Blythburgh, near Walberswick) and the like. The contrast with his work from the 1930s – and not only with the witty Surrealist collages, or the mildly uncanny photographs of graveyards, but with his large oil paintings – was striking.

In the work of the 1930s, the dominant note had been much stranger: as, for example, in *London in the Seventeenth Century* (1936), where the spectacle of dignified period architecture in the foreground is startlingly upstaged by a giant triangle – Newton's prism? – hanging in mid-air like something from a science-fiction movie about invading aliens. Then there were 'conceptual' pieces such as *The Origin of Colour* (1937: a tree growing from a polyhedron, not unlike the one in Dürer's

Melancolia I: vegetation out of crystal) and *The Birth of Colour* (also 1937: a hard, multifaceted ovoid nestling in leaves like a flower: crystal out of vegetation). At the other extreme from these fantasias were the dourly realist studies of 1930s industrial landscapes, often closely modelled on photographs that Jennings had taken in Bolton and elsewhere.

Plainly, the bucolic works he produced after 1945 were neither so exotic nor so gritty. The element of fantasy had not altogether disappeared: ploughing scenes alternated with large-scale imaginary portraits, including rather impressive studies of Karl Marx, William Morris and Edward Lear, and one or two imaginary landscapes, notably a vision of the Great Fire of London (see below). Nor was the urban theme entirely banished: from time to time, Jennings also reworked images that either came directly from his wartime films, or would have been quite at home there – for example, in two studies of a canteen tea lady (*c.* 1947), and what appears to be the audience for the Flanagan and Allen factory concert in *Listen to Britain* (*c.* 1949).

On balance, though, an unprepared viewer might easily conclude that the paintings of the 1930s and those of the 1950s are the work of two different artists. Above all, the presence of Surrealist influences in the later pieces is minimal to nonexistent. And yet the techniques are not old-fashioned; or, more exactly, only a little old-fashioned, to the tune of a few decades. Their manner of representing figures as delicately traced lines of movement and force is sometimes powerfully reminiscent of the Vorticist style that was thriving in London just before and during the First World War. In similar vein, the sketches Jennings made during these years, such as 'Horse and Plough' and 'Cornfield' (both *c.* 1948) also contain certain reminiscences of Cubism, and quarry jagged geometrical shapes from the moving parts of human and animal bodies. These preparatory studies are often extremely powerful – in fact, more striking than the finished paintings.

It's possible that Jennings was being self-consciously backward-looking here, pastiching pictorial styles that were ultra-modern in his boyhood to portray the familiar scenes of that time; and equally possible that the stylistic affinities are fortuitous, and that what he was really engaged in was rerunning the experiments of Wyndham Lewis, Picasso and Braque to quite different ends. Few viewers nowadays would be so resolutely anti-modern as to find these paintings harsh or difficult, and most of them are sufficiently easy on the eye to meet Matisse's (ironic?) requirement for a modern art capable of soothing tired businessmen. A few of them even risk that most devastating of verdicts on any work of modern art: 'pretty'.

Let's take three examples, all oil paintings, to stand for a much larger body of work.

Study of a Plough, 1947 Every inch of this landscape image is in some shade of off-white to silvery grey, with outlines done in faint, usually very delicate black strokes. The horizon, set slightly above the halfway mark, is perfectly flat, and divides a mottled grey sky from a bristling grey earth – the bristles being long grass. The landscape is all but featureless save for a giant plough, its sharp blade cutting into the earth like the prow of a battleship. There is no horse, no ploughman: the thing appears to be self-propelled. Jennings has made no attempt to give depth or contour to this machine – it has the two-dimensionality and slightly forced perspective of a diagram from an instructional manual. If you look very closely, you can see that there are traces of red in the four parallel tracks left behind the plough: again, these tracks are diagrammatic, geometrical. And if you look very closely at the grass, there are hints of yellow.

Harvesting, c. 1948 Again, every inch of the canvas is covered with a single, narrow range of colours – here, a wash of orange-yellow tones, mingled with pale pinks and white at the lighter parts and almost pure red at the warmest. The effect is of intense late-summer heat. Half a red circle to the top right represents a harvest sun; a barely perceptible line depicts a horizon sloping downwards towards the right, but there is otherwise little to distinguish the hot sky from the hot earth. Some dabs of deeper yellow and red towards the right suggest fires in the distance, though it would be equally possible to read them as clouds.

At the centre, outlined in thin, pointed brush-strokes of white and red, a stook: to its left, the rudiments of a human figure – a harvester. (The stook itself looks like it's on fire, or even exploding, with hints of an A-bomb mushroom cloud about its upper part.) To the left of the canvas, a wigwam shape that is evidently another stook. To the right, a cluster of unconnected lines that suggest strenuous activity – other farm workers, presumably – but do not quite gel into an image. Very close examination of the canvas shows the occasional dab or slash of grey-blue – a colour quite invisible from a few feet away.

The Great Fire of London, c. 1948 A tall, narrow picture, mainly dark grey but broken up with hundreds of thin, brightly coloured lines – yellows, reds, greens, whites – depicting the activity on a London street as the Great Fire takes hold. To the top of the image, curved flames jump up towards the sky that can just about be seen above the angled rooftops; to the bottom left, one Vorticist-style male figure runs towards the edge of the canvas, motive uncertain (running away from a blazing house to save himself, or into a blazing house to rescue its contents?); to the bottom right, another figure appears to be loading furniture on to a barrow, though the barrow's large wheel is the only unambiguous part of the structure. Between them, in the foreground, various geometrical figures suggest debris.

Verdict?

It would be unfair to pass judgement on the quality of these images alone, but it does seem reasonable to suggest that they tend to provoke responses more along the lines of 'interesting', 'agreeable' or 'thoughtful' than 'brilliant', 'dazzling' or 'profound'; and though they may be fascinating to anyone already engaged with Jennings's work, they seldom seduce the newcomer in the way that his films can. They are certainly not such strong, or such desirable, compositions as he was making in the 1930s.

My own view, or guess, is that they may perhaps best be seen as transitional works – transitional to a period that, in the event, never happened. The fact that Jennings painted a great deal in the last few years of his short life suggests, obviously, that he delighted in the activity; but as an intellectual, intensely aware of the newest developments in contemporary art as well as in himself, he would have been using this time of relative freedom to try out all manner of new possibilities and, perhaps, to forge new styles. We are looking at experiments, sketches, 'essays' more than at fully evolved works. Once again, we have to play the game of 'had he lived . . .'; had Jennings lived, might he have made the transition from film-making to painting as successfully as that other sometime labourer for John Grierson, William (later Sir William) Coldstream?

*

The novelist and screenwriter Gavin Millar recalls[21] a brief and not altogether happy meeting with Jennings at around this time. He, Lindsay Anderson and the other young critical Turks of the polemical film magazine *Sequence* had put together a drinks party at Millar's flat, where the guests of honour included a piquant mix of their fellow-writers – including the young Satyajit Ray (1921–92), soon to assist Jean Renoir (1894–1979) with the Indian locations for his 1951 film *The River* before launching his own, immensely distinguished career as a director – and their heroes, heroines and friends in the British film industry: the directors Robert Hamer (1911–63), Thorold Dickinson (1903–84) and Alexander Mackendrick (1912–93); the cameraman Douglas Slocombe; the sex-bomb Diana Dors; and Jennings. Millar managed little more contact with Jennings than asking him what he'd like to drink; Lindsay Anderson essayed a more substantial conversation with his hero, only to find him 'rather cold' – not that this froideur did anything to diminish Anderson's great admiration for his wartime work. It is sad, though, that Jennings and the man who was to be his most powerful critical advocate did not hit it off more cheerfully, and that Anderson never had the chance to play Eckermann to Jennings's Goethe.

In the late summer of 1949 Jennings travelled to Paris alone for a brief holiday. He wrote to Cicely: 'Oh and to my astonishment (or did I tell you this?) found my name on a poster and discovered they were running *Spare Time, Listen to Britain* and *Timothy* at an Experimental Film Festival – but in September!'

By this time, he had already begun work on the film which, though no one foresaw it, would be his swan-song: provisionally entitled 'Festival of Britain',[22] it eventually became known as *Family Portrait*. His earliest surviving notes, on British scientists, dating from June 1949, include some fascinating insights: 'Fleming the original discoverer of penicillin was a friend of Wilson Steer and an amateur painter . . . Green [one of the scientists Jennings had interviewed] himself pointed out later that the accidental discovery of penicillin was likely to be influenced by Fleming's interest in the colours of cultures.'[23]

Jennings took great pains over the preparation of *Family Portrait*, and others would inflict great pains on him in the course of making it. Chief among these was his old patron and antagonist John Grierson, now back in the UK after many years in Canada and working with the

Festival of Britain committee. Immediately on his return from Paris on Monday 29 August, Jennings found a letter from Gordon Smith indicating that the COI was unhappy with the long treatment Jennings had submitted for the proposed film. On the Tuesday he was summoned to see Grierson at the producer's flat. The two men then had a ferocious set-to, which Jennings reported to Ian Dalrymple the following day in a long and aggrieved letter.

On the face of it, what Grierson demanded of Jennings was not unreasonable: he wanted a short written précis explaining the 'philosophy' of the film – an explanation of what the longer document was meant to be outlining. But, even allowing for a degree of wounded pride, long-standing antagonism – 'It is, no doubt, silly to be hurt, particularly by a charlatan' – and chronic rebelliousness on Jennings's part, it seems clear that he was right to suspect that something else was afoot here: whether by calculation or just by following his instinct, Grierson had set out to take Jennings down a peg or two and remind him who was boss. His attempt to play Alpha Dog was, Jennings thought, all the more galling in being presented as a piece of humanitarianism – the demands for clarification of the original treatment being placed on him were supposedly

> for *my* benefit – to help me get wise to myself – and then [Grierson] paved out a mass of personal insults laced with insensibilities and backhanded compliments such as I have never been treated to even by Grierson. . . . This piece of writing of mine – full, no doubt, of clever literary allusions – but no shape – no form – no beginning middle or end – such philosophy as it had was 'fascist' – its scholarship thoroughly second-hand – its politics amateur – the confused product of a neurasthenic who had been living in the luxury of the feature world and who had now trailed his impracticability, desire to overspend, and self-pity across twenty-odd pages which would run to ten reels of film and £60,000 of production costs![24]

Jennings ended his letter to Dalrymple with a rueful but firm notice of his intention to resign from Wessex Films, effective from the end of September. Either Dalrymple's powers to sooth his employees, or his widely attested skills at keeping the Men from the Ministry off their backs, must have come into full play, for there was no further talk of resignation and within a matter of weeks Jennings had drawn up a substantial revision of his draft treatment. The episode is a reminder of how very different Jennings and his supposed mentor of the early days actually were; and it has the curious chance effect of book-ending Jennings's career as a film-maker. The man who had overlooked his earliest efforts at direction had reappeared out of the blue to stick an oar into his final work.

*

Family Portrait, like his other films, follows two distinct – though this time not wholly divergent – agendas. Its official task is to celebrate national achievements; to 'give ourselves a pat on the back', as the commentary puts it by way of introduction, and particularly to boost the image of Britain as a country in which the past was glorious, the present is bursting with technological promise, and the future has never seemed brighter. A director with a less acute or less idiosyncratic sense of history might have made of it a kind of *Look at Life* Tourist Board travelogue (and the film, to be sure, is not entirely free of such routine notes). But for Jennings, the commission offered a chance to return once again to the subject of the Industrial Revolution that had been obsessing him for the last two decades, and to create at least a simplified version of the epic vision of history that he had developed through working on *Pandæmonium*.

But the main theme of *Family Portrait*, the other agenda, can be most neatly inferred from the quotation from E. M. Forster that Jennings set by way of an epigraph at the head of his (almost) final version of the commentary, dated June 1950: 'the rainbow bridge that connects the prose in us with the passion'. His commentary dutifully elaborates on the title's cosy metaphor of the British people as a family, but it proposes – much as Orwell did in his famous essay on national identity – that while the British can indeed be thought of as a family, they are a deeply divided family: divided not only by class (Orwell's emphasis) or by region, politics or religion, but by their respective allegiances to what Forster calls Prose and Passion and what Jennings rephrases as prose and poetry. Only when these two national tendencies are reconciled and cooperate, he says, can great achievements follow. Hence his account of the birth of the steam engine:

it needed two sides of the family to meet . . . James Watt, crossing
Glasgow Common one Sunday morning, suddenly to see the
'separate condenser' in his mind's eye . . . and the skill of the John
Wilkinsons, the iron masters of the time . . . to get the steam-
engine made at all.

The meeting of scientific imagination and engineering skill . . .
a new kind of poetry and a new kind of prose.

Those who dismissively refer to *Family Portrait* as a kind of British
travelogue short in the soothing mode of the once popular *Look at
Life!* series might profitably ask themselves how many travelogues
encompass such recondite speculation. Moreover, Jennings goes on to
introduce his extended family circle to still more venturesome ideas,
such as his boldly imaginative assertions that 'Tolerance in Britain is
linked to the Royal Society's defence of free enquiry' – an insight as
penetrating as it is contentious – or that 'When we admire the sunset
we are using the eyes of Turner, when we switch on the light we are
tapping the mind of Faraday.' (Jennings, who knew his Ruskin well,
may deliberately have been echoing the Victorian prophet's obituary
verdict on Turner in *Lectures on Architecture*: 'Through those eyes, now
filled with dust, generations yet unborn will learn to behold the light
of nature.') And though most of the expected names of great Britons
are present and correct – Shakespeare and Newton and Darwin as well
as Watt and Turner and Faraday – Jennings modifies the standard
patriotic pantheon in two ways.

First, he extends the familiar roll-call by including slightly less well-
known, or all but unknown, heroes – Cayley, Gilbert, Trevithick –
culled from his private researches: 'in 1800 a Yorkshire squire called
Cayley had written down the laws by which the aeroplane flies'; 'Four
hundred years ago, Gilbert told the Queen that "the earth itself is a
great magnet"'; 'And then came Trevithick building the first locomotives in the world at a Welsh steam-foundry to take the place of
horses . . .' (How many Festival-goers would have recognized the
names of Cayley, Gilbert or Trevithick? How many students would
recognize their names today?) And even when the names evoked are
canonical, Jennings tends to consider their exploits from some mildly
oblique angle: 'when Drake was fighting the Armada . . . the Spaniards
said that he had a magic mirror in his cabin which revealed enemy

ships to him'; 'Captain Cook . . . [went] to the South Seas with the new chronometer for guide'; 'We can only thank heaven we produced a Blake, a Shaftesbury, a Dickens to proclaim love, and health, and light'; 'The very genius of Clerk Maxwell, Thomson and Rutherford shook the foundations of matter itself . . . The Elizabethan journey ended with the battle of Britain.'

In short, the potentially anodyne material of *Family Portrait* – and some of it is just that – is repeatedly shot through with threads of highly idiosyncratic scholarship, unconventional juxtapositions and bold imaginative leaps; the last qualities one could fairly write off as 'academic', which was Lindsay Anderson's final, withering verdict on the film from the perspective of 1981. In fact, though it is painful to say that Anderson's harshly limiting judgements on the film can be dismissed, they must be. True, the film isn't and couldn't have been as impassioned as Jennings's great war films; and it isn't even as elegiac or as tart as *The Dim Little Island*. Rather, it's a personal essay: a relaxed, elegant digression on subjects that Jennings found enduringly fascinating, and the most direct expression of themes with which his lively mind had been engaged throughout his years as a film-maker. There's a mood of optimism in the film which exceeds his set task of boosting the national image, and which makes talk of his personal dejection at this time seem all the more improbable.[25]

Kathleen Raine recalls a note of visionary optimism in Jennings's talk the last time she saw him, when they took one of their habitual walks together:

Half-way across Battersea bridge Humphrey paused and raised his arm in the old eighteenth-century orator's gesture; and the Thames, before that gesture (which embraced Dryden's *King Arthur*, the Triumphs of Gray and the *Masks* of Inigo Jones, the declamations of Los and the stance of Gainsborough's slender and elegant country gentlemen), became again Spenser's Sweet Thames, now the 'chartered Thames' for so long that its defilement and servitude had become irrevocable. And yet, Humphrey said, in that river, free from pollution, fish might breed again, silver salmon to feed the people of London. All kind of living silvery shoals once came there; and as he spoke the muddy foul waters flowing under us towards the Tower Bridge, Greenwich, and the docks where Humphrey had made his *Fires Were Started*, became transformed by Humphrey's inimitable magic into Blake's 'spiritual fourfold London Eternal'.[26]

*

But however grandly optimistic Jennings's vision of history may have become at this time, he had less reason to feel happy about his family life. For one thing, he had obviously begun (if, that is, he had ever stopped) having affairs again: 'In the late '40s, he used to ring up and say "I'm not coming back for supper"', and my mother would go absolutely berserk,' Mary-Lou recalled. In search of emotional comfort, or by way of rebellion, Cicely Jennings grew increasingly religious.

> My mother became a Catholic after my father died, but before then she had started going to services at All Saint's, Margaret Street, a very high [Anglican] church, built by Butterfield. My father found this very testing. I think this is one of the reasons their marriage came under particular strain at the end, because my mother was very drawn to this. But my father wasn't a militant atheist. I asked my mother about it once and she said, 'Oh, he believed more in a world religion.'

Almost every account of Jennings's life, no matter how brief, includes some measure of speculation about what he might have gone on to do, had he not died young. Would he have renounced film entirely, and somehow made his way as a painter? Found a new and significant role in the evolution of British television? Realized his ambition of making commercial features, been successful at it and emigrated to Hollywood? Returned to the theatre, or to academic life? Speculation on these matters, though not without point, tends to reflect more the prejudices of the speculator than the likely fate of the subject: for example, those who adamantly insist that he could never have made a dramatic feature are not to be swayed by the obvious retort that, in *Fires Were Started*, he already had.

What Jennings did in fact go on to do in the last weeks of his life is a matter of record. As noted at the start of this book, he had been asked by the United States Economic Cooperation Administration to direct one of a series of six films to be presented under the general title of *The Changing Face of Europe*. He opted for a project on health, provisionally entitled 'The Good Life', and set off via France, Switzerland and Italy for Greece.

His departure was marked by a sequence of curious omens; or so it seems in retrospect to those closest to him. In August 1950 he had briefly joined his family for a holiday in Devon, during which the children had unwittingly put themselves at risk when they found themselves trapped on a neighbouring beach by the incoming tide, so that they had to make their escape by climbing up a cliff. When Humphrey heard what they had done, Charlotte recalls, he exploded: ' "Never do that again! We always think that things happen to other people, and one day we find they happen to us!" ' Mary-Lou recalls that, though she and her sister were almost never allowed into his studio at 2 Regent's Park Terrace, he took her down one day a week or so before his departure and showed her three stacks of paintings: the first was the most important work, to be kept at all costs; the second pile was satisfactory work; and the third paintings consisted of paintings for which he had little use. Charlotte Jennings has a more dramatic story: looking back on the occasion, in 1970, she told the film-maker Robert Vas that on the day her father set off on his trip, she rushed out on to the street, threw her arms around him and begged him not to go. And a couple of nights before his fatal accident, Cicely suffered from a terrible nightmare from which she awoke with a large, angry bruise on her neck.

Still, it would be wrong to place too much emphasis on such notes of grim premonition. Mary-Lou now believes that the real reason he showed her the paintings that day was because the marriage was in a terminal state of crisis, and he expected to be leaving Cicely very soon. If Jennings had any inklings of his imminent fate, he certainly left no hints in the handful of letters he wrote home from his European travels, which are mainly chatty and genial: 'So far – except for a little toothache I feel fine – the sun shines solidly every day – we have not seen more than half a dozen tiny clouds in the last 5 days – The Greeks themselves are "working like beavers" – stripped of everything in the villages – but with a colossally high morale – laughing and signing over everything –'[27]

Then came the accident.[28] Mary-Lou recalls coming up the stairs that Sunday evening as the phone was ringing. The caller was Ian

Dalrymple, who asked to speak to Cicely. Mary-Lou passed the phone over, went into the next room, and then heard her mother scream.

On 6 October, Cicely Jennings wrote to I. A. Richards and his wife Dorothea:

> My dear, dear friends,
> Humphrey was killed accidentally in Greece last Sunday week 24 September while making a film for E.C.A.
> He had arrived in Greece with a unit about 10 days previously and had already seen a great deal – he had been as far as Iannina on the Albanian border and this Sunday had returned to Athens because of the usual camera trouble. He and his continuity girl, Dillon Barry, decided to go to Poros, an island about 3½ hours from Athens, to do a reconnaissance. Humphrey wanted to do sketches for camera positions. They were both climbing up a cliff to get a view from the top, when he grasped a rock which gave way, and fell onto the rocky beach below – not more than 25 feet actually but he struck his head and lost consciousness immediately. Thank God he never regained it and I think about 2 hours later died in the Naval hospital on the island. The doctors gave a blood transfusion but it was apparent to Dillon Barry from the first that there was no hope.
> He was buried in the English cemetery in Athens on the 28th.
> . . . I can't write about myself; I keep on thinking of all his friends and wondering what we are all going to do without him.
> . . . He had Trelawny's Recollections of Shelley and Byron in his pocket when he fell – he loved that book and read it constantly. I was reading it today – Shelley said – 'Death is the veil, which those who live call life; they sleep, and it is lifted.' He detested any positive statements about the spirit, but I think that is like him.
> My dearest love to you both,
>   Cicely[29]

Years later, Kathleen Raine wrote that on the night he died she had had a symbolic dream: 'the first occasion on which I was certain that some telepathic communication had reached me from the dead'.[30]

*

Jennings was well enough known to merit substantial obituary notices in the *New Statesman and Nation*, by Gavin Lambert, and in *The Times*. A memorial service was held at St Giles-in-the-Fields, Holborn, on Wednesday 4 October. 'Because he had died in Greece', Mary-Lou Legg recalls, 'my mother was mistakenly persuaded to have a service centred on Greek church music: the Kontakion for the Dead. This was so remote from my father, so wholly unlike his world and his ideas that the service, which might have been a comfort, was completely alien to us.' On the same day, a letter from Kathleen Raine was published in *The Times*. 'Your obituary notice of Humphrey Jennings paid tribute only to his work as a film director,' she wrote. 'Those friends who knew him best must point out the incompleteness of such a picture ...' And she went on to enumerate some of his other accomplishments: his edition of *Venus and Adonis*, his projected book on Thomas Gray, his brilliance as a critic of literature and art. 'At Cambridge,' she concluded, 'he was recognised by all his contemporaries as the most remarkable mind they had ever encountered.'

Cicely was devastated by Humphrey's death. In later years she confessed that, after many weeks of sheer numbness, she was overtaken by a sudden burst of intense rage. He had left her on her own so many times, and now he had left her alone for good.[31] Though she remained strongly loyal to his memory and sometimes fought for his reputation in later years, some of her rage found expression in a violent distaste for anyone and anything associated with Humphrey the aesthete or Humphrey the scholar. Before long, according to Charlotte, Cicely developed a powerful antipathy towards artists and intellectuals of all kinds, an antagonism no doubt founded in her memories of being snubbed by bright young men at Cambridge, but which deepened in direct proportion to her growing bond with the Roman Catholic faith. 'I remember an evening some time after his death when we were invited to dinner with Kathleen Raine. So we took a 45 bus down to Chelsea. John Hayward[32] was there, and some other literary people, and after a while they started to play a sort of literary quiz, quite harmless. But it made my mother furious – "I will *never* go to any of those intellectual evenings again – *wicked* people!"'

Humphrey had left her with little in the way of financial support. As Charlotte remembers, when Cicely went to her bank to withdraw money for their rent the week after his death, she found just £1 in their joint account – exactly the sum with which they had started married life. She also found that 'just before he had gone to Greece, he'd gone to an antiquarian book-shop and he'd bought a nineteenth-century book of parrots, engraved and hand-tinted; it had cost £25. Of course, she had to return it to the bookshop and ask for the money back.' The burden of looking after Cicely both practically and emotionally fell on her daughters, and especially on seventeen-year-old Mary-Lou, who was working in the wardrobe department of the Old Vic at the time. She was now the breadwinner and from her weekly wage of £2 before deductions she handed twenty-five shillings to Cicely. No one – a fact that to the present generation will seem horribly insensitive, if not borderline criminal – paid much attention to the feelings of the girls, or seemed to think that they needed any special consideration or help with their grief. This neglect had its sad consequences later in life; but they belong in another narrative.

Cicely's comment that Humphrey was buried in 'the English cemetery' in Athens is slightly inaccurate: this necropolis is usually known, in English, as the Protestant Cemetery. A photograph of his grave taken in 1958 shows a substantial white marble tomb with a cross in relief. Below it is the inscription:

HUMPHREY JENNINGS

BORN WALBERSWICK SUFFOLK 19–8–1907

DIED POROS 24–9–1950

And an epitaph:

DEATH IS THE VEIL WHICH THOSE WHO LIVE CALL LIFE
THEY SLEEP AND IT IS LIFTED

Sadly, that grave no longer exists.* When I went at the end of 1996 to the Protestant Cemetery – as well as to every other burial ground I could find within the Athens city limits – I spent wet and fruitless hours searching for some memorial to Jennings. It was only several weeks later, after a correspondence with the British Consulate, that I was informed that the grave had, in the official term, been

---

* July 2004: in fact the gravestone survives and is to be placed on the wall of the cemetery.

'reclaimed' a couple of years before, and that the plot was now housing the mortal remains of another non-Greek subject. It seems that a plaque will soon be put up in a nearby location, listing Jennings's name alongside those of all the other foreign subjects whose graves have been similarly repossessed in recent years.

Which would be one place to end the story, with an English poet's name writ in water. But in that the work of an artist can be said to continue evolving long after his death, Jennings's posthumous career was a good deal more eventful than most. For one thing, in 1950 only a handful of people had ever had so much as a glimpse of the huge prose project that some critics now consider a masterpiece to rival any of his films, and that was far and away the most ambitious of all his literary works. It would be another thirty-five years – half a lifetime, during which Jennings gradually became recognized by the *cognoscenti* as a film-maker of classic status – before anyone outside the circle of his friends and family would set eyes on *Pandæmonium*.

And so, rather than dwelling on the easy pathos of the fact that a great man now so little known to his fellow-countrymen should not even have a proper grave, let's recall Osbert Lancaster's last line of commentary in *The Dim Little Island*: 'Who can talk of an end, when we're scarcely at the beginning?'

Nine

Post-1950: Posthumous Career
and *Pandæmonium*

Too well aware of who and what they had lost, Jennings's friends, family and admirers set to work on arranging appropriate memorials for him. The most substantial of these was a pamphlet of essays and reminiscences by Ian Dalrymple, Kathleen Raine, Charles Madge and others, *Humphrey Jennings, 1907–50* – the first published commentary on Jennings other than brief reviews or magazine articles. The second was a smaller pamphlet, designed to accompany an ICA retrospective of his paintings. Kathleen Raine's piece for the ICA pamphlet began on a note of praise and lamentation so fulsome as to give pause even to the most fervent of her fellow-mourners and celebrants:

> Those who knew Humphrey Jennings took his genius for granted, as we do the sun. Natural phenomena cause no surprise; and Humphrey's mind had the quality of the Tao (not that he would have called himself a taoist, if only because 'the names that can be named are not the universal names'), the apparent simplicity of light, or the solar system. Only now that he is removed, we are aware that we shall never again know anything like it. His greatness, like that of Coleridge, is something that only those who knew him can fully realise; for it was the total phenomenon of his remarkable mind, activated by the most powerful imagination I have ever encountered in a living man, that made knowing him such a wonderful experience to those who came within measuring distance of understanding him.[1]

Charles Madge, opting for a cooler tone, took the occasion to elaborate the key concept which, he felt, was essential to any under-standing of Jennings's paintings, poems, films or other creative works: what Jennings called, misleading in its simplicity, 'the image'. This innocent word, Madge suggested, had a meaning personal to himself and bound up with his early researches into poetry and painting. His use of 'image' is not far off from the way it is used in psychology, in literary criticism and in surrealist theory, but it is not quite identical with any of these. It has resemblances to the psychological concept of the *gestalt*: 'the combination of many effects, each utterly insensible alone, into one sum of fine effect'.[2]

Madge took this last phrase, not from a gestalt psychologist, but from a passage in the diary of Michael Faraday for June 1850 – one of the passages Jennings had carefully tracked down for '*Pandæmonium*, his great collection of "images" chosen to illustrate the transformation in our way of looking at the world between 1660 and 1866'.[3]

A third pamphlet dedicated to preserving the Jennings legacy appeared later, in 1951. The Weekend Press of New York – in reality, pretty much a one-man printing and publishing operation run by a novice in the field, Jennings's old friend from Mass-Observation days, Ruthven Todd – issued a short run of his *Poems*. This is now an extremely rare book, and remains the only free-standing collection of his poetry to have been published to date.[4] Almost two decades later, Todd wrote: 'Looking back at the POEMS, I can only regret that I was not a better printer. I just taught myself and read all the handbooks I could find.'[5]

In addition to these loyal efforts on the home front and in the USA, there were one or two minor flurries of interest in Europe in Jennings's work. In his autobiography *Persona Granada*, Sir Denis Forman recalls the occasion when he flew the flag for British documentary by screening *Listen to Britain*, *Words for Battle* and *Fires Were Started* overseas:

> When these films were shown ... to Italian film-makers, who were in self-congratulatory mood because they believed that Rossellini's *Rome, Open City* and De Sica's *Bicycle Thieves* had laid the foundations for the new school of neo-realism, they were dumbfounded. 'Jennings discovered *verismo* ten years before we did,' they said, more in admiration than in envy, and it was true.[6]

But to highlight such moments of revelation is to paint too rosy a picture of Jennings's public standing at this point. Despite the continued or renewed respect for his work within professional film-making circles, despite all the eloquence of his talented friends and colleagues, it is quite possible – perhaps even likely – that Jennings might have been entirely forgotten by other audiences, and, over the coming years, have drifted away into the respectable obscurity of the reference books. The man who did more than anyone else to ensure that this did not happen was a fierce young film critic (and famous film director-in-embryo) who had barely so much as shaken hands with his hero but who saw plainly that Jennings stood for something rare and valuable in British culture: Lindsay Anderson.

The great turning-point in Jennings's critical reputation came in 1954, with the publication of Anderson's essay 'Only Connect' in *Sight and Sound* for April–June of that year. Often reprinted, this text was, and continues to be, the most influential single advocacy of his work; and Anderson's claim that 'it might reasonably be contended that Humphrey Jennings is the only real poet the British cinema has yet produced' must surely be the single most frequently cited pronouncement on his career. Half a century on, it still seems a fine piece of writing: on the one hand, wholly free of that smirking irony or cringing embarrassment about strong feeling that Anderson regarded as chronic failings of the English temperament; on the other, richly alive to all the strengths and weaknesses that typify Jennings's unique work. (It is sometimes hard, today, to grasp how acute and searching Anderson's insights can be, so firmly have they become established as orthodoxies.) Of Jennings's early wartime films up to and including *Heart of Britain*, Anderson observes:

> Ordinary people are sharply glimpsed in them, and the ordinary sounds that were part of the fabric of their lives reinforce the glimpses and sometimes comment on them . . .
>
> A style, in fact, is being hammered out in these films; a style based on a peculiar intimacy of observation, a fascination with the commonplace thing or person that is significant precisely because it is commonplace, and with the whole pattern that can emerge when such commonplace, significant things and people are fitted together in the right order.[7]

Of the later wartime films, the masterpieces, Anderson writes: 'They are committed to the war – for all his sensibility there does not seem to have been anything of the pacifist about Jennings – but their real inspiration is pride, an unaggressive pride in the courage and doggedness of ordinary British people.'[8] Of *Listen to Britain*: 'To Jennings this was a transfigured landscape, and he recorded its trans-figuration on film.'[9] Of *Fires Were Started*. 'No other British film made during the war, documentary or feature, achieved such a continuous and poignant truthfulness, or treated the subject of men at war with such a sense of its incidental glories and its essential tragedy.'[10] Of *A Diary for Timothy*: 'Not least among the virtues that distinguish Jennings from almost all British film-makers is his respect for person-ality, his freedom from the inhibitions of class-consciousness, his inability to patronise or merely to use the people in his films. Jennings's people are ends in themselves.'[11]

All this has been said elsewhere; but Anderson said it first, said it (one could argue) best, and said it most influentially. After passing some limiting judgements on the postwar films, he ends:

> For reality, his wartime films stand alone; and they are sufficient achievement. They will last because they are true to their time, and because the depth of feeling in them can never fail to communicate itself. They will speak to posterity, saying: 'This is what it was like. This is what we were like – the best of us.'[12]

There is a sense in which all subsequent writing on Jennings – including the present volume – is nothing more than an elaboration of this seminal essay, for Anderson's piece set in motion a minor critical industry that has thrived to the present day. 'Only Connect' did not exactly open the floodgates, but it did start a steady flow of commen-tary and analysis, praise and dispute; and though its exalted view of Jennings's achievement has been challenged from time to time, there has never been a serious attempt to relegate him to the obscurity of a minor or dated talent. No one who has taken a course in film studies at a British school or university has any excuse for being ignorant of his work. For good or ill, he is part of a broadly accepted pantheon of British directors.

The landmarks of Jennings film criticism in English – there has been no comparably large-scale analysis of other aspects of his work[13] – include Eric Rhodes's rather sceptical account in his collec-tion of essays *Tower of Babel* (1967); Jim Hillier's chapter in *Studies in*

Documentary (1972), now out of print but widely read in the 1970s; chapter-length studies of *Fires Were Started* in Anthony Aldgate and Jeffrey Richards's *Britain Can Take It* (1986) and Peter Stansky and William Abraham's *London's Burning* (1994), plus the recent short monograph on that film by Brian Winston for BFI Film Classics (1999); and David Thomson's short but characteristically brilliant assessment in his *Biographical Dictionary of the Cinema* (1975), to which the essential supplement is his much longer essay 'A Sight for Sore Eyes' in the American journal *Film Comment* (March–April 1993). Speculating on what Jennings might have done had he lived past 1950, Thomson ruminates:

> There might have been no place for Jennings's sharp but elusive talent. He might have become an eccentric or an outcast. But then I think of the imagery, the editing, the music he commanded; and above all, I recall his women. There are so many moments in his films when the world seems to hinge upon the stoic inward gaze of modestly pretty women. There is Timothy's mother, her face aslant on the hospital pillow after giving birth, not asleep or in pain, but dreaming of futures. There is the girl at the tea stand at the end of *Fires Were Started*, tousled, excited and laughing, as quickly seen but as hard to forget as the girl Bernstein saw in *Kane* on the ferry. There is Jacko's wife, not knowing yet, and another woman in *Listen to Britain* who watches children in a playground while she considers a photograph of her soldier husband. In every film, these glimpses of women enlarge the meaning of the work.[14]

Partly in response to this steady output of printed commentary, other media also began to pay attention to Jennings. There have been a number of short features about his work on radio. as well as at least one full-length documentary on BBC Radio Three. Television companies plundered, and still freely plunder, the wartime films of Jennings and his Crown colleagues for their own historical documentaries; admirers with enough leisure to watch daytime or late-night television claim that hardly a week goes by without their seeing some shot or other from *The First Days*, *Britain Can Take It* and the like, almost always broadcast with no credit to the original film-makers. But there have been one or two more direct and honourable acknowledgements of Jennings on the small screen, notably a memorable television documentary for the long-running *Omnibus* series, well directed by the Hungarian film-maker Robert Vas and transmitted by the BBC in 1970. The one unhappy consequence of Vas's documentary was that it gave rise to the legend that Jennings's death must have been suicide – this derived almost wholly, it seems, from Vas's fanciful idea that he must have suffered from some form of depression in the postwar years, a belief underwritten in the film by nothing more substantial than some vague and speculative remarks by Stuart Legg.

★

All this, plus the occasional short season of his work at the National Film Theatre and elsewhere, as well as the general growth of interest in film history, ensured that Jennings's reputation grew steadily if quietly in the three decades following his death, until a sudden burst of publicity early in 1982 when a major retrospective opened, celebrating his work, at London's Riverside Studios (7 January–14 February). This large and popular show was accompanied by an excellent illustrated catalogue, edited by Mary-Lou Jennings and published by the BFI, which reprinted the essays by Charles Madge and Kathleen Raine from the 1951 ICA booklet alongside Anderson's 'Only Connect', a rather dense new essay by the art historian David Mellor, 'Sketch for an Historical Portrait of Humphrey Jennings', and an extract from the editor and film critic Dai Vaughan's biography-in-progress of Stewart McAllister. When Vaughan's book *Portrait of an Invisible Man: The Working Life of Stewart McAllister, Film Editor* was published in 1983, it proved to be a thoughtful and ardent study ranging far beyond its apparently modest brief to ponder large questions of labour and leisure, individual creativity and collaboration, finance and art. Vaughan's research made it impossible for anyone seriously interested in Jennings's achievement to neglect the contribution made by this difficult, reclusive, fiercely talented Scot – something known all along by those who had witnessed at first hand their often stormy creative partnership on *Listen to Britain* and other films.

The Riverside exhibition attracted a good deal of attention from the media: major newspaper reviews, and an item on *Omnibus* – which at this time had broken from its traditional single-documentary format to become an arts magazine programme – presented by the ever-loyal

Lindsay Anderson. More importantly, discussions and meetings prompted by the exhibition led more or less directly to the publication, at last, of *Pandæmonium* by André Deutsch in 1985; the commissioning editor was Tom Rosenthal, whose sympathy for the project owed something, it seems, to the fact that he too had been a Pembroke man.[15] The secret masterpiece had been unveiled: thirty-five years after his death, the public was at last able to see the nature of the epic project at which Jennings had patiently laboured for more than thirteen years.

*

The correspondence file on the long and troubled publication history of *Pandæmonium* runs to well over seventy letters and covers three decades. One of the most revealing documents is the first: Jennings's assistant Dillon Barry's letter to his literary executor, Charles Madge, dated 22 January 1951:

Dear Mr Madge,

As you suggested I am writing to tell you the little that I know of Humphrey's wishes concerning 'Pandæmonium'. Curiously enough he told me all this a few days before he died; he remarked at the time that many of the finest expressions of English literature and thought have been published almost in spite of the author, often by persuasion or necessity. He quoted Darwin's Origin of the Species which he said was only a rough sketch for a final greater work which was never completed, and which was only published on the persuasion of friends.

He then went on to talk about Pandæmonium. He felt that it needed a good six months' full-time work to complete it, and he explained to me in some detail the important points he was bearing in mind. If I give you a seemingly arbitrary list I am sorry, but it seems the only way to put down the points which arose out of quite a long conversation.

– Humphrey wished to have the book published in a popular edition, such as the Penguin series, possibly in several volumes. He said that he had put aside an offer from a publisher who wished to have an abridged edition made.

– He said that the [seventeenth century] required the greatest part of the further research required, the rest was more or less complete.

– He wished to divide up the sections with introductions explaining the social & political background in the light of which the extracts are to be read – giving the contemporary climate of thought.

– He stressed that on no account would he cut down the extracts as opposed to eliminating them. Apparently when he first started on this work he had tried to condense the extracts & shorten them in some cases. He then found that in doing this, seemingly irrelevant facts were cut out, and then in the light of his later work he found that these seemingly irrelevant facts formed a vital part of the extract. In other words he made it a principle, & he was very definite about this, that one can take *out* an extract from a main work, but that in cutting it *down* one interferes with the basic structure of the thought expressed, and this one should not do.

– He wished the index to contain references to the *edition* in each case from which the extract was drawn. He felt that this was important because the actual date of publication even to a couple of years affected the flow of contemporary thought. Apparently most of this work he had already done.

– Finally I asked him about the purpose of the book. He said it was to illustrate the coming of the Machine using the words of contemporary observers. I asked him if he was entirely objective in the choice of extracts. Whether in fact, he chose them in praise or blame of the Machine alike, or whether he almost in spite of himself chose those that suited a theme he was bearing in mind. He hesitated over this, & then said that his purpose & choice was entirely objective, but that he found a theme emerging from the collection almost spontaneously – that the coming of the Machine was destroying something in our life.[16]

When Charles Madge found himself too busy with his duties at Birmingham University to continue with the task of championing the manuscript, the baton was passed to another old friend, Stuart Legg. Opening his campaign, he wrote letters in October 1953 to S. C. Roberts, the former Cambridge University Press official who was now

Master of Pembroke College (naturally, Legg emphasized Jennings's Pembroke connections) and to Allen Lane at Penguin. Legg also suggested to Cicely Jennings that they should make further approaches to Herbert Read at Routledge, even though the firm had shown no interest in renewing its original contract, and that they might get in touch with Rupert Hart-Davis, at the time a rising star of the publishing world. Both of Stuart Legg's letters quote Jennings's description of *Pandæmonium* as

> a series of images; that is, passages describing certain moments, events, clashes, ideas, occurring between 1660 and 1885 which either in the writing or in the nature of the matter itself have revelatory and symbolic and illuminatory quality; moments in the history of the Industrial Revolution at which the clashes and conflicts show themselves with extra clearness; moments of vision.

After a couple of months' consideration, in January 1954 Cambridge University Press politely but firmly turned the manuscript down, calling it 'almost unpublishable' because of its size, but suggesting others who might be interested: Mr Guest at Longman's, Ian Cox at Shell. Penguin also turned the book down.

On 16 November that year, Jacob Bronowski wrote a publisher's report on the text. He begins:

> I have read this ms. with exceptional interest. As Kathleen Raine says, I knew Humphrey Jennings (he and I were fellow-editors on 'Experiment' at Cambridge) and he had told me that he was making a source-book of England under the stress of industrial change. But until I read the ms., I did not know how deeply he had steeped himself in that time, nor how fierce had grown his sympathy with the working men whose lives were deformed by it. What happened to Humphrey Jennings, I now see, is what happened to me when I studied the rise of industry for my book on Blake; and the succinct way to describe this ms. is to say that it gives at first hand the kind of material on which the background chapters in my book are based.
>
> . . . But this, of course, tells nothing about the wonderful eye with which the extracts have been chosen, so that each centres on some telling phrase ('A Mechanical Muscle', 'The York Buildings Dragons', 'On Doubling the People in 25 Years', 'The

Concealed Yearning', 'The Vowel Flame', 'Darwin on Pigeons' followed by 'Darwin on Theology' and so on) and their sequence flashes with contrasts. Kathleen Raine, I notice, recalls the technique of cutting in films, and this is an apt simile. I have no hesitation in saying that the material is first-class, chosen from the best minds, and assembled so that it gives the sense and the scene of the rising industry vividly.

Bronowski then goes on to more practical considerations – the best format for the book, its possible readership. It should, he proposes, be addressed to the same intelligent general reader as Turberville's *Johnson's England* and Dorothy George's *London Life in the Eighteenth Century*. He then proposes cuts – 'too much Ruskin, too much Thomas Hawkins and Nathaniel Hawthorne and [the balloonist] John Glaisher – too much nineteenth century altogether for its balance' – which would reduce the completed book to some 350–400 'images', fleshed out with Jennings's own 'excellent' notes and 'an imaginative introductory essay'. This is almost exactly the form the book would take, three decades later.

Despite the enthusiasm so evident in Bronowski's report, no offers came forth, and efforts seem to have ceased for three or four years. Cicely Jennings, with the help on different occasions of James Reeves and Dillon Barry (now Mrs Dillon Usill) as well as Stuart Legg, tried once again to interest both Cambridge University Press and Herbert Read at Routledge, and was once again turned down. But events took a more optimistic turn after the publication of Bronowski's 'Recollections of Humphrey Jennings' in the journal *The Twentieth Century*. The editor of Hutchinson Educational, John Stevens, read the article and contacted Bronowski, keen to chase up 'its exciting reference to Humphrey Jennings' unfinished MS *Pandemonium*. 'Do you happen to have any idea who has the material now? It sounds like a perfect book for the brighter VIth former.'

So began an enthusiastic and frequent correspondence between Hutchinson and Cicely Jennings. By July 1959, the chances of publication were looking very good indeed: Stevens wrote to her discussing arrangements for royalties, and proposing as a suitable editor for the text a young tutor for the Oxford University Delegacy for Extra-Mural Studies called Raymond Williams, already fairly well known for his book *Culture and Society 1780–1950* (1958), the work that launched his career as the most influential and widely read British Marxist literary critic of the twentieth century.

Cicely knew little or nothing of Williams, so sounded out a mutual friend, Tony McLean, who wrote back to her in September saying, 'I ... have always held [Williams] in very high esteem', and mentioning that another friend, Francis Klingender, author of *Art and the Industrial Revolution*, had 'seen or read parts of [*Pandæmonium*]' and 'spoke of it with great enthusiasm'. Further reassurance came from Charles Madge, who had no objections to Williams taking over the editorial task, though Cicely, as she explained to him, still had her misgivings: 'I have tried to read his book "Culture & Society" but frankly found it very involved and dull – though I know I'm no judge, really. I am hoping to meet him and may like him better than his book, but I am still very much on my guard.' She would not mind calling the whole thing off if need be, she added. But by June 1960, Hutchinson, in recognition of the fact that 'Mr Williams is debarred by [contractual obligations to the publisher] Chatto from publishing before Autumn 1961 at the earliest', were proposing January 1962 as publication date.

Meanwhile, Mrs Jennings was approached with a quite different proposition. In April 1961, she received a letter from Mr Peter G. Plummer of Granada Television, explaining that he had, 'for some time, felt that the subject of the Industrial Revolution was one that might provide an exciting television series' and wondering whether *Pandæmonium*, which he had been discussing with Denis Forman, might 'possibly yield an imaginative basis'. Uncertain about the wisdom of letting Granada proceed, Cicely turned to Stuart Legg for advice. In his reply, dated 8 May, Legg poured cool water on the chances of *Pandæmonium* appearing as anything other than a plain anthology of documents, since Jennings left too little in the way of interpretative material for it to be realized in the way he had originally planned. He too was dubious about what television would make of the work, suspecting that access to the manuscript might simply serve as a handy substitute for original research, but he stressed that 'Granada are easily the sincerest strivers after good of the TV companies, even if their ideas of good don't satisfy, say Kathleen [Raine].' A week later, he wrote to Forman outlining the delicacy of Cicely's position: '*Pandæmonium* is something of a sacred cow to many of Humphrey's friends, and especially to the Cambridge literati. And if it were used in a way they thought profane, they could turn on Cicely for allowing it.'

But that summer, both projects crumbled away. Hutchinson wrote to Cicely informing her that Raymond Williams, who had just been elected a fellow of Jesus College, Cambridge, was now too busy to take on the job, and Granada dropped their enquiries. The correspondence between Cicely and Hutchinson grew ever less hopeful, and in January 1963 the publisher gave her back the manuscript. All was silent for the next few years, save for a single letter from Arthur Elton at the end of December 1964; Elton, who was re-editing Klingender's *Art and the Industrial Revolution*, was keen both to look at the manuscript and to put himself forward as a possible editor.

The next episode began in the spring of 1967. Bronowski, on a lecture tour of the West Coast, had run into his old friend Andries Deinum, who was an adviser on various projects for the University of California Press, including their journal *Film Quarterly*.[17] Bronowski had enthused Deinum about *Pandæmonium*, and Deinum had passed his enthusiasm on to a senior editor for the press, Ernest Callenbach. In his initial letter to Cicely, Mr Callenbach said that although he could foresee a number of practical difficulties standing in the way of publication, 'it certainly sounds as if an important work may be languishing, and that we should look into the possibilities'.

Once again, letters began to fly backwards and forwards between the interested parties; in one of them, Cicely explained: 'I think Humphrey *did* decide that he had finished – Pandæmonium – I have come across a sheet of paper with "The End" surrounded with flourishes! – but of course he would probably have gone on adding new images, even so.' The exchange went on for the better part of the year, but once again ended in nothing, or as good as nothing: the readers' reports for the University of California Press were, as Callenbach wrote regretfully, 'a bit ambiguous', and there was a feeling that too many of the passages by the likes of Pepys, Ruskin and Morris were too well known to sustain 'the strong documentary impression that the less familiar passages provoke', though Callenbach softened the blow by adding: 'My surmise is that they have become better known since HJ compiled them.'[18] Towards the end of the correspondence, Charles Madge wrote discouragingly: 'The philosophy of Humphrey's selection was so subtle and at the same time so consistent that if I or anyone else were to make major additions or subtractions the work would no longer be Humphrey's and might not really be worth while.' He suggested shelving the whole thing for a few years, and stressed that he had far too much work on his hands to consider being the editor himself.

Apart from a few minor exchanges – Kathleen Raine proposing Ruthven Todd as a suitable editor; Todd declining the offer, but wondering whether the American academic publisher Bollingen should be approached – all went quiet. Charlotte Jennings made an initial attempt to edit the files into publishable dimensions, but was soon overwhelmed by the scale of the task. Mary-Lou Jennings and Charles Madge took over, and selected a representative group of passages which they handed, in 1980, to the literary agent Hilary Rubenstein of A. P. Watt. Rubenstein willingly took up the task of presenting the manuscript to publishers; he was a great believer in the project, and once wrote that *Pandæmonium* might well prove to be as significant a work as E. P. Thompson's *Making of the English Working Classes* – a passionate work of reclamation already accepted as a modern classic even by historians who did not entirely share Thompson's unorthodox, humanist brand of Marxism. One by one, the publishers said no; but eventually, after almost three yeas of effort, Rubenstein finally persuaded a publisher to take a chance: André Deutsch.

The reluctance of those other publishers is understandable. They could not easily have foreseen the rapturous critical reception that the book was eventually to achieve on both sides of the Atlantic.

*

In the autumn of 1983, with the go-ahead from André Deutsch, Mary-Lou Jennings and Charles Madge set about the considerable task of sifting through the twelve red folders, containing well over a thousand pages of typescript and crabbed pencil notes making up the rough text of *Pandæmonium*. Realizing that there was no chance of the work being published in several volumes as Jennings had once hoped and planned, they weeded out hundreds of passages until the remaining pile was about a quarter of the complete archive; a familiar task for Madge, as well as a challenging one, as he had done almost exactly the same thirty-two years earlier, soon after Jennings's death. The surviving extracts, 372 in all, were then arranged in chronological order, or as close to that order as could be guessed, and divided into four parts: 1660–1729, 'Observations and Reports'; 1730–90, 'Exploitation'; 1791–1850, 'Revolution'; and 1851–86, 'Confusion'. But this was not the end of the editorial task. As Madge explains, Jennings had left a note entitled TO THE READER:

> There are at least three different ways in which you may tackle this book. First, you may read it straight through from the beginning as a continuous narrative or *film* on the Industrial Revolution. Second, you may open it where you will, choose one or a group of passages and study in them details of events, persons and thoughts as one studies the material and architecture of a poem. Third way, you begin with the Index – look up a subject or an idea, and follow references skipping over gaps of years to pursue its development.

Splendid suggestion; except that no such index has ever been found. Tentatively, Madge set about compiling lists of what he called 'theme sequences', isolating in each passage the major line of thought that seemed to stand out from its various subsidiary themes, and came up with the following headings: The Man of Science; Poetry and Science; Theology and Science; Industrial Man; Daemons at Work; Miners; Population and Subsistence; The Power to Come; Man – Animal – Machine; Music and Architecture; Earth and Creation; Light; The Railway; Men and Molecules; and London. (As Madge knew, the material could quite easily have been sorted into very different categories; but his own arrangement has proved both sensible and serviceable.) Finally, and again following some cramped and occasionally cryptic notes of Jennings's, the book was to be provided with illustrations, such as the 'Figure of the Water-Insect or Gnat' from Robert Hooke's *Micrographia* (1665) and John Martin's chilling vision of prehistoric predation from Thomas Hawkins's *Book of the Great Sea Dragons* (1834). This, too, was an admirable editorial decision, not least since it means that *Pandæmonium* can be seen – without too much stretching of terms – as a visual work as well as a visionary one.

Kathleen Raine was only the first of the book's many readers to agree with Jennings that *Pandæmonium* can be understood as a sort of literary 'film'. Almost exactly as in his films, Jennings's presence may be felt throughout in his approach to 'shooting' (selection of material) and 'editing' (relative lengths of extracts, surprise effects of juxtaposition). Unlike most of his actual films, though, *Pandæmonium* occasionally gives us his voice and his views direct, in odd moments of editorial commentary that flash out between the verse and prose extracts, and in an Introduction – assembled and partly rewritten by Madge from scattered notes – which both explains the scope and nature of the project and serves as a kind of credo or summary of his mature thought.

His explanation:

In this book I present the imaginative history of the Industrial Revolution. Neither the political history, nor the mechanical history, nor the social history nor the economic history, but the imaginative history . . .

I present it by means of what I call Images.

These are quotations from writings of the period in question, passages describing certain moments, events, clashes, ideas occurring between 1660 and 1886 which either in the writing or in the nature of the matter itself or both have revolutionary and symbolic and illuminatory quality. I mean that they contain in little a whole world – they are the knots in a great net of tangled time and space – the moments at which the situation of humanity is clear – even if only for the flash time of the photographer or the lightning. And just as the usual history does not consist of isolated events, occurrences – so this 'imaginative history' does not consist of isolated images, but each is in a particular place in an unrolling film.[19]

His credo:

Man as we see him today lives by production and vision. It is doubtful if he can live by one alone . . .

The relationship of production to vision and vision to production has been mankind's greatest problem.

Unless we are prepared to claim special attributes for the poet – the attribute of vision – and unless we are prepared to admit the work of the artist (that is to say the function of 'imagination') as an essential part of the modern world there is no real reason for our continuing to bother with any of the arts any more, or with any imaginary activity. No reasons except money, snobbery, propaganda or escapism. In this book however it is assumed that the poet's imagination does exist, that the imagination is a part of life, that the exercise of the imagination is an indispensable function of man like work, eating, sleeping, loving. I do not propose to ask the obvious next question 'What then is the place of imagination in the world of today?' I prefer to inquire what may have *been* the place of imagination in the making of the modern world.[20]

Though some of the implications of what Jennings is saying here may stand in need of further remark, the general drift is plain enough: he is interested not (or not only) in events and gadgetry but in feelings, sentiments, metaphors, states of mind; and he assumes not only that changed circumstances bring about changes of thought and emotion – say, new-found nostalgia for a countryside in the process of being ravaged – but that changes of thought and emotion may be a necessary precondition of grosser forms of change. So, for example, he cites an early passage from John Evelyn's *Diary* (9 July 1669) on the opening of Sir Christopher Wren's Sheldonian Theatre in Oxford, commenting:

> Note the attack on the Royal Society; and the parallel between the new secular building and the 'Fabrick' that 'rose like an exhalation' in the opening passage from Milton, which also compares the way Pandæmonium was built to the passage of air into the pipes of an organ. All organs had been removed from churches by an ordinance dated 1644, and it was a long time after the Restoration before they could all be replaced.
>
> The architecture of the Sheldonian, designed by Sir Christopher Wren, was based on a study of the classical theatre. Like St Paul's, and later in the Panopticon[21] and the Crystal Palace, it was an architectural symbol. Some of the classical rationalism which it expressed would later be borrowed for the purposes of science and industry. The word theatre reappears in the surgeon's operating theatre. The machinery of the theatrical masque reappears in the factory.[22] The division of labour in the musical orchestra has its industrial parallel.[23]

'Only Connect': part of the genius shown by Jennings in *Pandæmonium* is the genius of seeing hitherto unexpected connections

between apparently unrelated phenomena, just as he had once seen
(in Grierson's phrase) 'the Louis Quinze properties of a Lyons' swiss
roll', or the bald head of Darwin implicit in the dome of St Paul's.
Had anyone, before Jennings, made the imaginative leap from a
Jonsonian masque to the very different machinery of a factory? Perhaps
they had; but no one, surely, had ever produced such a wealth of
startling, fertile, occasionally bizarre links as is to be found throughout
Pandæmonium. And few cultural historians critics save William Empson
would have been prompted or able to hint at some occult link between
the suppression of church organs and the recurrent metaphor, from
Milton onwards, of architecture not merely as frozen music, but
specifically frozen organ music.

The richness of *Pandæmonium* can more adequately be hinted at
than displayed. Here, then, are some of the themes to which Jennings
devotes particular attention in his notes.

Part One (1660–1729) mainly concerns the birth-pangs of scien-
tific method, which came about with the formation of the Royal
Society and related developments. It begins with the building of
'Pandæmonium' by the fallen rebel angels in *Paradise Lost*:

> Meanwhile the winged Haralds by command
> Of Sovran power, with awful Ceremony
> And Trumpets sound throughout the Host proclaim
> A solemn Councel forthwith to be held
> At *Pandæmonium*, the high Capital
> Of Satan and his Peers . . .

Jennings comments: 'Pandæmonium is the Palace of All the Devils.
Its building began c.1660. It will never be finished – it has to be
transformed into Jerusalem. The building of Pandæmonium is the real
history of Britain for the last three hundred years . . .'

After Milton, the principal sources for Part One include Evelyn,
Pepys, Swift, Defoe, Robert Hooke, Newton and many less well-
known names from the annals of early science. Jennings not only
draws on many different literary genres but comments on the genres
themselves where pertinent: for instance, a disquisition on the
growth of diary-keeping in the late seventeenth century ends with the
observation, 'The idea of the diary as a form of expression is present
in the design of this book, since it consists of "images" – pages from a

mass-diary.'[24] And to a passage dated 1725 on the effects of lightning in Northamptonshire by one J. Wasse, Jennings appends a mini-essay which, in outlining the train of thought that prompted him to include it, indirectly explains much of the reasoning behind *Pandæmonium* as a whole:

> It is I think interesting to give the exact line of reasoning that leads to the inclusion of this image. It is this: when the 'bourgeoisie' took over in 1660, they began the final subjugation and exploitation of this island. They had amassed the necessary capital, 'fixed' the church on the laws of usury, tamed the power of the feudal monarchy.
>
> The tasks that lay before them were the taking of the land from the people by the Enclosure Acts, the creation of the factory system and the invention of machines and the means of power to run them.

Note, again, Jennings's belief that it is radical changes in social power which clear the way for technical and scientific progress, rather than the (more orthodox) other way round. Changes of power, and also changes of perception – he continues:

> Before any of these things could be done it was necessary to make an analysis of the materials and forces existing in nature and in these islands which would contribute to the scheme. Hence the financial backing of the Royal Society.
>
> Among these forces was electricity – not merely as a source of power but also as an essential part of the development of chemistry. Electricity was studied among other ways by the study of thunder and lightning. Before these phenomena could be studied a radically new attitude had to be developed towards them, and towards all natural phenomena. One of strict realism.
>
> In this image then we have a contributor to the papers of the Royal Society giving a cold, inch-by-inch analysis and reportage of the effects of a thunderstorm equally without reference to God or man. Without a trace of human feeling for the victim or on the other hand of the ancient awe with which 'the glance of God' had been regarded for centuries, even ages, past.
>
> To do this required a new attitude. This new attitude is so clear and so marked as to constitute, I believe, a fundamental

alteration of 'vision' parallel to that being developed by Defoe.
Realism.

Here then is a case of an alteration in vision already being
achieved not merely as the *result* of changing means of production,
but *also* making them possible.[25]

Part Two (1730–90) documents the first applications of the new
scientific mentality in the rapid growth of technology, and draws on
Voltaire, John Wesley, Thomas Gray (his old research topic), Christopher Smart, Josiah Wedgwood, Oliver Goldsmith, Erasmus Darwin,
James Boswell and James Watt amongst others. One of Jennings's
main themes in this section – and it is a constant motif of the book –
is the conflict of class interests brought about by the new order. Hence
his comment on a letter to Wesley (November 1739) which implicitly
identifies a community of colliers with 'Heathens': 'HEATHENS. In
this phrase resides the whole truth on England. Britain was seen as a
colony – its people the savages to be exploited – its wealth the property
of the conquerors – and its preachers the missionaries to dope and
convert the natives.'[26] And, following a letter from Josiah Wedgwood
to the porcelain manufacturer Thomas Bentley (9 October 1779),
Jennings observes:

> Here perhaps for the first time among these images there clearly
> appears the image of 'the mob'. I mention this not because it
> came into being now but because 'the mob' is one of the principal
> actors in the great struggles of the next seventy years – and the
> *transformation* of the mob into the ordered and disciplined dem-
> onstration of the 19th century is one of the clearest signs of
> increasing political consciousness. It is not too early to note here
> that the shooting begins on the side of the forces of so-called Law
> and Order: and that it produces immediate organisation, discipline,
> drum and colours etc.[27]

Part Three of *Pandæmonium*, which covers the years 1791–1850,
is the longest section as well as the most heavily annotated, with
more than twenty passages of commentary, some only a line or two
long and reading at times more like reminders to himself than comments to a hypothetical reader – 'Compare 157, Faraday's letter to his
fiancée in 1820. The house was in Upper Norwood. On the sunset
image, compare Turner who was a friend of Faraday. Turner died in

1851.'[28] Other such passages are more like miniature essays. His sources here include Jeremy Bentham, Blake (several times), Coleridge (several times), Wordsworth, Charles Lamb, Byron, Cobbett, Keats, Faraday, Tennyson, Carlyle (several times), Ruskin, Charles Darwin, Dickens, James Clerk-Maxwell, Herman Melville, and many much more obscure characters. The self-explanatory title of this section is 'Revolution'.

> When the enclosures forced the country-dwellers off the land they not only expropriated the people, but also expropriated poetry, which has its roots in the emotional links of man to the land and of man to man in a common society. They also *opened up* primitive land, cf. William Wordsworth. It is from this basis that Shelley spoke later of *words* quickening the earth ('Ode to the West Wind'). It is in this sense that poetry (and painting also) began in the 18th and 19th centuries to speak of the countryside as an area of holiness, connected with childhood – a garden of Eden which has been *lost*. It is the *recovery* and *saving* of this lost land that is behind very much of the imaginative writing of this period. It is in this way that the growing nostalgia for the country and the fading *glory* of childhood (compare Wordsworth's 'Ode: Intimations of Immortality from Recollections of Early Childhood') is connected with the political struggles of the expropriated working class: even when both sides are unaware of it . . .[29]

He goes on to discuss the summer of 1798, when Humphry Davy visited Dr Thomas Beddoes's celebrated Pneumatic Institute at Bristol – where the literati would repair to inhale gases and see visions – and began his adventures with nitrous oxide, and when Coleridge, influenced by a very different type of drug, composed 'Kubla Khan':

> The common factor [Jennings concludes] . . . who put up the money for both, and took both things, opium and nitrous oxide, was Tom Wedgwood.
>
> Xanadu is the palace of pleasure: the opposite of Pandæmonium. Now only a dream possibility, now only to be found in dreams or opium – only fragmentarily written down. It is the same palace as Blake's Jerusalem once builded on Pancras and Kentish-town, but now no more. Paradise Lost again.[30]

The fourth and final part, covering the years 1851 (the Great Exhibition) to 1886, is subtitled 'Confusion': 'The years 1849–51 should be the glorious climax of the story of Pandæmonium – the years of King Hudson [George Hudson, 'Railway King'] and the Great Exhibition. But in fact there is a strong feeling of disillusionment and compromise: a recognition of how short reality falls from the dream and the dream also from the reality . . .'[31] Besides additional passages from the authors already mentioned, particularly Ruskin, this section draws on Henry Mayhew, Charlotte Brontë, Alexander Herzen, Lord Shaftesbury, Thomas Huxley, Edward Lear (the subject of his uncompleted book), Lewis Carroll, Karl Marx, Gerard Manley Hopkins, Samuel Butler, Thomas Hardy, Arthur Conan Doyle and William Morris. As noted above, *Pandæmonium* ends by citing another end, the conclusion of Morris's *Dream of John Ball* (1886–7), where the sleeper awakes from his vision of medieval beauty to the grim, cold reality of Victorian London. To repeat:

> But as I turned away shivering and downhearted, on a sudden came the frightful noise of the 'hooters', one after the other, that call the workmen to the factories, this one the after-breakfast one, more by token. So I grinned surlily, and dressed and got ready for my day's 'work' as I call it, but which many a man besides John Ruskin (though not many in his position) would call 'play'.[32]

Slightly less densely annotated than Part Three, this concluding phase of the epic is studded with some of Jennings's most dazzling feats of connection:

> Sherlock Holmes's 'Book of Life', in *A Study in Scarlet*, stresses precisely the relation of the drop of water to the Atlantic – compare Valéry on the relation of the wine and the sea – the relationship of the individual to the crowd, of the molecule to the gas. It is also worth noting that the science of detection which is here seen arising from natural science was, so to speak, there all the time: Bacon's 'all learning for my province' schemes were precisely connected with the Elizabethan secret service – see Neale, *Queen Elizabeth*.[33]

> In 1871, the year of the Franco-Prussian war, Pissarro, Monet and Sisley were in England. Note the importance to Impression-

ism of 'the end of animism' in removing the symbolic animistic attributes of objects. Compare Cézanne: 'Le contour m'échappe.'[34]

The Chinese philosopher Chung-Tzu has the saying 'When justice goes out benevolence comes in.' Nasmyth escapes from strike-breaking into the dream-world of 'Everybody for ever' and benevolently exhibits works of art for the relief of the people his system has put out of work . . .[35]

'Realistic' reporting appears to supersede 'artistic' reporting but in fact realism becomes art. This is the identification of subject and object on a new plane.[36]

Other insights are commonplace enough (Jennings was not the first, obviously, to propose that the sentimental vein in Victorian culture was a return of feelings repressed by the harsher elements of Victorian economics), others are contentious or even cranky, and some are so brilliantly suggestive as to offer material for a dozen as yet unwritten cultural histories. Who else has possessed the sensibility and the gifts to assemble such a wonderful mass of fragments, and coax them into such eloquence? Taken as a whole, they offer not only the epic account of industrialization that is their ostensible subject, but a strange kind of self-portrait – at any rate, a portrait of the artist as polymathic magpie-scholar. And though unique, the work has spiritual cousins: Walter Benjamin's massive work on nineteenth-century Paris, the so-called *Arcades* project,[37] is no doubt the closest, but there are also strong affinities with Ezra Pound's poem-containing-history *The Cantos*, Charles Olson's *Maximus Poems* and other monuments of modern and postmodern poetry. Though the book has been the subject of one or two extended critical discussions – in a major article for the journal *Science and Culture*, for example, and in a largely hostile piece by the social historian Michael Saler – *Pandæmonium* has so far proved more popular with the intelligent general reader than with the professional scholar. Perhaps Jennings would not have been unhappy with this outcome, though: after all, the first real audience for his researches was a group of attentive, sympathetic Welsh miners.

On publication in 1985 it was given an exceptionally warm reception by the reviewers: 'A masterpiece of collage that reads like a novel' (*The Times*); 'An extraordinary and wonderful book' (*Sunday Times*); 'Like all great ideas, it is breathtakingly simple. And it has produced a book which is at once a treasure-chest of quirky, unusual pieces and a memorable account of the most devastating and exciting sea-change which has yet engulfed mankind' (*Observer*); 'It is what Ezra Pound called an 'active anthology', a book that sets ideas in motion and establishes a complex network of internal cross-references' (*New York Times*).

It also set in motion other enterprises. Professor Christopher Frayling, Rector of the Royal College of Art, was so excited by what he read that he made two major attempts to interest British film-makers in bringing *Pandæmonium* to the screen. Lindsay Anderson turned him down on the charmingly perverse grounds – taking Jennings's metaphor for reality – that it was 'already a film'; Ken Loach declined because he felt that Jennings had not adequately grasped the dialectical-materialist view of class struggle – in simpler terms, that it was not a properly Marxist history. Perhaps producers and directors of the twenty-first century will take a more positive view. Imaginatively handled, it could make a magnificent work of documentary film.

Epilogue

Since the publication of *Pandæmonium* and its subsequent paperback editions from Picador, Jennings's reputation appears to have held steady rather than noticeably declining or mounting. There have been one or two minor flurries of renewed attention: late in 1993, for example, when Carcanet Press published a collection of his letters, radio scripts, articles, notes and other writings that I had edited, entitled *The Humphrey Jennings Film Reader*, and on which I have drawn substantially for this book. The *Reader* was accompanied by an exhibition at the Mayor Gallery – still faithful to its old Surrealist links – and a day event at the Tate Gallery. At the same time, I also republished a facsimile edition of Jennings's 'original spelling' edition of *Venus and Adonis* of 1930 through my own small literary imprint, Alces Press. The *Reader* was reviewed by a fair number of national newspapers and one or two specialist journals, and most of these pieces showed both detailed knowledge of and deep affection for his work.

On 29 September 2000, Mary-Lou Legg unveiled a blue plaque at the old studios of the GPO Film Unit in Blackheath, London, commemorating the work of the Unit as a whole. Despite the best efforts of his elder daughter and others, there is, as yet, no blue plaque to Jennings himself, though I have heard rumours that English Heritage will soon be commissioning one, probably for display on his final London home in Camden.

Then there have been the various film retrospectives, in London and elsewhere, including a short one at the London Film Festival in 1995 showcasing the restoration of several short films (including *Making Fashion*, *Words for Battle*, *English Harvest* and *Family Portrait*) which had been restored by the BFI and the National Film Archive with funds provided by the Piper-Heidsieck company. I was subsequently invited by the National Film Theatre to programme a full season of films by Jennings and his contemporaries, which was screened in January 2000 – to my knowledge, the most complete retrospective held in this country to date, though a similarly full season had been shown at the Festival du Film Documentaire in Marseille during 13–22 June 1999, curated by the critic Laurent Roth and titled 'Un poète dans la guerre'. Others will no doubt follow: in Japan, for example, Hisashi Okajima of the Tokyo Film Archive – author of the first major Japanese-language essay on Jennings's work – hopes to mount a full-scale retrospective in his home town in the next couple of years.

When I organized the NFT season for January 2000, I was convinced that, with the inclusion of *Farewell Topsails*, *The Farm* and other minor works, it would be an exhaustive survey of Jennings's film career. I was soon proved wrong. On 20 September the same year, the Imperial War Museum held a day conference to mark the fiftieth anniversary of Jennings's death. The day included a screening of his 'lost' final film *The Good Life*, commissioned by the US Economic Cooperation Administration, which had recently been discovered by the museum's curators among a set of film archives handed over by NATO. The film had, presumably, been screened any number of times in the early 1950s, but had not been seen since, even by the most assiduous scholars of Jennings's work.

Since *The Good Life* was completed by another director, Graham Wallace, it is hard to be certain which of the sequences are by Jennings – especially since his cameraman on the project, Fred Gamage, was so upset by Jennings's death that his memories of the shoot are dim and confused. However, there are certain touches that seem unmistakably Jennings's, particularly the references to the world of ancient Greece with which the film begins and ends, and the visit to Missolonghi, where Byron had died of an 'ague' that was in fact malarial fever. (Jennings, recall, was carrying Trelawny's memoir of Byron and Shelley at the time of his death.) There is also an optimistic sequence of Greek girls performing a folkdance that is strongly reminiscent of the would-be hopeful finale of *A Defeated People*. And beyond these idiosyncratic touches, too, it seems that the film's general conception owes almost everything to Jennings: according to Fred Gamage and others, the new director felt that it was his job, not to impose his own interpretation on them, but to serve the original ideas as faithfully as possible. Even so – and without disrespect to his efforts – there is much in the film that is not, one suspects, quite as Jennings would have wished, beginning with its very first shot, a pan down from trees to ruins. Jennings, says Fred Gamage, would 'never have let me get away with that': he would surely have called for a static establishing shot.

In terms of content, *The Good Life* is straightforward. It begins with picturesque shots of contemporary Greece – ruined temples, an amphitheatre, a shepherd boy playing a pipe – while the voice-over cites the oath taken by doctors thousands of years ago in ancient Greece. A sudden cut to a Chevrolet making its way down a country road brings us instantly up to date – a doctor is travelling around the rural communities, inoculating the children against tuberculosis. (At this point, the voice-over yields to that of a Greek child, explaining how the youngsters reacted to this benign invasion and remarking that the BCG injection 'didn't hurt really'.) Rapid cuts to Vienna and Rome establish first the idea of the architectural splendours of 'our ancient continent', then the modern-day squalor that exists near, or even in, our ancestral ruins; will we have nothing to hand on to future generations but filth?

The mood lightens. We see a small disabled boy being taught to walk by a solicitous nurse (he's like a junior version of the injured airman Peter in *A Diary for Timothy*); the headquarters of the World Health Organization in Geneva, where officials are carefully monitoring an epidemic in the Middle East ('proof that disease respects no frontiers'); and an array of state-of-the-art medical equipment, from X-ray machines to the gadgetry of an Italian cancer hospital – all funded, the voice-over stresses, by the Marshall Plan, and made possible by technological cooperation between the nations of Europe.

We return to Greece – first to a traditional sheep farm ('This was going on in Homer's day'), then to the marshes of Missolonghi, where 'a certain Englishman' died: a shot of Byron's statue makes it clear who that Englishman was. Now, the voice-over enthuses, those lethal marshes are being sprayed with a wonderful chemical that will kill the mosquito larvae before they can hatch. That wonder chemical – the revelation draws a grim laugh from a twenty-first-century audience, raised on Rachel Carson's *Silent Spring* and other ecological jeremiads – is DDT. *The Good Life* concludes with an evocation of the ideal of a harmony between mind and body, both in ancient Crete (dramatic

Mycenaean wall-paintings of athletes and bulls) and in a modern summer camp, where the once neglected children of Greece's war are being offered sunlight, healthy exercise and recreations such as sculpting in clay. A penultimate shot of Michelangelo's *David* in Florence gives way to a last image – the last image, in effect, of Jennings's career, whether he filmed it or not: a close-up on the serious face of the same little boy we met earlier, slowly and doggedly learning to walk.

The Imperial War Museum's other premiere that day was of *Humphrey Jennings: The Man Who Listened to Britain*, directed by Kevin Macdonald, an hour-long documentary commissioned by Channel 4 and screened on 23 December 2000. I had been trying for the better part of seven years to persuade the BBC to make such a film, but had been turned down at least half a dozen times. That the film was ultimately financed by Channel 4 owes a great deal to luck: I had heard that the Director of Programmes, Tim Gardam, was an ardent admirer of Jennings's films; asked at a television festival to name his idea of a good documentary, he had nominated *Fires Were Started* – an admirable choice, though one that left younger audience members looking baffled. When I took the proposal to an initial meeting in the spring of 2000 and put forward my friend Kevin Macdonald as director, I was politely steered towards other possibilities – a policy that quickly and quietly changed when Macdonald won that year's Academy Award for Best Documentary with *One Day in September*, a thriller-like reconstruction of the Black September terrorist acts at the 1972 Munich Olympics. *The Man Who Listened to Britain* was an enormous pleasure to make, particularly since it gave me the chance to talk about Jennings with some of the practising film-makers who still admire him, still consider him an inspiration: Lord Attenborough, who spoke of how his use of a non-professional cast in *Fires Were Started* had revolutionized ideas of acceptable cinematic acting style for the whole British film industry; Lord Puttnam, who spoke of Jennings as an exemplary humanist; Mike Leigh, who said how deeply he had been moved by *A Diary for Timothy*, and how much it meant to viewers born, as he was, at about the same time as Timothy Jenkins; Terence Davies, who waxed eloquent about the National Gallery sequence in *Listen to Britain*; and the avant-garde documentarist Patrick Keillor[1] (whose highly acclaimed semi-fictional feature *London* directly invokes the name of Jennings), who discussed the implications of Jennings's work for those making films today outside the conventions of narrative cinema.

The range of accomplishment and interest represented by that short roll-call of modern British cinema speaks volumes about the respect with which Jennings is regarded by those within the industry a full half-century after his death. To this extent, Jennings is a living presence in contemporary cinema – one of the Old Masters who inspires, whether directly[2] or in more oblique ways, the shape and tone and content of the films that today's practitioners are making. Few of those who care about such matters would seriously dispute Lindsay Anderson's proposal that he is one of Britain's greatest film directors – perhaps, still, our greatest.

And yet the full value of his work, and not only his work in film, has yet to be acknowledged, let alone explored and built on. A substantial part remains inaccessible, even to the most assiduous viewers and readers: we still lack a complete set of his films on commercial video and DVD, a *catalogue raisonné* of his paintings, drawings, collages and Surrealist objects and of his extensive photographic work, particularly the Burmese pictures of 1947; an adequately edited edition of his poems; an academic press edition (no commercial publisher could attempt the task) of the complete *Pandæmonium* and perhaps a television series based on that epic work.

Jennings deserves an audience. Not just his present following, however august some members of that coterie, but an audience as broad as can nowadays be found for gentle, thoughtful, noble work in black and white. (Not necessarily such a tiny slice of the population as the cynic might predict: I have shown Jennings's work to gatherings young and old, American and Asian, scholarly and popular, and only once have I met with bored indifference.) His best work will surely live on in the twenty-first century for the reasons Lindsay Anderson outlined in 1954: as a unique and truthful vision of the greatest conflict of modern times, or of all time. And, as has been said elsewhere, Jennings is now part of that collective ancestral past which (as he argued in his radio talks on the laureateship in 1938) we must know about in order to know who we are.

But I also suspect that the most important aspect of his work lies not in what he accomplished for his time but in some of the tantalizing possibilities his life and work suggest for ours: an adult cinema of strong emotion, subtle ideas and poetic insight, instead of an infantilized and infantilizing entertainment industry addicted to coarse shocks, stale formulae and hollow fantasy; an uncynical, democratic humanism, founded in a vivid awareness of history and an uncompromising suspicion of the 'greed for money and power' in all its plausible disguises; a warm sense of patriotism untainted by its usual ugly siblings of arrogant insularity and racial contempt; the ideal of encyclopaedism, which, as Allen Hutt pointed out, Jennings both adumbrated and exemplified in his own person; a Ruskinian conviction that art, in all its traditional embodiments, is not the plaything of idle moments but an essential, if fragile, component of every society that deserves the name of civilization.

Jennings started some fires. It is for us to see that they do not go out.

Appendix

Letter from Jennings to William Empson

Dear Bill,

My reply has been delayed by Christmas with my in-laws, & a cold, and a visit to Paris etc: however I am now safely in the wilds away from the world, and will do my best for your questions.

(1) I think there is to be found in English poetry from 1580–1740 (from early Spenser to the revised 'Dunciad') symbolism or imagery (I take these terms as different but overlapping) derived from two things, (a) an extremely ancient philosophico-magical cosmological system, and from (b) the applications – partly ancient and partly contemporary (with the poets) – of this system, or branches of it. Note I take 'symbolism' to be derived from the abstract system, and 'imagery' to be derived from the applications (ritual etc) of it – or à peu près. Thus Spenser's two cantos on mutabilitie are mostly based on the philosophical abstraction: whereas the imagery in 'Tamburlaine' is mostly derived from what Marlowe had read of actual Roman processions etc, and also from the progresses of Queen Elizabeth. But there are philosophical abstractions in 'Tamburlaine' (e.g. 'Nature that made us of four elements') and also pieces of remembered or observed ritual in Spenser's cantos. That is, as I said, the two [illegible: 'contrasting ways of writing'?] overlap. Whether, in point of fact, the ritual came later than the first formation of the system or vice versa, or whether they grew up together etc I am not competent or prepared to say. But this can be said of English 'life and thought' (useful portmanteau phrase) in the 17th century, that four parts of what seem to be (or have been) a whole can be discerned. (i) They (Englishmen of intelligence 1580–1740) knew of statements by the ancients, Greek, Roman, Byzantine & later, of the abstract philosophico-magical system (which I will attempt to explain in a minute) as for example in Plato's 'Phaedrus'. (ii) There was still at that time (unsophisticated as yet by Madame Blavatsky) a semi-secret semi-popular adherence to the remains of the above system: to be found in various stages of decay among

Freemasons, gypsies, alchemists, Kabbalists etc. Marlowe & Raleigh seem to have been up to something of this kind when they were charged with atheism. It is here that the Tarot cards[1] come in, and also Milton's suspected addiction to 'Mortalism' (see Saurat[2] on Milton).

(iii) Parallel to (i) was the discovery in Roman authors and others of descriptions of actual ancient ritual connected with the system (iv) and finally the existence in 17th Century Europe including England, of actual ritual extremely similar to that described in (iii) of three main types [:] (a) that definitely sanctioned by the Roman Catholic church as Christian (b) popular pagan ritual (mumming, mayings etc) mostly condemned by the RC as pagan, and by the Protestants as 'Popery' and (c) the perpetual ritual of the lives of Renaissance princes (the progresses, 'royal entries', masques etc) much of which goes back to mediaeval ritual (and is not mere imitation of the Caesars).

All of these four parts and their sub-divisions overlap, and, as I think, the 17th century knew they overlapped. For instance Jonson in his masques and Milton in 'Comus' draw on practically all three sources: there is philosophical argument about Providence (the shape of things), there is the enchanter & the ritual of unbinding the spell. It is based upon the 'Odyssey' ultimately. It is a statement finally of Protestant chastity & yet ends with popular harvesters' dances which give place to the 'entry' of the Brothers & the lady

> To triumph in victorious dance
> O'er sensual folly & intemperance.

There is a pagan statement of Christian principles for you! Yet precisely the unity, the point, of 'Comus' is this identification of Milton's, of so many apparently various materials. And it can only, could only, be done because basically & originally these materials come from the same thing.

Which brings us to the system itself. Of the most broad characteristics of it I can hazard the following, which may be enough before going on with your questions.

(1) It is a cosmological business at bottom: a statement of the shape of the universe & the relation of the microcosm to the macrocosm.

(2) It seems always to be found in connection with agriculture: & hence in the shape of the universe & especially of the earth, the following points are emphasised. (a) the combats of one thing with another[,] hot & cold, winter & summer, Night & Day etc: in the most

abstract statements (Ovid 'Metamorphoses' I) it is the combat of the four elements. (b) Similarly in the microcosm there are combats, of the passions (see new book on 'Shakespeare's Tragic Heroes' by E. L. Campbell, of which the documentary part is excellent) & again, basically, a combat of the four elements or humours. (c) In all three combats one thing is constantly victorious over another and makes a momentary piece of ritual to celebrate. This ritual is itself an imitation of the deed performed. Enter Art.

(d) Between the microcosm & the macrocosm stands the King (see Frazer 'The Dying God'). As (a) the manifestation of the macrocosm & (b) the representative of the total tribe or community or of mankind itself, *his* combats are epic: definition of a hero. He is identified with the combats in both the sky and the earth. He is the sun & the wheat. His life is a perpetual ritual: both as microcosm & macrocosm he is *always* fighting combats: either as 'sunset' or as 'digestion'. Hence the predilection of early art for the upper classes.

(e) Now as for the actual shape of the ritual: the four seasons & the four cardinal points are the most important for agriculture. Hence, it seems, come the King's *four* supporters – holding the canopy – 'Matthew Mark Luke & John' (for going to bed is ritual: the sunset of the microcosm) etc etc. Out of these four supporters come, in Europe at any rate, the canopy of the throne, the posts of the bed. From war chariots (his *actual* combats) come two horses (active & passive, Night & Day etc). Other symbols added from elsewhere, to make the Tarot card called 'Le Chariot' & the ritual of the Renaissance princes & the entry of Tamburlaine 'drawn in his chariot by two captive Kings'.

That's as much as one can say for the moment: but probably enough to explain the earlier pages of this & to answer your questions.

To continue (e), I doubt if the fullest richness can be got from poetry employing this imagery or symbolism without knowing something about the system, but how much is necessary I am not at all clear. (2) & (3) Certainly the system collapsed generally in the 19th century: it collapsed first in the 'Dunciad', where the system is inverted. I quite agree it must either be revived by a real understanding or replaced. (4) Obviously from what I have said it was an aristocratic system. It is perhaps worth noting that Eliot's use of Frazer goes along with his Royalism.[3] I don't think it could be revived with the present state of agriculture, not merely the state of the farmers in England, but of mechanical farming elsewhere. In any case I think we are now in, or entering, or re-entering a period (a state of mind) not corresponding to the early stages of the system, but to *an earlier* state. The 'triumphs' correspond to [Herbert] Read's 'sense of glory': Read says there was a period earlier than his 'sense of glory' in which man was definitely afraid of nature & in which poetry & painting were protective instruments (spells, totems) instead of being *imitative* & celebration ritual (as I suggested the triumphs were indicating man's equality with nature). I suggest that poetry & painting are now back in their position of protectors, not to protect us from Nature (the macrocosm) but from ourselves (the microcosm). We may get to some state of equality with ourselves in the future & a sense of glory – victory of a mental Tamburlaine – return. This is hinted at in Blake: 'I will not cease from mental strife'[4] but we are not there yet. What is wanted *is* certainly a new system but it can't be found lying about. The difficulty of finding it, the battle against ourselves for it, the battle of the [*sic*] our four elements in our chaos, *are* the subject you are looking for, as I see it. Of Renaissance beauty Jonson said that

> There alone there triumphs to the life
> All the good, all the gain, of the elements strife.

but he is using there a system of *conquest* symbols. We have not conquered and I think the dream-symbols of the surrealists[5] & of Alice in Wonderland are on the right track.

I hope this is not too confused. I feel I have got it pretty clear in my own mind; but not so as to write a book on it – at least alone.

Write to me here, where I shall be for ten days, what you are doing on 'Alice':[6] & I will try & let you have some notes if I can.

Yours

Humphrey Jennings

You might keep this letter, for me if not for yourself, as I don't think I have written it out as fully before.

Select Bibliography

Aldgate, Anthony, and Richards, Jeffrey, *Britain Can Take It: The British Cinema in the Second World War*. 2nd edition, Edinburgh, Edinburgh University Press, 1994 (1st edition, Blackwell, 1986).

Anderson, Lindsay, 'Only Connect: Some Aspects of the Work of Humphrey Jennings', *Sight and Sound*, April–June, 1954. (Frequently reprinted: notably in *Film Quarterly*, vol. XV, no. 2 (Winter 1961–2), pp. 5–12; in Mary-Lou Jennings (ed.), *Humphrey Jennings: Film-maker, Painter, Poet*, with a postscript by Anderson dated October 1981; and in Macdonald and Cousins, *Imagining Reality*.

———, 'Reportage', *Sunday Times Supplement*, 15 November 1970.

Anon., 'Aubrey Leonard Attwater', *Pembroke College Annual Gazette*, no. 10 (June 1935).

Anon., 'A Welsh Village Makes a Film in Honour of Czech Lidice', *Picture Post*, 3 July 1943.

Armes, Roy, *A Critical History of British Cinema*, London, Secker & Warburg, 1978.

Barnouw, Erik, *Documentary: A History of the Non-Fiction Film*, 2nd revised edition, Oxford, Oxford University Press, 1993 (first edition, 1974).

Beveridge, James (ed.), *John Grierson, Film Master*, London, Collier Macmillan, 1978.

Blanche, Lesley, 'The True Story of Lilli Marlene', *Vogue*, April 1944.

Boorman, John, *Adventures of a Suburban Boy*, London, Faber & Faber, 2003.

Bradley, Fiona, *Surrealism*, London, Tate Publishing, 1997.

Bronowski, Jacob, 'Recollections of Humphrey Jennings', *The Twentieth Century*, vol. 165, no. 983 (January 1959), pp. 45–50.

———, 'Correspondence', *The Twentieth Century*, vol. 165, no. 984 (February 1959), p. 181.

Calder, Angus, *The People's War: Britain 1939–1945*, 2nd edition, London, Pimlico, 1992 (1st edition, Jonathan Cape, 1969).

————, and Sheridan, Dorothy, *Speak for Yourself: A Mass-Observation Anthology 1937–49*, London, Jonathan Cape, 1984.

Cameron, Evan, 'An Analysis of "A Diary for Timothy"', *Cinema Studies*, no. 1 (Spring 1967), Bridgewater, Mass., Experiment Press.

Carey, Hugh, *Mansfield Forbes and His Cambridge*, Cambridge, Cambridge University Press, 1984.

Carpenter, Humphrey, *W. H. Auden: A Biography*, London, George Allen & Unwin, 1981.

Carter, Miranda, *Anthony Blunt: His Lives*, London, Macmillan, 2001.

Chainey, Graham, *A Literary History of Cambridge*, revised edition, Cambridge, Cambridge University Press, 1995 (1st edition, Pevensey Press, 1985).

Chitty, Susan (ed.), *Antonia White: Diaries 1926–1957*, London, Constable, 1991 (paperback, Virago, 1992).

Clark, Kenneth, *Another Part of the Wood: A Self-Portrait*, London, John Murray, 1974.

Constable, John (ed.), *I. A. Richards: Selected Letters*, Oxford, Clarendon Press, 1990.

Crick, Bernard, R., *George Orwell: A Life*, London, Secker & Warburg, 1980.

Cunningham, Valentine, *British Writers of the Thirties*, Oxford, Oxford University Press, 1988.

Dalrymple, Ian, 'Personal Tribute' in Powell et al. (ed.), *Tribute*.

Del Renzio, Tony, and Scott, Duncan, *Surrealism in England, 1936 and After*, exhibition catalogue for the Herbert Read Gallery, Canterbury College of Art, May 1986.

Dickinson, Thorold, *A Discovery of Cinema*, Oxford, Oxford University Press, 1971.

Drazin, Charles, *The Finest Years: British Cinema of the 1940s*, London, André Deutsch, 1998.

Durgnat, Raymond, *A Mirror for England*, London, Faber & Faber, 1970.

Eddington, A. S., *The Nature of the Physical World*, Cambridge, Cambridge University Press, 1928 (reprinted: London, Routledge, 1978).

Éluard, Paul, *Oeuvres Complètes*, vol. 1, Paris, NRF/Gallimard, 1968.

Florence, P. Sargant, and Anderson, J. R. L., *C. K. Ogden: A Collective Memoir*, London, Elek Pemberton, 1977.

Forman, Denis, *Persona Granada*, London, André Deutsch, 1997.

Fussell, Paul, *Wartime: Understanding and Behaviour in the Second World War*, New York and Oxford, Oxford University Press, 1989.

Gascoyne, David, *Collected Journals 1936–42*, London, Skoob Books, 1991 (first two parts originally published by Enitharmon Press as *Paris Journal 1937–9*, 1978, and *Journal 1936–7*, 1980).

Germain, Edward B. (ed.), *Surrealist Poetry in English*, Harmondsworth, Penguin, 1978.

Goldsmith, James (ed.), *Stephen Spender: Journals 1939–1983*, London, Faber & Faber, 1985.

Graves, Robert, and Hodge, Alan, *The Long Week-End: A Social History of Great Britain 1918–1939*, London, Faber & Faber/Readers' Union, 1941.

Greenwood, John, 'Vale', in Powell et al. (ed.), *Tribute*.

Grierson, John, 'Humphrey Jennings', in Powell et al. (ed.), *Tribute*.

Grigson, Geoffrey (ed.), *The Arts Today*, London, John Lane/The Bodley Head, 1935.

Guggenheim, Peggy, *Confessions of an Art Addict*, London, André Deutsch, 1960.

———, *Out of This Century: Confessions of an Art Addict*, London, André Deutsch, 1980, New York, Universe Books, 1979.

Haffenden, John (ed.), *The Royal Beasts and Other Works*, by William Empson; London, Chatto & Windus, 1986.

———, (ed.), *The Complete Poems of William Empson*, Harmondsworth, Allen Lane/Penguin Press, 2000.

Hardy, Forsyth (ed.), *Grierson on Documentary*, London, Faber & Faber, 1966.

———, *John Grierson: A Documentary Biography*, London, Faber & Faber, 1979.

———, (ed.), *Grierson on the Movies*, London, Faber & Faber, 1981.

Harrisson, Tom, *Savage Civilization*, London, Victor Gollancz/Left Book Club, 1937.

———, *World Within: A Borneo Story*, London, Cresset Press, 1959.

———, Jennings, Humphrey, and Madge, Charles, 'Anthropology at Home', joint letter to the *New Statesman and Nation*, 30 January 1937. (Jennings later insisted that he had not taken part in the composition of this letter.)

Heimann, Judith M., *The Most Offending Soul Alive: Tom Harrisson and His Remarkable Life*, London, Aurum Press, 2002 (originally published by the University of Hawai'i Press, 1999).

Hewison, Robert, *Under Siege: Literary Life in London 1939–45*, London, Weidenfeld & Nicolson, 1977.

Hodgkinson, Anthony W., and Sheratsky, Rodney E., *Humphrey Jennings –*

More Than a Maker of Films, Hanover and London, Clark University/
University Press of New England, 1982.

Howarth, T. E. B., *Cambridge between Two Wars*, London, Collins, 1978.

Hynes, Samuel, *The Auden Generation: Literature and Politics in England in the
1930s*, London, Faber & Faber, 1976.

Isherwood, Christopher, *Lions and Shadows: An Education in the Twenties*,
London, Hogarth Press, 1938 (paperback, NEL Signet, 1968).

Jackson, Kevin (ed.), *The Humphrey Jennings Film Reader*, Manchester,
Carcanet Press, 1993 (paperback, 2004).

———, 'The Orwell of Cinema', *Prospect*, January 2001.

Jackson, Pat, *A Retake Please! Night Mail to Western Approaches*, Liverpool,
Liverpool University Press/RNM Publications, 1999.

Jeffery, Tom, *Mass-Observation: A Short History*, University of Birmingham,
Centre for Contemporary Cultural Studies, 1978 (revised edition,
University of Sussex Library, 1999).

Jennings, Humphrey, 'Song' in *Public School Verse*, vol. IV (1923–4), ed.
Martin Gilkes, Richard Hughes and P. H. B. Lyon, London,
W. Heinemann, 1924.

———, 'Design and the Theatre', *Experiment*, no. 1 (November 1928). Also
in Jackson (ed.), *The Humphrey Jennings Film Reader*.

———, 'Odd Thoughts at the Fitzwilliam', *Experiment*, no. 2 (February
1929). Also in *Reader*.

———, 'Notes on Marvell's "To His Coy Mistress"', *Experiment*, no. 2
(February 1929). Also in *Reader*.

———, 'A Passage in the "Progress of Poetry"', unpublished article, approx.
10,000 words, submitted to T. S. Eliot at *The Criterion*, early 1934:
Jennings family archive. (Eliot's reply, dated 20 April 1934, is also in this
file.)

———, 'The Theatre Today', in *The Arts Today*, ed. by Geoffrey Grigson,
London, The Bodley Head, 1935. Also in *Reader*.

———, 'Colour Won't Stand Dignity', *World Film News*, no. 3 (June 1936).
Also in *Reader*.

———, 'Surrealism', *Contemporary Poetry and Prose*, no. 8 (December 1936).
Also in *Reader*.

———, 'In Magritte's Paintings . . .', *London Gallery Bulletin* (name changed
subsequently to *London Bulletin*, since it then became a joint publication
of three Cork Street galleries, the London Gallery, the Mayor Gallery
and Guggenheim Jeune), no. 1 (April 1938). Also in *Reader*.

———, 'The Iron Horse', *London Bulletin*, no. 3 (June 1938). Also in *Reader*.

———, 'Do Not Lean Out of the Window', *London Bulletin*, no. 4 (July 1938). Also in *Reader*.

———, 'A Determination Not To Dream', *London Bulletin*, no. 4 (July 1938). Also in *Reader*.

———, 'Who Does That Remind You Of?', *London Bulletin*, no. 6 (October 1938). Also in *Reader*.

———, unpublished review of *The Anatomy of the Horse* by George Stubbs, *c.* 1939; Jennings family archive. Also in *Reader*.

———, 'Homage to Vulcan' (slightly edited version of his talk on James Nasmyth for the BBC National Programme in May 1939), *The Listener*, 8 June 1939. Original broadcast text in *Reader*.

———, 'Colorado Claro: Thoughts on the "Cleaned Pictures"', *Our Time*, December 1947. Also in *Reader*.

———, 'The English' (a review of *The Character of England*, ed. Ernest Barker), *Times Literary Supplement*, 7 August 1948. Also in *Reader*.

———, 'Paule Vezelay' (printed text to accompany an exhibition of Paule Vezelay's paintings at St George's Gallery, London W1, 1949). Also in *Reader*.

———, 'Working Sketches of an Orchestra', in *London Symphony: Portrait of an Orchestra*, ed. Herbert Foss and Noel Goodwin, London, Naldrett Press, 1954. Written in 1948; also in *Reader*.

———, (ed.), *Venus and Adonis; The Quarto of 1593*, Experiment Press, Cambridge, 1930 (reprinted Alces Press, London, 1993).

———, *Poems*, introduction by Kathleen Raine, New York, Weekend Press, 1951.

———, *Humphrey Jennings 1907–1950: Paintings*, London, Institute of Contemporary Arts pamphlet, 1951.

———, (with G. F. Noxon), 'Rock Painting and *La Jeune Peinture*', *Experiment*, no. 7 (Spring 1931). Also in *Reader*.

———, (with J. M. Reeves), 'A Reconsideration of Herrick', *Experiment*, no. 7 (Spring 1931). Also in *Reader*.

———, and Madge, Charles, 'Poetic Description and Mass-Observation', *New Verse*, no. 24 (1937).

———, and Gascoyne, David (eds and trans.), *Remove Your Hat: Twenty Poems by Benjamin Péret, with a note by Paul Éluard*, London, Roger Roughton, Contemporary Poetry and Prose Editions, 1936. (This is the slightly censored edition of *A Bunch of Carrots*, 1936; see the chapter on

Surrealism, above. The collection was reissued in an expanded edition by Atlas Press in 1986, with an introduction by David Gascoyne and textual notes by Alastair Brotchie; the references in the notes are to this edition.)

———, and Madge, Charles (eds), *May the Twelfth: Mass-Observation Day Surveys 1937*, London, Faber & Faber, 1937 (paperback, Faber & Faber, 1987).

Jennings, Mary-Lou (ed.), *Humphreys Jennings: Film-maker, Painter, Poet*, London, British Film Institute in association with Riverside Studios, 1982.

Jennings, Mary-Lou, and Madge, Charles (eds), *Pandæmonium 1660–1886: The Coming of the Machine as Seen by Contemporary Observers*, London, André Deutsch, 1985 (paperback, Picador, 1987).

Jones, David (ed.), *Essays and Reflections on the Perse School in Honour of Keith and Beryl Barry, 1936–1996*, special issue of the Perse School magazine *The Pelican*, Cambridge, May 1996.

Joseph, Noel, *The Silent Village: A Story of Wales – and Lidice*, with a foreword by Jan Masaryk; *Cinegram Review*, no. 14, London, The Pilot Press, 1943.

Lambert, Gavin, 'Jennings' Britain', *Sight and Sound*, May 1951.

———, *Mainly about Lindsay Anderson: A Memoir*, London, Faber & Faber, 2000.

Legg, Mary-Lou [*née* Jennings], 'Young Patriots with Spare Time', London, *Talk of the Town*, 18 May 2003.

Lovell, Alan, *Study Unit 11 – Humphrey Jennings*, London, British Film Institute, 1969.

———, and Hillier, Jim, *Studies in Documentary*, London, Secker & Warburg/British Film Institute, 1972.

Low, Rachael, *The History of the British Film 1929–1939: Film-making in 1930s Britain*, London, George Allen & Unwin, 1985.

MacClancy, Jeremy, 'Brief Encounter: The Meeting, in Mass-Observation, of British Surrealism and Popular Anthropology', *Journal of the Royal Anthropological Institute*, vol. I, no. 3 (September 1995).

Macdonald, Kevin, and Cousins, Mark, *Imagining Reality: The Faber Book of the Documentary*, London, Faber & Faber, 1996.

Mackenzie, Compton, *The Windsor Tapestry*, London, Rich & Cowan, 1938.

Madge, Charles, 'A Note on Images', in *Humphrey Jennings 1907–1950: Paintings*, London, Institute of Contemporary Arts pamphlet, 1951 (republished in Mary-Lou Jennings (ed.), *Humphrey Jennings: Film-maker, Painter, Poet*).

Madge, Charles, and Harrisson, Tom, *Britain by Mass-Observation*, Harmondsworth, Penguin, 1939.

Mairet, Philip, *A. R. Orage: A Memoir* (with an introduction by G. K. Chesterton), London, J. M. Dent & Sons, 1936.

Martin, Wallace, *The 'New Age' Under Orage: Chapters in English Cultural History*, Manchester, Manchester University Press, 1967.

———, (ed.), *Orage as Critic*, London, Routledge & Kegan Paul, 1974.

McBride, Joseph, *Frank Capra: The Catastrophe of Success*, London, Faber & Faber, 1992.

McLaine, Ian, *Ministry of Morale*, London, Allen & Unwin, 1979.

Mellor, David, 'Sketch for an Historical Portrait of Humphrey Jennings', in Mary-Lou Jennings (ed.), *Humphrey Jennings: Film-maker, Painter, Poet*.

Melly, George, *Don't Tell Sybil: An Intimate Memoir of E. L. T. Mesens*, London, Heinemann, 1997.

Mendelson, Edward, *Early Auden*, London, Faber & Faber, 1981.

Merralls, James, 'Humphrey Jennings: A Biographical Sketch', *Film Quarterly*, vol. XV, no. 2 (Winter 1961–2), pp. 29–34.

Millar, Daniel, *'Fires Were Started'*, *Sight and Sound*, Spring 1969.

Noxon, Gerald, 'How Humphrey Jennings Came to Film', *Film Quarterly*, vol. XV, no. 2 (Winter 1961–2), pp. 19–26.

Penrose, Antony, *The Lives of Lee Miller*, London, Thames & Hudson, 1985.

Penrose, Barrie, and Freeman, Simon: *Conspiracy of Silence: The Secret Life of Anthony Blunt*, London, Grafton, 1986.

Penrose, Roland, *Scrap Book 1900–81*, London, Thames & Hudson, 1981.

Peto, James and Loveday, Donna, *Modern Britain 1929–1939*, London, Design Museum, 1999.

'Pitman, George' [Allen Hutt], 'Men of Our Time, No. 8: Humphrey Jennings', *Our Time*, July 1944.

Powell, Dilys, 'Films Since 1940', in Powell *et al.* (eds), *Tribute*.

Powell, Dilys, Wright, Basil, and Manvell, Roger (eds), *Humphrey Jennings 1907–1950: A Tribute*, pamphlet for the Humphrey Jennings Memorial Fund, 1951.

Priestley, J. B., *Rain upon Godshill: A Further Chapter of Autobiography*, New York and London, Harper & Brothers, 1939.

Purcell, Hugh, 'Glory Traps' (on Timothy Jenkins, and his life since *A Diary for Timothy*), *New Statesman and Society*, 12 May 1995, pp. 19–23.

Raine, Kathleen, 'Writer and Artist', in Powell *et al.* (eds), *Tribute*.

————, 'Humphrey Jennings' in *Humphrey Jennings 1907–1950*, ICA pamphlet, 1951 (republished in Mary-Lou Jennings, *Film-maker, Painter, Poet*).

————, *Defending Ancient Springs*, Suffolk, Golgonooza Press, 1985 (1st edition, Oxford, Oxford University Press, 1967).

————, *Autobiographies*, London, Skoob Books, 1991 (first published by Hamish Hamilton as *Farewell Happy Fields*, 1973; *The Land Unknown*, 1975; and *The Lion's Mouth*, 1977).

Rancière, Jacques, 'Listen to Jennings', in Laurent Roth, *un poète dans la guerre*.

Ray, Paul C., *The Surrealist Movement in England*, Ithaca, NY, Cornell University Press, 1971.

Read, Herbert (ed.), *Surrealism*, London, Faber & Faber, 1936 (paperback, 1971).

Remy, Michel, 'Surrealism's Vertiginous Descent on Britain', in Robertson *et al.*, *Surrealism in Britain in the Thirties*.

————, *Surrealism in Britain*, Aldershot and Vermont, Ashgate Publishing, 1999.

Rhodes, Eric, *Tower of Babel: Speculations on the Cinema*, London, Weidenfeld & Nicolson, 1966.

————, *A History of the Cinema: From its Origins to 1970*, Harmondsworth, Penguin, 1978.

Richardson, Maurice L., *London's Burning*, London, Robert Hale, 1941.

Roberts, S. C., *Adventures with Authors*, Cambridge, Cambridge University Press, 1966.

Robertson, Alexander, *et al.*, *Surrealism in Britain in the Thirties*, exhibition catalogue, Leeds City Art Galleries, 1986.

Robins, Kevin, and Webster, Frank, 'Science, Poetry and Utopia: Humphrey Jennings' *Pandæmonium*', in *Science as Culture*, pilot issue, London, Free Association Books, 1987.

Roth, Laurent, *un poète dans la guerre, grandeur(s) d'humphrey jennings*, in the catalogue *Festival du film documentaire, Marseille 1999*.

Rotha, Paul, *Documentary Diary: An Informal History of the British Documentary Film, 1928–1939*, London, Secker & Warburg, 1973.

Saler, Michael T., *The Avant-Garde in Interwar England*, New York and Oxford, Oxford University Press, 1999.

————, 'Whigs and Surrealists', unpublished conference paper on *Pandæmonium*, 2000; gift from the author.

Sansom, William, 'The Making of *Fires Were Started*', *Film Quarterly*, vol. XV, no. 2 (Winter 1961–2), pp. 27–9.

Stallworthy, Jon, *Louis MacNeice*, London, Faber & Faber, 1995.

Stanley, Nicholas Sheridan, ' "The Extra Dimension": A study and assessment of the methods employed by Mass-Observation in its first period, 1937–40', unpublished Ph.D thesis, Birmingham Polytechnic, June 1981.

Stansky, Peter, and Abrahams, William, *London's Burning: Life, Death and Art in the Second World War*, London, Constable, 1994.

Stray, Christopher, *The Living Word: W. H. D. Rouse and the Crisis of Classics in Edwardian England*, London, Gerald Duckworth/Bristol Classical Press, 1992.

Sussex, Elizabeth, *The Rise and Fall of British Documentary*, Berkeley, University of California Press, 1975.

Swann, Paul, *The British Documentary Film Movement, 1926–1946*, Cambridge, Cambridge University Press, 1989.

Symons, Julian, *The Thirties and the Nineties*, Manchester, Carcanet Press, 1990.

Thomson, David, 'A Sight for Sore Eyes', *Film Comment*, March–April 1993, pp. 54–9.

———, *A Biographical Dictionary of Film*, London, André Deutsch, 1994 (revised edition of *A Biographical Dictionary of Cinema*, 1970, 1975).

Tillyard, E. M. W., *The Muse Unchained: An Intimate Account of the Revolution in English Studies at Cambridge*, London, Bowes & Bowes, 1958.

Todd, Ruthven, letter to Mary-Lou Jennings, 16 September 1978; Jennings family archive.

Trevelyan, Julian, *Indigo Days*, London, MacGibbon & Kee, 1957.

Vaughan, Dai, *Portrait of an Invisible Man: The Working Life of Stewart McAllister, Film Editor*, London, British Film Institute, 1983.

Vedres, Nicole, 'Humphrey Jennings – A Memoir', *Sight and Sound*, May 1951.

Watt, Henry, *Don't Look at the Camera*, London, Elek, 1974.

Webb, James, *The Harmonious Circle: The Lives and Work of G. I. Gurdjieff, P. D. Ouspensky and their Followers*, London, Thames & Hudson, 1980.

Weld, Jacqueline Bogard, *Peggy: The Wayward Guggenheim*, London, The Bodley Head, 1986.

White, Eric Walter, *Benjamin Britten: His Life and Operas*, 2nd edition, London, Faber & Faber, 1983 (1st edition, 1948).

Winston, Brian, *Claiming the Real: The Griersonian Documentary and its Legitimations*, London, British Film Institute, 1995.

———, *Fires Were Started* – , London, British Film Institute, 1999.

Wright, Basil, 'First Period 1934–1940', in Powell *et al.* (eds), *Tribute.*

———, 'A Note on Films', in *Humphrey Jennings 1907–1950*, ICA pamphlet, 1951.

———, *The Long View: A Personal Perspective on World Cinema*, London, Secker & Warburg, 1974.

Wyatt, Woodrow, *Into the Dangerous World*, London, Weidenfeld & Nicolson, 1952.

Notes

Prologue

1. For the full text of this letter, see Kevin Jackson (ed.), *The Humphrey Jennings Film Reader*, Manchester, Carcanet Press, 1993, pp. 177–8.
2. Ibid.
3. That is, for one of the other films in the *Changing Face of Europe* series, commissioned in 1950 by the US Economic Cooperation Administration.

Chapter One

1. David Thomson, *A Biographical Dictionary of Film*, London, André Deutsch, 1994, p. 373.
2. From the Jennings family archive.
3. Mary-Lou Legg has recently identified a photo of two boys taken *c.* 1920. She is fairly confident that the boy on the left is her father, Jennings, aged thirteen, and believes that the other may be Eric Blair, aged about seventeen (see Mary-Lou Legg 'Young Patriots with Spare Time). When Blair returned to the family home after his service as an imperial policeman in Burma, he found it humiliating once again to be treated as a child and an obvious failure (see Bernard R. Crick, *George Orwell: A Life*).
4. Letter in the Jennings family archive.
5. Letter to Cicely Cooper, February 1929, Jennings family archive.
6. 'Beyond the Life of Man', section 4.
7. Orwell, of course, was another connoisseur and celebrant of comic postcards.
8. See Jackson, *Reader*, p. 299.
9. Author's interviews with Rodney Jennings, who also supplied most of the other information about Frank Jennings's siblings.

10. Interviews with Rodney Jennings.

11. And one of his horse-shoes is in an Epsom pub. (I checked on both in the summer of 2000.)

12. An image sometimes said, following a hint from Kathleen Raine, to allude to the Tarot: see, for example, Alan Lovell and Jim Hillier, *Studies in Documentary*, London, Secker & Warburg/BFI, 1972, p. 66, which shows plates of 'Le Chariot' and 'La Maison Dieu'. When I interviewed Dr Raine, she unfortunately had no memory of her grounds for this attribution. As a reader of Eliot, Jennings would certainly have known about the Tarot, but if there is some esoteric dimension to his interest in horses, it is more likely to be founded in his study of the Triumph.

13. The full text is given in Jackson, *Reader*, pp. 231–2. Jennings's young assistant at the Crown Film Unit, Joe Mendoza, also recalls Stubbs as being one of the subjects on which Jennings loved to hold forth as they walked around London (interview with the author).

14. Also scrawled on the manuscript of 'The Prism' are some additional connections, of which the most legible reads: 'The Bank of England was founded in 1694 to lend money to William III and create & issue bank bills for the prosecution of the war with France.'

15. Mary-Lou Jennings and Charles Madge (eds), *Pandæmonium 1660–1886: The Coming of the Machine as Seen by Contemporary Observers*, London, André Deutsch, 1985.

16. Quoted in Philip Mairet, *A. R. Orage: A Memoir*, London, J. M. Dent & Sons, 1936, p. 40.

17. *The 'New Age' Under Orage: Chapters in English Cultural History*, Manchester, Manchester University Press, 1967, pp. 233–4.

18. See Christopher Stray, *The Living Word: W. H. D. Rouse and the Crisis of Classics in Edwardian England*, London, Gerald Duckworth/Bristol Classical Press, 1992, pp. 25–6.

19. Matters more fully discussed in Stray, *Living Word*.

20. Letter to Cicely Cooper, Jennings family archive.

21. From an unpublished essay written *c.* 1971, 'Humphrey Jennings 1907–1950', cited in Anthony W. Hodgkinson and Rodney E. Sheratsky, *Humphrey Jennings – More Than a Maker of Films*, Hanover and London, Clark University/University Press of New England, 1982, pp. 4–5.

22. *The Pelican*, May 1920, p. 45.

23. Letter from Mr. A. H. Gregory (nd).

24. Ibid., p. 1.

25. *The Pelican*, March 1925, p. 103.
26. Ibid., p. 3.
27. Mary-Lou Legg's account; there are no official school records for these misdemeanours.
28. *The Pelican*, July 1924, p. 43.
29. *The Pelican*, May 1926, p. 160.
30. Ibid., p. 161.
31. Letter from Mr A. H. Gregory (nd), p. 4.
32. Of which, unfortunately, no copies appear to have survived.
33. Letter to Cicely Cooper, Jennings family archive.
34. Undated letter [1999] in the Perse School archives.
35. Recollection of Mr Geoffry Smith, pupil at the Perse 1924–32, in David Jones (ed.), *Essays and Reflections on the Perse School in Honour of Keith and Beryl Barry, 1936–1996*, Cambridge, May 1996, p. 10.
36. One of the classic expressions of this tragic sense of anticlimax is, of course, Cyril Connolly's *Enemies of Promise* (1938).
37. The most charming epitaph on Jennings's schooldays, and one that strikes a more human note, comes, again, from Mr A. H. Gregory: 'He was a good fellow, Jennings. I can't think of anything bad to say about him. He would have made a great Company Commander but wouldn't have survived to 1945. I suppose he was more useful making propaganda films.'

Chapter Two

1. I have seen three versions; this one is adapted from T. E. B. Howarth, pp. 19–20.
2. A. S. Eddington, *The Nature of the Physical World*, Cambridge, Cambridge University Press, 1928.
3. Howarth, *Cambridge between Two Wars*, p. 93.
4. For a more adequate treatment of this subject, see ibid., especially pp. 84–140 and 182–208.
5. Cited in Hodgkinson and Sheratsky, *More Than a Maker of Films*, p. 6.
6. Empson's work was, for example, one of the key reference points for certain English poets of the 1950s, including John Wain and Donald Davie.
7. That is, in the notorious debate between F. R. Leavis and C. P. Snow in the 1950s.

8. See, among other biographical studies, Barrie Penrose and Simon Freeman, *Conspiracy of Silence: The Secret Life of Anthony Blunt*, London, Grafton, 1986, and Miranda Carter, *Anthony Blunt: His Lives*, London, Macmillan, 2001. Mary-Lou Legg recalls that Cecily Jennings was almost certain that Jennings and Blunt shared an enthusiasm for Poussin, who was the principal object of Blunt's mature work as an art historian. Some time in the 1930s, Jennings bought a large engraving of a Poussin from the Louvre, which now belongs to his granddaughter Anna Clarke.

9. Hugh Carey, *Mansfield Forbes and His Cambridge*, Cambridge, Cambridge University Press, 1984, p. 137.

10. Hodgkinson and Sheratsky, *More Than a Maker of Films*, p. 6.

11. Gerald Noxon, 'How Humphrey Jennings Came to Film', *Film Quarterly*, XV, 2 (Winter 1961–2), p. 20.

12. Ibid.

13. Undated document from the Jennings archive.

14. Julian Trevelyan, *Indigo Days*, London, MacGibbon & Kee, 1957, pp. 17–18.

15. Cited in Hodgkinson and Sheratsky, *More Than a Maker of Films*, p. 3.

16. The name for the examinations taken by Cambridge undergraduates; it is said to be derived from the three-legged stool on which candidates would sit in the Middle Ages.

17. Cited in E. M. W. Tillyard, *The Muse Unchained: An Intimate Account of the Revolution in English Studies at Cambridge*, London, Bowes & Bowes, 1958, p. 84.

18. Carey, *Forbes*, p. 64.

19. Tillyard, *Muse Unchained*, p. 76.

20. Ibid., p. 117.

21. Cited by Howard, *Cambridge between Two Wars*, p. 119.

22. Cited in John P. Russo, *I. A. Richards: His Life and Work*, Baltimore, Johns Hopkins Press, 1989, p. 93.

23. See Graham Chainey, *A Literary History of Cambridge*, rev. edn, Cambridge, Cambridge University Press, p. 327.

24. Cited in Russo, *I. A. Richards*, p. 93.

25. Ibid., p. 88.

26. Ibid., p. 93.

27. Tillyard, *Muse Unchained*, pp. 119–20.

28. See Russo, *I. A. Richards*, pp. 89.

29. Tillyard, *Muse Unchained*, pp. 78–9.

30. Edmund Spenser was the first of many English poets to have attended Pembroke.
31. Cited in Hodgkinson and Sheratsky, *More Than a Maker of Films*, p. 6.
32. Ibid.
33. Ibid.
34. *Cambridge Reporter*, 1926–7, p. 1391.
35. *The Pelican*, March 1927, p. 218.
36. The text of which may be found in John Haffenden (ed.), *The Royal Beasts and Other Works*, London, Chatto & Windus, 1986.
37. From the Jennings family archive.
38. *The Pelican*, March 1928, p. 282.
39. Dr John Constable, in *I. A. Richards: Selected Letters*, Oxford, Clarendon Press, 1990, has established that the appraisals of the first eight poems in *Practical Criticism* come from a course Richards gave in 1925; the remainder come from the 1927 lecture series. Jennings's presence is, at least, a fair likelihood.
40. Cited in Hodgkinson and Sheratsky, *More Than a Maker of Films*, p. 8.
41. Letter to Cicely Cooper, 1 April 1929, Jennings family archive.
42. This information is drawn from a letter from W. S. Hutton to Mary-Lou Clarke, 5 January 1979; in the Jennings family archive.
43. Pembroke College archives.
44. F. C. Happold wrote an account of this production.
45. *Cambridge Reporter*, 1928–9, p. 219.
46. Reprinted in Jackson, *Reader*, p. 181.
47. See ibid., p. 186.
48. Ibid., pp. 186–7.
49. *The Pelican*, December 1928, p. 40.
50. In the 1990s, Mary-Lou Legg edited a well-received volume of Bishop Synge's correspondence.
51. Humphrey once suggested that he should film her singing, but she would have none of it.
52. In 1893, her mother had been presented to the Viceroy of Ireland at Dublin Castle; he was obliged to kiss all the debutantes. The scene is described by Anglo-Irish novelist George Moore in *A Drama in Muslin* (1886).
53. Kathleen Raine, *The Land Unknown*, in *Autobiographies*, London, Skoob Books, 1991, p. 145.
54. *Disenchantment* by C. E. Montague, 1922; a classic of First World War

literature, comparable to works by Sassoon and Owen. Montague was forty-seven when the war broke out, but dyed his hair black and volunteered for the 24th Battalion, Royal Fusiliers. He was eventually invalided back to England.

55. In fact, Jennings's sole contribution to *The Venture* was a single sketch – 'Line Drawing, An Essex Group', in issue 2, February 1929, p. 88.

56. 'Lents' and 'bumps': annual intercollegiate rowing contests.

57. A character in Galsworthy – an Edwardian rebel artist.

58. Mary-Lou Legg, private communication.

59. This light aside proved oddly prophetic: see Chapter 8.

60. *Pandæmonium*, p. xxxix.

61. This line of thought, and the general distinction between sentiment and sentimentality, smacks strongly of the work I. A. Richards had been doing for his *Practical Criticism* book.

62. Cited in Hodgkinson and Sheratsky, *More Than a Maker of Films*, pp. 8–9.

63. As Jennings was later to explain in his radio broadcasts, in the classical world a Triumph was not an abstract success but something quite literal: a grand public procession including chariots, animals, captured prisoners and emblems of Empire. During the Renaissance writers took up the concept of the Triumph and transformed it into a literary genre, most famously in Petrarch's *Triónfi*.

64. Tillyard, *Muse Unchained*, p. 120.

65. Ibid.

66. Ibid.

67. Noxon, 'How Humphrey Jennings Came to Film', p. 21.

Chapter Three

1. Quoted in Hodgkinson and Sheratsky, *More Than a Maker of Films*, p. 10.

2. Kathleen Raine, *Land Unknown*, p. 145.

3. Cicely Jennings, handwritten note in the Jennings family archive.

4. Review of Mason's autobiography, *Before I Forget*, in the *Observer*, 6 September 1981.

5. A system of staging used in medieval religious drama, in which there were no changes of scenery and no curtain.

6. George 'Dadie' Rylands was one of the most flamboyant members of the English faculty and known well beyond Cambridge for his theatrical

productions. As a fellow of King's he was friendly with E. M. Forster and other Cambridge luminaries.

7. Letter dated 20 July (and almost certainly from 1930); parts of it are also reproduced in Mary-Lou Jennings, *Humphrey Jennings, Film-maker, Painter, Poet*, London, BFI/Riverside Studios, 1982, p. 9.

8. Noxon, 'How Humphrey Jennings Came to Film', p. 20.

9. A thorough account of the affair – the fullest we will have until John Haffenden's authorized biography is published – can be found in the notes to his *Complete Poems of William Empson*, Harmondsworth, Allen Lane/Penguin Press, 200, pp. 252–7.

10. Ibid., p. 255.

11. From the Jennings family archive.

12. Noxon accidentally calls him 'Macritte': 'How Humphrey Jennings Came to Film', p. 21.

13. Ibid., p. 21.

14. Ibid., p. 20.

15. Jacob Bronowski, 'Recollections of Humphrey Jennings', *The Twentieth Century*, vol. 165, no. 983 (January 1959), p. 50.

16. Letter to Cicely of 17 August 1931.

17. From an interview by Mary-Lou Legg with Julian Trevelyan, 3 October 1981.

18. Does he mean the 'Paradise' of the Essex farm, or is he recalling Hamlet's 'country matters'?

19. Letter postmarked 7 September 1931.

20. The Seizin Press was founded and run from Majorca by the poets Robert Graves and Laura Riding.

21. Presumably, with the reference to the Bodleian Library in Oxford, some form of research.

22. The journal *Cahiers d'Art* was enthusiastically read in Jennings's circle.

23. Noxon, 'How Humphrey Jennings Came to Film', p. 22.

24. Ibid.

25. According to the records, the first night of this production was 22 November 1926.

26. Kathleen Raine, *Land Unknown*, in *Autobiographies*, pp. 132–5.

27. Eugène Jolas (1894–1952): inspired editor of *transition*, perhaps the single most important of all the magazines to promote literary modernism.

28. An undergraduate friend of Jennings's who went on to work in publishing and became head of the publishers Methuen.

29. Empson had begun a three-year contract as Professor of English at Tokyo University of Literature and Science (Bunrika Daigaku) on 29 August 1931. See Haffenden, *Complete Poems of William Empson*, p. lxxii.

30. Gaston-Louis Roux (1904–88), painter associated with the Surrealists, close friend of André Masson, and noted as an illustrator of various texts by the Surrealists and their fellow-travellers.

31. From the Jennings family archive.

32. An unusual English version of the French term *artiste-peintre*, which distinguishes a painter of canvases from a painter of houses.

33. Private document, 2001.

34. See Constable, *I. A. Richards*, p. 75n.

35. The Revd John Jortin was an eighteenth-century biographer and essayist, the author of a life of Erasmus and a study of Spenser.

36. Interesting to see how early Jennings had caught up with this Surrealist favourite. His essay also includes a lengthy quotation from Tristan Tzara in the journal *Le Surréalisme au service de la révolution*, no. 6.

37. Samuel Johnson, *The Life of Gray*, in *Prefaces . . . to the Works of the English Poets*, 1779–81.

38. Milton, 'When the Assault Was Intended to the City', lines 10–14.

39. Constable, *I. A. Richards*, pp. 79–80.

40. The full text of this letter is in the Jennings family archive.

Chapter Four

1. Elizabeth Sussex, *The Rise and Fall of British Documentary*, University of California Press, 1975, pp. 110–11.

2. Cited, from an NFT programme note by Forman, in Dai Vaughan, *Portrait of an Invisible Man: The Working Life of Stewart McAllister, Film Editor*, London, BFI, 1983, p. 205; corroborated by author interview with Forman, 2000.

3. A phenomenon discussed in many social histories of the period; see, for example, Robert Graves and Alan Hodge, *The Long Week-End* (1941), pp. 19–35, especially p. 28.

4. Sussex, *British Documentary*, p. 1.

5. Or so the reference books tend to say. To be pedantically exact, Grierson used the word as an adjective: 'of course *Moana*, being a visual account of events in the daily life of a Polynesian youth, has

documentary value': *New York Sun*, 8 February 1926, reprinted in Forsyth Hardy (ed.), *Grierson on the Movies*, London, Faber & Faber, 1981, pp. 23–5. Grierson himself pointed out that he had first used 'documentary' adjectivally (Sussex, *British Documentary*, p. 3), but soon began to treat it as a noun, worth hanging on to because 'if it's so ugly nobody will steal it'.

6. Pick had provided employment for many leading modern artists, commissioning them to produce posters and the like in a variety of contemporary styles. For many members of the British public, or at least the London public, their first exposure to Vorticism, Cubism and Surrealism came by way of the Tube.

7. Cited in Forsyth Hardy, *John Grierson: A Documentary Biography*, London, Faber & Faber, 1979, p. 84.

8. Sussex, *British Documentary*, p. 21.

9. Ibid., pp. 41–2.

10. Ibid., p. 41.

11. See Paul Rotha, *Documentary Diary: An Informal History of the British Documentary Film, 1928–1939*, London, Secker & Warburg, 1973, p. 57.

12. Grierson, 'Films of Substance', *The Times*, 2 April 1932, p. 8.

13. Harry Watt, *Don't Look at the Camera*, London, Elek, 1974, p. 63.

14. Reported by Rotha, in *Documentary Diary*, p. 134.

15. Watt, *Don't Look at the Camera*, p. 65.

16. Sussex, *British Documentary*, p. 49.

17. Ibid.

18. 'George Pitman', 'Men of Our Time, No. 8: Humphrey Jennings', *Our Time*, July 1944.

19. Sussex, *British Documentary*, p. 53.

20. Ibid.

21. Ibid., p. 52.

22. James Merralls, 'Humphrey Jennings: A Biographical Sketch', *Film Quarterly*, vol. XV, no. 2 (Winter 1961–2), p. 32.

23. Noxon, 'How Humphrey Jennings Came to Film', p. 23.

24. Ibid., p. 23.

25. Ibid., p. 24.

26. Ibid.

27. Ibid.

28. Ibid.

29. Full text in Jackson, *Reader*, p. 3.

30. Ibid., pp. 3–4.

31. Cited in Vaughan, *Invisible Man*, pp. 60–1.

32. Watt, *Don't Look at the Camera*, p. 64.

33. J. B. Priestley, *Rain upon Godshill: A Further Chapter of Autobiography*, New York and London, Harper & Brothers, 1939, pp. 80–1.

34. Cited in Hodgkinson and Sheratsky, *More Than a Maker of Films*, p. 13.

35. Jennings's great-grandson, aged five, was much taken by *The Story of the Wheel* when he saw it at the NFT in January 2000.

36. The full text is reproduced in *Reader*, pp. 218–19.

37. Noxon, 'How Humphrey Jennings Came to Film', p. 24.

38. Full text in Jackson, *Reader*, pp. 202–18.

39. Though he did film extracts from one theatre performance of considerable historical significance: John Gielgud as Hamlet, for *A Diary for Timothy*.

40. Letter to Mary-Lou Legg, 16 September 1978, p. 1.

41. Undated letter to 'Anne', Jennings family archive.

42. Letter to Mary-Lou Legg, 16 September 1978, p. 1.

43. Presumably the same trademark coat that other contemporaries usually recall as ginger.

44. Letter to Mary-Lou Legg, 16 September 1978, p. 8.

45. Undated letter to 'Anne', Jennings family archive.

46. *Life and Letters Today*, vol. 17, no. 9 (1937), pp. 37–42.

47. From the David Low file in the Beinecke Library, Yale University.

48. See Roland Penrose, *Scrap Book 1900–81*, London, Thames & Hudson, 1981, p. 56.

49. Transcript by Charlotte Jennings of interview by Kevin Daly.

50. Trevelyan, *Indigo Days*, p. 80: 'I have often wondered,' he adds, 'what rites would have been performed by a conscientious Commanding Officer had he died in the line of duty with "Surrealist" as his declared faith.'

51. Alexander Robertson *et al.*, *Surrealism in Britain in the Thirties*, exhibition catalogue, Leeds City Art Galleries, 1986, p. 190.

52. See Jackson, *Reader*, p. 289.

53. Republished in ibid., p. 289.

54. Humphrey Jennings (ed.), *Remove Your Hat and Other Works*, London, Atlas Press reissue, 1986, p. 18. See also David Gascoyne's introduction, pp. i–xii, and Alastair Brotchie's textual notes, p. 77.

55. I follow here a handwritten version in the Jennings family archive; see

also Paul Éluard, *Oeuvres Complètes*, vol. I, Paris, NRF, Gallimard, 1968, p. 1003.

56. From a typescript in the David Gascoyne file, Beinecke Library, Yale University.

57. Michel Remy, *Surrealism in Britain*, Aldershot and Vermont, Ashgate Publishing, 1999, p. 74.

58. Paul C. Ray, *The Surrealist Movement in England*, Ithaca, NY, Cornell University Press, 1971, attributes the last-minute rehang to André Breton; Remy, *Surrealism*, suggests that it was Mesens who created the fuss.

59. Letter to Mary-Lou Legg, 16 September 1978, p. 2.

60. Reavey (1907–76) was an Irish poet and publisher, and translator from the Russian.

61. The incident was reported in the *Daily Mirror*, 20 June 1936; see Remy, *Surrealism*, p. 77, and his 'Surrealism's Vertiginous Descent on Britain', in Alexander Robertson *et al.*, *Surrealism in Britain in the Thirties*, exhibition catalogue, Leeds City Art Galleries, 1986, p. 27.

62. It is this, above all, that leads me to believe that Rodney Jennings must be muddling his chronology when he recalls seeing the picture in the Jenningses' cold and dingy Cambridge flat some five years earlier.

63. Not so; see p. 209.

64. From Kevin Daly's interview with Penrose, 7 October 1981, p. 2.

65. David Gascoyne, *Collected Journals 1936–42*, London, Skoob Books, 1991, p. 12; though Gascoyne later regretted his diaries' reticence on homosexual matters, the remark about 'purely intellectual' feelings is a plain enough disavowal of sexual attraction.

66. Susan Chitty (ed.), *Antonia White: Diaries 1926–1957*, London, Virago, 1992, p. 78.

67. Ibid., p. 80.

68. Ibid., pp. 25–6. Mrs Penrose's use of French was no affectation; a native of Gascony, she stubbornly refused to learn her husband's language for many years.

69. Ibid., p. 31.

70. Emily Holmes Coleman (1899–1974), unkindly described by her friend Peggy Guggenheim as a 'mad American girl', moved to Paris in 1926 and made something of a name for herself as a poet, publishing in *transition* and other avant-garde journals. After a brief period as secretary to the famous anarchist Emma Goldman, she followed Peggy

Guggenheim to England. She is remembered by literary historians and feminists mainly as the author of a single novel, *The Shutter of Snow* (1930), based on her experiences of post-partum dementia; and by gossips as the lover of Dylan Thomas in about 1934–5. In later life, she moved to Italy and converted to Catholicism.

71. See Jackson, *Reader*, p. 219.
72. Ibid., p. 220.
73. Ibid.
74. Ibid., p. 221.
75. Interview with Kevin Daly, pp. 3–4.

Chapter Five

1. From a photocopy of Jennings's original typescript, pp. 1–2, used as the appendix in Nicholas Stanley, ' "The Extra Dimension": A study and assessment of the methods employed by Mass-Observation in its first period, 1937–40', unpublished Ph.D thesis, June 1981, pp. 285–6.
2. Stanley (ibid., p. 6) suggests it is possible that these meetings began as early as the summer of 1936; he adds the names of Guy Hunter, Kathleen Raine, Ruthven Todd and Cicely Jennings to those already mentioned.
3. By chance, or some other agency, the Crystal Palace is one of Jennings's key 'images' in *Pandæmonium*.
4. Compton Mackenzie, *The Windsor Tapestry*, London, 1939, pp. 456–9.
5. The term used in Woodrow Wyatt, *Into the Dangerous World*, London, Weidenfeld & Nicolson, 1952, p. 36.
6. From his introduction to an unpublished work by Bob Willcock, 'Polls Apart', 1947, p. 2; cited in Tom Jeffery, *Mass-Observation: A Short History*, University of Birmingham, Centre for Contemporary Cultural Studies, 1978, p. 20.
7. Tom Harrisson, *World Within: A Borneo Story*, London, Cresset Press, 1959, p. 159.
8. Gascoyne, from a 1978 interview, cited in Hodgkinson and Sheratsky, *More Than a Maker of Films*, p. 35.
9. Stanley, ' "The Extra Dimension" ', p. 7; Mass-Observation Archive, file TC 69/5, Madge: 18 January 1940, p. 5.

10. Wyatt, *Dangerous World*, pp. 33, 34.

11. Ibid., pp. 34–5.

12. Trevelyan, *Indigo Days*, p. 85; also cited in Jeffery, p. 27.

13. Interview with the author, 2000.

14. 'Pitman', 'Men of Our Time No. 8: Humphrey Jennings'.

15. *Reynolds' News*, 1 May 1938; see Angus Calder and Dorothy Sheridan, *Speak for Yourself: A Mass-Observation Authology 1937–49*, London, Jonathan Cape, 1984, p. 73.

16. 'Poetic Description and Mass-Observation', *New Verse*, February/March 1937; 'Mass-Observation and the Social Narrative' and 'They Speak for Themselves', both in *Life and Letters Today*, no. 17, 1937.

17. Raine, *Land Unknown*, in *Autobiographies*, p. 168.

18. Ibid., pp. 171, 176.

19. Note from Mary-Lou Legg.

20. Jeffery, *Mass-Observation*, p. 7.

21. Winston Churchill's title for the first volume of his history of the Second World War; William Empson liked to joke that the Prime Minister had been guilty of plagiarism here: 'my second volume of verse *The Gathering Storm* means by the title just what Winston Churchill did when he stole it, the gradual sinister confusing approach to the Second World War': cited in Haffenden, *Complete Poems of William Empson*, p. 127.

22. Gascoyne, *Collected Journals*, p. 74.

23. Ibid., p. 93.

24. Alas, when I interviewed M. Cartier-Bresson in 2001, he had no memories to offer of this event, nor of Jennings himself: 'It's possible I met him,' he remarked apologetically, 'there were so many people at that time . . .'

25. Jennings family archive; Stanley, ' "The Extra Dimension" ', p. 306.

26. Jennings family archive; Stanley, ' "The Extra Dimension" ', p. 313.

27. Humphrey Jennings and Charles Madge (eds), *May the Twelfth: Mass-Observation Day Surveys 1937*, London, Faber & Faber, 1987, p. 415.

28. E. C. Large, 'The Coronation Mass-Observed', *New English Weekly*, 30 December 1937, p. 231. See also Hodgkinson and Sheratsky, *More Than a Maker of Films*, p. 38.

29. Letter to Mary-Lou Legg, 16 September 1978.

30. Evelyn Waugh, in 'Night and Day', *Spectator*, 14 October 1937.

31. Charles Madge, 'The Birth of M-O', *Times Literary Supplement*,

5 November 1976, p. 1395; also cited in Stanley, '"The Extra Dimension"', p. 30.

32. The poetic total awarded her by her biographer Jacqueline Bogard Weld, *Peggy: The Wayward Guggenheim*, London, The Bodley Head, 1986, p. xiii.

33. Ibid., p. 105.

34. Ibid., p. 11.

35. Peggy Guggenheim, *Out of this Century: Confessions of an Art Addict*, London, André Deutsch, 1980; New York, Universe Books, 1979, p. 159. Quite a few of Jennings's contemporaries thought of him as birdlike; but this particular avian comparison is, as far as I know, unique.

36. Ibid., pp. 159–60.

37. Ibid.

38. See Jackson, *Reader*, p. 247.

39. Ibid., p. 255.

40. Ibid., p. 272.

41. Ibid., p. 279.

42. Ibid., pp. 281–2.

43. Whose life has been given a highly entertaining monument in the shape of George Melly's *Don't Tell Sybil: An Intimate Memoir of E. L. T. Mesens*, though Melly mainly concentrates on Mesens's later years.

44. Melly, *Mesens*, p. 45.

45. Whose death was announced the day before I wrote this passage, 20 June 2001.

46. Full text in Jackson, *Reader*, p. 293.

47. Full text in ibid., pp. 226–9.

48. Mary-Lou Legg points out a family connection here: Jennings's father-in-law ended his career as the LNWR's Engineer for New Works. It was at this time that he became entitled to sit in George Stephenson's chair at Euston.

49. See Jackson, *Reader*, pp. 221–5.

50. Roland Penrose, *Scrap Book*, p. 78.

51. Cited in Hodgkinson and Sheratsky, *More Than a Maker of Films*, p. 19.

52. Thanks to the assiduousness of the BFI's archivists, both *Farewell Topsails* and *The Farm* were included in the January 2000 NFT Jennings season – the first time, as far as I am aware, that they had been screened in the UK since initial release.

53. Catalogue of the Jennings Exhibition at the London Gallery, 28 Cork Street (Second Floor Gallery):

1. The Cigar-Box (1930) oil
2. Odalisque (1933) oil
3. Femme au bras levé (1933) oil
4. Portrait of a child (1933) oil
5. *Collage* (1934)
6. Three Vases (1934) oil
7. Paysage diurne (1935) oil
8. Byron's House at Missolonghi (I) (1935) oil
9. Byron's House at Missolonghi (II), (1936) oil
10. Picture of London in the 17th Century (1936) oil
11. The Wild Horse (1936) oil
12. The Racehorse (1936) oil
13. The Origin of Colour (I) (1935–37) oil (*Lent by Mrs. Guggenheim*)
14. Drawing of a Woman (1936)
15. to 18. *Photographs* (1936–37)
19. *Collage* (1937)
20. *Collage* (1937)
21. The Origin of Colour (II) (1937) oil
22. Cap Canaille (1937) oil
23. The Origin of Colour (III) (1937) oil
24. Alpine Landscape (1938) oil
25. Bolton (1938) oil
26. The Locomotive (1938) oil

Prices may be had on application.

A footnote on the author concludes with the information that 'Pictures by Jennings belong to André Breton and Paul Éluard in Paris, and to Mrs Guggenheim, to Len Lye, Charles Madge, E. L. T. Mesens and others in London.' About 180 of Jennings's canvases are thought to have survived.

54. See Jackson, *Reader*, p. 230.
55. Cited in Vaughan, *Invisible Man*, p. 42.
56. Ibid., p. 43.
57. Ibid., pp. 43, 44.
58. Trevelyan, *Indigo Days*, p. 82.
59. Vaughan, *Invisible Man*, p. 37.
60. Cicely Jennings, letter to David Robinson, 1 November 1970.
61. Or was it ever intended as her final voyage? Whatever one of the film's

less well-known titles may say, the commentary ends with the assurance that the *Ionian*'s regular business trip around the Mediterranean will be repeated in just a week or so after her docking in London.

Chapter Six

1. Pat Jackson, *A Retake Please! Night Mail to Western Approaches*, Liverpool, Liverpool University Press/RNM Publications, 1999, p. 69.
2. In Angus Calder, *The People's War: Britain 1939–1945*, London, Pimlico, 1992.
3. Interview with the author, 1997.
4. Cooper, cited in Peter Stansky and William Abrahams, *London's Burning: Life, Death and Art in the Second World War*, London, Constable, 1994, p. 93.
5. The name was, it seems, proposed by Ian Dalrymple.
6. Stansky and Abrahams, *London's Burning*, p. 93.
7. Pat Jackson, *A Retake Please!*, p. 129.
8. Ibid., p. 90.
9. Interview with the author.
10. Forman, cited in Charles Drazin, *The Finest Years: British Cinema of the 1940s*, London, André Deutsch, 1998, p. 166.
11. Interview with the author.
12. Interview with the author, Milan, 2000.
13. Basil Wright, *The Long View: A Personal Perspective on World Cinema*, London, Secker & Warburg, 1974, pp. 199–200.
14. A germ, perhaps, of the justly celebrated 'One Man Went to Mow' sequence in *Fires Were Started*?
15. A conscious or semi-conscious echo of Quentin Reynolds's script for *London Can Take It*, one suspects.
16. Reprinted in Jackson, *Reader*, pp. 7–8.
17. Letter to Cicely Jennings, 27 March 1941; see Jackson, *Reader*, p. 15.
18. Easter Monday 1941; Jackson, *Reader*, p. 15.
19. Interview with the author.
20. In the course of a long and wide-ranging interview, Megan Dalrymple offered one suggestion which, to the best of my knowledge, is unique: that Jennings was on quite close terms with certain members of the Bloomsbury Group, and particularly Virginia Woolf. While I know of no

record to corroborate this, it is far from impossible: the artistic and intellectual Cambridge, in Jennings's undergraduate years, was often regarded as a sort of far northern colony of Bloomsbury, and there are any number of paths by which Jennings might have encountered these writers and artists. He would very likely have met both Keynes and his wife when working on *The Soldier's Tale*, for example.

21. A full text can be found in Jackson, *Reader*, pp. 285–6. 'Remember, France has always been an international meeting-place for culture. That's why I love France, and why I can only wait for the day when we shall all be free to rediscover the things which, for now, I can only savour in my imagination.'

22. Jackson, *Reader*, p. 16.

23. Ibid., p. 14.

24. The poet and sculptor Ian Hamilton Finlay once told me that he, too, had seen this wrecked plane covered with foliage, and admired the way in which Jennings's verse turns those leaves into a triumphal wreath.

25. Jackson, *Reader*, pp. 15–16.

26. Ibid., p. 16.

27. Ibid., pp. 17–23.

28. Letter of 13 September 1941.

29. Jackson, *Reader*, p. 29.

30. Even though the United States had yet to take the hint dropped in *Words for Battle*.

31. See Jackson, *Reader*, pp. 24–8.

32. Ibid., pp. 31–2.

33. Cited in Jeffrey Meyers, *Orwell: Wintry Conscience of a Generation*, New York, Norton, 2000, p. 171; from an article on Arthur Koestler, 11 September 1944.

34. Jackson, *Reader*, p. 85: from a letter to Cicely of 3 September 1943.

35. Ibid., p. 30.

36. Cited in Vaughan, *Invisible Man*, p. 97; from a paper read at a conference held in July 1973 at the Imperial War Museum, 'Film Propaganda and the War'.

37. Jackson, *Reader*, p. 59.

38. Edgar Anstey's vicious review of *Listen to Britain* in the *Spectator* (13 March 1942) has become notorious among Jennings's admirers. It concludes: 'By the time Humphrey Jennings has done with it, it has become the rarest piece of fiddling since the days of Nero. It will be a

disaster if this film is sent overseas. One shudders to imagine the effect upon our allies should they learn that an official British film-making unit can find time these days to contemplate the current sights and sounds of Britain as if the country were some curious kind of museum exhibit or a figment of the romantic imagination of Mass-Observation.' Mary-Lou Legg recalls that whenever she met Anstey in later life, he would try to put up a defence for this dismissal.

39. See Jackson, *Reader*, p. 38. A selection of Jennings's extensive working papers, including the full text of the fifth treatment, is reproduced on pp. 38–55.

40. To be scrupulously exact, *Fires Were Started* should read '*Fires Were Started* – '. To audiences of the time the phrase would have been immediately recognizable as the deliberately understated formula with which newsreaders reported enemy bombing (source: Mr Cyril Demarne).

41. See, for example, Lovell and Hillier, *Studies in Documentary*, p. 98; and Hodgkinson and Sheratsky, *More Than a Maker of Films*, p. 62. Jennings's friend William Empson had a lifelong fascination with what he once termed 'the Neolithic craving for human sacrifice'; part of his bitter argument with Christianity was that it was, in his view, the only major world religion to have 'ratted on the progress' away from the Neolithic blood-hunger that had been achieved by the cultures of China, India and the Mediterranean basin around 600–500 BC. See, for example, Haffenden, *Royal Beasts*, pp. 57–8.

42. William Sansom, 'The Making of *Fires Were Started*', *Film Quarterly*, vol. XV, no. 2 (Winter 1961–2), p. 27–8.

43. The author of a memoir of firefighting, *London's Burning* (see Select Bibliography).

44. Sansom, '*Fires Were Started*' p. 27.

45. Hodgkinson and Sheratsky, *More Than a Maker of Films*, pp. 60–1.

46. Stansky and Abrahams, *London's Burning*, p. 103.

47. Fred Griffiths, interviewed for the Robert Vas BBC documentary, 1970.

48. Jackson, *Reader*, pp. 57–8.

49. Sansom, '*Fires Were Started*'.

50. Ibid., p. 28.

51. Ibid., p. 27.

52. Ibid., pp. 28–9.

53. Ibid., p. 28.

54. This is perhaps the only moment in the film that smacks of the stagey: everyone likes to see a plucky English girl showing advanced stiffness of the upper lip. And yet Jennings's notes for the film suggest that her real-life original did indeed behave with exactly this degree of coolness. See Brian Winston, *Fires Were Started*, London, BFI, 1999, pp. 28–9.
55. See Lovell and Hillier, *Studies in Documentary*, especially pp. 66–7, 91–2.
56. Jackson, *Reader*, p. 59.
57. Sansom, 'Fires Were Started', p. 29.

Chapter Seven

1. Jennings was thirty-five: *nel mezzo del cammin di nostra vita*.
2. Broadcast of 26 May 1943. The full text of Jennings's talk is reproduced in Jackson, *Reader*, pp. 67–75.
3. Ibid., p. 69.
4. Ibid., pp. 71–2.
5. From his talk broadcast on the BBC Home Service, 26 May 1943.
6. Jackson, *Reader*, p. 74.
7. Ibid.
8. Stansky and Abrahams, *London's Burning*, p. 117; Public Record Office, INF 1/212.
9. Letter from D. D. Evans, dated 25 December 1942; Jennings family archive.
10. Undated letter, *c*. January 1943; full text in Jackson, *Reader*, p. 79.
11. The contract, countersigned by Herbert Read, is in the Jennings family archive.
12. Full text in Jackson, *Reader*, p. 81.
13. Ibid., pp. 80–1.
14. Undated letter, Jennings family archive.
15. *Picture Post*, 3 July 1943, pp. 16–18.
16. Undated paper in Jennings family archive.
17. Jackson, *Reader*, p. 83.
18. Letter dated 2 July 1943, Jennings family archive.
19. Jackson, *Reader*, p. 84.
20. See Joseph McBride, *Frank Capra, The Catastrophe of Success*, London and Boston, Faber & Faber, 1992, pp. 484–5. Sadly, McBride does not mention the meeting with Jennings.

21. It anticipates by four decades the (justly) famous BBC *Arena* documentary about 'My Way'.
22. A thankyou letter from Lesley Blanch on *Vogue* notepaper, dated 25 October 1943, remarks of her recent visit to his set: 'Such co-operation, such simplicity, is immeasurably helpful to the journalist, & one of the rarest things to come by, among film units, I've found . . .' It is signed 'Yours in admiration, gratitude, & immense curiosity'.
23. *Vogue*, April 1944, p. 90.
24. Jackson, *Reader*, pp. 95–6.
25. Curiously, Pitman is wrong about this; perhaps Jennings was sufficiently disenchanted with some of his fellow Surrealists to be by now inclined to play down the extent of his participation.
26. All citations are from 'George Pitman', 'Men of Our Time, No. 8: Humphrey Jennings', *Our Time*, July 1944.
27. Cited in Hodgkinson and Sheratsky, *More Than a Maker of Films*, p. 73; from an interview with Robert Vas.
28. Though Polish viewers, knowing all too well what was to happen to their nation as a result of the Soviet advances, may wince or grow justifiably angry at this scene.
29. Cited in Vaughan, *Invisible Man*, p. 138.
30. This was also, as I learned from interviewing Dr Jonathan Miller, something of a family joke. His uncle, Mr Julian Spiro, had worked for Crown during the war. When I went on to interview Mr Spiro about his memories of Jennings, he gave the single most hostile, and pungent, verdict on Jennings I have ever encountered. 'Humphrey Jennings . . . was . . . a shit.'
31. From the Jennings family archive.

Chapter Eight

1. Interview with the author.
2. Stephen Spender, in James Goldsmith, *Stephen Spender: Journals 1939–1983*, London, Faber & Faber, 1985, p. 71.
3. Ibid., p. 72n. A curiously ambiguous choice of document for the defence, this, since Peggy Guggenheim presents Humphrey as rather a ludicrous figure (see pp. 198–9), despite his obvious brilliance.
4. Ibid., p. 90.

5. See Jackson, *Reader*, pp. 101–2.

6. Mary-Lou Jennings and Charles Madge (eds), *Pandæmonium 1660–1886: The Coming of the Machine as Seen by Contemporary Observers*, London, André Deutsch, 1985, p. 134.

7. See Jackson, *Reader*, pp. 107–8.

8. None the less, Mary-Lou generally preferred the company of her father: 'He was positive, outgoing, wanted to talk about anything to almost anyone, including me. He conveyed light, excitement and a sense of exploration and adventure . . . He was fun, and sometimes very funny. My mother's personality was very negative: she was "against" ideas, talk, spending money – "We can't afford it" – and her initial reaction to any project was "No", and when asked why, "Because I say so." This wholly negative attitude to life was extremely damaging to us children . . .'

9. Fiona Bradley, *Surrealism*, London, Tate Publishing, 1997, p. 60.

10. For the benefit of younger readers: ITMA ('It's That Man Again') was a popular BBC radio comedy show of the war years.

11. The Crazy Gang was a popular English comedy troupe.

12. Raine, *Land Unknown*, in *Autobiographies*, p. 231.

13. See Jackson, *Reader*, pp. 110–11.

14. Ibid., p. 234.

15. Ibid., p. 236.

16. Ibid.

17. Ibid., p. 239.

18. Ibid., p. 238.

19. Ibid., p. 243.

20. Ibid., p. 118.

21. Millar, Gavin, *Mainly about Lindsay Anderson* London, Faber & Faber, 2000, p. 53.

22. Designed by the Government as a tonic for national morale, the Festival of Britain, held on the South Bank in London, would be a celebration of British innovation and accomplishment and would herald a bright techological future.

23. See Jackson, *Reader*, p. 157.

24. Ibid., p. 160.

25. These rumours appear to date from the time of Robert Vas's *Omnibus* documentary on Jennings in 1970.

26. Raine, *Land Unknown*, p. 232.

27. See Jackson, *Reader*, p. 178.

28. See Prologue.
29. From I. A. Richards archive, Magdalene College, Cambridge.
30. Raine, *Land Unknown*, in *Autobiographies*, p. 233.
31. Robert Vas documentary *Heart of Britain*, 1970.
32. English man of letters (1905–65); editor of the *Penguin Book of English Poetry* and most commonly remembered as a close friend of T. S. Eliot.

Chapter Nine

1. Reprinted in Mary-Lou Jennings, *Film-maker, Painter, Poet*, pp. 50–2; this extract from p. 50.
2. Ibid., pp. 47–9; this passage from p. 47.
3. Ibid.
4. The selection of poems published in *The Humphrey Jennings Film Reader* (pp. 289–300) reproduces the precise order of the New York *Poems*, but reverts to the text of the original published versions for the first five pieces. Some of his poems have also been republished in critical studies such as Hodgkinson and Sheratsky, *More Than a Maker of Films*, as well as in various exhibition catalogues, anthologies of Surrealist verse and the like.
5. Letter of 10 April 1968, in Jennings family archive.
6. Denis Forman, *Persona Granada*, London, André Deutsch, 1997, pp. 22–3.
7. Anderson, 'Only Connect', in Mary-Lou Jennings, *Film-maker, Painter, Poet*, p. 54.
8. Cited in ibid., p. 55.
9. Cited in ibid., p. 56.
10. Cited in ibid., p. 57.
11. Cited in ibid.
12. Reprinted, among other places, in Mary-Lou Jennings, *Film-maker, Painter, Poet*, pp. 53–9; this passage from p. 58.
13. Though there are a number of individual essays worthy of note: see, for example, Kathleen Raine's observations on Jennings as a poet in *Defending Ancient Springs*, Suffolk, Golgonooza Press, 1985, pp. 45–62; and Michel Remy on his paintings, photographs and collages in *Surrealism in Britain*, e.g. pp. 49–56, 189–92.
14. David Thomson, 'A Sight for Sore Eyes', *Film Comment*, March–April 1993, p. 59.

15. Interview with Mary-Lou Legg. Perhaps there was also an element of reparation involved – a few years earlier, when Mr Rosenthal was at Secker & Warburg, he had been obliged to reject the manuscript.
16. Letter in the Jennings archive.
17. This journal had run the special Humphrey Jennings issue: XV, 2 (Winter 1961–2).
18. Letter of 2 October 1967; in Jennings family archive.
19. Jennings and Madge, *Pandæmonium* p. xxxv.
20. Ibid., pp. xxxviii–xxxix.
21. Jeremy Bentham's ideal prison, famously discussed by Michel Foucault in *Discipline and Punish*.
22. A long-delayed echo, here, of Jennings's undergraduate ambition to stage a masque on the subject of industry? See Chapter 2.
23. Jennings and Madge, *Pandæmonium*, p. 15.
24. Ibid., p. 17.
25. Ibid., pp. 37–8.
26. Ibid., p. 50.
27. Ibid., p. 77.
28. Ibid., p. 250; and compare the famous remarks about Faraday and Turner in *Family Portrait*.
29. Ibid., p. 110.
30. Ibid.
31. Ibid., p. 253.
32. Ibid., p. 356.
33. Ibid., p. 348.
34. Ibid., p. 324.
35. Ibid., p. 298.
36. Ibid., p. 295.
37. See Kevin Robins and Frank Webster, 'Science, Poetry and Utopia: Humphrey Jennings' *Pandæmonium*', in *Science as Culture*, pilot issue, London, Free Association Books, 1987.

Epilogue

1. The director of a number of avant-garde film essays which occupy the ambiguous territory between documentary and fiction.
2. One could also cite Ian Sellars's grateful admission of the influence *Listen*

to Britain – and particularly its innovative use of sound – had on his movie *Prague*; while Mike Grigsby has quoted entire sequences of *A Diary for Timothy* in one of his recent films.

Appendix

1. This seems to be the only hard evidence of Jennings's awareness of the Tarot; see Chapter 1, n.12.
2. Denis Saurat, author of *Milton, Man and Thinker* (1925).
3. Presumably, Jennings is thinking of the notes to *The Waste Land*, which refer the reader to *The Golden Bough*.
4. The latest standard edition of Blake gives 'mental fight'.
5. To the best of my knowledge, the earliest reference to Surrealism in the Jennings papers.
6. What Empson was doing on 'Alice' ended up as a chapter in *Some Versions of Pastoral* (1935), 'The Child as Swain'.

Filmography

1934   **POST HASTE**
GPO Film Unit
Producer John Grierson
Director Humphrey Jennings
Length 10 minutes

PETT AND POTT
GPO Film Unit
Producer John Grierson
Director/Script/Writer/Editor A. Cavalcanti
Associate Directors Basil Wright, Stuart Legg
Sets Humphrey Jennings
Sound recording John Cox
Music Walter Leigh
Length 33 minutes

LOCOMOTIVES
GPO Film Unit
Director Humphrey Jennings
Musical Direction John Foulds
Music Schubert, arr. Foulds
Length 10 minutes

THE STORY OF THE WHEEL
GPO Film Unit
Editor Humphrey Jennings
Length 12 minutes

1936   THE BIRTH OF THE ROBOT
Shell-Mex BP
Gasparcolor
Producer/director Len Lye
Script C. H. David
Photography Alex Strasser
Colour decor and production Humphrey Jennings
Models John Banting, Alan Fanner
Sound recording Jack Ellit
Music Gustav Holst
Length 7 minutes

1937   FAREWELL TOPSAILS
Adrian Klein/Dufay Chromex Ltd.
Dufaycolor
Director Humphrey Jennings
Photography J. D. Davidson
Length 9 minutes

1938   PENNY JOURNEY
GPO Film Unit
Director Humphrey Jennings
Photography H. E. (Chick) Fowle, W. B. Pollard
Length 8 minutes

SPEAKING FROM AMERICA
GPO Film Unit
Producer A. Cavalcanti
Director Humphrey Jennings
Photography W. B. Pollard, Fred Gamage
Commentator Robin Duff
Diagrams J. Chambers
Sound Ken Cameron
Length 10 minutes

1938 THE FARM

Adrian Klein/Dufay Chromex Ltd.

Dufaycolor

Director Humphrey Jennings

Photography J. D. Davidson

Length 9 minutes

DESIGN FOR SPRING

(Also known as *Making Fashion*)

Distributor ABFD

Dufaycolor

Director Humphrey Jennings

Length 20 minutes

Made with the dress designer Norman Hartnell

1939 SPARE TIME

(Working title: *British Workers*)

GPO Film Unit

Producer A. Cavalcanti

Director/Scriptwriter Humphrey Jennings

Assistant Director D. V. Knight

Photography Chick Fowle

Commentator Laurie Lee

Sound Yorke Scarlett

Music Steel, Peach and Tozer Phoenix Works Band, Manchester
    Victorians' Carnival Band, Handel Male Voice Choir

Length 18 minutes

THE FIRST DAYS

(Alternative title: *A City Prepares*)

GPO Film Unit/ABPC

Producer A. Cavalcanti

Directors Humphrey Jennings, Harry Watt, Pat Jackson

Editor R. Q. McNaughton

Commentary Robert Sinclair

Length 23 minutes

ENGLISH HARVEST
Dufaycolor
Director Humphrey Jennings
Length 9 minutes

S.S. IONIAN
(Alternative title: *Her Last Trip*)
GPO Film Unit
Director Humphrey Jennings
Length 20 minutes
(A 9-minute cut was also released, entitled *Cargoes*)

1940   **SPRING OFFENSIVE**
(Alternative title: *An Unrecorded Victory*)
GPO Film Unit
Producer A. Cavalcanti
Director Humphrey Jennings
Photography Chick Fowle, Eric Cross
Script Hugh Gray
Writer of Commentary A. G. Street
Designer Edward Carrick
Editor Geoff Foot
Sound Ken Cameron
Length 20 minutes

WELFARE OF THE WORKERS
GPO Film Unit for the Ministry of Information
Producer Harry Watt
Director Humphrey Jennings
Photography Jonah Jones
Editor Jack Lee
Sound Ken Cameron
Commentary Ritchie Calder
Length 10 minutes

LONDON CAN TAKE IT
(Alternative title of shorter film for domestic distribution:
  Britain Can Take It)
GPO Film Unit for Ministry of Information
Directors Humphrey Jennings/Harry Watt
Photography Jonah Jones, Chick Fowle
Commentary Quentin Reynolds
Length 10 minutes

1941 **HEART OF BRITAIN**
(Alternative title of slightly longer export version: *This is England*
  Eire title: *Undaunted*)
Production Ian Dalrymple for Ministry of Information
Director Humphrey Jennings
Photography Chick Fowle
Editor Stewart McAllister
Sound Ken Cameron
Commentary Jack Holmes
Length 9 minutes

WORDS FOR BATTLE
Production Ian Dalrymple for Crown Film Unit
Director Humphrey Jennings
Editor Stewart McAllister
Sound Ken Cameron
Commentary spoken by Laurence Olivier
Length 8 minutes

1942 **LISTEN TO BRITAIN**
Production Ian Dalrymple for Crown Film Unit
Directed and Edited Humphrey Jennings/Stewart McAllister
Photography Chick Fowle
Sound Ken Cameron
Length 20 minutes

1943 **FIRES WERE STARTED**
(Alternative Title: *I Was a Fireman*)
Production Ian Dalrymple for Crown Film Unit
Director/Script Humphrey Jennings
Photography C. Pennington-Richards
Editor Stewart McAllister
Story collaboration Maurice Richardson
Music William Alwyn
Length 80 minutes

THE SILENT VILLAGE
Production Humphrey Jennings for Crown Film Unit
Director/Script Humphrey Jennings
Photography Chick Fowle
Editor Stewart McAllister
Sound Jock May
Length 36 minutes

1944 **THE TRUE STORY OF LILLI MARLENE**
Production J. B. Holmes for Crown Film Unit
Director/Script Humphrey Jennings
Photography Chick Fowle
Editor Sid Stone
Music Denis Blood
Length 30 minutes

THE 80 DAYS
Production Humphrey Jennings for Crown Film Unit
Director Humphrey Jennings
Commentary Ed Murrow
Length 14 minutes

V1
(Made wholly for overseas use with same material as
    The 80 Days but re-edited and with a new commentary)
Production Humphrey Jennings for Crown Film Unit
Commentary Fletcher Markle
Length 10 minutes

1944–45 **A DIARY FOR TIMOTHY**
(Released 1946)
Production Basil Wright for Crown Film Unit
Director/Script Humphrey Jennings
Photography Fred Gamage
Editors Alan Osbiston, Jenny Hutt
Sound Ken Cameron, Jock May
Music Richard Addinsell
Commentary E. M. Forster
Spoken by Michael Redgrave
Length 38 minutes

1945 **A DEFEATED PEOPLE**
Production Basil Wright for Crown Film Unit
(for Directorate of Army Kinematography)
Director/Script Humphrey Jennings
Photography Army Film Unit
Commentary spoken by William Hartnell
Music Guy Warrack
Length 19 minutes

1947 **THE CUMBERLAND STORY**
Production Alexander Shaw for Crown Film Unit
(COI for Ministry of Fuel and Power)
Director/Script Humphrey Jennings
Photography Chick Fowle
Editor Jocelyn Jackson
Music Arthur Benjamin
Length 39 minutes

1949 **THE DIM LITTLE ISLAND**
Production Wessex Films for Central Office of Information
Producer/Director Humphrey Jennings
Photography Martin Curtis
Editor Bill Megarry
Music Ralph Vaughan Williams
Commentary Osbert Lancaster, John Ormston, James Fisher,
Ralph Vaughan Williams
Length 11 minutes

1950   FAMILY PORTRAIT
Production Ian Dalrymple for Wessex Films
Director/Script Humphrey Jennings
Photography Martin Curtis
Editor Stewart McAllister
Sound Ken Cameron
Music John Greenwood
Commentary spoken by Michael Goodliffe
Length 25 minutes

1951   THE GOOD LIFE
Wessex Films, for the US Economic Cooperation Administration
Directors Humphrey Jennings, Graham Wallace
Photography Fred Gamage
Length 30 minutes (approx.)

Index